A MIRACLE A MINUTE!

The unforgettable story of a life lived with God!

James Clayton Pippin,
M.Div., D. Min., D.D.

CREATION
HOUSE PRESS

A Miracle a Minute!
by James Clayton Pippin, M.Div., D. Min., D.D.
Published by Creation House Press
A part of Strang Communications Company
600 Rinehart Road
Lake Mary, Florida 32746
www.creationhouse.com

Unless otherwise noted, all Scripture quotations are
from the New King James Version of the Bible. Copyright ©
1979, 1980, 1982 by Thomas Nelson, Inc. publishers.
Used by permission.

Scripture quotations marked KJV are from the
King James Version of the Bible.

Library of Congress Catalog Card Number: 2001090382
International Standard Book Number: 0-88419-782-4

01 02 03 04 05   8 7 6 5 4 3 2 1
Printed in the United States of America

❋ *Dedication* ❋

To Janet Diane Pippin

1954–1998

And to our daughters,
Anne Elizabeth Pippin and Beverly Allene Sutton

And our granddaughter,
Alecia Anne Marcum

And to my loving wife of fifty years,
Allene Hall Pippin

❊ *Acknowledgments* ❊

Space will not allow me to recognize everyone who helped make this book possible. But I'll give it a try. Almost weekly, I read each new chapter to the core members of our prayer meeting: Lois and Keith Johnson, Connie and Robbie Robertson, Ginger and Al Boles, Jerry Padberg and the late Bill Padberg, Geneva Walker, and Martha Jane and Sam Gillaspy; all of whom gave me constant encouragement and always looked forward to the next chapter! Thank you!

To Dr. Fred Hambrick, Dr. Douglas Baker and Dr. Woodrow Walton, three of my colleagues at the college where I taught for several years, who read the entire manuscript in its twenty-fifth draft and didn't offer a single change. Thanks a lot! (My apology to Dr. Baker, who let the reading of the manuscript cause him to miss the first Super Bowl game in fifteen years. He said he couldn't put it down!)

My appreciation to those who furnished photographs in the book: Penny and John Farris, Kathy and Roger Short, Patti and George Saylor, Juanita Pippin Daniels (who gave the picture of me as a boy on crutches that we used on the cover) and family members who took photos at our reunions.

Special thanks to my mama and papa, brothers and sisters and their spouses, who all helped shape my life and even save my life so I could grow up and become who I am. Thank you!

My appreciation to those dedicated teachers in grammar school, high school, Phillips University, Union Seminary and Columbia University, many of whom are in the book. Also to the Army officers and men with whom I served in the three times I was called to active duty: especially Col. Stephens, MSgt. Jerome Jacobsen, Bill Ruzensky, Mike Rakin, J.C. Lovett, Marie Smith, Howard Kite, Angela Barefoot, Chief of Chaplains, Maj. Gen. Charlie Brown, and Chaplain John Harris; all are a part of my story.

To my devoted wife of fifty years, Allene, who allowed me to go far away into the solitude of the study, and there to remain in "writer's reverie" for many hours, many days and many years to finish this mammoth task. (While I worked on my D.Min. degree, she earned the Ph.T. degree— "Putting Hubby Through!") Thank you, Sweetheart, for *everything*!

To our daughter, now with the Lord, Janet Diane Pippin who installed my second computer, Christmas 1996, and taught me how to make the thing work. The last day we saw her alive, after she drove away, I went back to my study and found a note stuck to the monitor. It read, "My darling daddy, you now have the whole world at your fingertips. Go for it! I love you!—Janet!"

Thanks to our special friends Sonny and Bonnie Ramirez, who recently purchased and installed my latest "PC," a powerful and amazing instrument. Sonny gave advanced lessons and is always on standby to come to my rescue.

Finally, my special thanks to Stephen Strang, president and CEO of Strang Communications; Allen Quain, manager of Creation House Press; the editors, Renee DeLoriea and Debbie Moss; the graphic artist, Karen Gonzalves; and the production crew, Jeanne Logue and Karen Stott.

❊ *Contents* ❊

❧ Foreword ❧

I have known James Pippin for more than fifty years. Evelyn and I have followed his and Allene's ministry, remaining close friends all this time. I have often told him that he is just about the funniest preacher I've ever known. In meetings I have conducted where he and Allene were present, I have remarked that James Pippin is the only person alive who can actually verify that I was ever in a college classroom. He tells the story about the day we first met in Mrs. Hale's psychology class way back in 1946, at Phillips University in Enid, Oklahoma. Ah! Those days.

Exciting times have always filled his life and ministry, so I knew that if he ever wrote a book, it would be a knock-out and well worth reading. In it he tells the amazing story of how I prayed for him to receive the baptism in the Holy Spirit, a prayer that was actually answered twenty years later! Then he was serving as senior pastor of the large First Christian Church in Oklahoma City, and I was in Tulsa following God's mandate to build Him a university.

I know this book will bless your life. In it he covers so many vital parts of a growing Christian's walk—including his early boyhood days, his school and college years, the building of one large church in the capital area, Washington, DC, and serving that unique, futuristic church of Oklahoma City. He also relates the often humorous story of his service to our nation, rising from the rank of private to that of colonel in the Army Reserve.

There is something here for everyone! His extensive travel, his preaching and teaching all over this planet, his experience in business and in all facets of the ministry, the lessons and secrets that life has taught him—all fit him well in his ability to expertly craft this piece of fine writing. But let me warn you not to start this book in the evening, for you will likely be up all night until you have read the very last page. The Rev. Dr. Douglas Baker said that because he began reading the manuscript of this book one Sunday afternoon, he missed the first Super Bowl in fifteen years!

As this book goes out to bless many, I am honored to recommend it highly as a book that will entertain, inspire, inform and strengthen you in your spiritual journey. You too can live an abundant life and experience *a miracle a minute!*

—ORAL ROBERTS

❊ Preface ❊

*H*ow does it feel when a person, who had no faith and no interest in the supernatural, takes a quantum leap that slams him up close, face to face, with a staggering miracle? I began finding this out late one afternoon when I placed my hand on a woman who was near death. After I had only prayed a brief prayer for Mary Wells, God suddenly stepped in. In less than a minute, this woman was well. Just after I left the room, she sat up in bed and called for the nurse to please give her something to eat. I share more about this amazing story in chapter one.

Years later, the month I resigned (was fired) from First Christian Church, a minister friend, Rev. W. L. McEver, who took my place on a national board, was asked why Dr. Pippin was not at the meeting. Mac stood up and said, "Jim Pippin sprained his orthodoxy and could not come!"

Laughter filled the room since most of those at the meeting knew what had happened. When Mac told me about this, I had a good laugh myself.

Sure, I may be a bit unorthodox now, but to tell you the truth, before I became unorthodox, it was my brain that was sprained *and* swollen. The big change began in me when God stooped over one day and told me that to Him there is no such thing as the supernatural—that everything He does is very natural. You may think it strange, but it was a most difficult thing for me, a clergymen, to believe that "with God all things are possible."

Yes, the leaders and top ministers of my denomination laughed at me. But I think I finally had the last and best laugh. I sure hope you will too, for this story is about how God grabbed me, shook me like a rag doll, turned me around 180 degrees and put me back down in a brand-new world. I became a so-called "charismatic fanatic" who believes that everything in the New Testament is true and that it all happened exactly as it was written. More than that, I believe you and I can do today all those things that Jesus did in the New Testament. Why? Because Jesus said so! And He cannot lie.

Well then, what about all those detractors who say, "The day of miracles has not only passed—and since we do not see any now, we must conclude that none has ever happened and none ever will."

I just give them the John Osteen answer: *They are all simply wrong!*

Another untrue statement of the detractors is this: "Oh, a few miracles may have happened in the New Testament, but all that ceased with the death of the apostles."

The answer to that statement of doubt is simple: Since the apostles did not give us the gifts of healing and miracles, these certainly did not cease with their deaths.

Hey, all of you detractors, you simply have to get over it; I believe in miracles! And I have lived a life packed full of them to prove it, and to me, that's what matters most.

Now the best good news I can bring to you is that beginning today *you* also can have a life that is filled with miracles. And here is the secret: One must love the Lord and be called to *His* purposes. (See Romans 8:28.) With these two key ingredients, miracles will begin to come in great abundance and in different sizes, some gargantuan, others so small that they often go unnoticed—small, like a mustard seed.

So, starting right now, if you are ready to begin this exciting life, stay with me and say, "In the name of Jesus Christ, my Savior, I too believe in miracles."

Then keep your eyes and ears open and keep your heart keenly aware, for I promise you that they are going to begin to happen. You never know at what moment a miracle will appear, but believe it—it can happen to you.

Just imagine! That moment can be right now!

I recently learned something new about a power that God has given to all Christians: You and I can also create! Wow!

That truth was right there in front of me all the time! But one day, God quietly dropped that marvelous secret into my lap, and then left the rest to me! So, not only are God and Christ creators, but They have given you and me this awesome power.

Jesus said it, I believe it, and that settles it. Where did He say it? Well, He said it with His life, but He also said it several times in the

New Testament, mainly in the Gospel of John. For example, John 14:12 says, "Most assuredly, I say to you, he who believes in Me, the works that I do he will do also; and greater works than these he will do, because I go to My Father."

So you see why millions believe with Dr. Norman Vincent Peale that it is God's will for all of us to live miracle lives. We will have a brief visit with him and Mrs. Peale in a moment.

Our Lord prayed that God's will be done on earth as it is in heaven. That prayer is being answered every minute, and God's will is often done through miracles. Starting with just a baby faith, you can become "a miracle magnet," attracting into your life the exciting joys of the works and the words of Christ. (See Matthew 17:20.)

The idea that "we are miracle magnets" always brings my thoughts to Dr. Peale, who probably said it first. Oh, how quickly God could cure this poor sick world "so barren of faith and bright hope, so filled with worry and fear." Far too many people today find this world to be a very sad place. It does not have to be. Our Lord's burning desire is to do a work in our hearts that will bring us constant joy. Through Christ we can become salt and light that will bring God's glory, convincing a sick world that He longs to make it well again. O glory!

The written Word (the Bible), the living Word (the Lord Jesus), the Holy Spirit and my own experience all convince me that our God is truly "the God of miracles."

Recently I was inspired by a sign I saw in a church foyer that read:

JESUS IS HERE, ANYTHING CAN HAPPEN!

This is the air of expectancy that God wants us to have. You and I can be involved in His "happenings."

Joseph Forte Newton said, "We have been given the freedom to make of our lives a masterpiece, a mixture or a mess."

Without Christ, our lives will become a series of very painful experiences, but being in Him and becoming His partner makes life a virtual heaven on earth.

It is as we will.

In a packed auditorium in Atlanta one winter night in 1942, I heard E. Stanley Jones say, "Without Christ in our lives, we are sunk; with Christ in our lives, we are unsinkable!"

Here's another secret; it was revealed at a luncheon with Dr. Peale. Get ready for something very thrilling because you are about to see that your life can reflect the radiance of Christ so strongly that you can light the lives of others who come your way. This key that unlocks the door to a life filled with joy was given to my wife, Allene, and me years ago. Our discovery began when Dr. Norman Vincent Peale and his wife, Ruth, were conducting a citywide service one morning just before Christmas. The service was being held in the sanctuary of the church where I was serving in Oklahoma City. Dr. Peale introduced Ruth, who gave an outstanding review of her inspiring new book, *The Adventure of Being a Wife* (Prentice-Hall, 1971.)

Afterward, a few of us gathered at a luncheon where Allene and I had the rare privilege of sharing a table with Dr. and Mrs. Peale. We immediately noticed how he and his wife Ruth both sparkled as bright as a Christmas tree! Ruth expressed thanks for the solo Allene had sung that morning before Ruth had spoken. Allene told them that years earlier she had also had the honor of singing for a banquet that had been held at their church, Marble Collegiate, in New York City. Dr. Peale asked how she had happened to be in New York. She explained that at the time she was studying voice in New York, singing at Brick Presbyterian and was a member of the chorus at Radio City Music Hall. She and I were pleasantly surprised that they remembered the occasion when she had sung at their church.

Then I said, "Dr. Peale, so many people believe that you and Ruth are living charmed lives. What is your secret?"

They glanced at each other and smiled. Then Dr. Peale looked at us and said, "Yes, my friends, we thank the Lord that Ruth's life and mine have both been filled to overflowing with the seemingly impossible. This should come as no surprise to anyone because the good Book is full of miracles and miracle lives. By believing in ourselves, in God and in Christ, we can all become 'miracle magnets' and make miracles happen. Remember though, these were put inside all of us by a loving God. Miracles are just sitting there waiting to leap forth as we exercise our faith. From what we have heard of your ministry here, James, we have learned that you two are also living lives that are familiar with miracles."

They both expressed a keen interest in our new walk in the Holy Spirit, so I said, "That's right. Allene and I have recently had an experience with Christ that landed us right in the middle of an exciting world of the fruit and the gifts that come to us through the Holy Spirit."

I briefly told them about our search for the Spirit and what had happened recently. Suddenly, their eyes brightened and their faces were covered with broad smiles, as though, maybe, they both had experienced something like that. For a few moments, we sat there in silence, looking at each other. Somehow, I felt that God had just made a miracle happen right there at our table. Allene and I tingled with excitement, feeling that Christ had united the four of us in an intimate spiritual bond that would last forever. For a few minutes, none of us seemed able to speak. Dr. Peale, his radiant face filled with the love of Christ, reached out for our hands and prayed a brief and moving prayer.

All too soon, they had to leave for the airport. As we watched our new friends drive away, Allene and I knew that the Light of the world, our Lord Jesus Christ, had just lighted our lives. A warm, fresh light had brilliantly shined anew in our hearts through the love that Ruth and Dr. Peale had radiated that day. We will always cherish those precious moments we spent with them.

The ministry and writings of Dr. Peale, Pastor Ralph Wilkerson, Brother Kenneth Hagin, Catherine Marshall, Billy Graham, Paul and Jan Crouch and many others have blessed Allene and me in our work for the Lord. Also, our close friendship with Oral and Evelyn Roberts, spanning more than fifty years, has constantly encouraged us and given me the inspiration to begin to write about my life.

Dr. Myles Munroe, who is the author of more than twenty fine books and the pastor of a large church in Nassau, recently spoke at Melodyland in Anaheim, California. He gave me a prophecy that jabbed me awake and made me finally decide to sit down and finish this book!

Dr. Munroe and I had never met before that night, and yet in the middle of his teaching, he came over to me, got up close in my face and said, "My brother, you have four books in you. You have a unique story to tell to glorify Jesus Christ. Don't you dare let them put you in your grave until you have written them."

Thanks Myles! And thank You, Lord Jesus, for Dr. Munroe's anointing.

It is my prayer that God will use this book to inspire you to do your own special thing before it is too late and that He will open the door of your life to an exciting, new world of miracles.

❀ *Introduction* ❀

*J*ust think. This very minute as you read this page, somewhere God is showing His deep love by healing a sick or dying person; His matchless grace is working in someone's life right now to bring salvation. Somewhere at this moment a broken heart has learned to forgive and has received great peace of mind, and somewhere, hungry hearts are being filled with the Holy Spirit.

I believe that this is one of God's greatest promises: Believers can experience His intimate presence wherever they are and in every moment of their lives. (See Matthew 28:20.)

This is true because Christ, in His glorified body, is sitting at God's right hand and is keeping His promise to send us the gift of the Holy Spirit. (See Colossians 3:1.) The apostle Paul attempts to describe God's nearness when he makes this startling statement, "God is closer to us than hands and feet, even closer than our breath!"

And then he quotes from an ancient poet, "In Him we live and move and have our being" (Acts 17:28).

Actually, all kinds of supernatural works of the omnipotent Christ are happening everywhere, minute by minute. Right now, in thousands of hospitals, tiny babies have just been born. What a miracle! In yonder green meadow a flower has bloomed; overhead the birds are singing, and if we could but hear it, they are singing a symphony of heavenly music to the glory of their Creator. God may be resting from His creating, but He will never rest from His sustaining. Once when Jesus was accused of working on the Sabbath, He said, "My Father is still working and I am also working." (See John 5:17.)

He not only worked in the lives of the men, women and children of the Bible, but that same Father and that same Lord are working right now!

A MIRACLE A MINUTE

I am absolutely confident of this truth: Christ's great miracle power is still working today. (See Hebrews 13:8.) If He were to withdraw that power for one second, the universe would self-destruct. Both time and space were created by Him, and they exist by His perpetual care.

The writer of Hebrews says that Christ is "upholding all things by the word of His power" (Heb. 1:3).

This very instant, somewhere in the stellar reaches of endless space, God could be making a brand-new star. We are told in the Word that He has not only given them a number, but He has also given each of them *a name!* (See Psalms 147:4.) Imagine, untold billions of stars in our vast universe and each has its own name!

Even though we may not hear it, the stars are all singing together a melody of praise to Him. Also, "all the sons of God [are shouting] for joy" (Job 38:7). Each of us can join in this chorus of praise. Our personal lives will begin to overflow with joy and the continuing works of the Father. He yearns in His heart for you and me to join Him in creating the abundant life for ourselves. But, alas, many people are either too preoccupied or too indifferent to notice, or maybe they simply do not care. As we grow from a child to an adult, something very sad happens to most of us along the way; we lose our sense of wonder. This modern civilization seems to work overtime trying to rob us of our capacity to wonder. Many have too soon listened to Frank Sinatra when he sang, "Put Your Dreams Away for Another Day."

We should never grow too old to dream. God provides us with many opportunities to dream big, to dream His dreams for us and for our world. He gives us innumerable opportunities to marvel, to be surprised, to be impressed and to be amazed. There are far too few exclamation points in the sentences of our lives. Our sophisticated and materialistic world has made wonder almost non-existent. Unlike little children who dream of gossamer things and hear the rush of angels' wings, many of us have forgotten that we all can wake up every morning in a brand new world. Those who have grown dull and despondent should let Jesus help them regain that lost sense of wonder, love and romance. Take Emerson's challenge: "Hitch your wagon to a star!"

In his sermon "The Roads to Bethlehem," I heard my brother Frank Johnson say, "Consider the wise men. They had not lost their sense of wonder. They were still chasing stars at age seventy! We should, like them, expect to travel all of our lives on a road of

Introduction

wonder, laughter and joy that glistens with new surprises at every turn."

It is not God's will for any of us to simply exist in what Macneile Dixon calls "The Human Situation," nor is it God's plan for us to just have a life. Our Lord said that He came that we might have life, yes, but that we might have it more abundantly—pressed down, shaken together and running over. (See John 10:10; Luke 6:38.)

I strongly believe that He is saying to us today, "Listen, My child, get a life! And while you are getting one, go ahead and get an abundant one, then to top that off—get the best, a life with Me that is an eternal one!"

David, filled with joy, said, "My cup runneth over!" (See Psalm 23.)

Only Christ can give us this quality life.

Only a growing faith *in* Christ can make it last.

However, this kind of life cannot come to the independent, the proud, the arrogant, the self-involved or the greedy. Jesus said that except we become as little children, we cannot enter the kingdom of God. (See Mark 10:15.) He is reminding us that His kingdom is a carefree place of innocence and trust, a place of perpetual wonder and delight. I ask you this: If we become keenly aware of the magic, mystery, brilliance and beauty of life, can every day be like Christmas Eve? Yes, I think so. Why stop trying to "catch a falling star" or pausing for a moment to enjoy a blazing sunset or a quiet rainbow?

Never, never let the devil get you in his trap and cause you to take God and His world for granted. Regain that childlike thrill of looking at the stars on a cold winter's night. So many of us have ceased to notice them. But we can be sure that if the stars came out only once a year, millions of us would drive far out into the country and spend all night on our backs staring with breathless awe up into the heavens. Only Christ Jesus can restore that lost radiance of which I speak—that rare, delicious enchantment of living, that lost sense of wonder.

In August of 1959, Allene and I found ourselves at midnight in the middle of the Mojave Desert. I stopped and cut off the engine. We got out of the car and looked up! O my God! The sky was filled with billions of bright stars. It seemed that we could almost reach up and touch them. Stars, stars from horizon to horizon in every direction! This magnificence of God's handiwork took our breath away. The desert was so deadly silent that I expected at any moment to hear what the poet has called "the music of the spheres." I had the strange feeling that were it not for our belief that Christ is in charge of our universe, some of us might go crazy with fear. I thought of that song with the erroneous line, "We are all out here, lost among the stars!"

To the contrary, we had seldom ever felt God's presence so keenly as we did that night. How could anyone feel lost in a loving Father's universe? That experience of deep reverence, that downright fear has never left us.

When we stopped and stared up at that awesome sky, I whispered to Allene, "There are so many billions, what keeps them all from crashing into each other?" Of course, we both knew the answer. (See Hebrews 1:3.)

We are told that there are more than 400 billion stars in our galaxy alone, and there are over 240 million known galaxies! The moment before we got in the car, a blazing star shot across the western sky. What a sight! As we drove off, I realized that this was the first time we had experienced the true meaning of "God Almighty!"

Even though we cannot see that many stars when we are near our large cities at night, we often forget the fact that they are all still up there. They are there just as they were in the desert that night, just as they have been there every day and every night since they were created billions of years ago.

I recently heard the utterly ridiculous statement made by a group of "great scientists" that concluded, "We have just discovered that the universe is much larger than we first supposed."

Much larger? My God, how blind and unreal can they be? There can be no end out there; there are unnumbered, unknown galaxies—too far away for us to ever see or go there! So if these researchers were to find the end of the universe, what would it be resting on?! Our finite minds cannot for long imagine infinite space or time. Do only those who have recently fallen in love look closely at the moon? Many others look only when there's an eclipse. The matchless grace and love of God are still flowing constantly toward us. And all of this has actually been going on every minute since the first day of Creation.

O my soul; we thank You, Lord! You are so very good! Praise Your name! Like the old country, Pentecostal preachers used to say, "I feel a spell comin' on!"

Are you also feeling His presence? Then pause with me and let us whisper a prayer.

Ah! His presence!

I am reminded of how in days of yore, the risen Christ revealed Himself in the breaking of bread to those two disciples one eventide at Emmaus. (See Luke 24:13–31.) Our Lord said that as often as we break bread or drink the cup, we should do so in memory of Him. I believe He meant more often than in a worship service. I believe He was also referring to eating and drinking in our homes or even at restaurants. This practice will greatly increase the times during the day and night when we remember Him and feel His presence. I cannot believe that so many of His children can day-by-day receive all of these promises and blessings without stopping often to feel His presence and breathe a prayer of heartfelt thanks to such a many-splendored God.

He is so very great, and yet so intimate. O my soul, our heavenly Father is so powerful that He dwells in the high and holy places, and yet He is so very personal that He also dwells within the person who is of a contrite and humble spirit. (See Isaiah 57:15.) He even cares for the little sparrow and for the beautiful lily, lovingly providing for their every need. Imagine, not even one sparrow can fall to the ground without our dear Father noticing. (See Matthew 10:29.) Every time I see a dead bird or animal, I say aloud, "Little friend, you did not fall without your Father's sight."

The psalmist says that God not only knows our names, but our caring Father is thinking about us right now. (See Psalm 40.) Jesus said that we are of much more value than many sparrows. These tender and heartwarming words fell from Jesus' lips to show us what kind of God we have. So loving a Father is He, that "a bruised reed He will not break, and smoking flax He will not quench" (Isa. 42:3). To the wicked who have rejected Him, He thunders in His wrath, but to those who humbly seek to know and please Him, He speaks in a still, small voice of tender love. (See Isaiah 19:9–12.)

Sometimes these quiet yet elevated thoughts bring feelings of ecstasy that make me vibrantly alive. They are often so moving that I have great difficulty putting them into words. Now really, in light of all this, how could any honest, intelligent person believe that this universe just happened? These so-called wise scholars and scientists have led our children to believe that it all came from the "Big Bang." Many young people leave home for college with a tender faith in God, but then at school they are often changed into hard-hearted atheists or agnostics.

They are told, "Grow up; stop being a weakling. Cease this foolishness of using religion or a belief in God as a crutch or an opiate; that religion stuff is for whiners and idiots who cannot make it on their own."

A MIRACLE A MINUTE

And when these young men and women have listened to all these lies, they have allowed their childlike wonder and innocence to be stolen from them and replaced by a fake "new reality."

Linda Bowles, in her column, "Creators Syndicate" (June 29, 2001), quotes Russian novelist Vladimir Nabokov: "Our existence is but a brief crack of light between two eternities of darkness."

Truly, the wisdom of the worldly wise is utter foolishness to God. His truth is hidden from these so-called scholars, but it is gloriously revealed unto babes. (See Luke 10:21.) Many of these "wonder killers" and "dreambusters" only value intelligence, wealth and power. When bad things happen, to whom do the agnostics go for help? When good things come their way, whom do they have to thank? Well, it's a fact that no agnostic can receive lasting help from a therapist.

Dr. Carl Jung has said that after over fifty years of counseling, he has never helped a single person unless he could get that person reconnected to his/her religious roots. Eric Fromme concludes that neither has he been able to help anyone unless he could restore in the patient the ability to give and receive love. I believe it was Voltaire who said, "If there were no God, we'd have to invent one to keep us from going completely mad."

Years ago, when I was a college student, I heard my brother Frank Johnson Pippin preach one of his greatest sermons. It was titled "Things That Money Cannot Buy." He closed that sermon with this moving poem by an unknown author:

> Five thousand breathless dawns all new
> Five thousand flowers fresh in dew
> Five thousand sunsets wrapped in gold
> One million snowflakes served ice-cold
> Five quiet friends, one baby's love
> One white mad sea with clouds above
> One hundred music-haunted dreams
> Of moon-drenched roads and hurrying streams
> Of prophesying winds and trees
> Of silent stars and browsing bees
> One June night in a fragrant wood
> One heart that loved and understood
> I wondered when I waked at day
> How—how in God's name—could I pay!
> —AUTHOR UNKNOWN

❊ 1 ❊

Jesus Appears to Mary Wells

*I*t had been a hard winter. Even on this late February afternoon, the sparsely melting snow could still be seen on the north side of the sanctuary. Sitting at the large oak desk that was centered in the middle of the plush study, I was deep in thought as I looked through the windows that reached from the ceiling to the richly carpeted floor. The sun was low in the west, and the trees that were scattered about the forty acres were casting long shadows on an empty parking lot.

My study was on the ground floor, underneath the chancel area of the large, imposing sanctuary of the futuristic First Christian Church, the "Church of Tomorrow" in Oklahoma City. The last rays of sun radiantly reflected on the clouds as if "God had taken His cosmic brush and with one bold sweep had splashed the western sky with brilliant hues of gold." As I thanked God for this inspiring twilight, my prayer and this wondrous setting brought a sense of peace and became the perfect backdrop for the close of the crisp winter's day.

Allene and I, with our daughters Janet, Anne and Beverly, had come to Oklahoma City two years earlier in 1964, after serving eleven years at the First Christian Church in Falls Church, Virginia. Although we were just beginning to feel at home in Oklahoma, the growing burden of serving such a large church was moving in on me by degrees. A New Year's resolution to leave my desk clear at the close of day had me checking off the phone calls, glancing through the mail and clearing away the leftovers.

Just as I pushed my chair back and stood up, the inter-office phone rang. Vera, my personal secretary, spoke in a quick and nervous voice. She told me that the nurse in the Cardiac Care Unit of Saint Anthony's Hospital was on the other line saying that Mary

A MIRACLE A MINUTE

Wells, one of our members, was at the point of death. Mary, a young and beautiful mother of two, was only in her early forties. She had been a faithful member of the church for years.

Vera continued, "The nurse said to tell you that you had better hurry or you'll never get there in time. Mary is failing fast."

As I hurried to the door, Vera handed me the room number and whispered, "Drive carefully now. I'll be praying that you make it there before she passes."

When I drove out of the parking lot, the sun had set and a light drizzle had begun. I had trouble keeping my speed down. Thank God, almost all of the lights were green. I sped into the emergency entrance, tossed my car keys to the security guard, and dashed up the north stairs. As I walked onto the second floor, the nurse on duty ran up to me. "O Brother Pippin, I'm glad you are here so quickly," she said as she took my arm and led my down the hall toward Mary's room. I noticed that the nurse had tears in her eyes.

She continued, "It's that precious Mrs. Wells, and she's about gone. It seems so unfair that such a young mother should die and leave two small children. The doctor has just left the room, so you can have a few moments with her alone."

With that, the nurse left. I closed the door and moved quietly to the bedside where Mary lay. Her eyes were closed, and her color was quite blue. She was on oxygen with intravenous needles in both arms. As I gently touched her hand, she opened and lifted her eyes to mine; then a weak smile covered her pale face. As she looked up at me through her tears, she seemed like a person who was ready to die.

In times past if I was in such a situation, I would have said a short prayer for God to receive her into His glorious kingdom. However, in that moment of time, a feeling of deep compassion swept over me. I suddenly refused to accept this as the final moment for such a young and needed mother. I was about to do something I had never done before, and I felt weak and shaky. But then I was suddenly moved to take a giant leap of faith and pray instead that Jesus Christ would heal Mary of her heart condition, right now!

I leaned over close to her face and said in a soft voice, "Mary, I have a strong faith that Jesus wants to heal your heart this very minute. Do you believe He can do this?"

As I said these words, her smile broadened.

She whispered, "Yes, James, I do."

As I raised up trying to further bolster my faith, I made a quick survey of this seemingly hopeless situation. Here lay a dying woman.

Her face and lips were as blue as the gown she wore. Wires were running from several parts of her chest to machines that measured a rapid and irregular heartbeat. There was little or no blood pressure.

I said to myself, "O my dear God, please help me! This woman is dying!"

It was now or never. I lifted my eyes, touched her shoulder, opened my mouth and these words fell out:

> Almighty God, in the name of your beloved Son Jesus Christ, Mary and I are prompted by the Holy Spirit and believe with all of our hearts that You can and will heal her this minute. Lord, she is too young to die and so needed by her family. Just give her a brand-new heart and touch her with a total and instant healing. We give You all the praise and glory and thank You now in advance for answering our prayer. Amen.

She smiled weakly and whispered, "Amen."

Since the doctor and nurses were about to re-enter the room, I gently placed my hand on her forehead, then turned and headed for the door. Glancing back over my shoulder, I smiled and said, "Praise the Lord, Mary. Keep the faith."

Without speaking, I shook hands with the doctor and nurse and went on out to my car.

It was dark when I drove home from the hospital that night. The rain was coming down much harder now. Suddenly, I was filled with a great peace that I could not understand. I had never felt quite like this before. Somehow, I knew that Mary was going to be all right. There was no sadness, no grief, no doubt in my heart, just a feeling of warm joy. No visit I had ever made to a patient in a hospital was in any way like this one had been. I just wanted to throw back my head and let out a great "Praise The Lord!"

What happened the very hour after I left the hospital will be difficult for many people to believe. I regretfully admit that it was also hard for me to believe. Even I did not know what actually happened until almost six months later. Mary did not share this with anyone for fear that I and others would think she had lost her mind. Her experience was so unusual that she had to write much of it down. She took courage and mailed her notes to me at the church and marked the packet as "personal."

As I began to read them, my arms were covered with chill bumps. I felt a charge of energy so strong that I finished her notes while pacing back and forth across the floor of my study. Now, of course, I remembered that she was much better and had gone home from the hospital within a few days after we had prayed. I had thanked God for her recovery, but I was not at all ready for her amazing story. Since her notes only hinted at what actually happened, I could not wait to hear the story in detail. So, I called her on the telephone and told her that I must see her as soon as possible. She agreed to drop everything and come immediately to the church. Within twenty minutes she was sitting in my study.

After I led in a brief prayer, she took a deep breath and at my urging began to relate her story:

"The next few minutes of that day after you prayed for me put the entire floor of the hospital in near panic. I raised up in bed, pulled the tubes from my nose and removed the attachments from my chest. The nurse must have thought I was dead. I am sure her monitor stopped working. When she ran into the room, she found me sitting up in bed, ringing my call bell and smiling broadly. She wheeled around and ran out to get the doctor on duty. Together they tried to get me to lie back down. Now the doctor and the nurse were pale, and my entire body felt as though it was covered with a rosy glow.

"I said to the doctor and nurse in a strong, happy voice, 'Please don't put those things back on me. Please get me something to eat, I am famished!'

"Then I began to chuckle at the looks on their faces. Soon, the room was filled with several doctors and nurses. After they fully checked me over, they began to glance at each other and shake their heads. They all concluded that something very strange had taken place. One of the doctors said that all of my vital signs were absolutely normal and that I seemed completely well. They decided, however, that I must remain in the hospital for another day or two *to make sure that I didn't have a relapse!* I refused to take any more of the fourteen different kinds of medications they had me on. Since I looked and felt completely well, they had no choice but to let me go home the next day."

"Brother James," she continued in a low voice, "I have never told this next part to anyone before, so you must promise to believe that what I say now is the gospel truth. As you prayed for me that day, I seemed to be lifted two feet off the bed. Then a few minutes after you and the doctor and the nurse left, I noticed a brilliant light behind the curtain of the window in my room. Slowly, this light changed into the form of a Person, and I knew that it was Jesus. He actually began to speak to me and said in a voice, warm and full of love, 'Mary, do not to be afraid. Your faith has made you well. I have healed your heart completely.'

"My heart and my entire body felt a sweet warmness but I could not speak. I just nodded my head and knew that what Jesus had said was true. I felt so good and full of joy. Then the light faded, and He was gone."

I looked at her, my eyes now blurred with tears. I knew that we were in the presence of a loving God who had given Mary her life back. There before me sat a living miracle. Mary had been at death's dark door, but Christ Jesus had healed her and sent her back to bless us all.

She then slowly began to relate the rest of the story to me in sentences that were interrupted first by sobs and then by laughter. All the while she seemed to radiate a thrilling joy, as though she were in heaven itself.

She continued, "Jesus came back to me again that night and then again the next morning. Each time He appeared in a glory of light behind the curtain. On these visits I saw more clearly the form of the precious body of our Lord. His words gave me great comfort and joy. He even included some instructions for me.

"He said, 'Mary, while the experience of My visits is fresh in your mind, I want you to read the story of My life in the Gospels so that you may become more thoroughly acquainted with the commands and teachings I gave while I was on earth. As you read, be much in prayer, conversing with our Father and abiding in His presence. Later, you must also begin sharing with others what God has done for you. I am the same Christ today that I was in the Gospels, but now able to be with My followers everywhere all at the same time through the Holy Spirit, the Comforter, whom our Father sent to be with all of you.'

"Before His last visit in the hospital room came to a close, He told me again that I was indeed completely well. He closed by saying that I must always remember that my faith had made me whole.

"James," she continued, almost in a whisper, "I feel so unworthy and ashamed to be blessed by an actual visit in person from the Lord Jesus. Please believe that every word I have told you is the truth."

She bowed her head holding her handkerchief over her eyes.

"Mary," I answered, searching prayerfully for the right words, "Mary, I believe you with all of my heart. But you must realize that no one can ever really be worthy of this. Just be forever thankful that you were favored with a personal visit from the Lord. I know that you will praise His name every day for the rest of your life for this special blessing."

She seemed unable to say anything more, and I did not want to break the sacredness of that moment with words. Very soon, she arose to leave. I continued to feel the presence of the Lord as we walked to the door of the study. Standing there that day in a half trance, I watched a miracle walk out of the church.

After the door closed, I did not know whether to laugh or to cry, for this was the first miracle of this kind that had happened in my entire life. As you would imagine, Mary was totally changed after her healing and her visits from the Lord. An all-consuming love for her Father and her Lord filled her life. She became more like Jesus each day to her husband, to her children, to all of her friends and to all whom she met in her daily round of life.

Of course, my own life and ministry were also radically changed. However, before I had arrived at this special place that gave me enough faith and courage to pray for Mary's healing, I had been on a long journey that was often filled with tragedy, suffering and defeat.

❋ 2 ❋

The Journey Begins— "Peter, Do You Love Me?"

I am sure that you must be wondering just how a minister of a large mainline church could rush to a hospital room where a member was dying of a heart attack, "lay hands on her" and ask God, in the name of Jesus Christ, to heal her instantly. In 1966, when this happened, there were very few ministers of the Christian Church (Disciples of Christ) who would have prayed for a dying person to be instantly healed. How I, a seminary graduate and the senior minister of a 3600-member church, could come to that place in my faith is the main theme of this story.

Something gloriously unorthodox had happened to my wife and me a few months earlier that brought a sea change in our lives and into my ministry. During the years that led up to that day, there was a time when I almost lost my faith. I even came very close to quitting the ministry. My theology, and especially my faith, had to change drastically before I could have said a prayer for the miracle healing of anyone. More than that, I would have had nothing to do with any person who would even think of doing such a thing.

My journey of faith began when I started attending Mama's church as a six-year-old boy. It was the Caney Creek Primitive Baptist Church in central Georgia, the "hard-shell, footwashing" kind. The men sat on one side, and the women and children sat on the other side of the old frame building. There were no fancy pews, only wood benches placed on wood floors. The room was heated in winter by one huge "potbelly" stove that sat halfway down the center aisle. In summer, all the windows were open and everyone tried to keep cool by fanning themselves with little, cardboard fans that were donated by a local funeral home.

Down the hill in back of the church flowed Caney Creek. This is where everyone who accepted Christ as their Savior was baptized by immersion. In those days very few churches had baptisteries in the sanctuary. Mama's church would never think of having such a thing as a tank of water in which to baptize people: All converts to the Primitive Baptist faith had to be immersed in running water, because this method most nearly simulated Jesus' baptism in the Jordan River. The season of year made no difference. In the dead of winter, I have even seen the preacher break the ice to enter the stream. All the church people would come down and witness the baptism. After the service, the people who had been baptized had to walk about a hundred feet to the church to change out of their wet clothing. Mama told me that she could not remember anyone ever catching the flu or even a cold from that exposure to the weather. She said that this was a miracle of God, and I believed her.

The preacher was "Brother Williamson." He had a long, white beard that I thought must be like Moses' beard. He was a very large man who overfilled the seersucker suit, so much so that the buttons seemed to be desperately struggling to hold everything together in front of his large "bay window."

One special day I was allowed to sit with Papa (who rarely ever came to church), and as the preacher walked in, Papa leaned over and whispered to me, "Son, I do believe the preacher is wearin' my seersucker suit!"

I looked up at him, smiled and nodded my head. When we got home he went straight to the closet, and after seeing that his suit was missing, he angrily confronted Mama.

She simply tilted her head and coolly replied, "Well, Pa, you never wear it, so I thought the preacher would get a lot more good out of it than you. But I must confess, I thought you'd never miss it."

Papa and I then looked at each other and laughed—because we both knew Mama was right.

Since Brother Williamson served four churches, he came to Caney Creek only once a month, but I thought that was quite enough to hold us, especially since every service lasted two or three hours. He never just took a text. Instead, he took a "crack at creation" and preached from Genesis to Revelation. I believed he could quote from memory the entire Bible, from cover to cover. As he began to quote the scriptures, he would often get stuck on a favorite text.

One Sunday, as I lay in Mama's lap, he came upon the words the Lord spoke to Peter on the shore of Galilee after the Resurrection. (See John 12:15.)

"Peter, do you love Me?" He said those words over and over, giving emphasis to each in turn.

"PETER, do you love Me?

"Peter, DO you love Me?

"Peter, do YOU love Me?

"Peter, do you LOVE Me?

"Peter, do You love ME?"

As he repeated these words over and over, I drifted off to sleep. Later, when I awakened, he was still bellowing out those same words.

I looked up at Mama and whispered, "Mama, did he?"

She answered, "Shhh! Sure he did, Son."

Half raising up, I said, "Well Mama, would you please go up there and tell him, so he can go ahead and finish that sermon?"

Mama put her finger to her lips, chuckled and shook her head at me. There was also muffled laughter from the row behind us. You know, I never knew why she just sat there and let the preacher go on like that.

With all that noisy preaching and stomping the floor and all those glasses of water he drank from the big pitcher on the pulpit, I thought of him as this huge locomotive getting up a head of steam, and he was soon sure to blow that whistle loud and long. I still remember so many of those scriptures that he pounded into my head with staccato blows. He preached so loudly that I probably heard all he said whether I was awake or half-asleep. Since the windows were all open, I imagined that he could be heard a mile down the road. However, it was on those Sundays at Mama's old frame church that I began to have faith in Jesus Christ. It wouldn't be long before I would really need that faith.

When I was about seven, I contracted a very serious kidney infection. The pain in my back was so severe that I could not walk. Mama brought all of my meals to my bed. She also prayed for me every day, and we prayed together every night before I went to sleep. My older sister, Annabelle, and my brother Jack took turns pulling me all over the house as I leaned back in an old wicker kitchen chair. Dr. O'Kelly was finally called and after checking my urine, he said the infection was serious. He told me that I must drink lots of water, eat lots of good food and above all, I must never touch another carbonated drink as long as I lived. After a few weeks and much prayer, I got well.

I now really began to thank God that our Mama was a praying

Christian. My older brothers called her "the praying fool." But they soon found out that she was the only really wise one among us. She took us all to Bible school and church every Sunday when we were children. We all thought she was a saint. She was always praying, reading her Bible and doing kind things for us and our neighbors. She used to whistle or sing all the old hymns of the church while she did her daily work. We knew that minding Mama was almost the same as obeying Jesus. Later on in life, whenever we received a letter from her, she would always turn our thoughts toward God. Every one of those letters was signed, "Lovingly and prayerfully, Mama." She did her best to teach us to lead a life that pleased the Lord.

Mama was almost always the first to get to church and the last to leave. She never heard a poor sermon, never knew a bad preacher and would not talk against anyone—nor allow us to do so in her presence. This virtue in her is all the more a sign of devotion when we think about how many church members today have "Roast Preacher" for Sunday lunch.

In one of her rare, firm statements she made sure she shed some clear light on the subject. One Sunday when all of us kids were having an after-church gossip session, she said, "Now, children, when you commit your life to God and are doing as much good as most preachers are, then you might have a small reason to be slightly critical. Until then, remember that our Lord said, 'Judge not, that ye be not judged'" (Matt. 7:1, KJV).

From then on, we watched our tongues when we talked about preachers, God or the church. Well, at least around Mama, that is. But even so, we still knew that Jesus was listening.

Once in awhile Mama would invite Brother Williamson to come to our house for dinner when he was calling on members in our area. She always served a great meal of all the things he liked. When we added the extra leaves to lengthen our table, it almost filled the little dining room of our house that was right by the tracks.

This one time when he was coming over, Mama got all of us kids together and told us to be on our best behavior, not to talk or make noise during the meal, and never ask for anything that we did not see on the table. Mama went to the door to greet the preacher and brought him in to shake hands with all of us. When we all sat down, squeezed together in that tiny room were Mary, Jack and me, then the preacher and Mama, Belle and Papa, and finally grumpy, old Aunt Genie who was visiting us at the time. She was Mama's sister and was like a matron at the jail, so we were all afraid of her. That day she was constantly looking, first at one of us and then at the other, to keep us all in line. I guess I was about six, Jack was eight, and Belle was about twelve.

Then Brother Williamson bowed his head, and we all got very quiet while he said the grace. Well, just as he finished, someone at the table let gas, quite loudly. In the midst of the deadly silence, while we were all holding our breath, biting our lips for fear we would laugh, Belle turned to Mama and with a serious look on her face, said in her little sing-songy voice, "Mama, somebody pooted!"

Now there was an even more agonizing silence, and everyone was about to explode. At this point, Brother Williamson shoved his chair back, lifted his red face toward the ceiling and, while slapping his knee, let out a laugh that rattled all the dishes. It was then that we all burst forth with peals of laughter. Now, the preacher did not laugh a "ha ha" kind of laugh. Instead, he took deep breaths and let them out with loud wheezes, which caused us all to laugh even more loudly.

Finally, he pulled his chair back up to the table and said, as he looked around at us all, "My sweet Jesus, bless this happy meal, to the glory of God the Father."

Well, we all calmed down. It was a meal and a time to remember. After this, we all saw Brother Williamson as a real person. Isn't it something that somebody's poot and the preacher's laugh could make me want to join his church and have him as my preacher? If I had not already decided to join the Methodist church, I do believe I would have become a Primitive Baptist, and he would have been my preacher for life. I probably shouldn't say this, but I've often wondered if it wasn't the preacher himself who was the culprit.

Then another miracle healing happened about a year after my bout with the kidneys. I developed excruciating migraine headaches. They began at noon every day and were so bad that Mama or my sister Mary, a registered nurse, often had to hold me and keep cold cloths on my forehead. Strangely enough, the pain always stopped just at sunset. One night, after this had continued for many days, Mama asked Mary, Belle and Jack to get in a circle around me and pray in earnest that the headaches would leave me. Then, when noon came the next day, the headache did not return. We all thanked God. But here is the real miracle. Jesus was such a powerful Healer that I have never had another headache in my entire life! However, I have been told that I have given a few to others along the way.

I was so thankful to God because of His care and healings during these two sicknesses that I wanted to get closer to Him. I had a great hunger for God and a yearning to know more about Jesus. I sensed that many people had a much closer relationship to God than I did. So, after I spent more time in prayer and reading the Bible, I finally decided to join the Methodist Church. However, while I was trying to make up my mind to do this, I was torn because of the great response Mama's preacher had made at the recent "laughing dinner."

But actually, I really didn't want to join Brother Williamson's church because I was afraid of his God. I thought that his God was going to "get me" sooner or later. Although Mama was a saint in my eyes, I finally decided to join my Papa's church. You see, he was a cigarette-smoking, bourbon-drinking, cussin', backslidden Methodist. I remembered that these were the very things Mama's preacher strongly spoke against. So, I thought I could get along with Papa's God a lot better since Pa had been a Methodist for many years and God had not "gotten" him or struck him dead yet. I guess I had the childish desire for an easy God of whom I was not afraid.

About this very thing, Mama told me in her sweet voice, "The fear of the Lord is the beginning of wisdom" (Ps. 111:10).

So, the next Easter, when I was almost eight, I was baptized in the Methodist church in Round Oak, Georgia. The main thing I remember about that day was that when the preacher wet his hand and put it on my head, the water dripped down my neck and soiled the starched collar of my brand-new shirt. By joining the church at that early age, baptism didn't have the impact on my life that I expected. My friends were being sprinkled that Sunday, so I simply went forward with the group.

The Round Oak Methodist Church was built on the foundation of the old Sunshine Methodist Church that General Sherman used as his headquarters on his march to the sea during the War Between the States. As he left the little town of Round Oak, he ordered his troops to burn the church to the ground. Even if my baptism was not that historical, the place where it happened was filled with history of the war.

Since Papa's church was close to our home, all of the Pippin children joined that church. There were nine of us born to George Thomas Pippin and Annie Eudora Jackson Pippin. Six boys and three girls made up the family, and I was the youngest. We were born in a six-room frame house that was located near the railroad tracks. Papa ran a large general store and was a rural mail carrier. He was about 5 feet 10 inches tall, and as far back as I can remember, he was a bit overweight. Like Brother Williamson, he also had a "bay window." He resembled his older brother Joe Frank, both of whom had the big "Pippin nose," but Joe Frank was taller and better looking in the face.

Papa had a thick head of reddish hair that came down within a couple inches of his eyebrows—he was a "beetlebrow," as was I. Papa made friends quickly, and everybody who came into the store and everyone on his route were his close friends. He was a kind, loving husband and father, always working hard to give us as good a life as was possible during those lean days while we were growing up. Mama was very short, and as a young girl, very slender and beautiful. But she had a "Pippin nose" even before she was a Pippin. As she grew older and brought nine children into the world, she never quite lost the weight she put on when she carried her babies. After I was grown, I heard the rumor that she had lost two by miscarriage. When I was a small boy and heard that word, I thought that "miscarriage" (Miss Carriage) was the name of the midwife.

Mama worked hard in the house, cleaning, cooking and caring for us children; she also worked in the yard, where she planted hedges, flowers and trees. She loved her own mama, Myra Childs Jackson, and her papa, Daniel Jackson, who were both Primitive Baptist saints. It was from them that she learned most of her virtues. I believed Mama was her parents' favorite, because it was to our home that both Grandma Myra and Grandpa Dan came to die. She was also the favorite among her sisters, for it seemed that they were always showing up for long visits at our house. She loved her family, but she kept reminding us that she loved the Lord most of all. One day when she was reading her Bible, she showed it to me, and I noticed seven check marks on a page. I knew this meant that she had read through that one Bible seven times.

Even with this love all around my brother Jack, very little of it seemed to flow into his head or his heart. He was two and a half years older than I, so we grew up together as close friends, uh, most of the time. What Huck said about Tom, "He told the truth, mainly," was true with Jack. He would often play tricks on me or say things that were not true. One day he told me that I was adopted, "but it was a family secret and I must not let anyone know that I found out about it." Although I knew it was not true, I sometimes felt adopted because I lived in a "hand-me-down world." I had to wear all of Jack's clothes when he grew out of them, and I rarely ever got anything new. As a matter of fact, the bottoms of my feet still look like his to this day because I had to wear his old shoes until I was fifteen.

A MIRACLE A MINUTE

One day when we were playing down in the woods, he got a flash of inspiration. He told me to go up to the house, bring wood, a hammer, a saw and nails, and to hurry back before his vision left him.

I kept bringing all the things he ordered, but I never knew what he was building, nor did he let me have anything to do with the project. This vision, when it became a reality, was a house he built up in a large tree in Dr. O'Kelly's pasture near our home. The tree house had two stories, and he and his gang were charter members of the "tree club." They held weekly meetings in the upper room, but I could not attend because I was not a member and not ever allowed to enter the upper level. That was reserved for the secret meetings of members only.

One afternoon, Papa came home from the store earlier than usual. When he looked down toward the tree house, he noticed smoke coming from the upper level. Thinking it was on fire, he ran down there, but quickly realized that the smoke smelled an awful lot like cigarette smoke. So he quietly climbed up to the first floor, and when he saw me sitting there, he placed his finger to his lips as a signal for me to be quiet. Feeling like a traitor, I smiled weakly and pointed to the upper level.

He nodded and silently proceeded to squeeze on up through the hole to their meeting room. As soon as he peeped half of his head in, he saw Jack and all the rest of the members of the "club" sitting around smoking cigarettes and cigars, and some of them were even chewing tobacco. When Papa stepped on up into the room, they froze, realizing that they had been caught cold in the act. Papa then noticed that there was quite an inventory of supplies of all kinds stacked up there on shelves: cigarettes, cigars, chewing tobacco, matches, candy and soda pop. Jack had stolen all of this from Papa's store when he had worked afternoons there after school.

Well, Papa flew into a rage, ordered all the kids to go home, pulled Jack down out of the treehouse, took him home and gave him the hardest whipping of his life. Papa then made him go back there that moment and bring every single item back to the house. Jack was barred from the store for a month after this tree incident. Although the meetings continued, the smoking ceased. So did the theft from the store. That night in my prayers I thanked God that I was not a member of that tree club. Papa was so upset about this theft and the smoking; we both felt terribly guilty, and neither Jack nor I ever stole anything from the store again. This lesson in honesty stayed with us from that day forward, but I do admit, we have wavered a bit now and then.

The Journey Begins—"Peter, Do You Love Me?"

Papa was an honest and hard-working businessman. He had four brothers and three sisters, all of whom learned these and other virtues from their dad, my grandpa, Thomas Clayton, who died before I was born but from whom I got my middle name. Papa's parents, Thomas and Susan Pippin, and all of their children were born at Pippin, Georgia, near Forsythe. The town of Pippin is no more, but in the late 1800s and early 1900s it had a post office, a store which Grandpa Thomas owned, a barbershop and, of course, a blacksmith shop. During that time the passenger and freight trains from the north, and from Atlanta to Miami, all stopped there at Pippin. As a small boy, I took pride in pointing out to my friends the spot that marked Pippin, Georgia on an old map that hung in Papa's bedroom.

Papa's oldest brother, Uncle Joe Frank, owned a large grocery and furniture store in Forsythe, Georgia, about twenty-five miles west of Round Oak. It was always a happy day when Papa took Mama, Jack and me to see his brother Joe Frank and his family. Forsythe was a big county seat town built on a square with the courthouse in the center, like so many small towns were built in those days. Next to Macon, it was the only big town Jack and I were ever in when we were small boys, so we were filled with joy on one of those special days we left home to visit Forsythe.

When we arrived, Jack and I flew out of the car and ran into the store yelling "Unka Joe Frank" over and over to the top of our voices. He would always pick us up and sling us around while he lifted his head and laughed loudly. Then his handsome sons and beautiful daughters, all much older than we were, would appear and stoop down to hug and kiss us both. When Papa and Mama came in, there were more hugs and much laughter. Uncle Joe Frank was taller and more slender than Papa. He had a ruddy face, a shock of red hair over heavy red eyebrows, a large hook nose and a high nasal voice, much like the one we are told Abraham Lincoln had. He wore a white shirt, brown shoes and suspenders that held up freshly pressed khaki trousers.

The store was always filled with delicious things, some different from Papa's. Even today, I can still remember the sounds and smells of that large busy store: the chatter from customers who were coming and going all day long; the cash registers constantly ringing…And, ahhh! the smells of the large bins of coffee beans, the big, round hunks of cheese, the leather scents from all the harness and saddles, and the most thrilling of all, the mouth-watering fragrance of peanuts roasting in the back of the store. Barrels were everywhere, filled with crackers, apples, peppermint candy and white pork side. Great jars were filled with pickled pig's feet, dill pickles and boiled eggs in brine. The Cracker Barrel chain of today must have been started by a Georgia cracker whose granddad had such a store.

There seemed to be no sign of the Depression in that store. Like Papa, Uncle Joe Frank most always had a cigarette in his hand or one hanging from his bottom lip. And like Papa, he loved his bourbon whisky, in moderation of course. He was a fair 'n square businessman, but a sly fox to those who tried to get to him on a deal.

In 1933, during the depths of the Depression, a large New York supermarket chain opened up a store across the square from him, in full view from his store. Well, word got to Uncle Joe Frank that they had arrived and aimed to put him out of business. As you might imagine, that did not set too well with Uncle Joe Frank, who had run the largest and finest store in the county for many years.

But, not to worry, he quickly changed the name from "Pippin Grocery and Furniture Store" to "The Pippin Penny Profit Store." He then proceeded to add only one penny of profit to everything in the store from a can of beans to the large sofa in the next room. Of course, he was forced to float a loan from the friendly town banker in order to make payroll and keep the store running. But then one morning a few months later, he looked over across the square and there sat two large vans being loaded. Two days later the giant Yankee chainstore was gone! In all the years Uncle Joe Frank was in business after that, no one else ever threatened him or dared to open a large grocery or furniture store in that town! Good thing Uncle Joe Frank wasn't in Forsythe the day General Sherman came through there. He'd have shot him off of his horse at first sight! He never used his popularity or power to raise prices or gouge his customers. Had he done so, that new store would have thrived and put *him* out of business.

I am happy to say that both he and Papa always priced everything fairly and were always ready to help anyone in need. They were not only selling groceries or furniture, but also providing honesty and fairness to all. They also had a strong desire to make a contribution to the prosperity of the region, giving everyone more goodness than groceries and more friendship than furniture.

Once when we were visiting the store in Forsythe, I saw a poor-looking couple walk out with a new sofa. After they left, I asked, "Unka Joe Frank, how can you trust that family to pay you for that sofa?"

His answer was, "Well, my sweet little feller, I got what I paid for it in the down payment!"

Papa burst out first, and then Mama, Jack and I all got a good laugh over that. He and Papa were also very patient with those who had a good reason to be behind in their monthly payments. They both met everybody with a big smile and a handshake and knew all their customers by name, including the names of the children!

I'd better not get started in contrasting this old-time attitude toward the customer with the atmosphere we meet in some of our large department stores in the malls today; that is, if we can find anyone to wait on us. We won't find many real friends there, even if we trade there for years, because just about the time we do get to know a person by name, she/he will be transferred to another store! Much of "Hometown America" has truly been lost. That is sad, but I suppose the owners, who are in tall buildings miles away, think that the shopkeepers might be a little too nice or might even go out of their way to do something special to bring us back. There are exceptions though, like Wal-Mart and J.C. Penney's.

During all the years we were growing up, Papa gave a lot of his time to his store in Round Oak, using all the friendly, caring attitudes of his daddy, Thomas Clayton, and his older brother, Joe Frank. He named it "Pippin Grocery Company." It carried everything from hardware to dry goods and groceries. But unlike Uncle Joe Frank's store, we didn't carry furniture. We did sell gasoline out front though.

When Jack got old enough, he began working in the store. He was very intelligent and quick to learn. So when Papa thought he knew enough about the business, he made him manager. Sometimes Jack would let me go to the store with him after school and hang around and watch him. This way, I began to learn "the tricks of the trade." Soon, the happy day came when he decided to teach me to do a few things in the store to help him. I was about ten years old then, and so short that I had to stand on a box of Early Bird chewing tobacco to be tall enough to work the cash register. It had about ten rows of keys to punch and then a handle to turn to ring up the sale and get the cash drawer to open. The first time I did this, the drawer hit me right in the chest and knocked me off the box and down on the floor. After that, you can bet I learned to catch the drawer before it hit me.

To me, it was such a big store, and there was so much one had to know. But it was in these preteen years that I learned a lot about people and about business. We had to know the location and price of every item in the entire store, how to sell to the customer and how to make correct change. Most important of all, we had to learn to keep busy at all times and work with little or no supervision. Papa taught us to be kind and patient and never cheat the customer. So, mastering all of these details about dealing with people and learning how a retail business is run proved to be very valuable to me later in life.

As Jack and I grew older, we began to overhear the night talk between Mama and Papa before we went to sleep. These conversations caused us to realize that they were very troubled and burdened, for those were the years of the Great Depression. Since Jack was born in 1919 and I in 1922, we grew up in those very lean times. By the time I was born, all of our older brothers and one of our sisters had gone out into the world to earn a living. Only Mary, Belle, Jack and I were left at home with Mama and Papa. Jack and I would often worry so much about Mama and Papa that we had trouble going to sleep. During many of those nights, I would whisper a silent prayer for them, even though I had no idea what was wrong. We were soon to learn the source of most of their heartache.

Papa had saved some money and planned to start a Chevrolet dealership in Round Oak. But the Florida Land Boom bug bit him, and like many others, he was caught up in the wild speculation on seaside Florida land. When a lot was bought one could sell it in a few days for twice the price. Then more lots would be bought and sold at huge profits. All of this came to a tragic end in 1926, when a killer hurricane roared in and destroyed most of south Florida, including the fortunes of thousands of people who were involved in the speculation. This was the end of the famous Florida boom, one of the greatest land scams in American history. Thousands of people lost all of their savings because of the dishonest companies involved and wild speculation.

I never learned how much Papa lost, probably several thousand. Later when Papa went down to Florida, he found that his lots were 100 feet out into the ocean. It took him a long time to get over this great loss. I recall as a small child that this was the subject of many of those late night talks he had with Mama.

Once we overheard Papa telling Mama, "Well, Ma, if I had not lost it in Florida, I probably would have lost more than that in the stock market crash."

Because the savings of so many people were lost in Florida, the Depression, which began in 1929, was all the more drastic for our family and many others. Those savings would have been as precious as gold then, so we all learned a lesson about avoiding speculation and saving up something for a "rainy day." But as for the Depression, it was a rainy decade. Many of us who came up during these years were later very cautious of the stock market and real estate deals. But these hard times were not without their blessings, for they brought us all closer together. We actually did not know we were poor. As I look back today, I realize how really lean those years were. Yet we were better off than most because of Papa's income from the mail route and the store.

In our little frame house, there was no hot or cold running water and no indoor toilets. We took a bath in a large wash tub once a week on Saturday nights "whether we needed it or not." Our house was heated by wood-burning fireplaces in each room. For light at night, we had coal oil lamps that burned kerosene. Later, we had Aladdin lamps that were much brighter. In 1930, Papa bought a 32-volt DC generator that was run by a gasoline engine. It was located out in the car shed, and it would go on and off all day and night as it charged the many batteries that gave us our electric lights. Ours was one of the few homes in Round Oak that had this luxury. There was only one naked light bulb hanging down from the ceiling in the middle of each room.

Our first party-line telephone came along about 1931. That year Papa also bought a large, battery-powered radio that had many large dials and lighted tubes. We could get only one station, KDKA, Pittsburgh. Later when there were more stations, the whole family gathered around the radio each evening and tuned in our favorite programs: *Jack Armstrong, Lum and Abner, Amos and Andy, Gail and Dan, The Inner Sanctum, The Lone Ranger* and *Dick Tracy*. Soon, the early soaps came along: *Ma Perkins, One Man's Family, All My Children* and others. Our favorite news reporter was Lowell Thomas. Even today, I can still hear his rich voice saying as he signed off, "So long until tomorrow."

The only things Jack and I got for Christmas were a few nuts, some fruit and popcorn; once we got a toy jumping jack that would climb a string. The Christmas tree was a small pine, cut from the woods near our house. Popcorn on a string and a multicolored paper chain were the only decorations on the tree. However, there were many things in our small town that brightened our lives, things that city kids never heard of—like a garden that provided fresh vegetables, chickens that gave us fresh, fertile eggs daily, and fresh milk from our three cows. We also had several pigs, and every January, when the weather was cold enough, we had "hog killin'." That furnished us with sausage and ham that were smoked in the smokehouse with oak chips. We only had to buy a few things from the store, like cheese, lard and coffee. Our flour and meal came from Mr. Granvill's old grist mill, two miles south of Round Oak. Often for breakfast we had biscuits, gravy, white side with a streak 'a lean and a large glass of sweet milk. Although those were hard times, I wish we had many of those good home-grown things to eat today.

Papa gave credit to the farmers and the black folks and anyone who needed anything he had in the store. Had it not been for his generosity, many families, especially the black people in our town, would have gone hungry during the long, difficult winters of the Depression. Even in the hardest of times, our dearly beloved Papa was generous to a fault. He started carrying the mail on horseback, then in a buggy, next on motorcycle and then in a car, first a Model "T" Ford, then a Model "A", and lastly a 1932 four-door Chevrolet. That Chevy was the most beautiful automobile I had ever seen.

Papa summed up all those years when he told Jack and me one night, "All the time that I carried the mail, I never stole a dime and never read anyone's mail, not even a penny postcard."

Jack and I were always watching for Papa to come home from the store about supper time. Often he brought us a surprise. When it was a box of Crackerjacks, we would spread newspaper on the floor, open the boxes, pile up the popcorn and peanuts, and then get down on our hands and knees and growl, pant and bark like dogs as we raced to see who could finish first. Sometimes Papa would bring us a 10-cent Baby Ruth candy bar, which in those days was as big as a small stick of stove wood. Jack would eat his real fast and then jump on me and take mine away from me. But I learned how to stop him from ever doing that again. The next time we got a "BabyRuth", I quickly unwrapped mine and spit all over it. After that I could always eat anything Papa brought us "slow and easy" and never again had to worry about Jack taking anything away from me.

One Christmas Papa gave Jack and me a bicycle he had "ordered on after" from Sears, Roebuck and Co. It was bright and shining, with large whitewall tires and a loud horn; oh, it was a beauty. Only one thing was wrong. Sears forgot to include the chain. So we learned to ride it by pushing each other all over town. We would find a hill, go flying down, and then have to push it back up again. Finally, the chain arrived and the first time I got on it, I rode at top speed all the way to Wayside, three miles away to see Frances Reed, my first sweetheart. I was so happy, I could not sleep that night. The next day I planned to ride it to Florida. Although Jack and I had many arguments about whose turn was next, that bicycle was our pride and joy for many years.

Papa started making some extra income when Dr. Ben White asked him to oversee several farms he owned near Round Oak. He was a physician who lived in St. Petersburg, Florida, but his wife and children spent almost every summer in Round Oak. Papa worked every Sunday afternoon preparing his weekly report of the happenings on all the farms, most of which were along his mail route. I can still hear those fast clicks on that old red Remington portable typewriter as Papa sat smoking and typing away. Touch typing was unknown to him, so "hunt and peck" was his method. During the summer months, Dr. White drove up to Round Oak almost every weekend, and he and Papa would spend Sunday afternoons driving around to some of the farms.

One summer Sunday afternoon, Papa let me go with them. We went speeding along those dusty, old country roads with Dr. White driving his brand new 1931 Cadillac convertible; Papa up front and I, a nine-year-old, sitting up on the edge of the back seat, surrounded by the comfort and smell of solid leather. As we pulled into the driveway of the last farm to be visited that day, we were met by the tenant who share-cropped the farm. Dr. White had mentioned to us that this man was a bit lazy. After some small talk with the sharecropper, the doctor looked around and noticed that the man had failed to do some things he had been told to do during the last visit. The farmer, a tall, skinny, white man, answered in a smart-mouthed way, saying that if the "Doc" wanted those things done, why didn't he come on out there and help do 'em himself. Being kinda new, he apparently did not know what a quick, hot temper Dr. White had.

Much to the tenant farmer's surprise, the doctor sprang out of the car, walked around to the farmer, and standing on tiptoe, caught him by the shirt and shouted into his face, "You just take back every one of those sassy words or I'll give you the thrashing of your life and throw you off my farm."

The tenant, in a quiet voice, said, "Dr. White, I am very sorry. I will never act like that again. I promise to work harder from now on."

Without another word, Dr. White climbed back into the car and we drove off. All was very quiet in the car for a few minutes.

Hoping to break the silence and to help ease the tension, I slid up on the edge of my seat and said in a low voice, "Well, that feller struck his match this time, didn't he? And it wudd'n wet neither wuz it?"

There was an immediate burst of laughter, first from Dr. White and then from Papa.

Dr. White glanced over his shoulder and throwing a thumb toward me, said, "George Tom, you've got a really bright and clever chap in that young'un of yours. Better keep your eyes on that boy, he's going places!"

Papa nodded as the laughter continued.

That day I learned for the first time that I had an exciting and valuable talent. I could say things that would make my papa and even a rich doctor burst into laughter. That sense of humor, the instinct for quick timing, that ability to always see the funny side of things, has been one of God's greatest gifts to me. Not only while preaching or teaching, but also in normal conversations. Even in times of crisis, this gift has often blessed others, my family and me. But the next few weeks would bring such good news that Jack and I not only laughed a lot, we jumped for joy.

❀ 3 ❀

Christmas in the
New House on the Hill

One night Papa called Mama, Jack and me into the living room and sat us down. He had a mad look on his face, so Jack and I were shaking because we thought Papa was angry. We sat there trying to remember if we had done anything wrong. Then Papa suddenly changed his countenance, started smiling and told us he had a big surprise for us.

"Guess what?" he began. "I have just bought the big, beautiful house up on the hill. Tomorrow, we will begin to move into a real mansion."

Jack and I both sprang up, ran and hugged Papa, then turned and hugged Mama, who had tears of joy in her eyes. Later, we were sent off to bed, but neither of us expected to sleep much. I said a prayer of thanksgiving to Jesus for giving us the very house that we had looked longingly at for years, wishing we could someday live there. I found out later that the combination of the mail route, the store, the garden, a large cornfield and the pay from Dr. White gave us the income that made that large home possible for us. Also, Mama made us remember that it was God alone who blessed us with that beautiful house.

So, in November of 1933, when I was eleven and Jack was fourteen, we moved into the large, two-story, ten-room house on the tallest hill in Round Oak. It was farther from the tracks than our old home had been, and it was on the east side. Although it was hard to leave the place where we were born, the new one was so much better that we soon got over it. The first time we walked into the house, our eyes bulged at those shining oak floors and the large rooms with higher ceilings. But our mouths really dropped open when we saw the indoor bathroom that had a large tub, sink and toilet...and hot and cold, running water.

A MIRACLE A MINUTE

Only a few months later, electricity came to rural Georgia. Thanks to President Roosevelt and the Tennessee Valley Authority, we benefited from a program to bring electric power to the rural areas of the Southeast. Gone was the constant put-put of the old 32-volt generator with its dim and blinking lights. Our lives were never the same after that move, especially after Papa bought Mama a refrigerator and an electric stove—both on the same day! Out forever went the ancient icebox and the iceman with his twenty-five pounds of ice each day; gone was the huge, old kitchen wood stove, and with it went the daily chore of cutting and bringing in stove wood.

Every room had a small, coal-burning fireplace, and during the winter, fires were kept going in them all day long right up until bedtime. The miracle of electricity had arrived, but we were years away from central heating and decades away from central air conditioning. At night, the fires were "banked," or covered with ashes, so they could be easily started the next morning. Every day Jack and I had to bring in coal and kindling or "light-wood," which Georgia people called "lie-dud." To build the fires the first time we would make several balls of newspaper that were the size of your fist, put the "lie-dud" on top of the paper and the coal on top of the "lie-dud." On a winter's night, we would lay the fire before we went to bed. Then in the morning, one of us would get up about daybreak, run and strike a match to the paper and scoot back into bed until the quick catching light-wood would ignite the coal and "bingo!" We had a big warm fire. Then we would grab our clothes and dash to the fire to dress for breakfast and school. The coal burned much hotter and longer than the wood we had used for so many years. At school, our heads were full of nothing but thoughts of our new home, and we told anyone who would listen all about it.

The new house had a beautiful oak staircase with a wide, shiny banister that led up to the second floor where there were three bedrooms, plus two more rooms that were unfinished. Jack and I had the small room on the west side. The roof was galvanized tin, which clattered loudly when it rained. One night during a storm, Jack and I got on our knees with our elbows on the windowsill and watched the grand display of lightning far out to the west. We could see clear out to "Fiddler's Rest," over ten miles away. We could never see anything that far away when we were at our old house. As the lightning struck, for an instant it looked like shimmering, bright, gold trees turned upside down. Then the rain started coming down real hard. We jumped at the loud thunder that sounded like huge stagecoaches rumbling over long wooden bridges that reached from the north clear to the south part of the dark sky. The loud claps of thunder, the brilliant lightning and the din of rain on the tin roof translated us into a private world of our own. When a bright flash of lightning came, it would light up the room as if it were broad daylight. Just for a split second when we glanced at each other, we looked pale blue and strange, as though we were ghosts. This sent shivers down my spine.

When we could stay awake no longer, we finally jumped into bed and pulled the covers up to our chins and stared frightfully into the darkness until we fell asleep.

On such nights, I would often whisper the prayer, "Dear God, please take good care of all the birds and the squirrels and the rabbits on this stormy night. Keep them all dry and safe 'til morning. Thanks for Papa buying us this good house that keeps us dry from the rain and safe from the storm. In Jesus' name, amen."

Our lives were so much happier during these carefree years in our new house. A special time of joy was when our older brothers and sisters came to visit. Frank and George came every Christmas. They turned the season into a bright and sparkling wonderland. Frank drove his old "Chivvy" from Oklahoma to Shreveport, Louisiana, where George worked. Then he and George drove to Round Oak in George's new Ford V-8. They would always take Jack and me to Macon, a large town that was twenty-four miles south of Round Oak. The four of us would pile into George's new car and race over dirt roads and around curves at speeds that took our breath away. We were all eyes when we got to Macon, with its stop lights, its wide paved streets and its many cars and tall buildings.

First, they took us to the barbershop downstairs at the Dempsey Hotel for a much needed haircut. Next, was the hotel coffee shop where we all got the "blue plate special," which was a meat and two vegetables served on a large blue plate, and included hot rolls, butter and a drink, all for the large sum of twenty-five cents. A slice of apple pie was five cents extra. After lunch, they took us to the large department store to buy our Christmas presents. It was a ten-story building, and each floor was a large store that carried only a special type of stuff. So there were ten departments or stores in that one building. This new idea came long before the shopping mall. It was really a mall that was stacked up on top of itself rather than spread out for miles. The two biggest differences were the whole thing was owned by one company and the elevator cut down on the walking. This was the first elevator Jack and I had ever seen; it was run by a pale, old, fat man who probably never saw the light of day.

The trunk of the Ford was jammed with gifts. One year George bought us a BB gun that was pumped up by a long rod that extended from under the barrel. Jack and I were ecstatic with joy during this entire day, a delight that continued as we arrived home at dark, unloaded all the presents and put them under the tree. After Mama served us all a great supper, I noticed that George started giggling and telling jokes. Then he went to the tree, got the BB gun, pumped it up, loaded it with a roll of BB shot and proceeded to go from room to room shooting out all the lights. All the while, Mama was following right behind him, pulling at his arm. She was trying to hide her smile as she shouted repeatedly, "You, George, stop it! Stop it, I tell you!"

That night, when we were upstairs in bed, Jack told me that George had been drinking and was feeling no pain. I didn't know what that meant. George was kinda wild in those days. Late that next afternoon, George came in with his girlfriend from Montecello. She was slender and pretty, and worshiped Brother George. Her name was probably Anna Grace, for we all called her Annagrafe. Jack and I came in from playing when it was about dark, and there sat George in a large wash tub in the middle of the living room and Annagrafe was giving him a bath. With a big smile on his face, he was holding on to the edge of the suds-filled tub and loudly singing a song he'd heard on the radio.

I turned to Jack and whispered, "He's feeling no pain?"

Jack nodded.

Well, although Mama greatly objected to this scene, I caught her laughing to herself when she went into the kitchen. He was about as happy then as the night he got tight and at 3:00 A.M., wearing only pajamas, drove off in Papa's Model T Ford to Montecello. He raced around the square as fast as the car would go, all the while whooping and hollering and singing loudly. On the fifth round the sheriff stopped him, parked the Ford and drove him home.

Frank told us the next night about what happened one time when they were driving back to Shreveport in Frank's Chevrolet convertible. George got tipsy and needed air, so Frank had to stop. George climbed up on top of the car and would not get off, so Frank took off and drove for miles at high speeds 'til George had enough air and shouted for Frank to stop. It's a wonder any of us ever lived past thirty.

George, like Frank, was good-looking enough to be a movie star. Actually, he, Frank, Jack and I all favored each other, and all of us looked like we were Jewish! You know—dark hair, heavy beards and large noses. (Excuse me, I'm smiling!)

As a matter of fact, when I was in the army, I ran into a captain late one Friday afternoon who yelled at me, "Pippin, what in the Sam Hill are you doing hanging around here? Don't you know it's Yom Kipper?"

I answered, "I know, Sir! I was just heading outta here."

For the rest of my army career, the Jewish men were my companions, and I always took the Christian *and* the Jewish holidays off. I kid you not!!

George was wild for sure in his younger days—lots of wine, women and song. But after he married Vera, a very pretty girl from Eatonton, he never drank another drop. From then on, he was a great husband and father, and worked like a Trojan. He and Vera moved to Oklahoma City in the early 1930s to be near Frank. George opened the "Rainbow Shoeshop" in the Paseo. He had no money, so his landlord made him pay his $30 a month rent daily. As soon as he took in a dollar, he would run over to the apartment office and pay that day's rent! Those were hard times a plenty, and George was straight as an arrow, but even so, George was always the life of the party. His favorite word to us all was, "Don't glum up on me!"

Frank Johnson was one of the other super characters in the family. Although Frank was a preacher, he kept us wide-eyed and laughing at his western jokes.

He'd ask us something like, "James, do you and Jack know how they milk cows in Texas?"

Of course, we chimed in unison, "No, we don't, Brother Frank. How?"

Then he'd answer, "Well, they put a big tub under her utters, get around in back and pump her tail!"

We laughed so hard we rolled on the floor. I recall about ten of these, but I will spare you. However, I can't resist Mama's joke on George.

He was not acting very good in cuddin' Gladys' third grade class, so she called him up to her desk and told him, "George, you know what your trouble is—you're spoiled."

He said, "No, cudden' Gladys, all of Mama's children smell this way."

Frank was good at those western jokes, but he was best at ghost stories and Bible stories. As we grew up, he dramatically acted out for us every important story in the Bible. He loved poetry and often quoted poems, a few of which he had written himself. When he and George were home together, there was never a dull moment for Jack and me. But before we knew it, Christmas and New Year's would be over, and they had to leave for Oklahoma.

One morning when they were leaving they came by the school and asked the teacher to excuse us for a few minutes. We ran out and jumped into their arms.

Before leaving, Frank stooped down, took me by both hands, looked me in the eye and said, "Son, I am expecting great things from you. So, be a good boy, study hard and one day your chance will come."

Then we four joined hands in a circle and Frank led us in a sweet farewell prayer. I am sure that they also said words of encouragement to Jack, but I only remember those moving words Frank said to me. When we were young, Frank and George always called Jack and me "Son." Later, it was "Brother James" and "Brother Jack." Tears were in all our eyes when they left. Jack and I watched them drive away until they turned the corner, then we sat close together sobbing and wiping our eyes. After waiting a few minutes to compose ourselves, we returned to class, but for the rest of the day we never heard a word the teachers said. Our minds were on Frank and George and their long, long ride out west to a place called Oklahom-a. Our older brothers and sisters were our heroes, and our dream was to become like them.

Round Oak was a very small town in Jones County. One winter when Papa was chairman of the PTA, he threw a big party for all of the parents, teachers, and kids. He personally prepared oyster stew on large stone heaters that were fired by charcoal. We all were like a large family. The teachers were our friends. But when we got a whuppin' at school, the news was passed to Papa—who then gave us another one.

A highlight of the year was when the schools in the county all entered the annual Forensics. Students from Jones and two adjoining counties were chosen to compete in several fields at an all-day event that included contests in poetry recitation, sports, debating and in declamation or speeches. Students from both junior high and high school were eligible to enter.

The year that I became twelve and entered junior high, my teacher, Gladys White (who was also our first cousin) wanted me to enter in declamation. Although older boys and girls would be entered in that category, she agreed to coach me and believed I would do well if I worked hard. I agreed to try it. I had to memorize a fifteen-minute speech and compete against about twenty students from large junior high schools in three counties. In the audience would be three judges, many parents, their friends and the general public. They all looked forward to this annual event that brought a large turnout to the high school in Forsythe.

Mine was a rousing, patriotic speech about great leaders of our nation such as Patrick Henry, John Paul Jones, Florence Nightingale and Abraham Lincoln. On the day of my speech, I was filled with fright, so to calm myself down while I was waiting backstage to take my turn, I bowed my head and whispered a long prayer. Then my turn came, and after they introduced me, I, a trembling little boy of twelve, stepped out to the middle of the bare stage, looked the large audience straight in the eye, and began my recitation. I spoke slowly and distinctly in a voice that gained volume and speed, giving it my very best. Without forgetting or stumbling on a single word, I ended with a strong close, speaking slowly and with deep feeling. When I stepped back and bowed, the entire audience stood up and burst out in applause.

There were shouts like, "Amen!" "Bravo, bravo, bravo!" "You really did it, Sonny!" "You will be President someday, young man!"

Well, you guessed it—I won first place. I was never so shocked. For months thereafter, whenever there was a gathering of any kind, including meetings at my Sunday school and church, or during intermission at the school plays or at halftimes at basketball games, I was always asked to get up and give that speech. You cannot imagine what this did for a little boy who had lived all of his life in the shadow of big brother Jack. So now I was not only a humorist, but I had also discovered that I could speak and deeply stir an audience. Although I cannot remember a word of that speech today, entering and winning that contest made a lasting impression upon my life.

The Lord must have known that I needed this boost of encouragement, because a great time of testing was coming. I would soon have an accident that would almost cost me a leg and bring me very close to the point of death.

29

❋ 4 ❋

The Possum Hunt That Changed My Life

I was thirteen years old that winter in 1935 when my brother Frank, who was at that time the minister of the Central Park Methodist Church in Oklahoma City, came home with his new wife, Ozelle. Annabell and Mary were also there. Frank wanted to take all of us on a possum hunt. Jack and I were almost jumping out of our skins because this was our favorite fun thing to do. Possum hunting is done on a winter's night, and when the moon is full and the trees are bare, you can see the big ole possums way up there silhouetted in the trees by the bright moonlight. So, on the night of November 10, we packed a basket of food, dressed warmly and struck out about dark for a full night of hunting. The party included Frank, Mary and Belle and their boyfriends, old "uncle Jim," Jack, myself and four dogs. Ozelle, a pretty city girl from Tulsa, stayed back to visit with Papa and Mama.

As we walked out of Round Oak, everybody else was talking and laughing, so I stayed close to Jim. I was thinking how glad I was that he could come with us. Like a member of the family, he had been the best black friend I had since I was just a small child, so he always kept an eye on me. Jim was Papa's driver on the mail routes when the roads were a foot deep in mud from the winter rains. As we walked along together that night, I was thinking of the time when he and I were hunting and we flushed out a rabbit that dashed off at full speed. Jim quickly reached down, picked up a rock and from a distance of over one hundred fifty feet, let that rock fly like a bullet, hitting the rabbit square in the head. Jim never took a gun with him when we hunted for rabbit.

When we got down in the hollow, all the chatter stopped and we did some serious possum hunting. Jim would climb the tree, grab the possum by the neck and throw him to the ground. Then the dogs would grab and hold it until Jim could put him in the croaker sack. We got eleven in the first three hours. About midnight, we stopped to build a fire, toast marshmallows and have sandwiches and hot chocolate. Ummm good! All food seems to taste so much better when it's eaten outdoors, especially at night. I sat there listening to the crickets, owls and whippoorwills while I ate. Just as we finished eating, Jim looked up in a nearby tree and spied a great big possum. But this tree was tall and too small for Jim to climb. He shook the tree and threw stones, but he could not get the possum to fall so the dogs could grab it. Although we already had eleven, we just had to get this big one for Jim.

Brother Frank said that since the tree was very slender, what we needed was an ax to chop the tree down. When Jim said he knew where he could "borrow" an ax, Frank sent him, Jack and me off to get it. Jack and I did not want to go; we wanted to stay around the warm fire and listen to Frank tell jokes and Bible stories. Nothing doing; we had to go. But Jack and I knew exactly why. Mary and Belle wanted to do a little smooching with their boyfriends. So, off the three of us went. We walked about a mile up to Bob White's house and Jim crept into the backyard and "borrowed" an ax.

On the way back, I slipped on a large rock and bruised my right leg just below the knee. It hurt a lot, but Jim looked at it and saw it wasn't bleeding, so it was OK soon. We got back, chopped the tree down and as it fell, the dogs grabbed the possum. Jim took it away from them and put it in the sack. Now we had a total of twelve, and since it was late, we put out the fire, called the dogs and headed for home. Jack and I were so worn out, I was asleep almost before I hit the bed. Oh yes, Jim returned the ax the next day!

For the rest of my life, I had more reasons than one to remember that night. In a few days my right leg started to hurt; every day the pain grew worse. It began to swell and throb just below the knee. In two weeks it was so painful that everyone had to walk softly in the room and could not sit on or shake the bed. Finally, at Mary's urging, Papa called Dr. O'Kelly. He told us that the leg did not look good at all and that I should be rushed to the Macon hospital at once. Mary and Belle carefully placed me into the back seat of Papa's 1932 Chevrolet. Then Papa jumped in and we all were off on the fast ride to Macon, where there was a very good hospital.

My sister Mary was a registered nurse there and Belle was in nurses' training, so I thanked God that they were home that day to go with us. When we got to Gray and the concrete highway, I felt a jabbing pain as we sped over each crack of that road. Before we left home, Mary called her favorite doctor, and he was waiting at the emergency room when we arrived. When Dr. Chrisman saw the leg, he told us this was very serious and immediately rushed me to surgery. Then he quickly went to a phone and called Dr. Newman, one of the best orthopedic surgeons in the South. Within the hour I was prepped, sent to the operating room and the surgery began. Mary called Mama and she called some friends, so my operation was covered by strong prayers.

Mary assisted the surgeon as he removed over three inches of the large bone just below the knee. When I woke up in the recovery room, I saw Mary, Annabelle, Dr. Chrisman and Dr. Newman all standing around my bed looking down at me with smiles on their faces.

"James, my boy," said Dr. Newman, "you came through just fine. Because of that bump on your leg, you developed osteomyelitis, a rapidly spreading infection of the bone marrow. I had to remove all of the infected bone and marrow so that your leg could be saved. This gives us the best chance that the infection will not spread nor recur. It's all behind you now, Son, so I'll turn you over to Dr. Chrisman and your pretty sisters. I will be looking in on you often, so don't worry; you are going to be okay."

I thanked Dr. Newman for saving my leg. He smiled, patted my shoulder and left. Dr. Chrisman told me that he would be in every day. After he walked out, Belle kissed me and had to leave, so Mary got me pushed to my room, which was actually the children's ward.

She stayed for awhile longer, held my hand and said, "Sugar, we just made it to the hospital in time; a day later, and you probably would have lost your leg."

Before she left, she assured me that all the staff were going to be real good to me.

Mary then brought the night nurse in who said with a big smile, "I'll be watching you every minute, Jamie boy. Just any 'ole thing your little heart desires, you just tell me, and it's yours!"

I gave her a weak smile. Then I think I drifted off to sleep.

As I looked back on it, I saw the clear hand of God in that entire situation: Mary got Papa to call Dr. O'Kelly just in time, she was a nurse at the Macon hospital, I arrived there in time to save my leg, and I was treated by an excellent doctor and an eminent surgeon, both of whom were immediately available.

However, the miracle that saved my life occurred later that night. About three o'clock in the morning, I awoke to find my bed surrounded by several nurses and three doctors who were all working frantically. When I raised my head up and looked down, I saw a dozen scissors sticking up from the incision. About an hour earlier, the night nurse had checked on me and discovered that the wound was bleeding profusely. She ran and phoned my doctors, who were there in minutes. It was not until they were able to stop the bleeding and had changed the sheets that I realized how much blood I had lost. Mary told me later that if the nurse had not faithfully checked on me, I probably would have bled to death that night. When I heard this, I knew that the nurse was my "guardian angel" whom God used to save my life. Early the next morning when she came to my bedside, I thanked her with tears in my eyes. One of our greatest blessings is to discover that God is always watching over us and has His hand on our lives. I heartily thanked Him for saving my life that night. I was there in the hospital totally bedfast for thirty days, with a cast on my leg from the toes to the hip.

I have just had a thought to hit me hard. You know, those two boyfriends of Mary's and Belle's almost cost me my leg and my life! But I didn't think of that then, and I'm glad.

In the children's ward, there was a thirteen-year-old girl at my end of the room whose bed was just across from mine. On my second day, she came over and said, "Hi, my name is Susan. What's yours?"

I said hi and told her my name. She told me that she had been there for several weeks. She was a very pretty little girl with black hair and sparkling brown, almost tiger, eyes. Her kidneys were failing, so the nurses had to wrap her body in hot sheets three times a day. Although she was not supposed to get out of bed very often, she would come over to see me and ask if I needed anything. I was flat on my back and could not move much, so I welcomed her attention. One night during my second week, she came over to say goodnight and leaned over and tenderly kissed me on the cheek. No one knew it, but we had quite a blossoming little romance going. Our friendship really helped make the days go faster and brighter for both of us. After lights out, we whispered little youth secrets to each other before we went to sleep. The next night she was halfway over on the way to kiss me goodnight when she heard the nurse coming. She quickly turned around and jumped back into her bed, pulled up her sheet and pretended to be fast asleep. After the nurse gave us fresh ice water and tucked us both in, she left. As soon as the door closed, we burst into the laughter we had suppressed until we were about to explode.

Every day we had good, long visits sharing things with each other about ourselves. Even though she knew she was dying and was growing weaker day by day, Susan was always bright and cheerful. This helped so much to lift my spirits. I thought how much I wished God would also give me her kind of courage in the face of death. When she would come over to tell me goodnight, since I could not raise up, she would always lean over my chest, so I could hug her tight and then kiss her. Lying there tethered to that hospital bed through all those long days and nights gave me my first experience in patience. Thoughts of sweet little Susan, her critical illness and what she was facing made my condition seem much less depressing.

One day my special Nurse-Angel came in and asked me, "Master James, aren't you tired of looking at that old ceiling? I am going to roll you out on the porch so you can see the street below. Ring your bell when you're ready to be brought in or need me. OK?"

I wished Susan could have come out with me. From the large screened-in porch, I could watch the cars and the people go by. One day I saw this young black boy come riding down the street on a scooter he had made. He had taken one old skate, cut it in two and attached one part to the front and one on the back of the bottom of a wide plank. Up at the front end, he had attached a three-foot post with a cross bar on it. He held the cross bar with both hands while he rode with his left foot on the scooter and pushed like blazes with his right foot. Then when he got his speed up, he would put both feet on the scooter and go flying down the gentle incline like he was on a speed bike. Those skates cut up quite a noise, while his shirt fluttered in the wind.

On the second day I whistled down at him. He looked up, gave me a wave and then sped off down the hill again. He became my little racer, and I was his audience. He came there almost every day at the same time. On those days when I heard his first ride down the hill, I would have the nurse push me out so I could again become his cheerleader, waving and spurring him on to greater speeds. If I did not appear right away, he would loudly whistle up to me until I came out to watch. But he continued to ignore my waving for him to come up to see me. I even had Susan come out and motion for him to visit us. No luck. After about two weeks, I did not hear him anymore. He disappeared without ever knowing how much diversion and downright fun he furnished me for much of the time I was there in the hospital.

As the days passed, I became very tired of the food. When she finished her days training at the hospital, my youngest sister, Annabelle, came after supper with her boyfriend Hoyt to visit me. Hid under her coat was a paper sack filled with two large hot dogs covered with onions, mustard and ketchup. I looked forward all day to their visits and to those hot dogs. While Hoyt watched for the approach of nurses, I had a great feast. Since then, every time I eat a hot dog or even smell one, I have a rush of memories of Belle, Hoyt, Susan, hot dogs and the fun visits we had until visiting hours were over and they had to leave.

Once when I was in Macon sixty years later, I talked on the phone with Hoyt who was then in his late eighties. He well remembered the visits and the hot dogs and his beautiful sweetheart, Belle.

Before we hung up, I asked him a question that had always bothered me. I said, "Hoyt, Belle was so pretty and you all were so happy together, why didn't you ask her to marry you?"

"Well...," he said slowly, with a tone of regret, "it really never came up."

I always thought that Hoyt was both good-looking and intelligent—but now I believe he was just a little too shy or maybe even slightly dumb to let beautiful Belle slip through his fingers!

I entered the hospital on November 24, and the doctors were kind enough to let me go home on Christmas Eve. Since the doctor felt that an auto ride might disturb the leg and possibly cause further bleeding, I was sent home in an ambulance. Saying good-bye to Susan was so difficult that I almost told the nurse that I wanted to stay a week longer. We had brought sunshine into each other's lives every day and had become very special friends.

That afternoon, as my stretcher was being rolled slowly out of the room, Susan quickly bounced over and, with great courage, stood on tiptoe and before everybody kissed me right in the mouth!

She then whispered close to my ear, "Good-bye, sweet James. I love you. Thanks for being my friend. Have a merry Christmas. Hope to see you again...someday."

The nurses were exchanging glances and smiling broadly, but she and I had big tears in our eyes. All of the nurses on that floor and my two doctors were waiting at the entrance to tell me good-bye. I could not keep back the tears, so they all quickly tried to turn them into laughter. Each of the nurses kissed me good-bye, and my two doctors reminded me that they would see me in a month, when I had to return to have my leg examined. My angel nurse helped Mary and Belle get me into the ambulance.

Susan was on my mind for a long time on the way home. Fortunately, Mary and Belle soon turned my thoughts to how happy I was going to be to get back home and see Mama, Papa and Jack again. I agreed, but even after I got back home, I still thought of

A MIRACLE A MINUTE

Susan and missed her every day, especially those sweet goodnight kisses. We exchanged a card or two, but then when she didn't answer my last card, I feared the worst.

Mary came to my bed one afternoon that week and gave me the very sad news that my precious little Susan had passed away. Knowing of our deep friendship, Mary sat on the bed and held my hand until I got my cry over. Although kids our age rarely ever talked about death or Jesus, I sorely regretted that I had not asked Susan about her faith. However, I was sure that since she was so sweet, she was now in the arms of Jesus and in a far fairer land than when she was in this valley of sickness and pain. It may be selfish of me, but I was so glad I was not there when she died. Jesus said, "Let the little children come to me, and do not forbid them; for of such is the kingdom of God…their angels always see the face of My Father" (Luke 18:16; Matt. 18:10).

My recuperation was a very long and arduous ordeal. I spent six months in bed, another six months in a wheelchair (which we called a rolling chair in those days) and six months on crutches. During all those long days and sometimes sleepless nights, I had plenty of time to think of Jesus, Susan and my future, and to read my Bible and pray. I learned to draw cars and to crochet—believe it or not. I also took guitar lessons twice a week from a beautiful girl named Waneata. I developed an enormous crush on my teacher, who was at least ten years older than I. She taught me a total of about fifteen chords and about two hundred songs. Each time she came, we drank a lot of iced tea and had a great time singing songs, talking and playing our guitars together.

I still remember one of the songs was "When I Had But Fifty Cents." It was about this guy Romi who took Julie out to dine, and she ate him out of house and home.

"She ate a this this this and a that that that and most everthang' you bet, ending up with a handful of mints, Romi owed what Julie et! Now Romi is crying still, 'cause he cannot pay the bill, He's now awashin' dishes, for he had but fifty cents!" Or something like that. After a few more weeks passed, she told me that I had learned everything she knew about the guitar and that she could not return. I cried. I never saw her again, but I still play the guitar now and then, and those songs make me dream of Romi and Julie and…Waneater.

Mama, Papa and Jack all cared for my every need, and so did Mary and Belle when they were there. Someone was always coming in and out to do things for me without ever seeming to mind or losing their patience.

36

I especially got very close to Mama during those days. She got in bed with me one night when I was depressed and in pain and said to me, "Jamie, I wish I could tell you just how much Papa and I love you. We are praying for you to get well every day and night. The Lord Jesus also loves you very much, and we know that He is going to pull you through this all the way."

Her love and faith increased my faith. And the Lord Jesus did just exactly what she prayed He would do, and things went a little better every day after that.

Finally, after over a year and several visits to the doctor in Macon, the cast came off and I began to walk on crutches. Then Belle, Mary and Mama took turns for many weeks gently exercising my leg. It had frozen straight at the knee joint. I was glad when it functioned normally again, although the leg had to be dressed daily during all those months. As I began to walk more and more on crutches, I learned to put a little more weight upon the leg, and after another six months I was walking without the crutches! O my dear Lord, it was so good to be out of that bed, out of the wheel chair and off those crutches. I tell you for sure, when this was all over I was not the same person as the one who was rushed to the hospital that frightful afternoon eighteen months earlier.

During my recuperation, I got the lessons from my teachers weekly, kept up my homework and did not miss any time in school. My second cousin Cecil Pippin built a wagon with small wooden wheels that was just large enough for me to ride in. So he took me to school and brought me back home every day while my leg was getting stronger.

That experience taught me many lessons that have never left me: It brought me closer to my family and closer to God, and closer to the church and the preacher at the little Methodist church who called regularly to visit and pray with me. I received "the milk of human kindness" through love and understanding from my family, my teachers, the students and so many other people. I learned that a friend is really one of life's greatest treasures, and I was taught the valuable lessons of humility and longsuffering. All those warm expressions of love shaped my life and softened my heart toward the Lord, and most important of all, this experience played a large part in my later decision to give my life totally to Jesus Christ and become a minister.

What happened next in my family was a near tragedy that gave me an even stronger faith and convinced me that God was very near and would answer my prayer. Although it was a prayer of a boy who was only fifteen years old, it saved the life of someone very close to me.

❋ 5 ❋

Father, Father, Save My Papa!

You will remember that Papa had two mail routes, the short one in the morning and the long one after lunch. Well, in late 1934 President Roosevelt consolidated many of these routes to save money, so Papa's routes were given to other carriers. Since Papa had carried the mail for over thirty-two years, he was forced to retire at the early age of fifty-five. This came as a tremendous shock, and it literally broke his heart to be retired with no notice at that early age. Rural Free Delivery (RFD) had been his pride and joy—his life. He was so good at it that he was named Georgia's "mail carrier of the year" several times and was once elected chairman of the Georgia delegation. The national convention met each year in a different large city. His great delight was to attend all of those conventions. Since his retirement pension was only one hundred dollars a month, that meant the end of his travel. What was worse, that amount was never increased for the rest of his life. Papa was always a very active and busy person, so he had great difficulty adjusting and was at a loss for what to do with much of his time. As a consequence, he began to worry a lot and drink more than usual.

One night I was alone upstairs in my room when I heard Mama scream. I ran down the stairs and found Papa slumped over with his face in his supper plate. Jack was working late at the store, but thank God, Mary was there that night and she and Mama were right behind me when I entered the room. Because of his color, Mary suspected immediately that Papa had suffered a heart attack. She ran to the phone and called Dr. Zackery, who lived ten miles away in Gray. He promised to be there as fast as he could. Then she and Mama got Papa to his bed, loosened his clothing and made him as comfortable as possible. I knew by the color of his face that he was in a lot of pain. His breathing was heavy and fast. None of us was able to do anything to help him, and it seemed that the doctor was taking forever to get there. Out on the porch, as I watched for the doctor, I heard a dog howling in the distance. This really sent a chill through me, because the black people in my community believed that when a dog barks like that at night, someone is going to die.

This was the first time I was moved to cry out in heartfelt tears to God, asking Him to hear and answer my prayer. I went out into the side yard of the house, and in the darkness of that August night, I fell down on my knees and prayed, "O dear Father, if You have ever heard a prayer I have prayed, please, please, hear this one now. Father, please do not let my Papa die. Speed the doctor to his side, and would You and the doctor please save his life? Please?? I ask this in the name of Your dear Son, Jesus. Amen."

As soon as I finished praying these words, the doctor pulled up and dashed into the house. I stayed outside and continued to pray fervently that Papa would live. I walked back and forth, wringing my hands while my heart was breaking. My throat ached and I had trouble swallowing. When I went back into the house, Mary put her arms around me and told me that Papa was resting much better and that Doctor Zackery had said that Papa was going to be all right. When I heard the doctor driving away, I ran upstairs to my bedroom window and watched him as he drove down the hill. With great joy in my heart, I thanked God that He had answered my prayer and saved my papa's life. I am sure that Mary and Mama were also praying the whole time, but I just knew that God had also heard and answered *my* prayer.

I walked quietly back downstairs, entered Papa's room and found Mama down on her knees by his bedside. As I knelt there beside her, we comforted each other and felt God very near. When we arose, I placed a tender kiss on my dear papa's forehead, turned, hugged and kissed Mama goodnight and then went back upstairs to my room. I knelt down and whispered another fervent prayer of thanks to God. Because I felt that Papa was going to be all right, I climbed into bed and fell fast asleep.

From that night on, prayer became a more vital part of my everyday life. I began to feel such a closeness to God and to Jesus that I started a plan to read the entire New Testament. I wanted more than ever to find out everything I could about Jesus' life and all the words He spoke. What I did not realize was that because of

A MIRACLE A MINUTE

Papa's heart attack, decisions were about to be made that would take me out of Round Oak forever.

My parents, Jack and I had vacationed at St. Simon's Island during several summers. When I recently saw the postmark on an old letter from there, I was reminded that in the early days the Island was called St. Simon Island, omitting the "s." The island is off the coast of Brunswick, Georgia, halfway between Savannah and Jacksonville. Each summer we spent two weeks there enjoying the beach, swimming in the ocean, going crabbing and fishing and just basking in the subtropical sun. Tall pine trees were everywhere, and mixed in were tall palm trees, and old live oaks with Spanish moss hanging from them. The four of us had fallen in love with St. Simon's and looked forward all year to returning there.

Since Papa had retired and probably would have a long time of recuperation, Dr. Zackery advised him to move to the island. He suggested that since the winters there were milder and the pace of life slower, Papa would be relieved of much stress. But what was to be done with the store? Jack might have to run it alone because I was still not yet able to be up on my feet for very long at a time. Jack had an idea. Mary had recently married Perry Nichols of Jesup, whom she met when she started working as head nurse at the Jesup hospital. Perry managed a large dry goods store there, but was not very happy with his job. So, at Jack's suggestion, Papa asked Mary and Perry to move to Round Oak. They arrived in the spring of 1937. A few weeks later, Papa turned the store over to Jack, Mary and Perry and started making plans to move to St. Simon's.

It was a hard decision for my parents to make. Neither of them really wanted to leave Round Oak, the town in which they were married, where all nine of their children had been born and raised, where all of their family and close friends lived and where so many of their relatives and friends were buried. Mama would also have to leave her beloved church, her favorite preacher and her sisters and brothers with whom she was very close. She saw them often and looked forward to meeting them each month at Caney Creek Church. This made it so much more difficult for Mama to leave than it was for Papa. But what was best for Papa was what they had to do. Since I was a freshman in high school, it was decided that I would remain in Round Oak until school was out and then I would join them. This was OK with me because I did not want to enter a very large school in Brunswick three months before school was out.

So, after thirty-five years in Round Oak, the day came when my parents packed up all they could carry in the four-door, 1932 Chevrolet and headed for St. Simon's Island. Although they both hoped that this would be a temporary move, they would live there for the rest of their lives. After hugs and kisses and reminders from Mama not to forget to do this and to remember not to do that, she and Papa got into the car and slowly drove out of the driveway. Mary, Perry, Jack and I all stood there waving as they pulled away. I held my composure as long as I could, but suddenly my eyes filled with tears and I began to sob uncontrollably, having a hard time getting my breath. Mary and Perry took us over to the front steps, and sat down and chatted with us until we had stopped crying.

The last few months of school went by quickly, so by June 1, I was ready to go. This boy of fifteen, who had grown up in a little country town, was about to be thrust into the busy life of a high school that was located in a large seacoast city. This year, 1937, was to be my most exciting year so far. I would begin to shave, my voice would change, and I would fall hopelessly in love with a very lovely girl.

❋ 6 ❋

Krista, My First and Lost Love

St. Simon's is a beautiful island off the coast, one of the "Golden Isles of Georgia." It is thirteen miles long and eight miles wide. In the winter the population was small, but during the summer the island was crowded with vacationers from all over the Southeast. The coastal town, which I considered to be a large city, was Brunswick. Its population was about eighteen thousand. The island was connected to the coast by a narrow causeway with several wooden bridges over the rivers that cut through the vast "Marshes of Glenn" in Glenn County, marshes made famous by our Georgia Poet Laureate, Sidney Lanier.

On that beautiful June afternoon in 1937, Mary and Perry drove me the two hundred miles to Brunswick. I could smell the refreshing salt air of the ocean even before we got to Brunswick. During that ride over the causeway with the vast marshes on both sides, the dappled sky of blue and white above, the view of the Atlantic Ocean and the tall white lighthouse far to the southeast, I began to feel like I was entering a brand-new world from which I would never want to leave. The years I spent there have ever after remained vivid in my memory. St. Simon's Island has the glow, aura, pace of life and romantic history that causes one to say of it what Hemingway said about Paris: He affectionately called her "a moveable feast."

Yes, watch your heart, my friend, for that magic island can cast a spell on you if you are not careful. Once you have spent the four seasons there, it will always remain with you as a sweet memory and a yearning that will refuse to go away until you return. You can never really leave, no matter how far you travel from there or how many years have passed since you were there. So, stay away if you don't want to be smitten by it for life.

This enchanting island paradise was made even more famous and romantically attractive by Eugenia Price. It was here that she made her home and where she wrote her many best-selling novels. If you read one of them, you'll read them all. But be sure to ask someone who has read them to tell you the proper sequence in which they must be read. Now, you see, I have given you a sweet little hint that will bring you much joy.

Perry, Mary and I arrived there in the early afternoon. It was good to be back again with my parents. Papa had already bought a home at Glenn Haven, about halfway up the island toward Fort Fredericka. All the cottages on the island were named, kind of like boats are. Our new home was a two-story frame house that Papa named "Bent Oaks." There were three oak trees in the front yard that grew up about six feet, then were bent over for about six more feet, and then grew straight up to form an "S." I was never able to figure out just how that happened. My bedroom was upstairs overlooking those bent oaks. For the first time in my life, I had a room of my own. We lived there until Papa finished a new house next door that was larger but all on one floor, which was better for his heart.

The summer literally seemed to fly by. I met new friends, went swimming in the large lake near our house, got as tanned as an Indian and just whiled away the days and nights with not a care in the world. I was to look back on that summer as the last absolutely carefree time I was ever to have. I did not have a job, and there were no chores because there were no cows, pigs, chickens and horses to feed or any fireplaces that needed daily coal. We had an oil heater and Mama had an electric stove. Oh, I forgot, there was one fireplace in Papa's bedroom that needed wood, but we bought most of this already cut.

O mine Papa, would today I could tell you thanks for that carefree world you and Mama gave me; no concern for bills, food, clothing or shelter; no job or career pain; no worries about the past or the future; and no concern for life or death—or taxes! The thoughts of youth are long, long thoughts, but surely they are certainly not often worried thoughts.

However, that easy summer life suddenly vanished that fall when, as a sophomore, I entered Glynn Academy, the large high school in Brunswick. The school bus stopped a block from our house in front of Highsmith's Grocery Store. Each morning at 7:30, I gathered there with several other students for the twenty-minute ride over the beautiful causeway to school.

A MIRACLE A MINUTE

One of the students who boarded the bus that first morning was a pretty girl with sparkling brown eyes and honey-colored hair that fell to her shoulders. Her name was Krista, and she was fourteen. I guess you could say that it was love at first sight, because we spent every possible waking moment together from that very first day. She and I always arrived at the bus stop early every morning so we could be together and chat. We always sat together on the bus, holding hands all the way. I didn't see much of the scenery for I wasn't really on that bus, I was in "luv!" As I think back, I can still hear the loud clatter the bus made as it crossed the rivers on those old narrow wooden bridges. Since we were in different buildings that first year, we could not see each other again until school was out for the day and we boarded the bus to go home.

After school we took long rides together on our bikes and often wound up by Dunbar River. As we sat there on the old wooden dock, as any pair of sweethearts would, we had long, long thoughts and long, long talks and dreamed of days to come. The very first time I really ever kissed a girl and the first time she kissed a boy was one afternoon on that dock. Though she was only fourteen, she had developed physically and mentally early and seemed to me to have the body and mind of an eighteen-year-old. Her mother was very strict with her and did not want us to be together very often or very long.

On the beach one night, as we watched a huge spring moon rise out of a calm sea and stood there holding each other, we learned what being deeply in love could do to one's life. So deep, it changed our whole world into a new, bright and sweeter place. Her presence filled me with such joy that when she was with me, though in a crowd, I felt we were alone, and when we were apart, though I was in a crowd, I was sadly alone.

One afternoon after school we were alone playing "pick-up-sticks" while lying on her living room rug. Our heads seemed to get closer and closer together when suddenly, she rolled over on her back and smiled up at me. Her breath was sweet, and her hair was fragrant and like fine silk. While leaning on my elbows, I gazed deep into her eyes at close range. I leaned closer and began to kiss her softly, each kiss seeming to last longer and longer. After awhile we stood up to embrace and discovered that we were both very weak and dizzy, feeling as if we were intoxicated. There was a popular song then entitled "But I Can Dream, Can't I?" that had a line in it that goes, "Your kisses taste like wine, and I am drunk with mine."

On that afternoon of ecstasy, we learned what that song meant.

Krista, My First and Lost Love

Although this may not be a romance novel, romance is what it was, big time. But in a real sense, this story is filled with romance. The long story of God's conversation with us is the greatest romance ever told. He has had a love affair with us across the centuries, and more recently He has tried, through Christ, to woo us back into His arms of eternal love. As a matter of fact, I do not think that it is possible to love anything or anyone deeply here on earth until we dearly love Him first.

Krista and I went steady for four years, and our love grew deeper with each passing day. Though we often engaged in what was then called heavy petting, during all those years we never made love. I must admit though, we came close several times. Actually, many adults find it difficult to believe that youth at our age could experience such a deep affection and yet have the strength to abstain from sex. But our love was so real and tender, so filled with devotion, that it was at a level far deeper than just the desire for sexual pleasure. Of course, the physical attraction was strong because that is the culmination of the deepest love, but we both were convinced that if that happened we would have displeased the Lord and destroyed all our chances of having His blessing.

So, the temptation to make love was never so strong that we had any real trouble turning away from it. We had a deep respect for one another, a relationship that was rare for a boy and girl our age. We did not want to yield to the carnal temptations of the moment that would spoil a love we just knew would last throughout eternity. Although Krista and I were in each other's thoughts most of the time, regretfully, we had to give much of our attention to our studies and student activities so we could get through high school.

How could any graduate ever forget Glynn Academy? It was a regular, public high school with a fancy name, wonderful but also very strict. Three of my teachers were "old maids." They were Miss Lott, Miss Bunkley and Miss Macon, who taught math, English, and literature *respectfully*. They really respected and deeply loved the subjects they taught. They were all in their fifties then, and they would stand for no foolishness. There was no running or loud talking in the halls between classes. The classrooms were quiet, everybody paid attention, and we got from the teachers exactly what we were there to get—an education. Maybe you are saying to yourself right now, "Oh, yeah, SURE!" But it's the gospel truth. The homework was so heavy that I can remember working up to four hours each night, all alone by the heater, often crying as I went to bed.

Today, as I recall those years, I am glad it was that way. We had to write detailed book reports on the great classics (oh groan!); many research papers to do; math problems to solve; sentences to diagram (groan #2); spelling words to memorize; and current events to stay abreast of. All of us were required to be on time to school, to our homeroom and in our seats for every class before the bell rang. None of us would ever think of walking into a room after the bell had rung and the door was closed. Well, not the second time anyway, that's for sure. If you did, the teacher and the entire class would stare holes right through you.

If you think the teachers were tough, just do something bad enough to get sent to Mr. Hood, the principal. He was often worse than a prison warden. He wouldn't touch you, but before he got through with you, you felt like he had beaten you half to death! Don't get me wrong, if you did your work and stayed out of trouble, he and the teachers were your friends. And, O my good Lord, was the grading strict! All students, both boys and girls, were treated alike—fairly, but roughly. Every student had to work like blazes for a "B" and had to be a five-star wonder to get an "A" out of any of them. No one could slide by, and no one was promoted to the next grade unless he or she passed with at least a C average. Believe it or not, we were constantly trying to please the teachers and working hard to improve our handwriting and to speak with proper English when we recited. The dropout rate was nil, with many grads going on to college. Student morale was high, mainly because we were made to work so hard. We took pride in our work and our school. Again, I know this all sounds too good to be true, but if you just ask anyone who graduated in the 30s and 40s and even into the 50s, they may say that it was even worse than I am describing—or better, depending on the way you look at it. I do believe that we were better educated with that high school diploma than many college graduates are today.

Oh, I forgot—we were not allowed to drive cars to school, and we could not leave the campus during school hours. We all had to eat lunch in the school cafeteria. Even if you brought your lunch, you still had to eat it there. The full lunch cost about twenty-five cents. Even in the depths of the Depression, no one ever heard of a free lunch furnished by the government. And it was nothing like this foolishness we have today at lunch, with the entire high school disgorging itself—four hundred seniors all piling into cars and speeding all over town eating at the fancy places and spending a small fortune before the year is out.

Those of us who entered the military in World War II were certainly prepared for the toughest drill sergeant and for the austere living after having dealt with that high school principal and sitting at the feet of those dear "old maids," God bless 'em and may God rest their gallant souls! Alas, they have all graduated to that glory in the heavens. Just imagine how those wonderful old girls shaped up *that* place!

During my high school years I was an active member of the St. Simon's Methodist Church, often driving Mama there on Sundays in Papa's '32 "Chivvy," southern slang for Chevrolet. The minister was Rev. James Webb, a tall, handsome, friendly man. I sometimes taught a class, sang in the choir and was president of the youth group, the Epworth League. On Sunday evenings, my friend Doyle Baldwin would borrow his Uncle "Mighty Fine's" '37 Cadillac limousine, pick me up, and then we'd go around and fill the car with pretty Methodist girls. But Krista was never with us; she and her parents were Episcopalians. This meant that I was sad, lonely and a bit depressed. To cover this up, I used humor and became the life of the party. I seemed to always see the funny side of everything, often keeping Doyle and the girls in stitches. Because I was sometimes crying inside, I seldom ever smiled, but I had *them* laughing so hard that tears ran down their faces. I always got a lot of joy in making others happy. Their laughter helped to cover up my loneliness. The youth group and the church became a vital part of my life all throughout high school.

That summer, I started hanging around the St. Simon's Airport. Jim, the instructor-manager, saw that I had a strong desire to learn to fly. He had "taken a likin'" to me, so I raked up the money and started lessons. I was on my eighth lesson in a Piper Cub when I was drafted into the army. While I was at Ft. MacPherson, I took two more lessons at the old Atlanta airport. I was into figure-8's, power stalls and shooting landings when I was transferred to Providence, Rhode Island. In the meantime, I lost two of my friends in plane accidents, so I never went back to flying. Not long ago I ran across some of those flying lesson receipts and could not believe that I only paid five dollars an hour with Jim, and at Atlanta, ten dollars! Today, lessons cost several hundred dollars for thirty minutes!

During my senior year I took a class in debating. Each year two senior boys were chosen to debate two senior girls. The question used for many years was, "Who was the more villainous, Macbeth or Lady Macbeth?"

For thirteen consecutive years the girls had beaten the boys. I was chosen that year, along with my friend F. H., to face the two brightest senior girls. They were so ferocious that if we saw them first in the halls or something, we avoided them until the day and time of the debate. We knew we had to work hard, so we practiced for long hours, and believe me, I sure prayed a lot.

Well, the dreaded morning for the great debate finally came. F. H. and I felt like gladiators, or worse, like "Daniels" in the lions' den. Of course, the girls from the whole school all turned out in droves, and the auditorium was packed solid with other students, teachers and visiting parents.

The girls led off. We sat quietly, looking bored, enduring their arrogance and premature assurance. F. H. began and greatly disorganized them; then when my turn came, I tore into those two pretty girls with no mercy. We provoked them so much they lost their tempers and in the end, during the rebuttal, they actually began shaking their fists and screaming at us.

In the closing summary, F. H. was absolutely splendid. Then I slowly moved to the center of the stage, logically dismantled all their points one by one, and really poured on the steam in the closing. I vividly pictured Lady Macbeth, that witch of consummate evil, during the darkest hour of that night, quietly stealing into the king's chamber, and with heinous delight, raising the dagger high and plunging it deep into her sleeping husband's breast. I described his royal blood gushing out and covering the treacherous hand that held the dagger.

In a loud voice, speaking slowly, I concluded, "What made this senseless murder all the more villainous? It was that this wicked *coward*, Jezebel—murdered the king *in his sleep!*—without giving him even a few seconds—to prepare to meet his Maker—thus damning his soul to an eternal hell! So, you see—we must now—find a new word that more befits the treacherous deed done by this so-called 'Laaa-deee'".

Staggering across the stage, I mimicked her, drunk with power as she gazed at her bloody hand, shrieking to the top of her voice, "OUT! OUT! DAMNED SPOT!"

Then F. H. and I slowly walked off the stage, I bringing up the rear, all the while frantically wiping my right hand with my left and whimpering over and over as if completely mad, "Out, out, damned spot...*OUT! OUT! DAMNED SPOT!*"

Well, in a flash, most of the audience jumped to their feet and broke into a loud roar and deafening applause. F. H. and I waited just a few seconds and then sneaked back on stage to our seats, looking very much as if we had faked a curtain call. This brought a second crescendo of applause. The judges were absolutely convinced that this year the boys had finally won a great victory, hands down.

Krista, My First and Lost Love

F. H. and I felt ten feet tall because everybody looked up to us for the rest of the year. That is, everybody except the senior girls! After the debate Krista was waiting for me at the exit. She was jumping up and down for joy and gave me a big hug while covering my face with kisses. She was so proud.

Lord, those long ago and fleeting high school years were sure some kind of special. I look back on them now as being some of my happiest times. If only we had known how to treasure that precious time! I wish our youth of today valued those four years more; then when or if they go into the military or to college, they will find the experience so much easier and more fun—just as it was for me, a proud grad of Glynn Academy!

You are probably shocked by the contrast between the 1930s and '40s school system and America's public education system of today. In those early years many of our high schools were this good and better. It makes me sad and even angry to know that many of our graduates today, especially in our large cities, know very little math, and many cannot even read or write, much less spell or speak proper English grammar. How can these young men and women expect to hold even an entry level job? I am both frustrated and greatly puzzled as to why so many of the public schools have disintegrated to this low level. What a waste of the student's precious, fleeting young years; how much the present system prevents them from having a productive and happy life, all because parents, school administrators and teachers do not *demand* discipline, hard homework or regular attendance.

Instead, students are passed on each year until those years are gone, leaving so many of them illiterate and uneducated. The system, teachers, and parents are cheating these students out of many of the satisfactions and joys that learning brings. Where do they go from high school? They will not make it in our better colleges, for they will not be passed on there; nor will those who cannot read nor write get a good job or support a family. An editorial in *The Daily Oklahoman* reveals the shocking fact that one out of three of our citizens could not correctly place Chicago on a map of the U.S. But sit down for this: Almost 80 percent of *college seniors* at many of our institutions of higher learning flunked a test on American history designed for *high school seniors!* But there's more: Although one out of three college students did not know that the Constitution establishes the division of power in our government, 99 percent of them could identify "Beavis" and "Butthead" as "TV cartoon characters!" (*The*

A MIRACLE A MINUTE

Daily Oklahoman, July 6, 2000, used by permission).

Parents, teachers and the system must all share in the dismal failure of our public schools and colleges to educate our children.

And all this socialistic government does is plead for more and more billions to throw at the school problem, while most of the parents, the Congress and the state legislatures stand by and watch the public education system grow worse and worse. Allene and I raised three girls, two of whom went to public schools. Our youngest, Beverly, went to a Christian private school. I would not let any of them go to public school today. I would send them to a private school, where they could get a high-quality education, even if I had to move or mortgage our home to do it. The U.S. cannot hope to compete globally in this century if these ill-prepared students continue to come out of the majority of our public schools. There are exceptional schools, of course, but these are too few and far between. I do not believe the government at any level should have anything to do with the education of our children.

I think it was Ben Gurion, a former prime minister of Israel, who said, "Know your teachers; forget about everybody else!"

For the life of me, I do not get what is going on. How can I but conclude that there is some sinister plan to *not* prepare the students to go out and make a good life in this land of opportunity, a deceptive scheme to graduate most of them directly into the welfare state. You see, if our grads cannot read or write, they cannot get and hold good jobs—the result of which is that the government will then have to provide for their needs. Oh, now I see; the light breaks upon me. (As if I hadn't known all along!) The hand that feeds and clothes them gets their vote. This "dumbing down" is tantamount to putting our students into a new kind of slavery, much worse than the earlier slavery of the old South. If this scheme is allowed to continue much longer, it will succeed in one of the major goals of the Socialists: *to destroy the middle class.*

The frightening thing about all of this is that if our public schools are not turned around soon, this "New Democrat Government" (which is supported by a burgeoning bureaucracy, a growing welfare state and all the like-minded liberals) will soon have the rest of us outnumbered—if they don't already. If many of the nation's conservatives and half of those Christians who are registered to vote insist on staying away form the polls (as they have done in recent elections), the liberals will soon have the majority vote, and it will be impossible to remove them from office. When this happens, not only we will have lost the vote, but we will have lost our country as well. The result? This spread of Socialism will first lead to a one-party system and finally to a nation led by a dictator who will destroy the middle class, take our guns away from us, ship all dissidents into concentration camps and put this once-free nation under martial law. Don't be deceived. It can happen here.

Just to think this might come to pass fills me first with chilling alarm and then with a white-hot desire to drive out of leadership (before it's too late) this sex-oriented, humanistic, Darwinistic, values-free, morals-free system of education and government.

Recently I heard a wise Milton Friedman say on TV, "Socialism is the most inefficient form of government known to mankind."

Socialism is a somewhat "intelligent" form of Communism, which owns and runs everything. Socialism lets us keep the homes, businesses and factories—that way we do all the work, and then the Socialist state comes and takes most of the profit in taxes. The government produces little more than obstruction, intrusion and red tape. For every dollar the welfare state takes from working Americans, only about twenty five cents gets to the "poor"; the bureaucracy gets the rest. The number of the "poor" is increased by raising the minimum wage and the per capita income. Let's say a family of four doesn't come up to the high level of that income. Then they are classified as poor and start getting thousands of dollars in benefits, full Medicaid coverage, and they pay no income tax! The higher the minimum wage and the average median income get, the more millions of "poor" we have in this land of opportunity and plenty. It becomes alarmingly clear that this tax-and-spend socialistic government seeks not to get these dependent Americans back to work, but instead seeks to *increase* the numbers on welfare, thus raising the income of all welfare bureaucrats, increasing their power and vastly increasing the number of votes they get.

OK, I'm about through with this, but before I go on with the story, let me give you the double-whammy! Anyone with any sense can see that all of the above drastically shrinks the working class, those of us who pay most of the taxes. Therefore, when the middle and upper working classes are eliminated, the entire system will collapse (because they have finally killed the goose)! That "goose" is us—those of us who work hard, produce the income and pay the taxes. As of the year 2001, the total amount of tax was over 50 percent of our income!

Please excuse me, my dear reader! Ohhhh, I'm probably just one of the "old fuddy-duddies" who is frightened to see our freedoms eroding daily. What started me on all this "vast right-wing conspiracy nonsense" anyway? What has all this to do with suffering humanity—or my life story? Let's get back to it fast!! Aaahhh, but you know what? Chances are I'll get off into a fevered pitch like this again before we're through with this.

Here we go now, back to the story: A few weeks after we both graduated from high school, Krista and I had what was to be our final date. As we sat there in the car in silence, both of us felt a strange sadness creeping over us.

Then, just before I walked her to the door, she moved over close to me and asked in a half-whisper, "James, do you believe that young people our age should get married?"

I hesitated, then put my arm around her and answered, "No, Krista, I don't. You know that I love you more than enough to marry you right now. But I've got the Army breathing down my neck and after that, we both should go to college. Maybe after I find out where I'm going to be stationed, we could get...but we probably should wait until after the war to get married. If we were to do that now at our age, I'd have no way to support you like I'd want to. Should we have a child, our lives and our future might be changed forever."

These words came falling out of my mouth as if I had anticipated the question and was fully prepared to give a wise answer. I think this was her way of saying, "Let's get married." And this was also exactly what I wanted more than anything on earth. But a world in conflict stood in the way. We both now feared that our deep love had come much too soon. I think of my days of loving Krista every time I hear that song Nat King Cole made famous: "They say that we were much too young, Too young to really fall in love."

Somehow, we both seemed to get the shocking message that soon our lives would be forced to travel down separate roads. That night in a dangerously changing world, we held on to each other tightly, our kisses mingled with our tears. There was now a kind of strange terror in my heart; I feared that our destiny had been seized from us and we were being swept away from each other by a swift tide of insanity that had engulfed the world.

As I am re-experiencing all of this right now, I am reminded of a line in *Doctor Zhivago*: As the bitter cold wind blows around the old frozen house and the hungry wolves howl on a hilltop not far away, and as they are clinging together in bed, Lara says to Zhivago, "O Lord, what a terrible time this is to be in love."

This swift tide of separation came all too soon for Krista and me. She and her family moved from the island to Sterling, a little town a

Krista, My First and Lost Love

few miles north of Brunswick. We saw less and less of each other. We did talk on the phone now and then, but every day we both felt that there was a large, empty sadness where our hearts used to be. I felt that I had suffered a great loss. The voice of my grief seemed to chant to me over and over: "It doesn't seem fair, It just isn't fair that we cannot spend the rest of our lives together."

This is how our Great American Love Story came to an end. It was so very simple and utterly unpredictable. In the summer of 1940 her dad bought a store that had living quarters in the rear of the building. The Georgia Highway Department (drat it) was resurfacing the road in front of the store. One day a tall, good-looking young man, who had a summer job on the road project, walked into the store and bought a soft drink. Krista waited on him. Then, during the next few minutes of that afternoon, a relationship began that cost me my girl. He was there; I wasn't. He asked her to marry him; I didn't. He won her; I lost her. This entire saga is made more difficult to relate because—OOPS, wouldn't you know that my gorgeous wife would walk in just as this part of the story is being written! And she is looking over my shoulder and her beautifully tragic eyes are reading this right now!! Shhhh! She just left the room! So I'll try to wrap this up quickly. Now, this is just between you and me, OK?

It took me many years to get over losing Krista. I could not imagine my life without her in it. My years of loving Krista did teach me this: I found out what it feels like to really be in love. So the rest of my young life, I never had to wonder about that. I would know it if it ever happened to me again because I could compare what I felt for any new girl with what I had once felt for Krista. But you see, she spoiled me. I soon began to wonder if I would ever meet a girl who could even halfway measure up to Krista. Thank God, I did. Wait just a little while and I will share with you the story of that wonderful event and all about the gorgeous girl who finally came into my life and became my first and only wife.

❋ 7 ❋

Brother Jack Comes Back

In 1939, just as I became a senior in high school, Brother Jack came back into our lives from Tulsa, Oklahoma. After he closed the store in Round Oak, Mary and Perry moved to Perry's hometown, Monroe, Michigan. Since Jack had leanings toward the ministry, Frank invited him to move from Round Oak to Tulsa and work with him in the fast-growing Eastside Christian Church, where Frank had been the founding pastor in 1935. He had started the church with only one family and met in a rented building. Jack did move to Tulsa to work with Frank. He taught an adult class and often preached on Sunday night. He planned to enter Bible college in the fall. After a few weeks in Tulsa, Jack sent us this telegram: "Have finally decided to enter the ministry. Please pray that this is God's will. Love, Jack."

The whole family was delighted when they heard this because Jack was gifted with many talents, including a brilliant mind. He made straight As in all twelve years of school and was the top senior student at Gray High School. Also, his command of the written and spoken word was outstanding for a young man his age.

Frank told us he thought Jack was happy and doing great. Then, something happened one Wednesday night a few months later. Just as Frank and Ozelle were getting into their car to go to the prayer meeting, Jack walked up. Frank asked him, "Brother Jack, we have been waiting for you. Aren't you going to church with us?"

Jack came closer to the car and answered, "No, Brother Frank, I think I'll pass tonight."

Frank smelled whisky strong on Jack's breath. Jack had been drinking some before he had moved to Tulsa, but had sworn off drinking months ago, right after he had decided to give his life in full-time service to the Lord. That night an argument started between Frank and Jack that soon became heated and included some loud words. At this, Jack turned and walked away.

Frank quickly got out of the car, took a few steps toward Jack and said in a pleading voice, "Jack, you are turning away from your promise to God tonight. And you are walking down a dark and dead-end street from which there may be no return. Please come back here now and let's pray that God will turn your life around once and for all."

But Jack kept on walking, and soon Frank could no longer see him in the darkness. Jack packed up the very next day and left Tulsa for St. Simon's. As far as I know, he never again seriously considered entering the ministry. I am convinced that his decision to walk away into the darkness that night was the turning point that shaped the rest of his life. It was actually a dead-end street.

So when Jack came to live with us that September, he seemed to be sad, alone and torn with guilt over what I thought was his decision to leave the ministry. But I was soon to learn the whole story. He began to stay up all night writing poetry and sleeping most of the day. His poetry was very good, some sounding like Edgar Allen Poe and some like Shakespeare. He wrote beautiful sonnets and long poems with deep meaning, many of which he read aloud to me. Some of his poems I didn't fully understand. He and I had long conversations late at night alone. He asked me to make him pots of fresh coffee, which he drank all night while he smoked one cigarette after another.

One night he finally told me all about a consuming love affair he had in Tulsa with a beautiful girl named Clara Anne. Her parents were against the relationship, and because they knew of Jack's occasional drinking, they had ordered her not to see him again. But Jack and she kept meeting in secret. He wrote her many poems of love bound in leather or fur that he made in a leather shop where he was working part time. Leaving Frank and the ministry and losing her had left him with a broken heart, bringing about a long season of sadness for him. He felt rejected and went through a deep valley of depression. I could relate to some of his pain, for I was going through those feelings in my loss of Krista.

Later that fall he moved into an old house up on Back River, on the north part of the island, where he spent the winter. The house was owned by a couple from Atlanta who were there only during the summer.

While he had been in Tulsa, Clara Anne (the girl he was grieving over) had introduced him to classical music. So when I visited him, often spending the night, we sat for hours on the front porch of that old frame house, with the moon reflecting on the river as we listened to the great symphonies. He would sometimes interpret the meaning of a composition to me. Soon I also became a lover of the classics, a devotion that has never left me. Even today, whenever I hear a great symphony, I remember Jack, and I am transported back to that old house on the river and to that time many years ago when he and I were both very young and very close.

On one particularly special night when I arose to check on him, I found him sound asleep on the couch near the window. A symphony was quietly playing in the background and the bright moon was shining full upon his face. His dark heavy eyebrows, thick black hair and large eyes now closed in sleep, were all in bold relief, burning a picture etched so clearly into my mind. My memory of this flashes back so strongly and in such detail, it seems as if I were there right now. After kneeling and saying a silent prayer, I gently covered him with a blanket and crept back to my bed. His writing, the music and my visits went on throughout that winter. Sometimes Doyle (my friend from high school who had the Cadillac) would go up there with me, and we would kill a few pots of coffee and have long chats.

Jack learned that the owners would be returning soon, so in April he moved back to our house in Glenn Haven. The house on the river was owned by Ed and Bit. When they came from Atlanta that May, they brought with them Bit's pretty niece, Sam. She was the third daughter born to her parents, who were Methodist missionaries in China. "Samm-ay" in Chinese means "third sister," so she was called Sam from birth. She had just graduated from high school. One afternoon Bit brought Sam in with her to buy groceries at the store near our house. Jack happened to be at the store when they came in. As soon as Jack and Sam were introduced and their eyes met, they were strongly attracted to one another. Jack began to date her that very night. After a whirlwind romance, he popped the question. Later, when her parents came down and met him, he asked for her hand in marriage and they gave their permission. So, they were married that summer, and Jack acted like a different person when he and Sam returned from their honeymoon.

One night Sam invited me over for supper. Later, as we sipped coffee after dinner, Jack got quiet and started glancing at me.

I broke the silence by saying, "Jack, you look like you've got something on your mind."

Brother Jack Comes Back

He smiled at Sam, and said to me, "Brother James, I got a proposition for you. Would you be interested in the two of us owning a grocery store? You know Mr. Andrews from Atlanta. Well he bought the store from old Mr. Highsmith, who suffered a stroke and had to retire. I've just learned that Andrews is not happy here and wants to go back to Atlanta. If you're interested, we'll ask Papa what he thinks, and if he goes along, maybe we can get him to help us buy the place."

I answered, "I would be interested in getting it, if he isn't asking too much and if Papa will back us. You know, that old Mr. Andrews is a tough cookie."

When Jack and I put the deal to Papa, he saw it as a good idea, so he bought the store for us at a good price—with the understanding that we would pay him back in three years out of part of the profits. We agreed, and in a few days after we signed all the papers, Jack and I were the proud "owners" of the "George T. Pippin & Sons Grocery Company." With the store came three frame cottages. Jack and Sam moved into one of these. Since I had just graduated from high school and Jack needed more income, we were both delighted with this opportunity.

It was a small store that offered a full line of groceries and had gasoline pumps out front. We bought grits, rice, several kinds of beans and peas, coffee, sugar and flour all in 100-pound sacks, then measured out different amounts of each into paper sacks. These items were taped, weighed, priced and placed on the shelves behind the counters. There was no such thing as self-service in those days. Every customer came up to the one long counter and told us the items they wanted or handed us a list. We then went behind all the counters, which were placed in a big "U" all over the store, to get the items, and place them in front of the customer. We also had a refrigerated case that offered a variety of meats.

Old Charlie Johnson, a man of about fifty five who had a face and nose like Jimmy Durante, was our first butcher. He not only taught Jack and me how to cut and price meat, but he also greatly broadened our knowledge of the world with his many tall tales about his days in California. When we were finished with most of our daily duties, and before the late afternoon rush came, we would take a break, brew up a pot of fresh A&P coffee and get ready to hear more of his amazing stories. Charlie kept us laughing hard as he told us about his bizarre past. (I'm sure he told us more than we should have known at our age about a part of the world we didn't even know existed.) Sam, who often came over to the store in the midst of one of these wild tales, was very impressed and seemed to believe everything Charlie said. She sometimes laughed harder than Jack or I. Mama also came into the store once in a while, but she took all his stories with a grain of salt. She also made him clean up his language. I regret that I didn't have the courage to do that. For someone who had not done a lot of traveling, Mama knew the Scriptures and could read you like a book. She was a wise old girl. But Charlie made the days go faster. He helped us a lot, and we sorely missed him when he went to work for Allene's brothers, George and Bobby, who ran a large grocery store down near the St. Simon's Airport.

After Charlie quit working for us, Jack and I did all the meat cutting. We called it "dressing the meat case," and it had to be done at least twice a day. We would buy a side of beef, which was half a cow, hang it up by the meat block and "take the side down." This meant cutting the whole thing up into various kinds or cuts of meat and steak. We ground our own hamburger meat fresh every day. After I had sold so many one and two pounds of burger, my hand became the scale. I could take a small tray, scoop in the pound or two, throw it up on the scale and never look at it— although the customer did. I could get the weight right on the mark every time! I could do the same with a pound of coffee.

Papa would come down most afternoons to give us his advice and the benefit of his vast knowledge of the business. But he left the actual running of the store to us. So that meant that we had to do all the buying, stocking, pricing, cleaning and waiting on the customers. Papa enjoyed just being there and would sit, smoke, have a "dope" (Coke) and chat with the customers. The most popular kinds of pop, which we called "soda water," were Coca-Cola and Dr. Pepper. These came in a wood case, twenty to the case. They cost us three cents for each bottle, and we sold them for five cents. Of course, there were also RC Cola and a tall "NE-High" Orange, but most people drank a "dope." Those who took the bottle with them had to pay a three-cent deposit, which we gave them back when they returned it. The pop companies charged us for each bottle that was not returned. They sterilized and re-used them!

Earlier, Papa had been appointed Justice of the Peace and held court once a month, actually conducting small claims trials and settling differences between spouses and other parties. Although he owned only one huge law book, he was gifted with a lot of common sense and would have made a good lawyer and judge. We were so fortunate to have him as our papa, sharing his life, knowledge and expertise after all his years in the grocery business.

Jack and I took turns at the pumps when a car drove up. The pumps were the old type that were operated by hand. A long handle had to be pulled back and forth to fill the glass container from the bottom up to the ten-gallon mark at the top. This was during the Depression, so most drivers would buy only two or three gallons of gas at twenty cents a gallon. Kerosene or "coal oil" was five cents. Some of the homes of the poor and the black people on the island were lighted at night with coal oil lamps. It would probably shock many of you to learn the price of some of the other items: Sliced bread, five cents a loaf; unsliced, four cents; coffee, fifteen and twenty cents per pound. Most everything was priced somewhere between five cents and fifty cents. One could come in, and for three or four dollars, buy enough groceries to feed a large family for a week.

Then I was given a gift that would enrich my life. Whenever our minister, Bro. James Webb, came by the store for a cold drink, Jack would divert him to the back while I snuck out and filled his car up with gas. One day in 1938, as I was filling his tank, I looked on the back seat and saw a book. Its red and yellow cover had gold coins on it. Near the coins were a top hat, cane, gloves and fancy white shoes. The title was, *Think and Grow Rich* by Napoleon Hill. The book so intrigued me that when Brother Webb came out to get in his car, I asked him about it.

He said, "Aw, Brother James, some friend at the barbershop just gave that book to me. I have no idea what it's about. Would you like to have it?"

I grinned and answered, "I surely would, Pastor Webb."

At that, he reached in, handed it to me and drove off. I stood there looking at it and handling it, little realizing that I held in my hands a veritable gold mine. Well, that book has been worth many tanks of gasoline to me. I devoured every page of it. Next to the Bible, it has been the most important book I have ever read. It has followed me throughout my life. As our story proceeds, you shall learn how the philosophy and principles taught by Hill in that book impacted my whole life.

About eighteen months after we bought the store, on the first Saturday night in December, Jack and I closed late. Checking our total sales, we found that we had just finished the best Saturday and the best week of the entire year. When Mama and Sam fixed supper,

A MIRACLE A MINUTE

Jack and Sam went home and I went immediately to bed, very tired. The next day was Sunday, and I slept late that morning. After Papa, Mama and I had finished a late breakfast, I went back to rest in my room. Suddenly, the music on my radio was interrupted with the unbelievable news that in a surprise attack, the Japanese had inflicted heavy damage on our Navy base at Pearl Harbor. All of us who heard those shocking words will always remember exactly where we were and what we were doing on the afternoon of that Sunday, December 7, 1941. That moment was to change all of our lives and all of history.

True to his fashion, Jack was the first person in Glenn County to enlist. He chose the Army Air Corps and was sent to Coral Gables, Florida to attend Officer Candidate School. It was called OCS, and the graduates, second lieutenants, were dubbed "Ninety-Day Wonders." Clark Gable was in Jack's group, and since they were in the same barracks for the three months of OCS, they became good friends. I kept my eyes open all my life hoping to run into Gable some day. I could see myself going up to him with a glad handshake, saying, "Hey Clark, I'm James Pippin, Lt. Jack Pippin's brother. You two attended OCS together."

And then I could hear him say, "Oh yeah, Jim, I remember Jack Pippin well! Kinda short, black hair, parted on the side, big brown eyes. Do you have time for coffee? We'll talk about the old days."

"You bet, Clark. I got the time."

But, of course, that never happened. I did not know him as Jack did, but I still wept when Clark Gable died. Since he knew Jack, I felt that I had also lost a friend.

After Jack finished Officer Candidate School, he was assigned to the Air Transport Command as a second lieutenant. Then, after a one-week leave, he was shipped overseas to the China-Burma-India (CBI) theater. Of course, at the time we didn't know where in the world he was. The only address we had for anyone who was shipped abroad was an APO #, NY, NY. Since all of his letters were heavily censored, he would let us know where he was and send us news by a code system that slipped past the censors.

Once he wrote, "If you want to know where I am, just ass Sam."

But we all knew that his wife, Sam, had no idea where he was. The censors thought he had only left out the letter "k" in spelling the word ask. So we figured it out that he was in Assam, which is in Burma! Before he had shipped overseas he had told us how he would send us lengthy coded messages in his letters.

"Remember," he said, "just count the first letter in every third word."

Even though some of his sentences made little sense, the censor never caught on. We had great fun figuring out his secret messages, but if he had been caught, he would have been in big trouble. But that was Jack's style—"live dangerously!"

Now, since Jack was overseas, the store fell almost entirely upon my shoulders. Had Mama not come to my rescue, I would have had great difficulty handling it. Then in a few days one of our customers, a kind, older man named Ed Fennel, came by at rush time. When he saw how desperately we needed someone, he offered to go to work for us. I hired him on the spot. He worked very hard for long hours and for little pay. We did let him have his groceries at our cost. So, with the three of us working together, the business ran smoothly from then on.

Ed was tall and thin, with sunken blue eyes and a protruding chin. His face always had a stub of white beard showing. He mostly wore a denim shirt and tan trousers. Ed talked funny, calling vegetables "wuhgetubbles." "Very good" became "werry gooed," and "Go to the store" was "Go at ta sto." "Unlucky" was "onlucky," "draining the radiator" came out "dreenin," and onions were "anguns." Before he began working with us, he had made a living part of the year selling fresh "wugetubbles" from his large garden door to door.

But Mama was the great surprise. She had only a fifth-grade education and had never worked out of the house in her life, except in the garden, planting flowers and earlier in her Pa's fields. Every part of the retail business was new to her. Although she was so short she could hardly reach the cash register, Papa and I helped her and she caught on fast. She kept the place spotless and made friends with all the customers; everyone loved her. She actually increased the sales and the number of customers, and best of all, she added a spiritual atmosphere to the place.

The war was ever heavy on our minds. Several years before Pearl Harbor, Brother Frank had entered the Civilian Conservation Corps (CCC) as a chaplain and had been called to duty in the Army before Pearl Harbor. The CCCs, a 1933 brainchild of FDR, were also called Soil Soldiers; 2.5 million strong, they planted millions of trees and built many bridges. Instead of putting them on welfare, FDR put them to *work*. Those who left the CCC as Frank did and went into the military made fine soldiers. As Frank put it, "The CCC made men out of boys." He was on a troopship filled with soldiers, some former CCCs, and was halfway to Honolulu when the Japanese attacked Pearl Harbor. The entire convoy was ordered to return to San Francisco, where his division spent several weeks in retraining and retooling before it resumed its voyage to Hawaii.

Our conversations, the newspapers and the radio were filled with the latest news about the war. Mama and Papa were very proud that two of their sons, Frank and Jack, were serving our country. Papa said over and over that we here at home must all "fall in" and work hard together to keep life going and win the war.

That winter, it was too cold for Ed to walk to work, so I bought an old 1932 "Model A" Ford truck for fifty dollars and began picking him up. This made me feel quite grown-up. That truck, my pride and joy, only needed a battery and a muffler; then it ran like a brand-new one. On those cold, windy mornings, I would get up at 5:30, six days a week, and go get him. Every night that the temperature was below freezing, I had to "dreen" the radiator and refill it the next morning. Ed always insisted that I come in. I followed him upstairs where he had a blazing fire going in a thin metal stove. It would be glowing red with a pot of fresh percolated coffee on top. We would chat a little while over a cup while he finished dressing. He sat there rolling a cigarette out of "Bull Durham," and that ubiquitous cigarette would hang from his mouth the rest of the morning. He would put on his socks, then take one old brogan shoe, turn it over and knock it against the bed-post. Although nothing ever came out of his shoes anymore, his unconscious habit forced him to do that all his adult life because his shoes had always been full of dirt from working in the fields and in his garden all day.

One winter morning as I sat there drinking my coffee, rain started pouring down. The clatter of the rain on his old tin roof was so loud I could hardly hear a word he was saying. Hearing that clatter flooded me with memories of our house at Round Oak. A Nor'easter blast hit the island, and the high wind rattled the windows and shook that old, two-story frame house so hard that it creaked like a ship caught in a storm.

Sitting there, listening to Ed and the rain, and looking into my half-empty coffee cup I said to myself, "Here I am, a young, nineteen-year-old man—the sole owner of a great truck and a part owner of a thriving grocery store, with my Papa, Mama and Ed to help me successfully run it while 'our boys' are over there saving the world for democracy."

Brother Jack Comes Back

For the first time in my life, I felt really mature and in the thick of the things that made the world tick. I poured myself another cup of coffee, and soon Ed and I were off, headed for the store in a downpour of rain.

As I drove on, I continued half aloud, "You have come a long way from that little boy who followed Jack around like a puppy only a few years ago, James Clayton. I believe you have finally become a man."

It was a good thing, for in a few short months my manhood was going to be sorely tested by something I thought would never happen. I would answer my country's call, don the uniform and become a proud soldier in the Army of the United States!

❊ 8 ❊

I'm in the Army Now!

ecause of my injury some years back, my right leg was over an inch shorter than the left. Therefore, I had been classified as 4F, fit only for limited service. Everybody seemed to be going off to war but me, and I was depressed about being left behind. Krista was already married; Frank, Jack and most of my friends were already in; and I thought Uncle Sam would never call me up. During the lonely nights that summer, I read *No Time for Sergeants* and laughed my head off all through the book. Although I knew I was needed at home to manage the store, I had a secret desire to get into the service. Then, in the fall of 1942, the Army began drafting men with minor disabilities. I could hardly sleep the night that news came out. Only a few weeks later I got the familiar letter that began, "Greetings."

I received orders from Washington to report to Fort McPherson, near Atlanta, on the sixteenth of October, 1942, to take my physical. I immediately began to get ready to leave and, if I could pass the physical, saw myself beginning "the adventure of a lifetime." Papa, Mama and Ed were a little shocked, but they assured me that they could handle the store. I think they felt that I would not pass the physical, but I was convinced that I would.

On that morning, I boarded the brand-new "Nancy Hanks" train for Atlanta. I arrived at the mammoth Atlanta terminal station in the late afternoon, and then gathered at the entrance with a large group of recruits. There, waiting to take us to "Fort Mac," was an Army bus. The next two days were spent taking a complete physical. After all the tests were finished, I went before the doctor who would check the tests, look me over and make the final decision. While the doctor examined my leg and asked about it, I told him about my strong desire to be accepted for duty. I also told him that I experienced no pain in walking and no restriction in movement.

He looked at me and smiled. Then, as he stamped a big "accepted" on my records, he said, "Pippin, I think you'll make a good soldier. Go get dressed and give these to the chief sergeant. Young man, you are in the Army now!"

With a broad smile on my face, I shook his hand firmly and went to put on my clothes. While I was dressing I kept saying over and over, "I can't believe it—I'm really in the Army!" I felt a great joy, as if I had achieved an impossible goal. This was an answer to my many prayers. Getting into the Army would shape my life for the better in so many ways, and I thanked God for it all.

While I was dressing, only a thin partition separated me from the next stall, so it was easy for me to overhear a conversation that was taking place just inches from me. A doctor was talking to a recruit who had just finished the exam.

The doctor quietly asked the man, "Do you want to enter the Army?"

The young man answered, "No sir!"

Then I heard the doctor say, "Shhh! Keep your voice down. How bad do you want to stay out?"

The recruit answered, "Sir, I'll do anything to stay out!"

The doctor replied, "Well, I can fix that. If you have a couple hundred with you, I will mark your records 'unfit for service for psychological reasons.' Go get dressed and drop back by here."

The young man whispered, "Doc, you got yourself a deal!"

I was dumbfounded. I sat there trembling. I could not believe my ears. I went to the officer in charge, a colonel, and told him the whole story. He took me by the arm and asked me to lead him back to the cubicle where I had dressed. We sat there silently and sure enough, soon we overheard this same doctor making another deal, this time for five hundred dollars. We crept out, and the colonel, with a sad look on his face, took my name and asked me if I would stay over one extra day and give a deposition to the CID (Criminal Investigation Division).

When I agreed, he shook my hand and said, "Private Pippin, you must keep this to yourself. Don't say anything to anyone about this. Don't worry; your name will be kept out of the matter. For notifying me and giving your statement, I will change your orders so that you may report back for duty two days later than your orders read."

I agreed and smiled. As I shook his hand, I promised to be at his office the next morning. I gave the secret deposition describing all I had heard, word for word. Doing this meant that I would have sixteen days of leave back home to get ready to return. I was very pleased to have the extended time, and I was glad I had the courage to turn in that "doctor."

I learned later that upon my statement and other evidence furnished by the colonel, the doctor, who was a civilian, was dismissed. His license was also revoked for five years, and he was barred from ever working for the military again. Though I never saw his face and never knew his name, I felt truly sorry for this stupid, professional man. To think that he ruined his reputation and career, and would probably carry that deed with him for the rest of his life—all for a few hundred measly dollars. On the train ride back to Brunswick, I said a prayer for him, asking that a merciful God would lead him to repent, receive forgiveness from Jesus and never do anything like that again.

When I arrived at the train station in Brunswick, George was there to take me home. I was glad that he could meet me because I was nervous about having to break the news to Mama and Papa that I had been accepted. After I greeted them with hugs and kisses, Mama went to the kitchen and returned with fresh coffee for George and me.

While we sat there sipping our coffee, Papa broke the silence. "Well, Son, what's the verdict? You in or out?"

I hesitated a moment, put my cup down, stood up at attention, glanced around at the three of them and answered, "Well, my dears, you are looking at Private James Clayton Pippin, a soldier in the United States Army. I have to report for duty in two weeks."

George smiled, Papa shook his head and frowned, and Mama put her hands to her face and began to sob. In a moment though, while she dried her tears, she said, "Son, you know that we all will miss you sorely, but you must do your duty for our country. You going in makes three of our sons that are now to be in uniform."

George made us all feel better when he added, "James, you could have probably got deferred, but I, like Mama, also feel that you must do this. So don't worry about things here. God will go with you all the way and also remain here with us."

He placed a hand over on my knee and continued, "Son, I will be here to help in every way I can. If I weren't married with three kids, you can be very sure that I'd be right in there with you."

I had orders to report back on November 2, so this gave me just over two weeks to get ready and say my farewells to everyone. Now that I was accepted for service, I actually had mixed feelings about leaving. Those of us who entered the military to serve in World War II knew that we were putting our lives on the line and that many of us would never return. Knowing the injured would outnumber those killed in action, we could also see ourselves disabled for life. But I pushed these thoughts to the back of my own mind as I was swept up into the thrill of joining Frank, Jack and sixteen million of our men and women who were off to see the world, fight to defeat our enemies and make the world "safe for democracy."

My outlook on life was radically changed when I realized that I would not have to sit this war out behind the counter of a small grocery store as I had feared I would. Saying good-bye is always hard. And this one was most difficult. We tried not to think about my leaving, until the time had fully arrived. Jack was in Burma and Frank in Hawaii, so I could not imagine where I would wind up. Since Mama, Ed and I had worked closely together for the past year, I was confident that the Lord would make all things go well. Papa would be there some during the day and always be available by phone to answer any question they might have.

Then too, Brother George, his wife, Vera, and their three boys had moved from Wilmington, Ohio to St. Simon's the year before and had bought the shoe repair shop in downtown Brunswick. George had sold his shoe shop in Ohio because he and Vera wanted to be in a warmer climate and nearer Mama and Papa. They were faithful in their visits and would be there to do many of the things I had done.

One afternoon when Papa, Ed and I were alone in the store, Ed came up to me and placed his long, bony arm around my shoulder. Knowing of my concern, he told me not to "werry" because they would hire another person to help if they needed to.

When Papa saw the look on my face, he motioned to me to come sit in a chair near him. He put his hand on my arm and said, "Son, to help your spirits and to give you a release from your ties to the store, you know that the business has already begun to fall off since so many of our boys are away. You also know that the war is not going well for the Allies right now. It's so bad that they may have to draft older and maybe even married men. The need for personnel is becoming so great that the military may very soon even have to draft women. Because of the critical need, you must not worry about anything here. What you are doing for our country is far more important than running this little store. Carry with you in your heart all the things that Ed, George, your Ma and I have said to reassure you. You go and make the

Army the best soldier you possibly can. You'll never regret it."

Then after he had also patted my arm and gave me one of his famous winks, I knew that everything was OK. What Papa said was so true. He was a man of few words, but we all were quiet whenever he spoke. The Lord seemed to confirm to me that what they all had said permitted me to now turn my back on what was there and look to the future where I was really needed.

So, early on the morning of November 2, 1942, after I had finished packing what few civilian clothes I was allowed, I said all my farewells. Just as we had gotten through the hugs and kisses and the tears were all dried, I looked up, and as if on perfect cue, George was at the front door to take me to the train station. Mama and Papa walked us to the car and stood there attempting a weak smile as we drove off. I looked back and gave a final wave, and through tears, I saw the images fade of the two most important people in the world to me.

We didn't talk on the ride to the station, only breaking the silence as we parked. After I went in to get my ticket stamped, George and I walked out on the platform to the train. I was deeply touched to see tears in his big brown eyes as he told me good-bye.

In about a minute the conductor shouted, "A-l-l a-b-o-o-o-a-r-d!!"

George quickly thrust a fifty-dollar bill into my hand and said, "God speed, Son. Take care of yourself. Don't forget to write, and don't worry."

I smiled and climbed aboard. As I turned to wave, I yelled, "Thanks, Brother George, for everything! God bless you. Kiss Vera and the boys for me. Watch out for Papa and Mama. I love you. Good-bye!"

He was nodding OK when the train pulled away.

For the first hour, I sat alone by the window. I was caught up in deep thoughts of all I was leaving behind and excited about what lay ahead. While I watched the tall south Georgia pines pass quickly by, I recalled a statement by Oliver Wendell Holmes that my high school English teacher, Miss Macon, used to recite for us:

> What lies behind us and what lies before us are tiny matters compared to what lies within us.

That morning long ago, I began to understand that what was important was not the past or the future, but what God helped me bring to this present hour—that is what would guide me aright in whatever the future held.

I'm in the Army Now!

The "Nancy Hanks" clicked the miles away. It seemed no time until we arrived for a brief stop at the Macon terminal. When I looked up I was pleasantly surprised to see Ray, my oldest brother, coming into the coach to greet me. Ray worked for the Railway Express Company there at that station for many years. Papa had phoned to tell him that I was on the train. Ray sat down, and we chatted for a few minutes. He was sorry that his wife, Laura, could not be there. He was very proud of Wilbur (Billy), their only child, who was in the cavalry stationed in Texas and doing well. He showed me a picture of Wilbur, that handsome son of theirs, sitting in full uniform on horseback.

When I stood to tell Ray good-bye, he hugged me tightly and told me he loved me. I think that was the first time he had ever said those words to me. Ray and I had never spent much time together because he left home the month I was born, so when I was growing up, I only rarely saw him, Laura or Billy. Just as he turned to leave, the train began to move and he had to jump off. He waved good-bye to me as my train pulled out of the station.

I arrived at the Atlanta terminal at about 8:30 P.M. The same bus and the same driver that had been there two weeks earlier now took a very quiet group of young men to the Induction Center at Fort Mac. It was after 9:30 P.M. when he pulled up in front of the mess hall and yelled, "Anybody hungry? OK men, fall out for chow."

My first meal as a soldier in the Army wasn't much. But it was late and all of us were starved, so it didn't matter. We went through the line holding shiny, stainless steel trays. The sleepy cooks slammed some hot navy beans, two pieces of toast, a carton of milk and some canned fruit on the partitioned tray. After we ate, we were driven to a small shack.

The driver, who was a sergeant, said loudly, "OK, all twelve of you lucky fellows get out here. This is where you will billet 'til you're shipped out. Be sure you don't leave anything on this bus. I will wake you up at six in the morning to take you to breakfast."

The twelve of us walked into a small, one-story building. There were six double bunks in it. I marveled at the sergeant's efficiency in knowing just exactly how many beds were in that shack. I chose the bottom bunk at the far end near the window. We all quickly undressed, climbed into our beds, and after very little chatter, the other men all drifted off to sleep.

I got up and cracked open the window a few inches. It was much colder there in North Georgia. As I lay there listening to the cold night wind blow around that little shack, I thought, *Well, Private Pippin, you are sho 'nuff in the Army now. So far so good.*

What with the three free train rides, the free food when we were being examined, the late night snack and the good Army bed with clean sheets and warm GI blankets, I was suddenly surprised when a feeling of complete security swept over me. I was comforted by the confidence I had that the Army would take care of all my needs until the war was over.

I lay there in bed, remembering how many times I had heard the story that when the Non-coms were trying to sell the Army to recruits they would yell at them, "Hey you guys, you get free food, clothing, shelter, good pay and thirty days leave a year—and don't forget the free medical and dental!"

This feeling, which I had never really had before, led me to make an important decision. In return for all the Army was giving me, whatever it took in hard work, study, patience and obedience to those in authority, I would give the military my best and become the very finest soldier possible. Somehow, I knew that this commitment I made that first night on active duty would direct my course and keep me focused while I was in the Army and even beyond.

As I look back on my decision that night, I see it as a turning point in my young life. I believe this pledge firmly set an attitude and began an approach that helped shape me into who I was to become. It was a paradigm shift—the turning over of a glass, a watershed, a moment of truth, the turning of a page—that directly influenced my military, business and ministry careers for the rest of my life.

As I thought of totally giving of myself to my country and reflected on the happenings of the past few weeks, I could not drift off to sleep without making that same dedication to Jesus my Lord and my Father God. So I said a fervent prayer to Him, a prayer that I repeated almost every night while I was in the service:

> Dear Lord, in the name of Jesus, please watch over Frank, Jack, Papa and Mama, Ed, George and Vera and all my family. And keep them and all my loved ones safe and well 'til we meet again. Amen.

The next morning our sergeant woke us up at 6 A.M. sharp. He told us to shower and shave over in the next building. After that, he told us to get dressed and be ready to fall out and go to breakfast at 7 A.M. We quickly threw on fatigues and shoes, showered and shaved, and then hurried back to our barracks to get dressed for breakfast. The food was great at the Induction Center, especially breakfast. Hot oatmeal or dry cereal, pancakes with butter and syrup, scrambled eggs *or* bacon—never the two together, too much protein they said—a carton of milk and lots of good, freshly brewed coffee.

From there, we went to the large supply warehouse where we were issued a full supply of clothing, including shoes, belts, ties and three hats. We folded and placed all this in a large duffel bag that would be our only suitcase for the duration. Then we returned to our barracks.

A little later when the Sergeant showed up, he pulled a complete olive-colored drab uniform out of one of our bags and showed us just exactly what to wear and how to put on our brass. This he said, would be our duty "uniform of the day" until we arrived at our basic training post. So, we all put them on and got some good laughs when we looked at each other. In fact, we were a happy, though sloppy, bunch of recruits.

Since the uniforms were wrinkled and did not fit well, I ran my other duty uniform over to the tailor shop to be altered and pressed. Two mornings later, I took the other uniform in and picked up the altered one, dressed at the tailor's and appeared in the breakfast line in my newly fixed outfit. Man, did I look sharp. But talk about hoots and whistles and groans—I really got it from the men.

One guy yelled out, "Hey, Pippin, you bucking for sergeant er sumthin'? You don't belong in here wid us peons. You even look like one of them there occifer's!"

The sergeant in charge yelled out, "At ease, you dog faces! Shut up and eat your breakfast. Wouldn't hurt any of you to also shape up and look like a real soldier."

The mess hall got very quiet. I went on through the line and sat over at a table by myself. No one would even speak to me. But in a few days, all of them "followed suit" and got their uniforms fitted and pressed. Then we all looked like real soldiers and were friends again.

After breakfast we were briefed about what the next few days would be like before we were transferred. First, we were taken to a large classroom and given a battery of Army General Classification Tests.

The sergeant in charge said, "OK, men, listen up. These tests you are about to take are very important. The test grade you make will determine the schools you will attend, the quality of duty to which you will be assigned and your MOS number (Military Occupational Specialty). So be at ease, listen to me and do the best you can. I will give you the cue of when to start. You have one hour."

After his instructions he said, "Good luck," and went to the front of the room and sat down. He blew his whistle, and we were off and running!

I didn't feel very stressed about taking all these tests because when Jack was home on a short leave after completing OCS, he had given me a lot of good advice about the military in general. He had focused on these tests in particular, just in case I was ever called up.

That night he had been dressed in his sharp officer uniform with his gold second lieutenant bar shining on his shoulder. As he looked at me over his cup of coffee, he began to explain in a tone of seriousness, "Now Brother James, listen carefully. On the morning of the tests eat a moderate breakfast, go to the latrine just before you go in to begin the test and then drink a Coke. This will help to keep you alert. Pay close attention to all of the instructions given by the test supervisor and notice the time the test starts."

He continued, "First, go through the entire test and answer all the simple questions, those that you think will not take much time. Avoid the long or complicated questions until after you have finished the easiest ones. Then go back through and answer only those difficult questions that seem the quickest to solve. Use the last minutes you have left to check all of your answers. As you go back through that last time, go ahead and guess at those hard ones that you did not answer. Since the tests are multiple choice, you have a one in four chance of guessing the right answer. Don't leave any of them blank. But on the guessed ones, try to eliminate the choice that seems most wrong. Remember that all of the questions count the same number of points, so the short ones count just as much as those long and complicated ones. Think you can remember all of this?"

I answered, "I think so."

Then he had me repeat as much as I remembered of what he had said.

When I finished he said as he laughed, "I believe you are gonna make it fine, lil brother!"

I am confident that my test results were much higher because I carefully used all of Jack's suggestions. Not to brag, but I made high marks on all of them!

I hope that this book has just become more valuable to you and your children or grandchildren! I throw this and all other information of this nature in at absolutely no extra charge! So, remain alert. You never know what choice pearl the Lord will give me to drop next. By the way, if I have any knowledge, wisdom or smarts, I give all the credit to Christ, our Lord of miracles. Also, for any joy, pleasure, instruction, entertainment or other good thing I bring to you in this entire story, I also give all the credit to Him, without whom I would be nothing. What a blessing it would be if you could also tell me about the unique and special things He has shown you or done in your life. Feel free to write to me if you want to.

The day after we completed all these tests, we went to the dispensary for our shots. You would be amazed how much these grown men were whimpering and moaning. Especially when you realize that these are the very same men who, on a field of battle under enemy fire, would display rare acts of bravery that required tons of courage. But not that day. As we got in line to receive our immunizations, some of them were actually trembling. One big tall guy went to the back of the line and started to sob, big tears streaming down his face!

Your silly, fearless author, Pvt. Pippin, marched bravely to the head of the line, turned to the group, and said with the Sarge's tone, "Men, calm down, this won't hurt a bit. *Just watch me!*"

I took a step forward, raised my head and stood at attention. Then two gargantuan medics in white coats marched up to me. Each one of them had a pistol-type "Shot Facilitator" in each hand. While one shot me in my right arm, the other one shot me in my left arm at the same time. I turned, smiled victoriously, flipped a salute to the men, took two steps forward and fell flat on my face. I had that coming, but I found out later that one of those shots was for tetanus, and many men are prone to faint a few seconds after they get that shot.

Boy, did I learn a lesson in humility that day! I don't think I was ever that brave (arrogant) again. I prayed that none of these men would ever see me again in this life. Not a chance though. That week, three of them went to the same post I did, and you're right, they never let me forget that little scene! They nicknamed me "hot-shot" and used it in the mess hall and in other most embarrassing places.

I spent the rest of the time waiting for my orders telling me where in this wide world I would be sent. In a few days my name was finally called. I jumped and my heart was up in my throat with anticipation when I ran up to get my orders. My hands were shaking as I tore open the big, brown envelope. My eyes went racing through the orders, searching to find out to which exotic and far away place I would be sent.

And there on page three was the bad news. I was not going to see the world from the window of a train or through the porthole of a troopship that would carry me to a place in India or Kathmandu or some far-flung island down under in the South Pacific where I could dress like Hemingway and become that fine soldier of fortune I dreamed of. Oh, no!! Instead, I was loaded into a *bus* and transported only twenty-five miles away to Lawson General Hospital! O my soul, was I disappointed! There I was right in the northeast part of the metro area in the city of Atlanta, instead of living out my dream of transcontinental adventure.

There, with about two hundred of some of the ugliest old men I had ever seen, I began a crash, basic-training course that lasted nine weeks. Were they ever a sordid bunch of misfits! Almost every one of them had some handicap. One had no thumb on his left hand; another had lost all of the ends of his fingers on his right hand; one even had a glass eye! Some of them looked and talked as if they were fifth-grade dropouts. They reminded me of the cast of characters in Treasure Island. Then I finally said to my self, "Self, knock it off; you are also handicapped. Show 'em that large scar on your right leg."

It was the sight of this motley crew of older recruits that confirmed to me that things must be going really bad for us in Europe, just as Papa had said. Believe it or not, before those nine weeks were up, I found out that they were a really great bunch of soldiers. Those of us who were handicapped, even if only slightly so, as was I, seemed to be more committed to doing our best.

This was my first close encounter with Army drill sergeants. These men were definitely of a different breed. They barked at us from 5 A.M. until lights out at 9 P.M. Up to now, I just thought I was in the Army. Why do they have to yell so loud and be so mean? Our day began with reveille at 5 A.M. One of the drill sergeants would come to the door of the barracks and flip on all the lights. Then he would yell so loud he could be heard in hell, "Fall out." And "fall out" we did— out onto the company street. After breakfast, we made our beds and cleaned our personal areas. Then our training started with their fiendish desire to wear us out. Early-morning calisthenics were immediately followed by an hour of hard, fast, close-order drill.

Then we were allowed to crash into a chair and be bored to death with long, dry lectures for the rest of each day. They droned on about splints, braces, tourniquets, first aid, how to bandage all parts of the human body (excluding, of course, the sergeant's big mouth), simulated intravenous and morphine injections, litter bearing, water purification and personal hygiene. Plus, the chaplain gave us a lecture on how to avoid catching venereal disease! (Ha, Ha.) As you can see, 'twas a busy day.

The chaplain came by once a week to invite us to chapel services that were aimed at how a soldier could remain close to God while he was preparing to kill the Sarge—oops—the enemy. The "Chappy," as he was fondly dubbed, was very close friends with the sergeant, and so they had a special way of guaranteeing the chaplain would have a good crowd in chapel.

Here's how it went: We would all fall out on Sunday morning, and the NCOIC (non-commissioned officer in charge, alias Sarge.) would yell at us, "Those of you who want to go to chapel services, remain in place. The rest of you fall out over here to be assigned to kitchen detail."

Of course, we all remained in place! Our mamas didn't raise any foolish chillun! Then he marched two hundred greatly relieved soldiers to the front door of the chapel and shouted, "Fall out, enter the chapel, take a seat and keep your mouth shut!"

You can imagine the broad smile on that chaplain's face when all two hundred of us sat down and he began the service. He immediately announced that all Catholics could proceed to the room in back of the chapel where the Catholic chaplain would conduct Mass. Jewish soldiers had their services on Friday evenings. The vast majority of us benefited greatly from these brief Sunday services. Most chaplains were super persons, and getting to know them paid off rich dividends in the long run.

Almost before we knew it, the nine weeks were over and we marched to the theater, got in line and took our turn standing before the commander of the hospital detachment, Major McCoy, and Lt. Jameson, his XO (executive officer). The major briefly interviewed us. This included asking us to describe in detail just what we did in civilian life. Later, each of us was assigned to a duty station. I was sent to the Personnel Records Section, where I learned to prepare the service records for the large graduating classes of medical technicians who were in school in the big buildings across the road and to the north of the hospital. Most of these men would be immediately shipped overseas to England or Europe as corporals to serve as advanced medical technicians in the first aid stations and the hospitals that were located near the front.

During the next few months, I made friends with my section boss, Lt. James Stephens, head of the personnel section, and Corporal Jerome Jacobsen, who kept our personal record cards, Form 20, up to date. He had a very small office just to the right of my desk. About the only really bright day I had was the day I was promoted to Pfc (Private First Class). I believe I was more proud of that promotion than I was years later when I was promoted as a chaplain to full colonel.

I wasn't at Lawson long before I met a very lovely girl, Anne Puryear. Her daddy was French, but her mother had divorced him and married a pediatrician from Nashville, who was stationed at Lawson as a major. Her mother was also a very beautiful woman, who liked me a lot. Anne had a lovely figure, long fine, blond hair, stunning green eyes and the longest eyelashes I had ever seen on a woman. She was also a great dancer and had a large wardrobe of very fancy clothes. She always dressed as if she were going to meet the president. She drew the looks each time we were out. We were very fond of each other and had great times together, but when I left Lawson, we started to drift apart. The strain and long separation of the Army didn't do our relationship any good.

To relieve my intermittent boredom with my duty, I applied for OCS training. I was interviewed by a board made up of majors and one colonel. I was rejected, partly because I had no college and partly because when one of the majors asked me where Afghanistan was, I answered, "I think it's in Africa!"

I really doubted if in those days anyone on the board even knew where it was, except for that smart little major who asked the question. But as I look back on it now, I believe the real reason I was not accepted was because I had no clean socks to wear that day. Wearing a dirty pair of socks made me feel ill-dressed and gummy all over. I became extremely distracted when I noticed that my socks kept falling down, but even more so when the board members started rubbing their index fingers under their noses. I just knew they could smell my dirty socks. I have often wondered if those socks changed the course of my future. From that day and for the rest of my life, I have always made sure I had a pair of clean socks to wear to every interview.

❋ 9 ❋

Yankee Fathers and a Southern Nazarene

Since my IQ at that time was 123, I was selected for the Army Specialized Training Program (ASTP). Thousands throughout the Army were being selected and sent to ASTP. I was "busted" back to private and given orders to transfer in July of 1943 to Providence College, Providence, Rhode Island. During my last two weeks at Lawson, I dated Anne every night. She gave me a large picture of herself, which I took with me.

A total of eight hundred of us had been selected from all over the country to be put through a nine-month crash course to become engineers. Upon completion, we would be promoted to second lieutenant and shipped to Europe where engineers were in great demand to rebuild bridges at the front. Some of us had high hopes that we were finally going to get the chance to become officers and get into the thick of things.

However, the professors at Providence College seemed to have a different idea. It was a Catholic school located on a beautiful campus not far from downtown Providence. All of our teachers were Catholic priests. This Georgia boy was painfully deep in Yankee land. Nothing was the same.

Practically all we had to eat was rabbit food, lots of congealed salads with a lot of shredded stuff in them, cooked vegetables served half raw, canned fruit, bread that was cold and hard and Yankee cornbread that was much too thick and so sweet it tasted like cake. One lunch they served something I had never seen before. It looked like white grass with little bitty green tadpole heads on the end. I later learned that this was bean sprouts, but I still wouldn't touch it. Almost all of the meat served had been baked or broiled and had no flavor. The chicken was often about half done, what we called "slick chicken" down home. All of my life since I was a teenager, I always told Mama and later my wife or a waitress, "I don't want no slick chicken. I want it fried 'til it's brown and done."

Until I got to Providence, I had never seen so much broiled, baked and steamed stuff. I guessed all those Catholic seminarians that attended that school had to be Yankees. I was lonely for Georgia meals, or even some real Army food, and starving for some fried cat-fish, fried chicken, biscuits and red-eye gravy, grits and turnip greens, and cornpone and buttermilk. Even the coffee was warm, weak and old. O my good Lord, deliver me from this! Those large women (civilian cooks) never heard tell of banana pudding, sweet potato pie, chicken-fried steak, hearty chili or beef stew!

Now, the Fathers, Ahhh the Fathers! They were all Ph.D's, dressed in long black robes with a generous supply of beads swinging from them. They all spoke sternly and with a thick "Bahston" accent. We rarely saw them, except in class. We had to be in our seats before they entered, and remain seated until they left the room. They did not stay back for any questions or discussion. They were all business, very serious and void of even a speck of humor. Their orders from the Army were to "give them soldiers a four-year college education in nine months and by God, do it if it hairlips the devil!" So our classes began at 7:30 A.M. and went until 8:00 P.M or even later. We only had short breaks for those horrible lunches and dinners. All of the Fathers had to cram about three hours of regular instruction into each fifty-minute, crash-course lecture.

Twenty minutes into the lecture, each of them would fill up a chalkboard with formulas, charts and other unintelligible material. When one board was filled, another would be pulled down, spanking clean, ready for some more stuff that to me resembled Greek, Japanese or worse. There were three such double boards across the front of the room, and they filled them all! Hey, if you dropped your pencil on the floor and reached for it during class, you might as well get up and go to your room because you would never catch up with him. Before you had a chance to look up with pencil in hand, he and his lecture had turned the corner and were gone.

Even though most of us had only finished high school, we were being taught advanced courses in trigonometry, physics, calculus and the new world geography. They all loved to assign loads of home-work, while each of us sat there pondering when on earth they expected us to do it. By the time we got to our rooms after the last class, all we could do was to fall in bed, often sleeping all night in our clothes. It was a wonderful plan, that is, for super bright graduate students who had a Ph.D. in math. One bright spot was the long letters I got from Anne. But I was always so beat that I didn't write to her very often.

They did give us Saturday afternoons and Sundays off. My heavy schedule gave me little time to write and almost no time to think of Anne Puryear. She wrote often at first and sent me another beautiful picture of herself. I ran with three good-looking Jewish men, for they always had exciting weekend plans that included great food, dances and movies. Along with that, a very pretty Jewish girl was always invited along to be my date.

Few women are as uniquely attractive as young Jewish girls. They were bright and beautiful, had blue eyes and black hair, were good dancers, and they treated their dates like kings. However, just about the time one of them and I were getting to know each other enough to smooch a little, she'd find out that I was not Jewish and would push me off the sofa and onto the floor. That was the last of that. I look Jewish enough that they had to be told, or they would never have suspected. Maybe it was my southern accent or my kind of sweet, southern kisses that blew my cover! Oh well, 'twas good while it lasted.

In October 1944, when the first quarter grades came out, a total of five hundred of the eight hundred of us failed and were dropped from the program. We were shipped out in two days to different Army bases far and wide. The military was so angry with us that they ordered all five hundred of us to go back through basic training. William Ruzensky, a friend from Hartford I had met in class, and I wound up sitting together on what resembled a cattle train. We were bound for Rockford, Illinois, ninety miles northwest of Chicago. On this train there was no diner and no bunks. All we had were plain wood seats and very little heat, and boxed meals were our daily fare. Sometimes we could buy a hot dog and a Coke from the "butches" who were barking outside the windows whenever we stopped. They were not allowed on the train!

According to our orders, we were to be assigned to Camp Grant, for eighteen weeks of medical basic. We were not so dumb that we couldn't figure out that after we finished this basic, the Army was going to get even with us now by sending us as medics to the front— so the Germans could kill us! I just knew that some smart little majors in G-1 at the Pentagon were livid because their brainchild had miserably failed when they were unable to create thousands of engineers overnight. Bill and I were shocked and angered. We thought it was very unfair to be sent back through this excruciating experience of basic, particularly since we had been in the Army over a year, had already taken our basic and had even recently lost our stripes. On the long train ride from Providence, Bill and I became friends, so when we arrived at Camp Grant and were assigned to barracks, we were glad that they kept us together.

The corporal who took us to our building didn't even ask us our names and failed to tell the first sergeant that we were new arrivals. Camp Grant was a very large installation, consisting of companies, battalions, regiments and a division. We were assigned to Company C, 28th Medical Training Battalion. However, we were not told to report in to the first sergeant or to the company commander, because when we came in that Saturday afternoon they were not there. When reveille was called on Monday at 5 A.M., Bill and I fell out with all the rest of the troops in our platoon. Each company had four platoons, one to each barracks. Our sergeant called the roll, but our names were not on it. We said nothing.

We expected him to then ask, "Is there anyone whose name I did not call?"

But he didn't.

After we went to breakfast we fell out with the rest and were marched to our first class of the day. There they called the roll, and again, our names were not on the class roster. We didn't much like all those lectures, classes and movies the first time around, so we surely didn't want to suffer all that again. So when the class was over, Bill and I hid and did not fall in for the next class.

Outside, behind the barracks, we looked at each other, smiled and both said at the same time, "Guess what? They don't know we're here!"

We had the white-hot adrenaline to say to the Army, "We'll show *them!*"

So we fell out each morning with the company, and if they still didn't have us on the roster, we sneaked out of the area after breakfast. Now, I knew this was wrong and very dangerous, and I had not forgotten my pledge to be a good soldier, but we were so angry that I just couldn't see myself running in and reporting to the first sergeant. The Army was angry at us, but we were more angry at them. To keep from being stopped and put on random details, we each got a clip board, put some old orders we found in a trash can on it and put a pencil behind our ears. Everywhere we went we walked fast, as if we were on an errand for some colonel. No one ever stopped us. We would come back to our company only to eat lunch and dinner.

Each day we'd try to think of something new to do. We went to the train station 'way down at the edge of the base, sat by the hot stove and read the morning paper. We'd sit in the library almost every day, I must have read six books in those two weeks. One sunny day we even went out into the fields, lay down in the tall grass and took a nap. Often in midafternoon, we'd fast-step it up to the USO Restaurant and have coffee and cherry pie! Yes, we were AWOL (Absent Without Leave) for about two weeks. That took a lot of foolish courage.

But this all came to a screeching halt one morning as we were finishing breakfast. The first sergeant stomped into the mess hall and yelled, "Ateennn-chutt!!"

Then he barked, "At ease, no talking! Are James Pippin and Bill Ruzensky in this room?"

Chill bumps covered my entire body. With bowed heads, we both slowly stood up.

"Would you two men kindly come forward and follow me? Your company commander would like to have a little chat with you, if you think you can spare the time."

We walked out amid a howl of laughter from the men.

The Sarge shoved us along to the orderly room as though we were convicts. He then said in a loud gruff voice, "You two criminals sit down, shut up and do not move. The corporal here will take you in when the Old Man is ready. You two bums are in heap big trouble. He's mad enough to chew you up and spit you out, and I hope he does!"

When the first sergeant stomped out and slammed the front door, Bill and I jumped as if he had shot us. We were shaking all over.

When the corporal turned his head to answer the phone, Bill looked at me and spoke in a shrill whisper so fast I could hardly keep up with him, "Pip, you gotta get us outta this. You can present our case much better than I can, and man, you better reach down into yourself and come up with charm like you've never used before in your whole life. I just know the Old Man's gonna throw the book at us for this. We could even be court marshaled! O my Lord, why did we ever do such a stupid thing!" He looked as if he were about ready to cry.

I replied, "Bill, would you please just calm down and dry up. You know I'll do my best. But I can't promise anything. I am as scared as you are. Hey, you'd better not start any of that crying in there. If you believe in that Lord you just called on, you'd better start prayin' right now. I've been prayin' since the first sergeant came into the mess hall. If we had done a little prayin' earlier, we'd not be in this awful mess; we'd have turned ourselves in."

At that instant, the commander yelled through the door, "Corporal, send those two men in here, and do not disturb me until I'm finished with 'em."

Ruzensky pushed me in ahead of him and closed the door behind us. While Bill stood at attention, I popped my heels together, gave him a sharp salute and said, "Pvt. Pippin and Pvt. Ruzensky reporting as ordered, SIR!"

Bill and I had never seen him before. He stood up, and we saw that he was a short, slender captain with gray eyes and a handsome baby face. His uniform was clean and sharp, and his brass was sparkling.

He spoke in a tenor voice, a bit too loud. "Stand at ease. Now would you two professional goof-offs mind telling me just where in the hell you have been? How long have you been on this post? Do you know that I should throw you both in the brig for this? Why didn't you report in to me the instant you arrived? Speak up! And it better be damned good!"

I quickly and quietly told the Captain, "Sir, if you will give us just a few minutes, I can explain the whole thing."

He sat down, shrugged his shoulders and said, "Oh, you can, can you? Then pray let me hear it!"

I whispered a short prayer, took a deep breath and started, "Sir, this is the gospel truth about what happened. We've been in the Army for over a year, and both of us have already been through basic. They took away our stripes and sent us off to attend ASTP, promising us a commission in nine months. But only a genius could have passed those advanced courses. Most of the eight hundred of us couldn't hack it, so they kicked us out and are punishing us by sending us back through basic. We arrived just about ten days ago, and no one even knew we were here. We think our records must have gotten lost on the way and finally showed up."

I paused, looked him straight in the eye and said, "Captain, Sir, Bill and I know we've done wrong, but we checked the training schedule daily and saw that we had already been through all those classes, so we skipped them. And Sir, I swear we have not been off post, and we've stayed out of trouble. But Captain, if you will just give us a chance, we'll show you what good soldiers we can be. Since we have been in the Army over a year and were Pfc's, we can be a real asset to your company. We give you our word that we will not only stay out of trouble, but we will also make you and the first sergeant proud of us. We promise to become 'super troops' and make you glad you gave us a second chance."

The commander slowly rose out of his chair and smiled. He then walked around the desk, came over to me and said, "Pippin, your explanation and your commitment changes the picture. You both seem to know the seriousness of what you have done. You two seem like pretty good troops to me. Look, you guys, I am going way out on a limb here, and I am going to give you that chance you asked for. But, I swear, if either of you screw up again, the first [sergeant] and I will have no mercy on you. Do you understand? And, by the way, you keep your word, and this incident will not appear on your records. That's all, you're dismissed. Now, get out of here and show me what you can do!"

We popped to attention, snapped him a sharp salute and said in unison, *"Yes, Sir!"*

We did a curt about-face and leaped for the door. Outside, as we took a deep breath, we felt like criminals sentenced to the electric chair who had just been pardoned.

On the way to class that morning, Bill said, "Pip, you did a swell job in there. I knew you could sweet talk that captain!"

I told him, "Hey, Pard, don't give me any credit. Thank the good Lord. He was smiling on us today! That captain could have ruined our careers. Now we've got to keep our promise and really make God and the captain proud of us."

We were better than our word. Beginning that hour, and for the rest of the time we were there, we more than measured up to our vow.

The next day I heard that the major was coming down Saturday morning from Battalion Headquarters to put the company through a rigid inspection. So, I went to supply and checked out a field manual. Then early that morning I fixed my footlocker and my area as good or better than the manual described. My bed was tight and smooth; my extra shoes and boots were all tied, shined and lined up under the bunk; and my wall locker was perfect. I cut white paper to fit the partitions in the tray that sat up at an angle in my footlocker. All my toilet articles were placed just so in the tray. But I couldn't get the heavy Gillette double-edged razor to stay in place. It kept sliding down. However, I discovered that if I licked it, it would stay put—that is, for about five minutes. When it got dry though, it would slowly slide to the bottom of the tray and ruin the symmetry. So, I knew what to do about that. But I did everything so perfectly that my time ran out before I could wash my filthy mess gear. I sighed and said under my breath, "Well, there's nothing I can do about that now!"

Somebody yelled that the major was on the way. We all made a dash for our bunks and stood at attention. I heard him hit the stairs. I quickly stooped, licked my razor and had just regained my position when he walked in. Our wonderful little captain-friend was right behind him.

The first sergeant yelled, "Attiiiiinnn-chuuut!"

The major ordered, "At ease, men."

I was first in line, so he came directly over to me. I popped to attention. He looked me over and then glanced down at my bed and my area, and then at my footlocker. He asked me, "Pippin, is this your footlocker?"

I answered, "Yes, SIR!"

Then the major turned and said to the captain and the first sergeant, "Have all the men fall out, come over here and gather 'round this footlocker."

The major then said, "Sarge, I want you and the men to look at this footlocker and this area. This bed is as tight as a drum, you can see your face in those shoes, and this floor is so clean, you could eat off it. It's about the best I've ever seen. I know I do not need to look at his mess gear or anything else. Look, Sarge, the captain and I are going to the mess hall for a little coffee and will return in forty-five minutes. I want every footlocker and every personal area in this barracks to look just like this one."

As he turned and shook my hand, he continued, "And Captain, give Pippin here a three-day pass, starting bright and early in the morning."

The captain said, "Yes, Sir."

The first sergeant then screamed at the men, "Fall to and get this house in order, you lousy dog-faces! If this place is not shining perfectly in forty-five minutes, I will personally grind every mother's son of you into hamburger and sell you to the Nazis!"

I didn't like the looks on the men's faces. So after the officers left, I walked out close behind the first sergeant. I felt kind of like a traitor. I had not only lost all my friends but made for myself a building full of enemies. I ran to the supply room and checked out my small suitcase. Later after the men were in class I went back to my barracks, packed and got ready to get off that post.

Since my sister Mary was a registered nurse who then lived in Monroe, Michigan, a short distance from Detroit, I called her collect and told her I was coming to see her. I asked her to meet me at the Detroit train station. She seemed delightfully surprised. On my way back past the orderly room, the first sergeant came out and handed me my pass.

He said, "Pippin, although your pass isn't supposed to start 'til in the morning, the Old Man is so proud of you that he is giving you permission to leave anytime you're ready. Do you realize that in all of my Army career you are the first soldier I've ever known who got a pass during basic training? So you better be careful, stay sober and return on time. We'll see you in three days. You are one lucky son-of-a-gun!"

Little did he realize that it was not luck, it was just the Lord!

I was out of there like a streak of lightening. An Army bus took me the few miles north to Moline, Wisconsin, where I caught the Twentieth Century Limited nonstop to Chicago. There I changed to the Burlington and Northern Express through-train to Detroit. Those trains were fast, clean, comfortable and absolutely beautiful. As we pulled out of Chicago, I sat there and had a hard time believing all this had happened: I was changed from a "convict" into a hero in only a few days!

I whispered, "You know, Lord, I think I'm close to fallin' in love with this man's Army!"

Later, I felt so good I was strutting all over the train, feeling like a general, visiting with the passengers, eating in the diner and sipping that great coffee the large, smiling waiter poured from a solid silver pitcher. While watching the beauty of the countryside pass quickly by the large window, I was surprised at how much respect and kindness the passengers had for a common soldier. They would ask you to go to the diner with them, offer you a drink, or start up a conversation wanting to know, "Where do they talk like you talk?" or, "Now, come on, be honest with us. What's the Army *really* like?"

I also spent some of those hours just sitting alone, reading my little Gideon New Testament and praying and praising the Lord for His great love and His most recent blessings.

In what seemed like a few hours, I arrived in Detroit and Mary was standing in front of the station waiting for me. We had a good visit on the beautiful drive to Monroe. Then for two nights, after she got off from work, we ate at a fancy restaurant and mostly reminisced about the "good old days" in Round Oak. Mary had always been very sweet to me, but now that I was grown and in the Army, she treated me as if I was her favorite brother. I told her about how I got the pass, and she was so proud that I had used it to come to see her.

But the time passed too quickly, and long before I was ready, I had to leave. When she told me good-bye at the Detroit train station, she gave me a great big hug and pressed two twenty-dollar bills into my hand. I really believe that morning was the first time I actually thanked God aloud for my sweet sister Mary who was so dearly loved by everyone in the family. Since I was "the baby," they all treated me like somebody special, and this gave me that extra push I needed to succeed.

I retraced my steps back to Rockford and back to good 'ole Camp Grant. I think I spent less than twenty dollars on the entire trip. I had to be careful that I did not strut as I walked back into the company area and to my barracks.

About a week after returning from my pass, the captain called me into his office, and he and the first sergeant pinned an "Acting Corporal" band to my shirt sleeve. I was sure shocked and glad. From then on to the end of basic, I did my best to show the captain, the sergeants and those "raw young recruits" what a real soldier looked like and how he acted. I was, at least, a whole three years older than they! Most of them were just out of high school. I felt that I had more authority with that little, black corporal armband on than if I were a real sergeant. The troops were more afraid of me than they were of the real corporals, but I was much nicer to them. They worked harder for me that way and were proud of the way their area looked. Now that morale was higher, they finally all completely forgave me for the "footlocker incident."

As winter began to move in on us in late November, Ruzensky was transferred to Regimental Headquarters where he was briefly assigned to the finance department. Shortly after that, he was sent to a post near his home in Hartford. I missed him. We had been through a lot together, and when he left our company, we promised to keep in touch with each other. And we have.

In January, 1944, I was transferred to Company C, 29th Battalion. I was promoted to section leader, but still remained an acting corporal. All my buddies in my other company had finished basic and had been sent overseas. I remember most of these men, and a few of them were my friends. Since I was still stateside, knowing that they were in Europe and in the thick of the war brought a new and deeper sense of commitment to me. I was getting a little depressed, partly because of the bitter cold of northern Illinois, but more so since I had been pulled to do guard duty one night during a near blizzard. My acting corporal stripes meant nothing to the sergeant of the guard. Even though I had put on practically all the clothes they issued me, I was still cold. Those of us from the South had never known cold like this. The temperature was fifteen degrees below zero, and there was a thirty-mile-an-hour wind. I was a Georgia boy and felt like I had water in my veins, while the Yankees had real thick blood in theirs. They were used to these North Pole winters.

Out on guard duty at 3 A.M., the ice crunching under my boots was the only sound in a night of winter silence. The driven snow whirled past the lonely street lights and hit my face like flying needles. I had never felt so alone. The vehicles behind the high fences were lined up in long rows and covered with canvas. Now under two feet of snow, they looked like ghosts sleeping in fresh covered graves. "Brrrrr!" I trembled and shook until my teeth chattered.

Whenever I related this part of my Army career to my three young girls and said, "Man, was it cold!", they would sing out in unison, "Well, Daddy, just how cold was it?" Then I would answer, "It was so cold that if you blinked your eye the lashes would stick together; if you inhaled, the hairs in your nose would freeze; and if you spit, it would bounce!"

Then they would cackle out as if they had never heard it before. I now believe they were laughing at me, not with me.

That winter, I was also cold in my spirit. I was depressed, a long way from home, knew hardly anyone in my new company and even felt shut off from the Lord. In my Gideon Bible, in the lives of Christians I knew personally and in books I had read, I sensed that many of these men and women had much more of God than I did. I didn't think the church could have made it across the centuries and up to my time on what I had. I became convinced that what they all had was the Holy Spirit. I believed that the Spirit had everything to do with a person's devotion to God, and it was only the Holy Spirit who gave them great joy in serving Christ. I also noticed a difference in the chaplains. Some of them smoked, drank and used swear words. But one day I met a Nazarene chaplain, and immediately I saw a vast difference in the way he conducted his life and talked about Jesus. The Pentecostal chaplains also seemed to me to be more dedicated. I sensed that they had found just what I was longing for, the secret to a victorious Christian life.

As I began to read my New Testament, I saw the major role the

A MIRACLE A MINUTE

Holy Spirit played in the daily lives of those early Christians. So I became more interested in getting closer to God and even receiving the Holy Spirit, although I was not sure what that meant or how to receive Him. I also began to attend chapel services more regularly, and my little Bible became more valuable to me the more I read it. The Gideons furnished them at no cost to the military. Their edition included the entire New Testament, Psalms, Proverbs and a few hymns. A most helpful part was suggested readings to suit the soldier's need. Such as, "When you are lonely, read verses…" and gave the verse or paragraph in the Bible that referred to that need.

Many of our men and women in uniform say that their faith was maintained or their lives were even changed by that precious little Bible. It is still available today in the New King James version to anyone, at no cost. Many World War II soldiers would say in unison today, "God bless the Gideons!" The chaplain asked me to hand out the Bibles during the chapel services and to take enough to pass out in the barracks and the mess hall, so most of us had one or two of them.

The story got back to us that a soldier in battle "over there" had one in his jacket pocket when he was fired upon by the enemy, and the bullet hit that little Bible, stopping at John 3:16. It saved his life. After that, many infantry and medic soldiers would not go into battle without at least one of those little Bibles in their shirt pockets.

Each night after lights out, I would continue to read mine, under the blanket with a penlight in hand. One night I came upon the verse in Matthew 10:32, where Jesus says, "Whoever confesses Me before men, him I will also confess before My Father who is in heaven."

I suddenly realized that I had never done that. I had joined the Methodist church, sure, but I had never confessed Christ as my personal Savior before anyone, anywhere. Could this be why I felt so spiritually cold? Maybe.

So I said to the Lord, "Next time I am in church or in a prayer meeting, Lord, I am going to do just that."

But I seemed to hear Him answer, "My son, I want you to do that now!"

"But Lord, there are no men here. They are all asleep and the lights are out."

Then in my spirit I heard the Lord say, "What about those other men?"

He was referring to the men who were in the dayroom at the end of the barracks. I never knew why they called it the dayroom, because no one was ever allowed in there in the daytime.

"But Lord, I have already heard that motley crew in low voices cursing and laughing, telling dirty jokes, smoking and playing cards. They have already used Your name in there several times. One even called out, Jesus Christ! Lord, certainly not those men!"

"Yes, those very men."

I thought to myself, *Well, OK, Lord, if I'm gonna do this, I gotta do it right.*

So I crept out of my bunk, quietly opened my footlocker, got out the brand-new pajamas and robe Mama gave me and put them on. Then I stepped into my new pair of slippers. In all of my time in the Army, I had never seen a soldier wearing pajamas, a robe or slippers. Oh well, this was a special night. But I had to move fast before I lost my courage. I picked up my little Gideon Bible, put my index finger in it on the text and marched in, closing the door behind me.

As I glanced around the smoke-filled room, I moved over in front of the only vacant chair and got their attention by saying, "Men!"

Now, I should have said, "Hey, fellers" or "Look, you guys." I should not have said "Men!" because that's what Sarge called them. Anyway, I really got their attention. They all stared at me and froze. They could not believe their eyes—a soldier in pajamas? A robe? Slippers? And to top it all off, holding a Bible?

I just knew they all were thinking, *What on earth is this—an apparition, an angel or just a crazy GI?*

Trembling and stuttering, I took a deep breath and said, "Well, g-g-guys, I've been rrreading my B-B-Bible, and Jesus says in here in the Gospel of M-M-Matthew that if a person will confess Him before men, He will confess that p-p-person to the Father who is in h-h-heaven."

I calmed down a bit and continued, "I want to do that right now. I want to confess Jesus Christ as my personal Lord and Savior before you men tonight."

At that point, my knees buckled and I fell back into the chair. My head was bowed and tears covered my face. Not a soul moved, and no one said a word. The silence was deafening for what seemed like an hour.

Then out of that deathly silence, like a bolt out of the blue, there came a hand clap and a loud "Praise the Lord!" It came from one of the soldiers. He rushed over to me, fell on his knees beside my chair and with one hand on my knee and the other raised high in the air, he began to pray, real loud: "O Lord God Almighty, the angels are singing somewhere tonight, for this prodigal who has spent his life out in the sin-filled world in riotous living has come home."

Even though I had not been that bad, I let him go on because his words were sweet music to my ears and such a great blessing to my soul.

He continued, "O there is great joy in heaven tonight because a sinner has repented. And one sinner who repents covers a multitude of sins. Praise You, sweet Jesus. Thank You, my Father! Hallelujah forevermore! Amen and Amen."

At that point, I peeped around the room. All the guys were still frozen, in place.

The soldier who gave that beautiful prayer then stood, pulled me up out of the chair and shook my hand. He then looked me dead in the eye said, "You are now also a son of Abraham."

But I didn't want so much to become a son of Abraham as I wanted to become a Christian. But whatever... I felt very good.

As he and I moved over to the door, the men broke their spell and began slowly moving out of the room. Each one shook hands with both of us, as if they had been to a church meeting and were greeting the preachers as they left.

The last man out was a short, slender, black-headed Catholic boy from Boston. As he strongly shook my hand, his eyes began to fill with tears. He said, "I wish to God I had the guts to do what you just did."

Now there were more tears in my eyes.

After "the meeting" broke up, the man who prayed for me introduced himself as J.C. Lovett, from Jackson, Mississippi. I thought he was a preacher, but no, he was a Nazarene layman. He was short and very slender, and had thin, reddish hair and blue eyes. He was so dedicated that he did everything the preacher told him to do, and more. He went out into the neighborhoods of his town, and with excitement and deep love, he preached on the streets, invited people to accept Christ as Lord and tried to get them saved. Everyone he met was asked, "My friend, have you had a born-again experience with Jesus Christ?"

I learned later that J.C.'s presence there was nothing short of a miracle. He had never been in that room before that night and was never there again at night. He was married and lived off the post and was on separate rations. He had been there waiting to go on duty at midnight as a night KP (kitchen police). He said he had thought he was in that dayroom to minister to some of those men and try to get a few saved. But instead, God had sent him there to receive my "good confession."

Had he not been there, I would have had to stand alone in that silence with no one to "pray me through," to hear my confession or to receive me as a born-again Christian into the kingdom of God. But God knew what I was going to do that night, so He sent me what I felt was an angel. J.C. also saw it as a miracle. I felt a refreshing, a washing that night, and I do so now as I relate this to you. God is so good, He cares for us as He cares for the little sparrow.

In the following months, my life was more greatly blessed with peace of mind. I became more content with where I was and who I was than ever before, and best of all, I began to attain a "joy unspeakable and full of glory." But to sustain that level of Christian ecstasy required much more than I ever thought I could give. I almost failed but, praise God, I stuck it out all the way. You shall now discover the exciting experience I had when I "took up" with the Nazarenes.

❧ 10 ❧

I Break Fast
at Breakfast

In those days the Nazarenes were very strict and ultra-conservative. The women wore no makeup, jewelry or slacks, and they did not color their hair. The men and women did not smoke, chew tobacco, drink alcohol, dance or go to the movies. They did not even chew chewing gum and did not drink "pop." (These days, I think some of them may drink a little Coke, because I hear their headquarters has stock in the company! Oh, no—just kiddin'!) They carried their own Bibles to Sunday school and church and spent a lot of time every day reading them. I do not relate all this to make fun of Nazarenes. How could I, when God gave me a great blessing through them? I do so to show the drastic contrast between their personal devotion and that of some church members who belong to the mainline denominations.

J.C. could not wait to take me to Sunday school and church and to meet his devoted wife, Maurice. Almost every Sunday after church they would take me to lunch. She was a very sweet lady, had a good job and was as dedicated as he was. J.C. also introduced me to his preacher and found great delight in telling people at church the story about how I got saved in that dayroom. The congregation rejoiced when they heard it, and this made me feel like I was a member of their happy family.

Nazarene church services were quite unlike anything I had ever experienced, far different from the Methodist or the Primitive Baptist. The Nazarenes had actually broken off from the Methodist church many years ago. They had no choir; however, the men and women sang as if they were the choir. That first Sunday, when the time came for prayer, the preacher went to the pulpit and began praying. I was on the front row, and when I looked around I was startled to find that the entire congregation had disappeared! I thought they had all left or had been raptured. But no, they had turned around and were down on their knees with their elbows resting in the pews praying. Then they all began to pray in English as loud as the preacher.

I whispered, "No one is listening to the prayer the preacher is praying!"

Then after the preacher finished his prayer, as if on cue by the Spirit, they all suddenly arose, turned and sat down. Instantly, the church was full again! After the prayer and the preacher "took up" the offering, he began to preach—very good, but very loud and very long. I thought of dear old Brother Williamson in Mama's church because this preacher knew his Bible just as well. The Sunday and Wednesday nights were more of the same. Soon, I was right in there with them, kneeling with my elbows on the pew and praying out loud, and then singing at the top of my voice.

I actually began to look forward to these lively services. I guarantee you, no one was ever bored. From then on, and for as long as I was at Camp Grant, our schedule every evening and all weekend was filled with one desire: to get closer to Jesus Christ and to God. Most of that time was spent reading the Bible and praying.

After a few weeks of this regimen, I asked J.C. how I was doing.

He told me, "You are doing fine, dear Brother, but we've just got started. Remember, you told me that night in the dayroom that you wanted to get closer and closer to God. You later said that you also wanted to receive the Holy Spirit. For this to happen, you must first become entirely sanctified. So now we have to do a very important thing."

So I said, "J.C., we have been to church every time the door was open; we have prayed so much that I have begun to think that we need to give God a rest; we have read the Bible every spare moment; passed out Gideon Bibles and gospel tracts all over the post; and we've talked to many strangers about the Lord! What else on earth is there for me to do?"

He said with a beaming face and broad smile, "Just one more step, Brother James. You must now learn to experience the blessings and joy of fasting."

"Fasting? J.C., I am a Methodist. We don't know anything about fasting."

He then became very serious. Lifting his hand and pointing a finger at me, he said in a firm voice, "That's the whole problem, Brother. Some of the large denominations have ceased to practice the New Testament ways of the deeper Christian life. So many have forgotten how to love, serve and please God. Tomorrow morning, I challenge you to join me in the New Testament act of fasting."

Then he came up to me, smiled, put his arm around me and continued, "If you agree, we can use Wednesday as our day of fasting each week."

I was ready to do anything, pay any price for the love, peace and joy of God that I had been seeking since a boy. So I said, "OK, J.C., I have wanted all my life to become entirely sanctified. And I have longed for the baptism of the Holy Spirit. J.C., I'll do it, I'll take the plunge, I'll go all the way. But you are going to have to walk by my side on this."

He smiled, shook my hand and said, "Jesus and I will be right there with you, so be not anxious."

The next morning he came to my bunk very early and whispered, "Good morning, Brother James, wake up. It's Wednesday and a beautiful day. This is the day the Lord hath made for us to begin our fasting. So get up now. I'll go into the latrine with you, and while you shave, brush your teeth, put on Vitalis and brush your hair, I will talk with you about the Lord."

As I yawned and stretched I said, weakly, "Hallelujah."

After I dressed, we walked to breakfast. He said on the way, "Now, you must not reveal to anyone that you are fasting. You must do it in secret, then God will reward you openly."

This was my very first time to fast, so I was in uncharted waters. Now, the Nazarene fast is different. Different—and hard. It is a twenty-four-hour, total abstinence fast. You start the day eating breakfast. Please don't tell J.C., but I would advise you the first time around to have a very large breakfast. Then you go through the lunch and dinner hour with no food. You do not drink anything or take anything by mouth. You can brush your teeth, but you can't swallow the juice!

Get ready, for that is the day when everyone around you seems to be eating candy bars and drinking pop. And this is the very afternoon when one or more of your buddies will come up to you and invite you to go to the USO to have a cup of coffee and a big slice of apple pie—with ice cream on it—on him! What are you going to say? Well, you can't hit him, hate him or tell him you're fasting. I know, take a rain check, find him tomorrow and say to him, "I'll take that pie and coffee now!" But then he cannot be found. Besides, you will not want it nearly as bad tomorrow. J.C. told me to be on guard because all those offers for food were just Satan trying to get me to break my fast.

While everyone is noisily and happily eating lunch and dinner, you spend that time alone or with your fasting partner praying, reading the Bible and talking about the things of God. During the early evening hours, you begin to get real hungry. You haven't had any coffee since breakfast, so by now you probably have an enormous headache. Actually, several times you have smelled the aroma of food and coffee drifting in your window from the dining room, but this is the time when you begin to get serious about your faith. J.C. and I spent many Wednesday nights upstairs in the field house, in the small projector room, down on our knees. I figured that we must be trying to get Dwight L. Moody knees. They say his knees were as callused as a camel's from his long praying. It didn't hurt him or J.C. to kneel for hours.

Shut away up in that room, you could cry your prayers out loud to God, you could groan, moan, shout or speak your mind to Jesus— anything the Spirit led you to do, because you knew you could do it without being heard by anyone but J.C. and God!

On that first Wednesday, about midnight, the silence was deafening. I heard a dog barking in the distance and a train whistle that sounded to me like a funeral dirge. I almost wished I was on that train, going anywhere. Just then J.C. turned to me and whispered, "Brother, you should be having visions about now."

I sat down on the floor and with a sheepish smile said, "J.C., why are we whispering? Visions? I have been having visions since about eight o'clock."

"What! Tell me about what you saw."

I dropped my head, weakly smiled and said, "My mama's fried chicken, hot buttered biscuits and gravy, corn on the cob, banana pudding and a big mug of fresh brewed COFFEE!!!"

He laughed, shook his finger at me and said, "No, no, Pip! Sometimes you may think there is no hope for you. But never you mind, lil Brother, you will soon get out of that flesh, and have meat to eat that others know not of."

I told him that I was sorry. He smiled and we continued worshiping God until it got very late and he decided that he needed to go home. I was so glad because I was ready to go to bed. That first night while I tried to go to sleep, I kept thinking about those peanut butter crackers I had in my footlocker.

"O, groan! Satan, in the name of Jesus Christ, get out of my sight;

you're not going to get me to break my fast, so there!"

So I firmly set my jaw and resisted. During those few hours of sleep, I think I dreamed of nothing but food and coffee all night.

The next morning, J.C. came to my bunk and shook me at about 5:25 A.M. I felt like I had just gotten to sleep. He whispered for me to come join him in the dayroom. He told me that our fast was almost over. There we had a brief time of prayer. I had shaved and showered the night before, so I only had to wash my face, brush my hair and get dressed. He fell out with us for reveille.

As soon as we were dismissed, J.C. quickly grabbed my arm. He seemed to sense that I was cocked and ready, like a race horse leaping out of the gate, to make a mad dash for that chow line. But, in a sweet and almost feminine voice, he said, "No, Brother James, we must wait back and let the entire company go into the mess hall before us. We need to get the full benefit of our fast."

But, O my Lord, was I hungry! I do believe that at that moment, I would have given a five-dollar bill for one cup of hot, freshly brewed coffee.

He said softly, "Brother James, all the men are in. Now we can go in and break fast."

Suddenly, I realized that this is where the first meal of the day got its name. Of course! Break-fast! Breakfast. When we got our food and sat down, J.C. said a brief word of grace. As I began eating slowly and sipping that great cup of coffee, the Spirit of Christ led my mind to the time in centuries past when the early church, and later the priests and nuns, would daily break fast with that early morning meal. I felt that in the Spirit, J.C. and I were among that vast unseen company reaching back through the ages and around the world who were this very morning breaking their fast with us.

I do believe this breakfast in that mess hall with J.C. was my most meaningful meal. I strongly sensed the presence of Christ, who seemed to be saying to me personally, "My Son, as oft as you break the bread and take the cup, you do so in memory of Me."

My eyes were brimmed with tears. Truly the fasting changed that meal into a sacrament, almost as much as if we were among a group of the first disciples, taking the bread and the wine with Jesus Himself.

So, this was fasting the Nazarene way. It wasn't easy, but what a blessing it was! J.C. and I continued to fast every Wednesday for many weeks. Gradually, it became a little easier, but never did it lose all of its bittersweetness. We learned the great benefit of denying the flesh so that God might feed the soul. Wednesdays thereafter were entirely different from any other day. On that day I felt more alive than on other days. All my senses seemed to be so much sharper, the Lord seemed so much closer, prayer seemed so much more personal, and O, the Word of God, when read on that day, was as if it were written just to me. The songs of the birds, the sun setting, the moon rising, even the breeze caressing my face— all were newly different. It was after a few weeks of fasting that miracles began to happen more and more frequently in my life, some very small but all unforgettable.

A few days later, on the eighteenth of December, our battalion was given two weeks leave to go home for Christmas. It was snowing hard the afternoon we arrived at the whistle stop near Moline. I ran into the little store to get warm and wait for the train. Glancing around, I saw a three-dollar, satin pillow with the word "Mother" stitched on it. I only had a twenty dollar bill in my wallet. I gave the pillow and the money to the pretty, young lady cashier as the train was stopping. In her haste, she only gave me change for a ten! Later, on the train, I discovered that I had only seven dollars left to get me all the way to Brunswick. One of my buddies graciously loaned me money for dinner. I arrived too late that night in Atlanta and missed my connection, so I had to check into the YMCA next door to the terminal. It cost me a dollar for the last bed available, an upper bunk. This left me six dollars, the exact train fare home.

My bed was on the second floor of a large barracks-like room filled with six rows of double bunks. The room was almost completely dark. I silently crept down to my bed. I knew that the wall lockers would make a lot of noise, so I undressed, hung my pants and jacket on the posts at the foot of the bunk, and hung my other clothes on the post at the head.

Then, as I was drifting off to sleep, I felt the bed move. When I sat up, I saw the dim figure of a man walking quickly away. I suddenly remembered that I had foolishly left my wallet in my pants pocket, so I jumped down and checked. Surely enough, my wallet was gone. I ran to the large, tall doors of the room, down the wide stairs and out onto the freezing street—in my underwear! But I saw no one. I slowly walked back up the stairs, sat down on the first step and began to weep.

I knew nothing else to do but pray, so I blubbered out my plight, "O my blessed Lord, You know that my furlough papers, ID and train fare home are in that wallet. What can I do? Where will I go? I am desperate, Lord. Please, p-l-e-a-s-e, Lord Jesus, hear me now and come to my rescue. You are my only hope!"

While I was thus crying and praying my heart out, I heard the big door open at the bottom of the stairs. Through my tears I could see a young man walking slowly up toward me. He stood in front of me for a moment and then reached into his pocket and handed me my wallet. Startled, I took it.

Before I could speak, he said, "I stole your wallet. But when I opened it to take the money, I saw that picture of Jesus you've got in there and I just could not do it. I had to bring it back to you. Forgive me, and will you please forget that this happened?"

He then quickly turned and walked back down the stairs.

I called after him, "Thank you and God bless you."

After the big door slammed, I looked up and sobbed, "I thank You, Father, for it was that picture of Your Son Jesus that brought my wallet back to me."

I sat there for a moment, looking at and loving the Person in the picture. It was the "Sallman's Head of Christ" that Mama had put in my wallet when I left home for the Army. Sallman saw this face of Jesus in a dream, woke up, made a quick pencil sketch, and finished it the next morning; now we have this most popular face of Christ. Printed on the back of my picture is the famous tribute to Jesus, "One Solitary Life," written by Dr. James A. Francis. Very few people know the author of this amazing tribute. Most often when it is printed the author is listed as "unknown." Years ago Dr. Ralph W. Sockman, a personal friend who spoke for us several times at First Christian in Falls Church, Virginia, told me the author's name. Because that wallet was a reminder that God really answers prayer, I kept it long after it had worn out. I still have that same picture of Jesus in my wallet today.

After I returned to my bunk and put my wallet in my pillowcase, I continued to thank the Lord for this miracle. As I drifted off to sleep, I prayed for that young man whose tender heart toward God was touched by the beautiful face of Christ. I claimed his soul for the kingdom because I felt that God had also worked a miracle in his life that night.

The next morning I arose early, went downstairs to the large bathroom, shaved, showered, came back up and dressed. Then I was off to the terminal where I bought my ticket and boarded the train to Brunswick. I had the strangest sensation when I put that empty wallet in my pocket. I didn't even have enough money for a cup of coffee, and yet somehow I wasn't the least bit worried. After the train pulled out, a man sitting next to me asked if I'd go to the diner and have breakfast with him! I must have looked cold, broke and hungry. As we sat there in the diner having that first cup of morning coffee, I thanked him. Then I told him about the wallet, and he smiled and said that he was also a Christian. But by his generosity, acts and words of love, he had already proven that to me. When he asked me to also join him for lunch, I knew that all he did for me that day was not a coincidence. It was Jesus keeping His promise to care for us.

When I arrived in Brunswick late that afternoon, Ed Fennell was waiting to meet me and take me home in the old '32 Ford. It was so good to see him. We had a good chat and some laughs on the way. After I warmly greeted Mama and Papa, I could not wait to tell them the miracle story of the wallet and the kind man on the train.

Papa wiped his eyes and Mama laughed, saying over and over, "It seems that God has always looked out after you, James. He is so good and faithful to answer our prayers!"

But she just had to shed a few more tears when I gave her that precious little pillow. Then she hugged me all over again.

After coffee, I told them about the girl who shortchanged me.

Since I knew the name of that little shop near Moline, Papa suggested that I send her a special delivery letter asking her for the money she owed me. I did, and in a few days I received a sweet letter from her.

She wrote, "I was ten dollars long in my register that night. Sorry. Enclosed please find a check for ten dollars! Happy New Year! See you on your return? Kristen."

Thank you, pretty Kristen, thanks Papa, and *thank You, dear Lord!*

This was just a continuation of the many miracles that have followed me all of my life, especially since the night I confessed Christ as Lord in that dayroom and experienced a real live and loving Lord to whom I pray. The regimen of fasting with J.C. Lovett seemed to show the Lord that I was serious about my faith and love, that I wanted to get closer to Him as a personal Friend and that I wanted to be deeply committed to His will.

Christmas 1944 was one of my best. It was good to have leisure time with Mama and Papa, who told me all the news. Jack's wife, Sam, was spending the holiday with her parents. It made me happy to hear that the store was still doing well and that Mama and Ed were working well together. Sam also helped when she was there. I visited the store and chatted with Ed and Mama. I also spent several evenings with George and Vera, savoring her great dinners. Almost every day I went into town and visited with George at the shoe shop and over coffee at "ye ole Brunswick cafe," where we brought each other up to date on the rest of the news. I could tell by the looks on all their faces and their tone of voice that they were very proud of their son and baby brother and to have three Pippin boys wearing the uniform.

Those exhilarating days sped by, and soon I was back in the car with George, chatting on the way to Brunswick, where I caught the train for the long ride to Atlanta and Chicago and to that whistle-stop near Moline. I ran into the gift shop, gave pretty Kristen a big hug and thanked her for sending me the money. She laughed, we both blushed, and then I ran out to board the waiting bus to Camp Grant. I planned to ask her for a date real soon.

In late February of 1944, our company spent eighteen days and nights on field maneuvers. Each soldier was issued only one-half of a pup tent, so J.C. and I shared a tent together. He and I dug out a rectangle about eight inches deep, the exact size of the tent. This gave us much more room. But you must trench the tent well all around, because if you don't and it rains, you will wake up half-drowned in a miniature swimming pool. Of course, you never touch the tent with your finger while it is raining because if you do, a stream of water will come flooding down in your face.

This field duty was hard, but strangely enough, it seemed easier since "the Nazarene experience." All the training was dead serious and modeled after real battlefield conditions. We had field showers, got hot water from the 55-gallon drum near the field kitchen and shaved in our steel helmet pots. Following combat procedure, we stayed ten feet apart as we passed through the chow line and when we sat on the ground to eat. We slept in sleeping bags, but the latrine was about a hundred feet away from our little tent. On those cold winter nights we had to dress to go out, so this trip was quite a miserable chore. But, thanks to the Lord, people our age seldom get up at all during the night.

Starting after breakfast in the early morning, we practiced the duties of a medic in battlefield conditions until lunch, and did it again all afternoon. Then after supper, we had map-reading exercises that had us stumbling over miles of rough terrain in pitch darkness until about 10 P.M. If you survived eighteen days and nights of this without losing your mind or going AWOL, you knew for sure that you had become a soldier!

I Break Fast at Breakfast

About halfway through, some of the men started moaning and groaning. When the first sergeant heard this, he yelled, "Hey, you guys cut out that chatter. This is nothing compared to what our fighting men are going through in Europe." And then he thundered, "And you will be joining them soon! These field maneuvers here are designed to help you carry out your mission over there. Quitcha bellyakin'! None of you have been shot at or killed by enemy fire yet, have you? So, this vital training is preparation for fighting and is teaching you how to stay alive as combat troops so you can care for the wounded and play a vital role in winning this war. So, would you please spare me any more baby noise."

Although he sounded like he had said these words to medics hundreds of times before during his duty at Camp Grant, you can bet your life we men listened and remembered every word. On the nineteenth day the maneuvers were completed, and we were back in comfortable barracks with hot showers and eating great food inside the warm mess hall.

One week later the battalion was ordered to prepare to ship out. Since I was on limited service because of my leg, the commander struck me from the orders. I was upset and went in to see him. Even though I reminded him that my leg had not prevented my carrying out any of my duties during the training, he still told me I could not go with them—no matter how much I pleaded with him. His orders were that I could not go overseas with my company. I was crestfallen and depressed.

That last Sunday, I went with J.C. to our dear old Nazarene church. He had taken Maurice to the train to Jackson on Saturday. After our quiet and lonely lunch, he wanted to go say good-bye to some of his and Maurice's friends, so we parted, but we agreed to meet back at the barracks after supper. When he arrived, I got the key from the orderly and we went to our memorable dayroom for our final time. It was a place that had become almost sacred ground to us. We concluded with a special prayer for his safety and protection and that our Lord would take care of his dear wife while he was away. Since we all had to wake up very early for orientation, he went to his bunk to finish packing. Later, I noticed he was not on the floor and had not come back before I turned in. I did not hear him when he crept back to his bed. I figured he had taken a long walk in the night and had a quiet talk with the Lord.

The next morning after breakfast and orientation, and just before the battalion fell out to board the convoy, I went around the area and said farewell to those men I knew best. When I came to J.C., we embraced and had to fight back tears.

He said, "Good-bye, old friend; keep all of us and Maurice in your daily prayers."

I took both of his hands in mine, looked him in the eye and said that old and familiar benediction: "May the Lord watch between me and thee while we are absent one from the other. God go with you all the way and bring you safely back home, J.C."

His eyes filled as he quickly turned and ran to the end of the convoy to climb aboard his truck. I stood there alone, waving as the long convoy pulled out. J.C. was sitting at the gate in the last truck, and we threw each other a snappy salute as he went by. The roar faded and was gone as the trucks turned north toward Moline, and to the train that would begin their long journey. Final destination: GERMANY!

Now the area was empty and deadly quiet. How can I share the reality of the feelings of loneliness I had as the sun began to set that day and I walked through those vacant barracks, cutting off all the lights. I came back to my empty building and sat on my bunk for a long time, remembering and praying. Right there was my blessed footlocker that had won me a pass to see Mary months ago; over there is where J.C. slept during his last night at Grant. I heard a lonely whippoorwill chirping loudly in a nearby tree, trying to distract me and attract his lover. I did not want my mind to flash back to last night. Then, the barracks were filled with the sounds and smells of troops who were busy doing the things troops do when they are headed for the front. I had no yen to bring that on my heart—but I lost control—and just could not shake the thoughts of that last night when I had been surrounded by men I had come to know as friends.

The smell of boot polish; the snap-snap-snap of the shine cloth; sounds of the scurry to finish packing; the singing of the old songs that soldiers have sung for so many years in so many training camps in so many wars; the familiar but oddly loud sounds coming from a crap game at the end of the room; silent men, sitting on their footlockers, pen and paper in hand, head down, writing words of love to those most loved; one quiet, lonely man sitting near me stopped frequently to wipe away tears that he hoped no one noticed; laughing men, hollow laughs a little too loud, trying to keep back the tears. With months of memories racing through my mind, I had a hard time getting to sleep. Finally, I felt much better when God reminded me again that He could be there with me, and also with J.C. and all those men at the same time; be with me here and with them—all the way to the front and back; be with them all the way home here or all the way home *there*.

I'm glad I didn't know it then, but for most of those men it was *there*. They never again came home here. They entered France after D Day, during some of the heaviest fighting, and the majority of them were seriously injured or killed in the Battle of the Bulge. J.C. was assigned to Headquarters in England and served for the duration in a general hospital near London as a medical technician, rising to the rank of tech. sergeant.

In a recent phone conversation, he shared with me the awful condition of many of the injured when they arrived at the hospital from the front. But the skilled doctors, nurses and technicians worked with them, often around the clock, going as long as three days at a time without sleep. It was a miracle of modern medicine and the healing Christ that almost all of the ones who made it back to the hospital returned home well and able to carry on normal lives. In late 1945, when J.C. came home without injury, I was keenly aware that I was speaking with a hero, a very tired and much decorated medic who had helped save the lives of thousands.

The few of us who remained at Camp Grant were assigned to Cadre. Since I was still an acting corporal, one of the old first sergeants who was retiring asked me to take charge of his orderly room. I accepted even though there was very little to do. It was a welcomed change after eighteen weeks of basic and eighteen days of field maneuvers.

One Saturday morning, after a few days as an orderly, I was called to Regimental Headquarters and told by a captain that I would be shipping out to Fort Lewis, Washington on Tuesday. I asked him how long he thought I would be there. When he told me I would probably be there for the duration, I almost fainted.

"But sir," I responded, "who made this decision? You are not giving me much notice; how long have you known this? I really need to return to Lawson General Hospital in Atlanta. I have just learned that my brother, Lt. Jack Pippin, who was injured in Assam, India, has recently been shipped back to Lawson for extensive surgery. Sir, this is a compassionate request…"

The captain cut me off and stood up. As he shook his head and extended his hand, he said, "I'm sorry, Pippin; I don't know the answers to your questions. But that decision has been made, your orders have been cut, and it is much too late for me or anyone else to do anything about it now."

A MIRACLE A MINUTE

I dropped my head, feebly saluted and almost staggered out.

The very thought of being shipped to Fort Lewis, Washington, so far from home, sent chills down my spine. The rest of the day and into the night hours I was in panic, at first. Then I was in fervent prayer to God. I slept very little. I did not want to go! But my orders were already cut.

"What on earth is going on?" I kept asking God. "What can I do?"

What I needed now was another miracle—*a great big miracle.*

After chapel services on Sunday morning, I told the chaplain about my dilemma. He said, "Pippin, I see little or no chance that anyone can help at this late date. Maybe you can get transferred to Atlanta after you get to Ft. Lewis. I promise that I will keep you in my prayers. If you think that there is anything I can do, please call me."

I thanked him and left.

After Sunday lunch was over I poured myself another cup of coffee and sat alone in the mess hall. While I prayerfully clutched my mug in both hands, I gazed down at the coffee and spoke softly to God. "Father, everybody says it's too late and that no one can help me. But I know You can help me, for all things are possible for You. I only have one day to get those orders changed. I'm sure You understand my plight. You are my only hope. Please guide me and help me. What is Your will for me? Lord, I know that I am only one among the millions of people in the service who need You right now, but is there any way that I can get my orders changed at this last minute so that I can go to Lawson to be with Jack and nearer home? If so, please show me how. If not, then I will try my best to be at peace about it."

I held my coffee cup in both hands, took a sip from the cup, and at that very instant the words our Lord spoke at the last supper came into my mind: "As often as you break bread or take the cup you do so in memory of me."

At that moment Major Stephens, my old boss back at Lawson, flashed into my mind. I remembered that he really liked me.

I thought, *Is this Your leading, Lord?* I whispered to myself, *I bet he is a lieutenant colonel by now! And Chief Sargeant Leonard Jacobsen, who was my friend, is probably a Master Sargeant! My desk in the records section was just outside his door. But there's so little time. I'm scheduled to ship out to Lewis on Tuesday morning. Lord, this is Sunday afternoon. How can I possibly get in touch with Stephens? Please tell me, Lord.*

Then I arose to leave, and as in a flash, God showed me just what to do.

"That's it! That is it! Thank You, Lord Jesus. I got it. Of course, that's the only way. I'll do it!"

I ran from the mess hall, and in minutes was at the Western Union office on post. I stumbled in all out of breath and wheezed, "Lady, I'd like to send a telegram to Atlanta."

"Sure thing, Soldier," she said with a broad smile. "Here's pen and paper. Sit over there and write it out and we'll have it on its way in a flash."

As I started to write, I whispered a prayer. Then I thought, *Since he's probably a lieutenant colonel by now, I'll call him Colonel!*

I had seen his name a hundred times when he signed service records while I was working there. So, here goes:

> Colonel James P. Stephens, Personnel Records Section, Headquarters Detachment, Lawson General Hospital, Atlanta, Georgia.
>
> Colonel Stephens,
>
> Sir:
>
> I, James C. Pippin, worked your department several months one year ago. Just finished 18 weeks Medical Basic, acting Corporal, Section Leader. On orders ship out Tuesday AM Ft. Lewis Washington. But Sir, brother, Lt. Jack Pippin, is patient there with serious injury sustained in CBI theater. Earnestly desire come work for you be with him. Will do best to be asset to you. If you want me, please expedite request for transfer.
>
> Thanks, God bless.
> James C. Pippin, Acting Cpl.
> Regimental Headquarters
> Company "D", 26 Bn. MRTC,
> Camp Grant, Rockford, Ill.

I kissed the paper and gave it to her. She sent it while I stood there. I paid the kind lady and walked slowly back to my barracks. Now, as it is so often with us humans, I began to doubt and started mumbling negative thoughts like, "There is very little chance that he will see my message in time, and even so, there's even less of a chance that he will act upon it."

Even though I knew what I had done was by God's leading, many negative words continually plagued my mind that afternoon and evening.

"Suppose he is not there now—maybe he doesn't even remember me—what if he is sick tomorrow? I cannot wait until Tuesday."

I must admit that I really didn't have the faith for the size of miracle that I needed. I knew in the wisdom of the Spirit where this thinking was coming from, so I came against the evil one. By bedtime, I had regained control of myself and positive thoughts had begun to flood my mind.

Jesus seemed to say, "Son, you prayed in My name, and you know what the Father told you to do. You did that. Now, please leave the rest to Us and go to sleep."

A sweet feeling of peace came over me as I continued to pray until I fell asleep Sunday night.

On Monday morning while I shaved, showered and dressed for duty, my fervent prayers were going up to God. As I sat alone after breakfast I said almost aloud, "Lord, You already know the time is short, that I must hear from Atlanta by noon today. Increase my faith and help me to be at ease and completely trust You as I go about my duties today."

I was shaky all that the morning. By the time lunch came, I noticed that the palms of both hands were sweaty. It seemed like the longest morning I could remember. Oh, how proud God would have been of me had I been filled with the assurance that my prayers had already been answered and that my request for the transfer had been acted upon.

After lunch, I felt much better when I returned to my office in the orderly room; I wasn't shaking, my hands were dry and calm, and I had no indigestion! I just relaxed and sat at my desk, still nervous but in an attitude of prayer.

I kept glancing at the clock. Each minute seemed like an hour.

Then the phone rang. I was so startled that I almost jumped out of the chair. I quickly grabbed the phone.

"This is M/Sgt. Parker, Regimental. We're looking for a—uh—James C. Pippin, your company, I need to talk to him, pronto!"

My heart leaped up into my throat. I finally managed to squeak out the words, "Yes, Sir! This is him speaking."

"Hey, if you are James C. Pippin, man, you'd better get up here, on the double, Col. Wilson wants to talk to you."

Without a word, I slammed the receiver down, hit the street and ran all the way to Col. Wilson's office. A grinning M/Sgt. Parker waved me right in. I stepped up to his desk. Breathing heavily, I rigidly saluted and identified myself. He was a tall, stout man with white hair, a white mustache and bright blue eyes. When he looked up and smiled, I saw that he was a lieutenant colonel.

He said, glancing again at his desk, "Hehhyesssiree, hat hease, Pippin."

When he stood and came around the desk, his smile broadened, revealing a mouth full of white teeth.

At that moment I thought: *This simply has to be the most beautiful person I have ever seen in my entire life, even if he does talk kinda wheezy!*

"Say son, hee, hee, hew've really got a friend down there hin Hat-lanna hin that Col. Stephens. He sounds like a puurrince of a feller. Hue'll be glad to know that hat his request, *wheee have changed hyour horders*. Ya, haaaaa! What doo hue think of thaatt! We're sending hue to Hat—lanna, Boy! Hyour travel horders har in there."

He shoved a manila envelope into my stomach and continued, "This here is hyour records jacket. Keep hyour heyes on this and hand deliver hit to Col. Stephens. Hyour new horders are effective himmeejettly, so you are—free—TOOO—L-E-A-V-E!" As he said these words in his shrill voice, he stood up on tip-toe to his full height and punched me in the stomach, but I tell you it was the most lovely voice I ever heard.

I began to shake all over. A broad smile crept across my face.

"Sir, I want to thank…"

"No, no, no…doan menchun hit, Pippin, gerr-laad to be of help. I hear that things are pretty tuff hright now over there hin the CBI hayreah. Rest hassured that that brave brother of yhours his hin good hands, Lawson Gen'rall his one of hour best."

Sobbing with tears rolling down my face, I said, "Colonel Wilson, you will never know how much this means to me. I pray God's richest blessings on your life and your family."

He smiled and gave me one of his, "No, ho, ho's." As we walked to the door, he put his arm around my shoulder. He then took my hand and wished me good luck and happy landings.

I felt ten feet tall as I left the building. I was loudly thanking and praising God with every breath. I wanted to run and leap and dance around like a little child, but too many people were watching! Walking briskly back to my company with my miracle "horders" clutched in my left hand, I had difficulty controlling myself. As you can tell, I'm having difficulty controlling myself right now!!

I was utterly amazed by how quickly God had brought all this about—Sunday morning I was a quivering mess; Sunday afternoon, the telegram was sent; Monday at 1 P.M., Col. Wilson called, and now at 1:30 P.M., *I am free to leave for HATLANNA!* God is indeed a good God!

The song "His eye is on the sparrow, and I know He watches me" kept running through my mind. This miracle was a valuable lesson in faith. What seemed to me to be absolutely impossible was so simple for God. Even through my wavering faith and fervent prayers, He made a way where there was no way. And, O my soul, He doesn't need much time to do it either, does He?

Later that Monday afternoon I said good-bye to my sergeant and packed all my gear. Then bright and early Tuesday morning, I said a sad farewell to dear 'ole Camp Grant. When my Army shuttle bus passed through the area, past Regimental Headquarters and headed for the open highway and Moline, I was surprised at my mixed feelings about leaving the place. The winter of 1943–1944 had been the coldest and most miserable winter I had ever experienced. Depression and loneliness had dogged my tracks off and on starting from the first week Ruzensky and I arrived at Grant. But our little foolhardy stunt of hiding out, my confession of Christ in the dayroom, J.C. Lovett and our deep friendship and our fasting and devout search for a closer walk with God—all had greatly lifted my spirits. More than this, a peace of mind and heart came to me that continued throughout the rest of the time I was at Grant, including those awful eighteen days on maneuvers. Because so many good things had happened to me there, I will never forget old, bare and ugly Camp Grant. I won't forget its warm mess halls full of good food, the acrid, constant smell of burning coal during that bitter winter or my good friend Bill Ruzensky.

As I rode on the bus, taking in the lush green countryside of Illinois, a brief feeling swept over me. I suddenly felt like I was going off and leaving God at Grant. But later, on the train to Chicago, I realized that God was "in that place" and, indeed, everywhere at the same time. After I changed trains to Atlanta, the thought of seeing Jack again and the anticipation of what awaited me in the days ahead made the time go faster and gave me a sweet feeling of joy. By Wednesday afternoon I was grabbing an electric bus and riding from the Atlanta terminal to Chamblee and the entrance to Lawson General Hospital.

❋ 11 ❋

Jack and the
Battle of the Bulge

When I arrived that afternoon at Lawson on July 16, 1944, I phoned M/Sgt. Jacobsen from the front gate. He was there in minutes. On the way to Col. Stephen's office, he said, "Glad to have you back, Pippin. You'll be surprised at how much things have changed around here. I'm sure you're dying to know what happened on this end on Monday morning when my colonel walked in."

"I sure am, Sergeant, and don't leave out a word."

"OK. Well, when Col. Stephens walked into his office Monday morning and sat at his desk," he said, glancing frequently over at me, "your telegram was on top of his stack of mail where I had put it earlier. He read it, then called me in and told me to get G-1, Head of Personnel Section, Regimental HQ, Camp Grant, on the line. Your Col. Wilson must have been walking into his office just as the phone was ringing.

"When he came on the line, Col. Stephens told him the situation and then asked, 'Colonel Wilson, do you see any problem with sending this man to me?'

"Wilson's voice came back so loud that I heard every word from across the room. Col. Stephens was very amused at Wilson. He had a big smile on his face as he tilted the phone away from his ear the whole time that Wilson was talking. He and I thought that Wilson had a—uh—slight speech impediment?"

At this point, Jacobsen began in a sing-songy way, trying to mimic Wilson's wheezy voice, his way of speaking and his silly laugh.

"O, ho, ho, ho, although hide'd love to have Pippin stay here and work for me, hive habsolootely nooo problem hat hall, Sir! I'm honely too glad to do hit for hew, Col. Stephens...as soon as we hang up, Hiall have Pippin's horiginal horders rescinded and cut new ones to return him to hew…Aw, it's HOKAY, don't menn-chun hit Sir…hallways ready to put two brothers back together, Colonel, especially hunder these hregretuble circumstances…Wal, hue'd do the same for me, herr-right?…Yesss Sirrreee, and thuh same to hew, Sir, hand…good luck! Don't chew hezzetate if you hever need henneythane helse from this hend? Just hue hask for me, HOKAY? Wilson, here, standing huhready, hover and hout Sir, Buh-Bye."

Then Jake glanced at me and went, "How'd hue think hi did, Pip, he, he, hole boy?"

I told the sergeant, "Jake, you can cut up all you want to about that lieutenant colonel, but to me, that man was an angel. He and Col. Stephens were having the most important phone conversation about me that has ever happened."

I sat grinning at him, thinking how very clever he was and that he just might be a skosh jealous. I clutched my records securely in both hands and was just glad to be there.

He continued, talking normally this time, "No, really Pip, I feel like I'm driving a celebrity here. You sure got clout with top side. You are the very first private, er scuze me, I mean, acting corporal, I ever knew, that had two colonels fightin' over him!"

Now I felt that he was trying to make me feel good.

I came back, "Thanks, Jake, but my clout, if I have any, is a bit higher than top side. And thanks to you for your vital part in it. The Lord had a hand in it, too."

"Ohhh meee, now! Have you gone up there and got religion?"

I glanced at him and noticed his rather large nose, his reddish hair and his bright blue eyes. I wouldn't dare miss this chance, so I said gravely, "Now, Sgt. Jacobsen, I shouldn't have to tell you about the goodness of our God of Israel!"

Then he got real serious on me. "Yeah, I know. But I doubt that this God of 'ours' is all that interested in the day-to-day life of us peons."

Since we were driving up to the colonel's shack, we had to cut our talk short. I just said, "One of these days soon, over coffee, I need to share with you a few of the things that have happened to me since I left Lawson."

As we neared the door, he said, "OK, you buy me a cup—one of these days."

I was still smiling broadly when Jacobsen and I walked into the building. As we entered Col. Stephens' office, he seemed glad to see me. He smiled and rose from his desk. He was very tall, slender and had a small mustache and salt and pepper hair. His uniform crisp and clean and his brass sparkling bright. He was every inch a colonel. Looking and speaking like Joseph Cotten, he lifted his hand and told us to have a seat.

I first thanked him for what he had done for me. We talked about the trip, and he wanted to know all about Jack's injury. He said he had called down to the ward and told them that I was arriving today. The nurse had told him that Lt. Pippin was anxious to see me, but since he was pretty tired right now, it would be better for me to come see him in the morning.

Then he said, "It's good to have you on board again, Pippin. Where would you like to work?"

I asked if Major McCoy was still there.

He nodded.

I told him I would like to work for him if that was OK.

He came around the desk, grabbed my hand in both of his, smiled and said, "Give my regards to your brother Jack. If there is anything else I can do for you or for him, just let me know."

After I warmly thanked him, he turned to M/Sgt. Jacobsen and said, "Jake, take my sedan and drive Pippin up to see the major. Help him with his gear. Tell McCoy that I hope he has a good spot for him."

We both saluted and left. Before we went to the car, I asked Sgt. Jacobsen to go with me across the hall so I could see where I had worked the first year I was in the Army. I showed him my desk just outside the door from his old "office" that was now a supply closet! His present office was almost as large as the colonel's! There was not one soul left there with whom I had worked.

When he saw the look on my face, Jake said, "Like I told you, things have changed one hell of a lot since you left, Pippin."

I nodded my head, and we went on out to the sedan. As we drove away, I felt like I was the M/Sgt. and Jake was the private. I told him that I thanked God that the colonel was still there! He grinned.

I turned to him, winked and went, "He, he, he!"

Major McCoy had not changed one whit. He also seemed glad to see me. After he and Sgt. Jacobsen had a few words, he called me in for a brief chat. I told him about Jack, and he told me to take the time I needed to visit or do things for my brother. Then he asked me to take charge of the insurance office. I was given a large room in the headquarters building. I had it all to myself, complete with a private entrance and a class A phone. The only way I can explain all this VIP treatment was that since the J.C. Lovett experience, I felt I was now "one of the King's kids!" But I wouldn't dare mention that to Jake.

My new first sergeant, McClure, was a clone of William Holden. He had his corporal help me with my gear and take me to my barracks and bunk. He left, and as I looked around, I felt at home again. The hospital buildings were mostly one story. They were completely finished inside and now had nicer latrines and better beds. Along with this, they had large exhaust fans, and the heating was more modern. I unpacked and went to supper. I had forgotten how much better the food was there than it had been at Grant. The hospital had garrison rations; Grant had field rations.

After supper, just on impulse, I went to a phone and called that sweet Anne Puryear. She answered the phone and seemed to be mildly glad that I called. I asked her to have a cup of coffee with me on Friday night. That sounded nice to her, so the date was on.

The trip for the past two days was kind of tiring, so I needed no rocking when the bugler sounded "call to quarters" and when at nine o'clock it was "lights out."

As I slipped between clean sheets on a firm innerspring mattress and a twin bed, I prayed, "Well, dear God, here I am back where I started. Thank You again for all You have done these last few days. You are my miracle, Father, and Your Son is my dear Friend and Elder Brother. Help me to be of good service to the major and of good cheer to Jack, and to gain a stronger faith in You, Lord, every day, that I may better serve You."

Before I drifted off to sleep, I thought about the year I had been away from Lawson—I had been a lot of places and done a lot of things. What a difference a year had made, just twelve little months. I felt I had a lot more "praise praying" to do that night, but when I woke up the next morning, I couldn't remember whether or not I had prayed at all.

Soon after breakfast, I was on my way down the covered corridor to Brother Jack's ward. I felt good and rested, and it was a beautiful day, but I was a bit apprehensive about this first visit. I had not seen Jack since June of 1942, when Belle and I had taken him and Sam to Jacksonville to catch his plane overseas. That was over two years ago. Since I did not know how he was progressing or the full extent of his injury, there was no way to tell just what kind of reception I would receive.

Most all of the hospital wards looked exactly alike, but each patient was assigned to a special one that treated his particular injury. As I entered Jack's ward, I noticed that a clean but medicinal smell pervaded the long room.

A pretty young lieutenant dressed in starchy white walked up to me and said, "Lt. Pippin is getting better every day." Then she said with a smile, "It's easy to tell that you are his brother."

I grinned back and replied, "All of us Pippins favor. But don't you think I'm better looking?"

She laughed and led me down to Jack's bed.

As soon as he saw me coming, he smiled. When I moved to the side of his bed, he extended his hand. His cast looked like a thick, white life jacket. It went from across his shoulders to his hips. A white stick extended from his left side out to his left elbow. His left arm was raised out to the side with the elbow bent to a 90-degree angle. I could only see the tips of his fingers. Hugs were not possible, so I leaned over and kissed him on the face.

"How you doin', Brother Jack? It's so good to see you."

"A lot better since you got here. I was delighted when the colonel called down and told me you were coming back to Lawson."

He smelled fresh and clean and talked in short sentences, as though he had difficulty breathing.

"Pull up that chair...it was good to get back to the States. But the ticket was much too high! I came over on a hospital ship—in pain every mile of the way. The doctors have already done several surgeries. They'll probably do some more. I'm in less pain now. But the morphine helps a lot."

"Well, you look pretty good this morning."

"Yeah," he answered as he shifted in bed, "these sweeties have really been working on me. Every day they give me a bath, a massage, a shave and change my bed. And the food is super. I really do feel a lot better today. As a matter of fact, the nurses want me to move around some each morning. So why don't you get that wheelchair over there and let's go to the canteen for a little visit. Do you have time?"

I nodded as I got him out of his gown, put on his pajamas and a robe, and carefully got him into the chair. His legs were fine, but he was still a bit too weak to walk that far.

A climate or attitude of kindness pervaded the entire hospital. As I pushed him to the canteen, people in the corridors cleared the way and anyone near us stopped to hold the door open. The chair rolled smoothly since Jack had lost weight and there were no bumps at the doors. Because we wanted to talk privately with no one sitting near us, we were both glad that the canteen was almost empty. I pushed him over to an isolated corner of the room. He ordered hot tea and I asked for fresh coffee.

I spoke first, "What's with the tea?"

The morphine made him speak with a slight slur, "Got to drinkin' it out in India. When I get this cup fixed just exactly the way I like it, I want you to taste it. I'm gonna get you off that coffee—and on to tea! Much better for you. Drinking tea is a time-honored tradition all over India. But tea really got started in China—as a medicine over five hundred years before Christ. Then as a beverage it spread to Japan. Early in the 1800s the British East India Company encouraged the cultivation of tea in India. Now it is Southeast Asia's favorite drink. At midmorning and midafternoon for much of that part of the world everything ceases—commerce, work, pleasure and even the war."

This was vintage Jack, giving me that brief history of tea as a medicine and then as a beverage.

He continued, "By the way, we heard that General Montgomery and all his senior officers even broke for tea the afternoon of D Day! Ain't that just like the British?! Each afternoon in India they also have high tea, with scones and delicious little sandwiches. I was stationed out in a large tent near our air strip—close to the town of Dibrugarh, on the Bramaputra River, in Assam."

I smiled and said, "Oh yes, you sneaked that info to us about where you were stationed. We all got a bang out of your coded letters."

He chuckled and continued, "I was with the Air Transport Command in charge of on-loading those C-46 commandos that were flying tons of supplies and ammo over 'the hump,' the Himalayas, to the Chinese troops who were fighting the invading Japanese. Pretty good duty. That is, if you don't mind the heat, interminable monsoons and being slap-dab in the middle of world headquarters for all of the lethal insects God ever made."

He pulled out a cigarette. I picked up his lighter and held him a light.

"Then one afternoon while I was working in the compound a 'Jap' sniper, probably with a telescopic lens, almost blew my left arm off. Like to have bled to death. My arm was just dangling when I was found and carried to the field first-aid station. A little later the medics and the surgeons at the field hospital saved my arm and my life...but I think that's about enough of all that right now."

The details of how he was shot shook me, and I had trouble controlling my reaction.

I wanted to respond in the right way for him, so I said with a lump in my throat, "Back here, we all had been praying for you every day. We had no knowledge of your being injured 'til you were on the way home. I thank the good Lord and the medics and doctors for saving your life and for your safe, though very painful, trip."

He nodded, glanced toward the Red Cross lady and held up two fingers. She came over with a pot of fresh coffee in one hand, hot water and tea bags in the other, and refilled our cups. We smiled and thanked her.

Then his voice turned more soft, "My sweet Sam came up for a short visit the other day. But she left just before you arrived. She said that Mama, Papa and Ed were doing great at the store. They are all looking forward to the two of us coming home soon. By the way, I got some good news this morning. After my next operation, the doctors are going to let me go home for a week or two. Maybe you can come down just for the weekend."

He brightened up a bit, and then reached over and put his hand on my arm. It was almost as if that instant was the first time he fully realized I was there.

He said, "My, my, Brother James, you look wonderful! I am so glad you're here. It's really great you got to come back to Lawson. You smarty, how'd you pull off that transfer?"

I told him a brief history of my life so far in the Army, including how well I did on the AGCTs (army general classification tests) because of his help. I ended by telling him about the miracle transfer back to Lawson. While sipping his tea, he listened with keen interest. When I finished, he smiled weakly and began to shake his head slowly from side to side.

I finished by adding, "The good Lord made it all possible."

That word about the Lord caused him to slowly turn his face toward the window. He had a faraway look, as though his thoughts had transported him back into the past, maybe back to Tulsa, to Clara Anne, to Frank and to God.

After a brief pause, he looked at me with misty eyes and said in a husky voice, "You know, Brother James, the Lord has always seemed to smile on your life. So many wonderful things keep happening to you."

And then as if to change the subject, he glanced at his watch and said, "We'd better get back. Say, can you believe it's almost time for lunch?"

From then on I visited him almost every day.

A MIRACLE A MINUTE

Friday afternoon I cleaned up, changed clothes and was on Anne's porch at 5:30.

She hurried to the door, saying, "Pip, Pip, where in the world have you been?" As she invited me in, I hugged her briefly but omitted the hello kiss. As always she was gorgeous. She was wearing a pink dress with a white pinafore cover and a big bow at the back, pink pumps and black hose. She had two little pink ribbons on either side in her fine blond hair. We sat and chatted awhile; then her beautiful mother came in, and I stood and gave her a little hug. After greetings were exchanged, I asked if Anne wanted to go out for a while. She nodded, so after bye-byes we were off. We walked down the hill to Peachtree Street and caught a bus. As the bus pulled away, I said, pointing, "That's where Margaret Mitchell lives." She laughed and said, "I know!"

In a moment, I took her hand and said, "How would you like to go to the Top of the Henry Grady for dinner instead of just for coffee. Are you free to do that?"

She answered in her soft, sweet voice that had a slight Tennessee drawl, "Pip, I think I'd like that. I have saved the entire evening for us. Don't you think you and I need to talk a little bit?"

The blue room at the Top of the Grady was lovely and comfortable. The food was great, and the band came in at about eight. We were seated near the rail, right over the back of the dance floor. I remembered what she liked, so I ordered a glass of white wine for each of us. As we touched glasses and sipped our wine, we began that little talk we needed to have.

She went first, "Pip, you will never know how much I missed you those first few weeks you were gone. I wrote and wrote, even sent you another picture, and I got precious little response from you in return. Your few letters confused me, for I thought we felt the same way about each other."

I quickly tried to explain, "My dear Anne, I loved your letters *and* your picture. They were a bright part of my three months of hell there. The few times I did write, I tried to express the grueling time we were going through."

"Oh, I know, but you could have at least taken a moment to call or something. I thought you just forgot all about me," she replied.

"Impossible! Then when we were failed out and I was sent way out to Rockford, Illinois, I felt I was at the end of the world. I know I should have called or written more often. I'm so sorry. I had a few dates in Providence, but believe it or not, I did not have a single date during the seven months at Grant."

She nodded kind of like she understood, then the waiter arrived and we ordered. I got steak and she ordered salmon. It was good to have food that was not cooked in the mess hall. After more wine, an excellent dinner and lighter conversation, the band arrived just as we were sipping our coffee. I got up and reached for her hand. As I watched her walk to the dance floor, I realized that I had almost forgotten just how lovely she was. When we embraced to dance, I noticed just a faint hint of a rare fragrance. I was pleased at how she followed my lead with the slightest touch. In her high heels, she was almost as tall as I was. It was so pleasant to be with her again.

Once while we were out on the dance floor, I stepped on someone's foot. When we turned, we saw it was Bob Hope!

I said nervously, "Sorry, Mr. Hope."

He shot back, "That's OK, Soldier."

And then just before he and his partner danced away, he pointed his left hand to an empty space on the floor and said with a big smile, "We've already been over there!"

Anne and I blushed and laughed because we knew he meant for us to keep our distance! Bob Hope never lacked a clever response to any circumstance. Once when he was performing before thousands, a little kitty cat walked across the floor and stopped right in front of his feet. The audience laughed.

He smiled as he looked down at the kitty and said, "Say, you furry little thing, this is a monologue, not a catalog!!" Of course, the crowd roared!

The rest of my evening with Anne went very well. We talked and danced a lot, and the evening passed quickly. But our little recaptured romance was short lived, indeed.

Our second date was really the coffee chat. We sat in her living room, and after we had our coffee and talked about this and that, she asked me what I was going to do with my life. The answer cost me the girl! I moved over closer to her, took her hand and briefly related the Camp Grant experience with J.C. and the Nazarenes.

I then said, "Anne, I have decided that I am going to become a minister, possibly a Christian, a Methodist or an Episcopalian. What do you think?"

I shouldn't have asked.

She said, "Well, Pip, all that must explain part of the reason why you have not kept in touch with me. As you would imagine, I have dated some this year while you have been away, and I am mildly interested in a young man I met in Nashville. But even if I wasn't interested in anyone, I would never marry a man who was going to be a minister. That is just not the life for me. Although you are one of the sweetest men I have ever known, I cannot see myself in that role. I'm sorry."

That was that. We visited a few minutes more, then she walked me to the door and I was gone. When I was in Nashville a few years later, I called her mother. She said she was glad to hear from me, but she also told me that Anne was married and happy as a lark. So all is well that ends well…sometimes.

As I went in and out of many of the wards on my rounds as an insurance counselor, I began to realize what a unique environment the Army general hospitals were during those years of that tragic war. Though Jack's injury was serious, words cannot express the awful condition some of these men and women were in when they arrived at the hospitals. The officers, the enlisted men and the enlisted women of all of the Army branches were treated in separate wards.

Although most of the injured preferred not to talk about their recent experiences in combat, I had good long visits with some of them. One afternoon, I visited with an infantry major about his insurance needs. Before I left, he seemed to want to talk. He was looking past me, as though having been just transported in his mind, miles and months away.

He began, "As quickly as possible after I had been injured, I was brought back from the FEBA (Forward Edge of the Battle Area) by the medics to the first-aid station, then to a field hospital near the front. Had our medical support men and women not been the best in the world, many of us who were injured would have surely died. It was nothing short of a miracle what the surgeons, nurses and medical technicians were able to do for us in those field operating tents. Often these folks worked around the clock until exhaustion forced them to take time to sleep. Over 95 percent of our injured whom the faithful medics brought back to the doctors were saved. As soon as I could be moved, I was transported back to a Port of Debarkation, loaded onto a hospital ship, transferred to a plane and flown here to Lawson."

I wish now that I had used a recorder or could have taken short-hand so I could have made a detailed record of these chats. I visited this major several times before he went home.

In the summer of 1944 and in early 1945, thousands of our men and women arrived daily at Lawson and our general hospitals all over the nation. Many of the injured had been hit either on D Day or in the Battle of the Bulge. When the arrival of their planes was announced at Lawson, often in the middle of the night, all the nurses and those of us who were trained as medics were immediately called out. We were relieved from regular duty and were waiting there at the U. S. Naval Air Station when the old DC 3s pulled up to the off-loading area. Then we carefully transferred the wounded to the waiting ambulances and rode with them to their hospital wards.

These faithful old workhorse planes (that were the most used and the safest that ever flew) arrived at all hours of the day and night. The pilot pulling her up and cutting the engines, the sound, the look and the smell of that old sweet plane will always be firmly etched in my mind. I can clearly see, hear and smell it now as I write. But the military personnel were only a part of the total support. Joining the medical teams in the general hospitals were the American Red Cross, the USO, the library personnel and thousands of volunteers, all of whom were on hand around the clock to care for the needs of the wounded.

One day I happened to walk through one of the senior officer's wards just as the afternoon coffee was being served. I looked over and saw an older chaplain, a colonel, who had a cast that covered his whole body except his head and his toes. He signaled me to come over to his bed and asked me to have a seat. He called for an extra cup and asked his nurse to serve me coffee. The nurse patiently helped him drink his through a straw. After I took care of an insurance request, he asked me to mail some letters for him that he had dictated earlier to a Red Cross lady. As I took the letters from the nurse, I told him that I was thinking of becoming a minister, and later a chaplain, when I got out of the service. I asked him if he would share with me a few of his reflections on his duty overseas.

Surprisingly, he agreed. "Well, since you are leaning toward the chaplaincy, I'll share a few thoughts with you. When I got hit, I was alongside the medics, right up at the front. Up there with us were several other chaplains and their assistants. I encountered so many of these dedicated men of God, from every mainline denomination, including Catholic, Protestant and Jew. We were always up there by the side of the troops as they were taking enemy fire. You will be happy to learn that many of the men and women had an experience with God while they were in the heat of battle. I think the statement that Chaplain William T. Cummins, made on Bataan in 1942 is true: 'There are no atheists in the foxholes.'"

He continued, "It's not difficult to find a soldier who had a 'foxhole conversion.' The chaplains comforted the wounded and the dying with familiar scriptures from the Sacred Word, said prayers for courage and heard their confessions of sin and confessions of faith. I have often seen a chaplain holding a dying man in his arms, heard the chaplain praying or giving Last Rites, watched him close the eyes of the dead and after carefully laying his body down, he would then jump up and trot along-side another soldier that was being carried on a stretcher to the rear, to safety and into the hands of the surgeons and nurses."

The tired, older servant of God kept on for a few more words and then gradually drifted off to sleep. The nurse smiled at me, put her finger to her lips, thanked me silently and waved good-bye as I left.

When I could get the wounded to talk about those tragic hours, which was not often, they would tell me stories I cannot forget. A chaplain's assistant shared with me that the Twenty-third Psalm and the Lord's Prayer could be often heard all up and down the line in the middle of night. He said that many of those assigned to the chaplain branch and the medical corps went without sleep for days, treating more persons in a month than they had back home in a year as civilian doctors and clergymen. Although these troops made many very close friends who brightened up those dark days of hard-ship, misery and death, the great joy for them was to get back to the States and see the faces of their loved ones at the general hospitals. Of course, their finest hour was the day they got to go home!

I was surprised to find that in the officers' wards at Lawson the severely injured, many of whom were in constant pain, could order dinner from a menu where steaks, chops, seafood and other gourmet items were offered. This practice was approved by the hospital com-manders at most posts. This was an attempt to show them how much we all appreciated what great price they had paid for our freedom. Also, an alcoholic beverage, if they so chose, was served them before dinner. Nothing was too good for these brave men and women. Each officer who requested it was allowed to keep a fifth of his favorite whisky in his wall locker.

Especially in the paraplegic and quadriplegic wards, the officer's desire was the hospital's command. A paraplegic was a soldier who had lost either both arms or both legs. A severe quadriplegic had suffered the loss of both arms to the shoulder and both legs to the hips. To conserve precious space on ships and planes and make it possible for more of the injured to be brought back to the States, many "quads" were placed in small wicker baskets. Thus the phrase "basket case" entered our vocabulary. I will never forget the absolute shock and sorrow I felt the first time I saw an injured soldier who was returned from the front in a short, wicker basket. O God, what a price for victory!

One of the greatest miracles of the war was what the doctors, nurses and technicians, who teamed up with the rehabilitation and the prostheses departments, were able to accomplish with those patients who had lost a part of their body in combat. With superior and professional skill, actual miracles were wrought in the replacement of teeth, arms, legs, eyes, noses and hair pieces. The miracles accomplished through cosmetic and facial surgery even included the restoration of one side of the entire face. The vast majority of these long-suffering and traumatized men and women were able to return home feeling well and whole. In a short time, most of them obtained good jobs, developed great careers and were lovingly accepted by everyone, including their girlfriends, wives, families, friends and employers. When we think of the hundreds of military hospitals that were releasing thousands of patients all at the same time every day during those months, we can truly say that "a miracle a minute" walked out those doors and headed for home.

But these injured men and women would be the first to say that they are not the real heroes of this war. It is rather their buddies who paid the greatest price, the ones who did not make it back. Those "who gave the last, full measure of devotion"—they are the real heroes. The faces of their comrades who died by their side or in their arms can never be shaken from their memory.

How can our nation ever begin to repay those who were injured, or more, those who are no longer with us in this world? How can a grateful America ever begin to say thanks to the millions of support personnel, from the brave medic to the most skillful surgeon, who worked as a team to save the lives of many of the sixteen million men and women who served in World War II? All of these played a premier roll in the horrible drama of that Great War, a war that was to become the main centerpiece of the history of the twentieth century.

We who wore the uniform in this and other wars were told that we fought in order to "make the world safe for democracy." But the combat soldiers I knew were instead fighting to save their life or their buddies' lives, with nary a thought about "democracy."

Excuse me, but did we make the world safe for democracy? What is happening to our freedoms and to our democracy? What kind of nation do we and our children live in today? Is it really a true democracy? Is there real justice or safety for all in our courts today, on our highways and streets, or in our schools and colleges?

Are the freedoms that thousands of Americans fought and died for slowly eroding in the face of increasing Socialism? After being a nation in solid unity that won the war, what do you think of the daily sinister effort to divide this country into many factions of distrust and even hate? It is difficult today to find a simple, devoted American citizen, a patriot, born on the 4th of July, a proud member of a great *United States of America!* We have become a nation of Native (Indian) Americans, African Americans, Latin Americans, Jewish Americans, women Americans, children Americans, gay Americans and straight Americans. Soon, I guess, I will become an English/German American, my wife a Scottish American, and then most of us will soon probably have a word in front of our citizenship such as French, Russian, Spanish, Canadian, Mexican and even a South American American—for heaven's sake, we all came from somewhere else, including the Indians! But we all must be citizens of the *United States* and not a hundred scattered groups, each to its own selfish agenda. The socialist goal is to sharply divide us all into hate groups before they take over the country; then the United States we once knew will be no more.

Allene and I were watching a TV movie recently in which an older black woman told a fifteen-year-old white girl: "What's wrong with this country are the g—d—whites!"

What would have happened if that movie line had been "the GD blacks, Spanish, Indians; or the GD Jews, or the GD Communists! A howl so loud it could be heard around the world would have gone up from the press, TV and even the pulpits. You can bet your life that movie would have been quickly seized and burned. But it was aired several times over a three-month period, as was *Mississippi Burning*, which also engenders racial hatred. The frequent airing of *Roots* does not help the progress many of us hope to make toward total racial healing and unity. And have you ever wondered what happened to the movie, *Amerika*, shown on television years ago? It related in detail just how the Communists took over America! I can't even find that movie any longer!

I have been told that I am now a member of a vanishing breed: A WASP! I think this stands for a White Anglo-Saxon Protestant. But Christian bashing is real popular right now, and few seem to object.

I heard a liberal member of Congress say recently, "The Christians don't deserve a place at the table!"

Just think what would have happened to him if he had said that about any other group. Ah! But we Christians deserve a place at the Christmas Table and at the thousands of shopping malls all over this land. We don't hear much bashing of Christians at Christmas! The cash registers of the nation's chain stores are playing "Jingle Bells" then. These retail stores do the vast majority of their business between November 24 and December 24. Yet, prayer, Bibles, the Ten Commandments and everything Christian have been banned from our public schools. Even Christmas carols cannot be sung in our public schools anymore. In the midst of all this, the church choirs are welcome to our malls at Christmas time to sing any of the carols. I have often wondered why these socialists, liberal politicians, the ACLU, the Secular Humanists and other atheistic groups who own national retail chains don't go ahead and ban Christmas. They wouldn't dare though, for they all know what a steep dive their earnings would take *if there were no Christmas or Easter!!*

The goal of the secular humanists and their kind is to ban Christ, God, the Bible and the Constitution. They aim to then close all the churches and synagogues and turn them into museums. This land of the free and the home of the brave is beginning to look and act a lot as the Soviet Union did before it collapsed. They banned God and Christ from everything until, at the end, the country was starving to death. North Korea, a communist stronghold, is in rags and starving. However, Russia is now welcoming Bibles back and placing the Ten Commandments on the walls of their schools. The churches that were closed and turned into museums for years are again packed with Christians who stand for hours, singing and praising God.

The Soviets learned their lesson just in time and are now pleading for God to return. But at the same time, many in the U.S. are trying to throw all those same things away. Will we ever learn? Socialism/Communism has never worked anywhere. Nothing seems to work for very long where God is banned. History has shown us that God doesn't like it when a person or nation slams the door in His face. And Jesus Christ had rather be re-crucified than to be ignored or rejected. The Scriptures are unanimous in warning us that a hell of eternal misery awaits those who reject God. And O glory, there is a kingdom of eternal joy awaiting those who love Him and await His appearing. (See Hebrews 6.)

And those who didn't make it back from all our wars, did they really give their lives in vain? I am sure that some people who read this may find it all a bit morose. But most of us either don't know, don't care or have forgotten all too soon the great lessons of history.

❊ 12 ❊

An Angel
Rides in the Storm

*J*ack recuperated so well from his last surgery that the doctors gave him two weeks leave. He was now able to walk short distances and no longer needed a wheelchair. The day before he went on leave he called me at the insurance office and asked me to take him for a ride. It had been a while since he had been off-post, so I was delighted for the chance to spend some time with him. That afternoon we borrowed a car from one of his many friends in the ward, and I drove him around to see some of north Atlanta, much of which was made famous by Margaret Mitchell in *Gone With the Wind*. We actually drove by her house on Peachtree Road, located just up the hill from where the trains to Atlanta used to stop so the residents could get off near their homes. It is so hard to realize now that we could have called on Peggy Mitchell and, since Jack was injured, she would have gladly had us for tea! If you've never read her book, please do; but read her *"Letters"* first.

Before returning, Jack and I stopped at a restaurant in Buckhead for tea and coffee. Jack entered first and, of course, picked a table in the farthest corner from the door. For security reasons, a lot of men I have known who had been in combat would never sit with their backs to the door when they were overseas or out among civilians. Some of them continued this precaution unconsciously long after returning to the States, especially those who had been wounded as Jack had been. So he kept his eye on the door to alert us at the approach of "the enemy." As I sat facing him, I thought for a second that in his subconscious mind he and I might be in downtown Dibrugarh, India! This precaution must have made him more at ease. Plus, no one else was there but the waitress: Wounded soldiers were very uncomfortable when civilians stared at them.

An Angel Rides in the Storm

Since he was feeling so much better these days, we laughed and talked of many things while enjoying several cups of coffee and tea. We talked of Round Oak, St. Simon's, Clara Anne, the store, Sam, Mama, Papa and the family. Then we chatted about more recent events like his time at OCS, knowing Clark Gable, and the coded letters. He also shared more details about the beauty and the beast that is India.

Finally, he paused, looked me in the eye and said, "Brother James, the way the war seems to be going, you will be out of the Army soon. What do you plan to do with your life?"

The face of Anne flashed into my mind! I blinked my eyes and answered, "Well, Brother Jack, I have thought and prayed about this for a long time. I think I have finally decided to become a minister."

He replied, "Are you certain? How were you able to bring yourself to this decision?"

I paused, a little too long, so he looked at me and crooked his finger for me to continue.

After the waitress refilled our cups, I began, "I guess I decided partly because of a vision, sort of. I saw life as this long passenger train headed for the kingdom of God. As I stood watching it pass by, I noticed that there were very few persons in the coaches up front. As the cars kept passing, I was puzzled to see that there were very few young folks even on the train. Almost all of the passengers were old, some very old. So the thought hit me hard—this doesn't seem right: Why should we who are young grow old before we jump on the train? Most of us usually wait for the last few coaches. It seems a shame for so many to wait until they are middle-aged or old and worn out to decide to serve the Lord. Must we live the best part of our lives for self alone, and then decide to serve Christ? If we ever intended to answer His call to live a life fit for the kingdom, I figured we ought to quit playing around and get with it and board early. I feel that God wants and deserves our best years. You remember that old song [I sang him the melody]:

> Give of your best to the Master,
> Give Him the strength of your youth.

"Brother Jack, I believe that God has very carefully and joyfully prepared a breath-taking kingdom for all of us. I believe that we should live so that we can enter that kingdom. Jesus said that it is His Father's good pleasure to give us the kingdom. It breaks His heart when we reject Him and His Son Jesus and put no value on His plan for our lives. The kingdom is of such great value, Jack, that we should

125

do everything we possibly can to enter in. No earthly prize or treasure should be so precious that it causes us to miss being in that
eternal kingdom with our Father. Many of Jesus' parables stress this
great truth. So, we can never say good-bye to God. He is our forever
Father, Jesus is our forever Divine Friend and Elder Brother and the
church is our forever family.

"So I made up my mind that if I was going to catch that train at all,
I should get on board early and thus become the most effective servant possible, a servant that the Lord Jesus could really be proud of. I
thought that it was most unfair if I decided selfishly to spend most of
my life doing all the things *I* wanted to do and waited 'til the last
minute to try to grab the caboose as it passed by, therefore doing as
little as possible just to squeak in. If I did such a shameful thing, I
thought I would really deserve to slip and fall on the tracks and be
left in darkness at the station."

He chuckled and looked at me for several moments. Then he
spoke almost in a whisper, "Man, I have never heard it put that way
before. You talk as though you believe that God is real, that all the
things you read in the New Testament are true and actually written
to you. Do you feel God's presence this strongly every day?"

"Almost. Brother Jack, the cattle on a thousand hills are His and
the gold therein."

He swallowed hard, cleared his throat and said with misty eyes,
"My dear Brother James, I wish to God I had your faith!"

"God loves you very much, Jack, and wants to give you a strong faith.
I am sure you felt His presence the day you were hit and through this
long ordeal of your recuperation. But, you know, the Bible tells us that
even the disciples lacked a strong faith. They said to Jesus, 'Lord, we
believe, help Thou our unbelief.'"

I asked him, "You remember the mustard seed story and how He
said, 'Ask and you shall receive'?"

He nodded and smiled.

At that instant, it became very dark outside. After a loud clap of
thunder it began to rain hard. He quickly arose and went to the register. I guess he thought that after such a heavy sermon, I would end
it with an offering or an invitation! We paid the bill and left the
restaurant. I pulled the car up close to the door and covered him with
a newspaper so his cast would stay dry. As we drove away in that
downpour, I told him that I was sorry to give him such a long testimony. But he told me, no, that it was beautiful.

Then I said that the loud clap of thunder and the hard rain

brought back to mind a story I read from a history book recently. "Once Socrates, while sitting on his front steps, was being loudly and continually badgered from upstairs by Zantippi, his wife, who pleaded for him to hop up and go do some chore. When he didn't move she poured a large vase of water down on him. He glanced up at her, his hair and face soaking wet, and said, 'Me thought that such a thunder storm was sure to produce a shower!'"

Jack laughed louder than I had heard him since his return to the States. On our drive back to his ward, the weather began to clear. There was a bright rainbow over the hospital. I did not mention it since he seemed to be deep in thought. We said very little.

As we neared the gate, he reached over, put his right hand on my knee and said in deep earnest, "Brother James, I want you to know just how much our visit this afternoon has meant to me."

He held my left hand with his right as we walked up the wet steps and entered the ward. His cast prevented my giving him a hug, so we just shook hands.

I said, "Love you, Brother Jack."

He smiled and I turned to leave.

As I reached for the door, I just barely heard him say, "Ditto!"

Then one rainy afternoon a few weeks later, something happened that I thought was going to cause both of us to board that kingdom train early! When I was home on leave from Lawson and Jack was there between operations, he came over to the house and asked me to take him to Brunswick. The wind speed and rainfall had been increasing over the past few hours. The radio had warned that a hurricane was moving north off shore, now located forty miles north of Jacksonville. I mentioned this to Jack, but he was adamant. He said that he just had to talk to George before he closed the shoe shop. Mama, Papa and Sam also tried to dissuade him from going out in this heavy rain with that cast. But true to his nature, he still wouldn't listen.

So while Sam got him into an old raincoat, I pulled Papa's Chevy under the open car shed. We managed to get him in the car without getting wet. On the way over on the causeway, I could not get my eyes off of those dark clouds in the southeast. The rain and wind had increased a bit, but we made the trip over there OK. Papa had called George at the shop to see if we made it and to tell him to make us stay over there until the storm moved farther north. As we ran next door to the cafe, George told Jack that we were pretty dumb to be out in this storm. They sat at the counter and ordered coffee.

A MIRACLE A MINUTE

I knew Jack wanted privacy, so I sat in a booth and had the waitress serve me there. She came over, poured my coffee and, since no one else was in the cafe, sat the pot down on the table. She wore a short, white cotton dress that buttoned up the front and had a neat little pink apron around her waist. The buttons on the top of her dress were barely able to stay buttoned. Then she put her knee up on the seat across from me, leaned back against the booth and seemed to want to visit.

As I sipped my coffee, she said, "I think I know you. When you and George came in, I was certain you were his younger brother."

"That's right, where did you know me?"

"I graduated from Glynn Academy the year you did. You never noticed me because you couldn't take your eyes off Krista."

"Ah, so right you are! My days of loving Krista. And your name?"

"Cindy. I knew Polly, Krista's best friend. So sad about her early death."

As I reflected, I said, "Yeah, it took a long time for Krista and a lot of others to get over sweet Polly's death. One of the last times I was with Krista, we went out to see Polly's grave. Sit down a minute?"

"Oh no, my boss'll be here any second. That your other brother over there? Man, this storm is gettin' bad. Y'all will probably be stranded in here…want a refill?" Now she had a broad smile on her face.

Cindy leaned over a bit too far and filled my cup, turned and stooped to pick up nothing off the floor so I could get a good look at her. Then she walked back over to the cash register. I gazed down into my cup and thought of Krista and Polly and how very fragile life was. I glanced over at Cindy, and thought what a sweet and pretty girl, a bit too classy and attractive to be in this dull cafe. She looked lonely. Now and then she threw a quick glance at me and then quickly turned away when I returned it. Probably had a sweet, little girl over at her mama's house because some jerk had passed through, gave her his line and after a few months, kept on going. "'Have to be a waitress, for the rest of my life,'" she's probably thinking.

I raised my hand and beckoned Cindy over. She came and poured me a fresh cup. I bucked up my courage and said, "Cindy, we were talking about Polly and Krista and I was just thinking how fragile life is. I hope you won't think me nosy, but do you know the Lord? Are you taking your little girl to Sunday school and church?"

"Oh yes, I've been baptized. But how'd you know I had a child?"

"I just guessed."

She explained, "I don't want Sonja to have to live her life as I have mine. If I had prayed for the Lord's direction, I wouldn't have married that Don Juan from California that snowed me and after two months was on his way."

"I don't mean to be giving you advice, Cindy, but a bright and lovely girl like you ought to get into college, go for a degree and choose a career that will get you out of places like this. Also, will you join me in praying for God to send you a good man who will take care of you and your little girl?"

She responded with a chuckle, "I sure will. By the way, what you doing the rest of *your* life?"

I smiled and said, "You flatter me, my dear. I am going to be a preacher! How about that? Yeah, when I get out of this man's Army, I plan to go to college and serve the Lord, if He'll have me."

She flinched at a big strike of lightening and a loud boom of thunder, and then said, "I kinda figured that when you asked me about the Lord. No one has ever mentioned that subject to me, especially in here. Oh, George and your other brother seem to be about through. Gotta go, hope to see you again soon."

I smiled and shook her hand.

As I got up, I noticed that the wind speed was getting higher and the rain was coming down harder. George stepped over to the phone, called Vera and told her that he would not be home until after the storm.

Since he and Jack had finished their coffee chat, George went to the register. The wind and rain were shaking the big windows of the cafe. While George was paying Cindy, they swapped a few words as they glanced over at me. Just before George left, he told Jack and me not to try to go back to the Island in this storm.

After he left, Jack walked over and said, "I'm through here, Brother James. Let's go."

"Jack, you seem to be totally oblivious of that storm out there! Remember Papa and George warned us not to leave in this storm."

"I know, but I forgot to bring my pain pills. I told George that I just had to get back to the house."

I foolishly gave in to him. I asked Cindy to help me with his raincoat and to go to the car with me. It was hard to get him in and keep the cast dry, but we made it. Then I ran around and got in the car. After I wiped my face with the towel Cindy gave us and cleaned my glasses, I noticed as we pulled away that she was standing under the awning waving good-bye, while the wind blew her hair every which way. I planned to come back before I left for Lawson and take her out to eat—or something.

I had only driven a few blocks when Jack pulled a pint of bourbon out of the glove compartment and took a hefty swig.

"Jack, please don't drink any more until we get home. It's going to be hard enough to get you back into your house if you are sober."

I could barely see the radio station, WMOG, as we drove by. He said, "Brother Jame," that was his nickname for me, "member all those years I had my program of words and music at that station…?"

I responded, "Yeah, but it seems like ages ago, doesn't it? You called it 'Moonriver.'"

As he nodded, I began to quote from the closing lines he used at the end of each program:

> Moonriver, silently under a moon so bright
> Silver ribbon in the hair of night
> Rest on, float on, care will not seek for thee
> Sleep on, drift on, Moonriver, to the sea.

Jack looked over at me. We both had tears in our eyes.

The wind and rain were increasing by the moment. Soon, the windshield wipers could not keep my vision clear. The car radio warned that the hurricane had just turned and was heading directly toward Brunswick. It was then that I got shook. As I looked ahead, I could see the old, long wooden bridge we had to cross being whipped so hard it looked like a huge black snake. How, in God's name, were we going to make it across that bridge? I could imagine our car together with that thing being swept up and away, leaving only the piling stubs sticking up where the bridge once was. Just before we got to the bridge, the wind was so strong, the car began to drift to the left. I stopped. It continued to slowly slide off the road.

"Brother Jack, if this car goes off the road, we will wind up in thirty feet of water. It will go under and if we get out, that cast is going to melt in two minutes and you might loose your arm. In this storm we both could be swept away! I think it's time for us to pray."

As the car began to slide a little more, I dropped my head and said, "Lord, this looks like the end. There seems to be no way out. Please help us. We are not safe in this car or out of it. I was just talking about how fragile life is, but, Lord, I never thought ours would end today. I now commend our spirits to Thee, our Father."

While I kept praying, Jack was also busy talking to God. "God, if you'll save us, I'll never touch another drop. I'll clean up my mouth and my life. I promise, O good Lord, I promise with all my heart. Just don't let us have to get out of this car. I will lose my arm, I'll drown. Oh, God, if you have ever heard me, hear me now! Did You bring me all the way back from India, just to drown me in this storm?"

He opened the glove compartment, took out the bourbon, all his cigarettes and even his lighter. He rolled down the window a few inches and tossed them all out as the rain covered his face. Then he bowed his head and began to sob.

As we sat there, the rain came down even harder, now in great horizontal sheets, rocking the car as if it were a baby buggy. I closed my eyes and asked the Lord to forgive us both of all our sins, and sensing that this was it, I said what I thought was my last prayer, "Please, Father, remember us when You come into Your Kingdom."

When I opened my eyes I could not believe what I saw. There, parked within a few feet of our car was a big, yellow tow truck, its lights blazing! How in the world did he get out here across that storm-swept bridge? The driver's voice could not be heard over the storm, so he started making motions to us, trying to tell us that he would turn the truck around, hook us up and try to get us to the island.

In a few minutes we were slowly being towed across the old bridge. In the middle of the bridge, I started praying again—telling the Lord that if we don't make it across this wildly swaying bridge, we're finished! I had never been that scared in my life, and nothing has ever even come close to my sheer fright since that day. About every few yards, a board or two were missing and we could feel the car bump as we crossed. The sides of the bridge were being whipped off at places and went flying across in front of us. Even though at times our car was almost blown off the bridge and later, off the road, our driver kept slowly chugging along and somehow, by the grace of God, he was able to pull us all the way to the island! Talk about a staggering miracle!

The driver got out, unhooked us and disappeared. He didn't even come close enough for us to clearly see his face, much less to thank him. Since we were shielded now by the tall pines and big live oaks, we made better time. We were both sobbing for joy that at the point of our greatest peril, God had sent us what we ever after considered to be an angel tow truck and a brave angel driver. We drove on home slowly but safely.

For years Jack and I tried to find out who that driver was and how he got there. Was he really an angel sent by the Lord? We both con-cluded he was exactly that and praised the Lord mightily for it. Although Jack didn't stop drinking or smoking, I never chided him about it. Papa, Mama and Sam, who were waiting, watching and praying, were weeping for joy when we drove in and they realized that we had made it. When we related the tow truck story, they started crying all over again. Mama told us that she had been on her knees almost the entire time we were gone, praying for our safety. I am sure that you realize what an impact this great miracle made on my life and also on Jack's. My faith was made stronger to know that here again all things really are possible with God.

While Jack was hospitalized, he underwent a total of eighteen operations in about eighteen months, each one giving him better use of the arm and hand. Now, he began to spend more time on leave at home with Sam and their first child, little Daniel Jackson Pippin II. At first, Jack just sat around at the store and visited with the folks, but he was delighted when the cast was removed and when in a few weeks he was strong enough to go back to work full time.

By October 1944, the wounded were returning from overseas in such large numbers that the hospital was packed to overflowing. Those of us who were of the headquarters detachment were ordered to vacate all our buildings and barracks, which were rapidly con-verted into additional patient wards. This made it possible to accommodate the increased number of wounded. When they moved us to the far north end of the post, we were shocked to learn that we were to be quartered in the small buildings that had been erected there during the First World War! They were one-story, wood-framed buildings. Each one was covered on the outside and on the roof with green tar paper. They were unfinished on the inside, like the buildings at Camp Grant.

Handsome Sgt. McClure had married a very pretty girl and retired, so a Sgt. Mercier from New Orleans was shipped in as our new first sergeant. A devastating contrast to McClure, he was short, fat, almost bald and had no bottom teeth. He looked as strong as a bull though, and I felt that with little provocation, he would charge. He always exuded a very bad attitude. He had enlisted during World War I, so he was a leftover from the old brown shoe army. He had already served for more than thirty years and was long overdue for retirement.

Major McCoy was still detachment commander. He was a Roman Catholic, and he was dark, handsome and five-foot-ten. His office was just off the large central room. Mercier's desk sat out in the middle. His orderly was Corporal Rakin, a short, burr-headed kid from the Bronx who had a nose so large it preceded him everywhere he went! There were two smaller rooms at the north end of the building. Major McCoy asked me to use the larger of the two as an insurance office. Sgt. Mercier asked Rakin and me to take the other room as our living quarters "in order to secure the building." But I learned later the real reason we were asked to take that room.

There was a large potbelly stove in the main room and a smaller one in my office. Beginning late that fall, I started building a fire in mine as soon as I got up. As the winter moved in, Sgt. Mercier ordered Rakin to have a good fire going in his stove when he arrived each morning about 7 A.M. This fire became Rakin's cross. Sometimes Mercier would arrive early and find me and Rakin still asleep. Then he would go to Rakin's bed, grab it by the side, dump him off on the cold bare floor and walk away shouting in his booming Cajun voice, "Get up, you lazy bum, and build us a fire!"

For some reason, the sergeant never said an unkind word to me.

After I realized that he often arrived early, I began to dump my ashes and prepare my fire at night. I would get up first and light my fire while my teeth chattered and I shook all over—with nothing on but my underwear. I would then dress and once again show Rakin how to build his fire. But being a city boy, he never got the hang of it. Even if I built his fire for him, he would later throw so much coal on it that he'd put it out. He could seldom get his fire started, much less keep it going. Since it always gave off pitifully little heat, Major McCoy would visit back in my office early in the morning to get warm, to have his morning cigar and chat awhile. This made Mercier very angry at Rakin. I "borrowed" a three-pound can of coffee from the mess hall and always had a fresh pot of drip coffee on the stove in the morning.

The Major became fascinated by the large map of Europe I had hanging on the wall behind my desk. In bright colored ribbon, I showed the latest advance of our Allies against the Germans, with the positions of each of the Allied and the German armies in different colors. Each morning as we chatted, he fired up that stogie and had a good cup of coffee while I gave him an unofficial briefing on the latest news of the fighting.

During one of our morning chats, Lt. Jameson, his executive officer (XO), burst in by the back door of my office. He flushed when he found the major sitting there by my fire. He was tall and slender, starched and pressed and very erect, and had blond hair and bright blue eyes. He always carried a swagger stick that caused him to look very much like he was bucking to become the commander of Hitler's Gestapo.

He glanced at both of us, at the glowing stove and our coffee cups, and at my war map. Then he interrupted the major's conversation, and blurted out in a somewhat harsh voice, "Major McCoy, when are you going to give your XO this office?"

"I'm not, Lt. Jameson. For the third time, I am telling you, I want you down there nearer the troops."

Jameson bristled and stomped out. He seldom entered the building after that, except for staff meetings. When I first came to Lawson in 1942 and met him in the theater, he was a first lieutenant. Almost three years later, when I left Lawson, he was still a first lieutenant! I guess it takes all kinds to make up an army. So now we knew the reason why Rakin and I were asked to take that other room: to keep Jameson from getting it for his office.

The fighting in Germany exploded in the early morning hours of December 16, 1944, when from out of the snow-covered forest of the Ardennes, Hitler threw three of his best armies in a thunderous counterattack into Belgium and Luxembourg. This proved to be his final frenzied drive to stop the Allied advance. He caught the Allies completely off guard at their weakest point as his armies blasted a large hole in our front, sixty-five miles deep and up to twenty-five miles wide. Hitler's bold plan was to divide the Allies and destroy our Armies. Our casualties were greater during those few days than at any other time in the war since D Day.

The radio said that it was snowing almost as hard in Atlanta as it was in Germany. Early every morning I would build a fire, dress, put on the coffee and then trot out in the snow to buy *The Atlanta Journal.* Using the *Journal's* excellent coverage, I meticulously updated my multicolored map. All the nation and especially all the stateside military were watching with bated breath the bold advance of Hitler's December surprise. The radios in every American household were blaring out a play-by-play description of the daily situation. A few of our men began to drop by the office to catch my daily update, with McCoy always sitting up near the stove, sipping his coffee, slowly drawing on his fragrant cigar, and Mercier and Rakin sheepishly watching just outside the door. In my starched uniform and shined shoes, wielding my pointer stick, I came on so strong that one would have thought I was at the Pentagon briefing the Joint Chiefs of Staff! Needless to say, I think I was showing off.

An Angel Rides in the Storm

In the first few days of the fierce fighting, it looked as though Hitler's blitzkrieg would accomplish its mission to capture Antwerp. This would inflict a devastating blow to the Allied advance, especially to the British Army. It was reported to be one of the darkest days of the war; as he paced back and forth at his staff meetings, the visibly worried Eisenhower desperately needed a miracle.

Then, it came to him in a flash of inspiration. He ordered Lt. General George S. Patton, Jr. into the battle. Just what Patton was waiting for! Like Ike, he was also pacing back and forth in a frenzy, sweating bullets to get back into the thick of the war. Old "blood and guts" really needed to shine, and man, he did more than that! He turned his Third Army around and sped toward Bastogne. Unmercifully pushing his weary troops without a hot meal or sleep for forty-eight hours, Patton arrived just in time to rescue the trapped 101st Airborne Division from the Germans! On December 26, his Third Army liberated Bastogne, and then turning south, he caught the German armies by surprise from the rear, inflicting heavy casualties and taking thousands of prisoners. By the end of the week, Patton and his troops were the heroes of the free world. However, they took no time to celebrate.

Greatly encouraged by Patton's unprecedented victory, the Allies all along the front bravely charged toward the east, completing the second most destructive advance of the war, a battle that raged for days. Objective: to destroy the last of Germany's finest trained armies. This hard-fought encounter also cost the Allies dearly, but they quickly broke the back of Hitler's military might, completely destroyed his armies' morale and brought his Third Reich finally to its knees. Patton then helped to inflict such utter destruction on the few larger units that were left that they turned and routed in full retreat. By the last day of December, Germany's crippled, sick and scattered armies were in hopeless confusion and disarray. The Allies and the whole world knew that this was the beginning of the end. We now know Hitler's great winter disaster and our stunning victory as The Battle of the Bulge.

General Patton, still on a roll, had reached the Rhine River. He called Eisenhower at dawn that morning with the news that he was standing on the west bank and taking a leak into the river. He begged Eisenhower for the permission to go charging ahead all the way to Berlin, capture Hitler and win the war.

The answer? A resounding, "NEGATIVE, George! Roosevelt has promised Joe Stalin he could have that honor!"

A MIRACLE A MINUTE

We are told that Patton slammed down the phone and flew into a rage. Those who stood by tell us that he swore in all the words he knew when he was a boy and then added all he had picked up along the way as a man. After he spit them all out, he continued like a volcano, and the greatest quote of his entire military career was recorded as he shouted, speaking at the top of his high tenor voice, giving strong emphasis to each word in turn, "I am fighting to win a war! I care nothing at all for stupid political promises! The very insane idea of bringing our Armies all the way over here, and then ordering these brave men to halt and stand back while we let that communist butcher take Berlin, the top prize of the entire war in Europe!!"

If Ike had not cut off his fuel, I do believe that grand old soldier would have blazed ahead to Berlin anyway, even against Ike's orders. Patton perceived our real enemy to be the communists.

Army Colonel John Beaty, Ph.D., Columbia, a five-year member of the Military Intelligence Service at the Pentagon and author of a dozen books, shocked millions of veterans, including many general officers in the early 1960s, when he uncovered this piece of news:

In 1937, Hitler sent a communiqué to Churchill and Roosevelt urging them to meet him at a place and time of their choice to discuss his plan to have the great military might of the United States, Great Britain and Germany unite to fight Russia and destroy the Communists. In the message Hitler strongly stated that he did not want to fight the Americans or the British—his only enemies were Russia and France.

Colonel Beaty states that the message from Hitler was never delivered to either Churchill or Roosevelt, whose copy was buried somewhere, probably in the State Department. This communiqué was discovered and finally came to light ten years later—in 1947! Remember this offer came in 1937, before the bombing of Britain, before Hitler's drive across Germany's boundaries in a frenzy to take Poland, Austria and most of central Europe, before his waterloo with Russia and long before his white-hot hate to destroy the Jews.

Stalin, to gain absolute power, killed four million Poles and fifteen million of his own people. Stalin also put to death over two million Jews before Hitler ever built his first concentration camp. If the Congress and the American people had known the real Stalin, how he came to power and how he remained in power, they probably would have made FDR accept Hitler's offer. But, alas, as far as we know, FDR never saw it. Patton thought that we were going to have to fight Joe Stalin and the Communists sooner or later, so while the United States had the conventional tools of war—the men, the artillery and air power—over there, he wanted to go ahead and finish the job then and there and get it over with.

In retrospect, even some senior officers I have talked with think that Patton's idea of using only non-nuclear weapons to defeat Russia would have cost us all much less in the long run than did the fifty-year "Cold War." I believe that many Americans would agree, especially when we recall the enormous cost the U.S. had to bear in the manufacture of costly stockpiles of nuclear weapons and the added millions we spent to maintain a large number of troops and conventional weapons in Europe and all around the world. Plus, at a cost of more billions, our top secret B29 flights armed with multiple-nuclear warheads flew the route from Plattsburg Airbase in New York to an airbase near Seattle—back and forth for years, being re-fueled in flight, ready in an instant to counter attack if the Soviets made a first strike. I know few will agree with me, but I would sleep better tonight if they were still up there!

I know that some may see this as a child's fantasy, but just imagine for a moment with me if history had worked out another way. Had the U.S. and Great Britain received and accepted Hitler's offer and joined Germany to attack communist Russia, the Soviet armies would have surely surrendered immediately against the awesome power of that united front. All of the Allies, Germany and even Russia, would have suffered much fewer military casualties, less destruction of their cities and millions less civilian casualties.

And now the most important point of my thinking is this: I really believe *there would have been no Holocaust.* O my dear Lord! Just think—*no Holocaust!* Most of Europe's creme de la creme—those millions of beautiful, intelligent, men, women and those precious little children who only had a tiny taste of life—sent to their deaths by Hitler's madness! Think of the poets, the artists, the physicians, the writers, playwrights and divas whose great talents were buried forever; their voices and dreams are hushed, their songs, still-born. Now this poor world is forever deprived of the great blessings these lost millions would have brought into all of our lives and into the lives of generations to come!

In the light of this irreparable loss to the world, Hitler's offer doesn't seem such a bad idea after all: *We should have been willing to do anything to avoid the greatest act of genocide in history!* Those who buried that communiqué must share in the guilt for the death of so many Jews and so many troops and civilians on all sides who were wounded or killed.

Why was Hitler and most of Germany furious with the Jews? Many reasons, but mainly because they felt the Jews were successful in getting the United States into both World Wars. Hitler also blamed them for the reason Germany lost World War I. But much more than that, when World War I was over and the defeated German armies returned from the trenches, the troops discovered they had been stabbed in the back. While Germany was fighting the U.S., Britain and France, the Russian Communists—Germany's greatest enemy—had slipped in through the back door and taken control of Berlin, Munich and other population centers. Had it not been for the Free Corps, which killed some of them and chased the rest out of the country, Germany would have been overrun in a matter of months. The military and the majority of the German people would have awakened to find that they had not only lost the war but had also lost their Fatherland to the Communists, who had already made giant strides in their plan to seize and take total control of a weak, starving and defeated Germany.

It was not until the tide turned in Hitler's attack upon Russia, and he saw that he was going lose World War II that his fury turned to destroy the Jews. He saw them as "that evil group that not only plotted to seize his country while he was a Corporal in the trenches, but had brought the U.S. into the war to bring his final downfall." Had Hitler's plan been accepted by Roosevelt and Churchill, he would have still disliked the Jews, but he would never, never have needed his pogrom to try to destroy the Jews. World War I and World War II caused Hitler to believe that the Jews were baiting the U.S. and Britain into both of these wars that would once and for all bring the complete destruction of all Germans and all of Germany!

Because there would have been much less need to rebuild any Allied country, especially Germany, the U.S. would have had only a small part of Russia to rebuild. Since our two main enemies of World War II, Germany and Japan, were completely defeated at a cost of untold billions, they both had to be rebuilt mainly by the U.S. at a cost of more billions. Ironically, the super intelligence of one Jew alone, Albert Einstein, together with U.S. financing gave us the Manhattan Project, the atomic bomb. Its use brought the immediate surrender of Japan and the end of the war in the Pacific, which saved millions of lives on all sides.

History has shown the world that if any nation wants to get rebuilt all brand-new, it need only get into a war with the U.S.—and lose. The Marshall and MacArthur plans would have cost the United States about 10 percent of what was expended in rebuilding Japan, Britain, France, Germany and the rest of Western Europe, which the Allies destroyed in order to kill as many Germans as possible, get Hitler and divide and destroy Germany once and for all.

To add to the insults of the Versailles Treaty, the ultra injury for Germany was when the premier of France said at the start of World War II that there were twenty million too many Germans in Europe. He wanted the U.S. and England to come and help the French to kill them all. When Hitler learned of this statement, his hate for the French increased a thousandfold. That French premier's stand was no worse than Hitler's, who wanted the U.S. and Britain to come help him to kill all the Communists. All of this utter destruction was brought to that part of the world because of what many senior military advisors called "the unnecessary World War." Our war with Japan, when added to the cost of reconstruction of Japan and of Russia, plus the costs of the Cold War, just about bankrupted the people of the U.S., who had to pay for all of this through a long period of heavy taxes.

I have believed since I came off active duty in the army in 1946 that the U.S. should have levied a graduated 5 percent tax on the Gross National Product of every country we rebuilt. Our Lend-Lease plans were neither lend nor lease. We were never repaid even ten cents on the dollar of the billions it took to prepare and fight the war and then at its end, to restore the carnage of the wars. The tax could have begun in 1948, starting with 1 percent, then increasing 1 percent each year until it reached 5 percent, and it should have continued for fifty years. No wonder the U.S. dollar has become weaker and weaker against most currencies, especially the pound, the mark and the yen.

Let me throw this in before I forget it: I am surprised that the U.S. dollar has any value whatsoever, since the U.S. has taken so many very expensive "TRIPS." Uncle Sam took a trip to France in World War I; another to England, Europe and Japan in World War II. He went flying to the moon, and then in the Apollo venture he went out into deep space. He recently sent a robot to the region of Mars. Then this old wandering vagabond, Uncle Sam, went to Korea, then Vietnam, next to Granada, next a quick trip to Kuwait, then Haiti, Bosnia and Kosovo—and don't forget that little soirée to Somalia. All of these excursions cost you and me billions or trillions or gazillions of dollars in taxes. We had to print money to finance these trips, which resulted in a weaker dollar and rampant inflation. I think Uncle Sam ought to have his passport cancelled and be restricted to his quarters for awhile, since he doesn't seem to know his headquarters from his hindquarters! Did Lee say that about Grant?

After World War II, we built for those countries, who were our arch enemies, brand-new factories, buildings, airports, streets and highways, refineries, hospitals, hotels, homes and schools—all those things we destroyed to get Hitler and his men. Remember, we had to win the war wearing out our older factories to build armament to fight Germany and Japan. Then after the war, while we were building those countries back new, much of our own great industrial power became second class or worse, obsolete. Just look at Germany and Japan today, two of the strongest nations on earth, with brand-new factories, air-lines and everything else. They are importing to the U.S. much of what they make in those new factories, selling their imports in compe-tition with what our American workers are making. After all of what we have done for these nations, that 5 percent tax on their GNP would be little enough recompense for what it cost us in taxes and in the loss of the lives of our men and women who were killed in combat.

Using NATO as a shield, we were spending millions again while the generals and the president sat in their plush armchairs and air-conditioned suites and sent our Air Force off to billion-dollar waves and waves of three-mile high bombing of Yugoslavia, raining utter destruction upon an entire country just to get the man whom they were already calling a Hitler. This is more stupid than destroying a beautiful building in order to kill a rat that's hiding in the basement.

I think Bill Clinton probably got up one morning bored—and scared personally about a looming charge of high treason—and said to himself over his cereal, "I think I'm gonna start me a war!" So now thousands of troops went in the dead of winter into that awful terrain to do what? Those countries have been fighting each other for four hundred years. Now the U.S. taxpayer has got to foot the cost of going over there and rebuilding that country we destroyed. But what's so sad, we can't bring back a one of those innocent civil-ians who were killed on both sides.

China and Russia are angry about our sticking our noses into their sovereignty. The U.S. doesn't have many real friends, and we surely do not need those two to be our enemies. Our wars seem racially biased because we looked (and continue to look) the other way while millions of Africans in Sudan are being slaughtered by their enemies. Ms.

Albright said that help for Sudan was "not marketable to the American people." Clinton had this sneaky little deceptive way of drastically downsizing our military and then dispersing what was left of our troops all over much of the world so that we did not have the strength to defend Taiwan, South Korea or any other country against a juggernaut attack of his "friends" China and Russia. Just as the U.S. sold scrap iron and steel to Japan in the months leading up to the attack on Pearl Harbor, with which they made airplane engines to kill our soldiers, we have shut our eyes while our missile secrets have been sold to or have been stolen by the Chinese.

Well, so much for all that!

To get on with our story, Ike understood and admired Patton and gave him his fourth star, but Patton's impetuosity, his upfront candidness and what some of his detractors called his big mouth all probably worked together to prevent his becoming one of our five-star generals. The likes of Patton will not soon come this way again. It is my fervent prayer that we will never again need such a dedicated warrior. Although it makes me sad to say it, I think we will, but I surely pray it does not come in the lifetimes of the veterans of the second World War; we who served and the widows and orphans of that war do not deserve to have to go through the agony of watching World War III on TV. There are only 5 million of us left and we are dying at the rate of 1,000 per day!

Many Americans believe that such strong patriot generals as Patton and MacArthur would not have stood for the huge costs of lives and materiel (i.e., everything used by the Army) paid for by us in losing the Korean and Vietnam wars. We are still paying a staggering price today for stopping at those parallels. Most of the World War II generals I have known, or read about, would think it grossly insane to fight a war in which our troops were not permitted to win.

I might be called an alarmist, but I believe that a third world war could be triggered any day now by the need to fight to prevent Communist China from seizing Taiwan, while at the same time China could throw its military might into a battle to assist North Korea in taking South Korea. Current peace efforts between North and South Korea should be watched with great caution. Many of the North Koreans are almost starving now. If we continue to give them billions in aid, they will use the money to rebuild their economy and military forces until they are strong enough to fight. When China gets fully armed, including a powerful nuclear capability, she will become a threat not only to Taiwan and South Korea, but also to the

A MIRACLE A MINUTE

Philippines, most of the Pacific Rim and finally to the U.S. (Most of the paragraphs above were written in August 1997.)

But what really concerns me most is how on earth can we come to the rescue of even one friendly nation when our military strength is being downsized and scattered all over the planet in social and peacekeeping efforts that often do not really involve our national interests? We are so weak that I fear we cannot launch a strong effort anywhere, certainly not on two fronts at the same time.

After serving over 36 years in the Army reserve, and retiring with the rank of Colonel, I feel that something would be sadly lacking in my character if I did not express the deep concerns I discussed in the previous pages.

One summer a few years ago, when I, as a reserve officer, was Acting Post Chaplain at Fort Chaffee, Arkansas, I had the good pleasure of talking with Gen. Patton's son, Major General George S. Patton III. As he was leaving an officers' dinner in his honor, I said, "General Patton, my brother served with your dad in Europe."

He quipped, chuckling, "Well, didn't everybody!"

When we all finished laughing, I responded, saying, "General, my brother was one of your dad's chaplains."

He quickly turned, came up to me, shook my hand and expressed warm interest. He wanted to know more about it, so as we walked to the door. I told him, "My brother, Major Frank J. Pippin, served in Third Army under your dad during the Battle of the Bulge."

"Well, what do you say! Chaplain Pippin, as you know, my dad had a very warm spot in his heart for all chaplains. They helped him in so many ways, especially with troop morale. Glad to meet you, Colonel."

Now that we were outside, I popped to, gave him a sharp salute and said, "General Patton, sir, the pleasure is mine. God go with you."

He smiled, flipped me a salute, boarded his sedan and was driven away.

❊ 13 ❊

A Farewell
to Arms

During the rest of that winter, it was hard to keep those old, drafty buildings warm, so I continued to get more coffee from the mess hall and each morning make it fresh on my hot stove in my little drip pot. The major continued to come in, and I poured him a cup, which he enjoyed along with his morning cigar. After he went to his office, I would take a cup to Sgt. Mercier. Rakin had a Coke bottle in his hand most of the day.

As I write now over fifty years later, I still vividly recall those cold winter nights, with that north Georgia wind whipping the snow around the old frame headquarters building and those frigid mornings, starting a fire, the warm stove, the smell of coffee brewing, and my cozy little insurance office where a Major and a Pfc. would often sit, have a cup, a good chat and become friends.

In a few weeks, my name came out on orders promoting me to corporal. I was sure those stripes came mainly from that good, warm fire. Of course, the fresh coffee, my war map and the daily briefings didn't hurt a bit. Never in a million years would I have dreamed that those early morning fires I learned to build as a child so long ago would get me a promotion to the glorious rank of corporal in the Army of the United States. I was truly glad that my buddy, Corporal Rakin, made sergeant on the same orders.

One morning, while he was still asleep, I woke him up by singing him a little song, over and over:

> If you could learn to make a fire,
> You would be staff-sergeant now,
> Get up, get up, you sleepy head,
> Or Mercier'll toss you out of bed,

A MIRACLE A MINUTE

If you didn't hail from Yankee land,
Your fire'd be blazing to beat the band!

He jumped out of bed, grabbed a chair and with an imaginary whip chased me from the building, screaming, "Yi---Yi---Yi." Although he would never admit nor show it, Rakin and I were close friends. As Mercier's orderly, he often helped me in ways that only he could. We often took turns loaning each other money near the end of the month to pull us through. He was a genius at making a perfect daily morning report, a huge task in itself. Many nights, before we cut off the light, Rakin and I would have long talks about religion, his and mine, and about the past and the future.

A few weeks later a staff sergeant from Tocoa dropped by the office to try to sell me his 1938 Buick Century coupe. He was being released early and needed the money. Though he asked for more, he accepted a check for $850.00, so I became the proud owner of my first real car. It was dark blue with a "straight eight" engine, stick shift and wide white-wall tires. The trunk was as long as the hood. That car so changed my life that I wondered how in the world I ever got along without it.

One April afternoon after work, six of us piled into a friend's car and headed to a cafe in Buckhead to have a snack. I remember that I was sitting up front in the middle.

As we pulled up and parked, the music on the car radio was interrupted with these shocking words: "Ladies and gentleman, we interrupt this program to bring you the sad news that President Roosevelt has just died from a cerebral hemorrhage at his home in Warm Springs, Georgia. That is all we have now, but we will give you more details as they come to us."

I felt like I had been stabbed in the heart with a dagger. The date was April 12, 1945. The time, about 4:30 P.M. Just as we all remember where we were that day when Pearl Harbor was hit, so it was with that tragic day our beloved president died. We six men looked at each other and all began to cough and fight back the tears. I felt as if I had lost my father. In a real sense we all had. The whole nation and the entire world seemed to be mourning in unison, deeply stricken with grief.

His body was to be shipped the next day by special train from Warm Springs to Washington. Requests were made for military volunteers to come and stand by the tracks at intervals of fifty feet on the entire route. A light rain was falling as I took my place beside the tracks near Buckhead. It seemed that the very heavens were weeping with us. In just a few minutes, the train approached. I was at attention, holding a salute as it passed slowly by. Then, at the end of the train in the observation car, clearly in view, I saw his flag-draped casket. I could hardly see it for the tears. My heart was up in my aching throat and I could not swallow. I turned slowly as that last car with his body passed by, holding the salute until it rounded the curve and disappeared out of sight. Then the image flashed into my mind of that long line of men and women in uniform who were taking their places and standing at attention all along the tracks from Warm Springs to Washington.

Standing alone there in a drizzle of rain, I put both my hands to my face and wept. A few moments later, I waved at the soldier who was fifty feet further up the tracks, then I turned and walked to my car.

We will probably not see a president of FDR's stature again. For me, he ties in first place with Ronald Reagan. Like Patton, FDR was a brave and gallant warrior. He was stricken in early manhood with poliomyelitis that paralyzed him from the waist down. Even still, he went all the way to the White House and became the only president elected to four terms. He made life very exciting for most Americans during his historic time in the White House. All of us in uniform were so very proud to be Americans, serving in the armed forces with him as our commander-in-chief.

Sure, he had some faults and made some mistakes, but we have never had a president who was perfect. But the vast majority of historians attribute to him alone the bringing of our nation up out of a devastating depression, even if as he did so, he and his administration opened an ever-widening door to Socialism. But at the time, we thought all of those measures he used to get us out of the Depression were temporary; at least the administration said they were! In retrospect, many agree that two of the most far-reaching of his mistakes was when he gave the Soviet army the privilege of taking Berlin, and then later at Yalta, with Churchill looking on, he so casually handed over to Joseph Stalin territorial rights to all of Eastern Europe! This fateful decision doomed millions of people to fifty years of misery and poverty as slaves under the Communists. But on balance, this nation and all of the free world owe to FDR a debt that can never be paid.

By late April of 1945, the number of wounded coming to Lawson began to decrease rapidly, and at the same time many people were being released from the military. Sgt. Mercier was the first in our group to get out. Before he left he came into my office and said some kind things, shook my hand and left. The rest of the enlisted men were notified that we would be transferred to other installations where the Army was short of personnel.

A MIRACLE A MINUTE

In July of 1945, I was ordered back to Fort MacPherson, where I had started! After I cleaned out my desk, rolled up my map of Europe, packed and told Rakin and Major McCoy good-bye, I drove over to Headquarters at Fort Mac in my '38 Buick. It was a very hot and humid afternoon.

They were waiting for me. Within a minute, I was introduced to Capt. Roger Follette, a tall, skinny, sallow man from New Orleans. He was the officer in charge of the personnel division, who wasted no time assigning me to the payroll section. After a few words of welcome he arose and ushered me out of the building with, "See you at 0730 hours in the morning, Corporal Pippin, ready to go to work."

As I was leaving, a short, very slender and good-looking sergeant, Howard Kite, came up to me. He was wearing a perpetual smile that was punctuated by a dangling cigarette. He offered to show me to my room. It was on the ground floor of one of the huge, old, permanent brick and marble buildings that were erected there before the first World War. Though Kite wasn't my boss, as chief NCO of records section, he gave me an idea of what my duties would be. I was pleased when he asked me to go to supper with him. We hit it off so great that he became my closest friend in the Army since J.C. Lovett.

The pace really picked up the next morning when I met my immediate boss, Marie Smith, chief of the payroll section. She was a lovely, young, buxom, redhead. She had large blue eyes and full lips, and when she smiled, which was often, she revealed a narrow split between her two front teeth. She wore a thin beige dress cut two inches above the knee with a matching belt tied tightly around her small waist. She showed me to my desk and standing there with clipboard in hand, gave me a brief job description.

In closing, she said, "As you can see, Corporal Pippin, there are eighteen persons in this corner of our large room who make up the section, a few of whom are civilians. They are a happy, efficient group who will make you feel at home from the start. In due time you will get to know all of them well. Feel free to come to me anytime you have questions or if you should have a problem of any kind."

With this, she quickly turned and stepped off, clicked those high heels, and confident that I was watching, she gave me what we guys called "that fifty-dollar walk!" I soon got to know the section, mainly at our daily coffee breaks at midmorning and midafternoon. Sgt. Kite often was among those who sat with me, but after a few days my pretty boss Miss Smith would often come over and join us.

One morning about a month later, she came over to my desk and asked me to remain there for the morning break. I sensed her delicate fragrance before she sat down.

She had our coffee sent in and after the room cleared, she pulled her chair up close to mine, sat, crossed her legs, dropped her voice and said, "After observing your work closely these past few weeks Cpl. Pippin, both Captain Follette and I agree that you are the person we have been looking for to replace me as Chief of Section. I plan to quit in a few weeks, but I will remain in the section until then. I know you are new here and that this comes as a surprise, but if you will accept the position, I will train you myself."

Golly! I could hardly believe my ears. I was a little shaky when I responded, "Miss Smith, I am honored, but I notice that there's one staff sergeant and several buck sergeants in the section. How will they take to working for a corporal?"

"Well, most of them have just returned from overseas and won't mind. But that brings me to some more good news. Capt. Follette has agreed to promote you to sergeant before you become chief." She tilted her head, her silken red hair falling to her shoulder, winked and said, "How does that strike you, Corporal Pippin?"

"Well, Miss Smith, of course I accept! But you'll have to promise that you'll be patient with me and stay close to me until I'm on top of everything."

Since the crowd was coming in from break, she rose, shook my hand and said, "So, it's a deal then?"

I nodded. She smiled and all eyes were on her as she walked away.

In two weeks I was very proud to be a three-striper, or "buck" sergeant. Marie trained me well, having me meet her back at the office to work alone, sometimes until near midnight. After about two weeks of this, she turned the section over to me. That first monthly payroll was almost as big as a Sears and Roebuck catalog, containing names of over two thousand soldiers. With Marie's continued help, the second payroll was a snap. I was then on my own. That job and her friendship made my last few months in the Army some of the best. As you have already suspected, we became sweethearts. It happened one night when I took her home. At her door she came over to me, embraced and kissed me. So, after this, Marie and I, Kite and his girl, started to double-date frequently.

Kite and I became almost inseparable; it was "Kite and I" and "Pip and I" at the beginning of most of our sentences. I believed that we could read each others' minds. We kept ourselves and anyone who was with us in stitches with our repartee. Often, when I spent the night at his home, his sweet mom and dad would have a great breakfast ready for us at 6:30 each morning. I can still taste the bacon and eggs, hot biscuits, grits, gravy and fresh coffee. Then to finish up, a third cup of coffee and a third biscuit covered with his mom's homemade pear or peach preserves. Kite and his parents were really like a second family to me.

Since my first cousin, Claude Pippin, was the senior agent at the Railway Express Agency, I got Kite and me a holiday job there, from November 1 through New Year's eve. The REA was a part of the Atlanta terminal. Our hours were from 5 to 11 P.M. We routed hundreds of Christmas packages that were placed on roller-racks, sending them straight into the waiting trucks. Then the trucks were moved to flat cars that carried them "piggyback" to destinations all over the USA. We also drove the REA delivery trucks, taking packages to local business and homes.

I was delightfully surprised that Christmas Eve when Brother Frank, now a major just back from Germany, found me there. He stood over in a corner watching me route packages. When he came over and grabbed me from behind, he said that he just knew I would be in charge of the entire terminal by now! I was so glad to see him. Since it was time for my supper break, we went by to see Claude and went on up into the terminal to eat. He had lost some hair while he was in the Army, but looked very sharp sitting there in his fitted uniform, sporting those shiny gold leaves. We talked a mile a minute, with so many miles and so many months to cover. Since he was on leave, waiting to be released, he went on to the Island to see Mama and Papa, George and Vera and the boys. After New Year's, I got a three-day pass and had a great time with Frank and the family.

This brief duty with the REA changed me into a taxi cab driver, from sane to crazy. I called it "fast but careful." Your eyes are constantly moving in all four directions almost at once. You watch for cracks in the traffic and bluff a lot! No one wants to tangle with a REA truck. Of course, this was before the day when trucks carried a big sign on the back: IF THIS DRIVER IS DISCOURTEOUS, CALL US!

Even today, Allene hates to ride with me. She is always stiff as a board, holding on to the door handle. She still says what she began saying over fifty years ago when we were on our first date: "James! You are a reckless driver; you drive like a ravin' maniac. You are scarin' the livin' daylights outta me!"

I countered with, "Sure I'm reckless! A reck-less driver has no wrecks!"

She mumbled, "Taint funny."

If a car blows its horn within three blocks of where I am, she glares at me and screams, "What in heaven's name are you doing wrong now?"

But I can't seem to break the habit of driving fast. The way she acts, you'd think the car was bummed up on all sides, but I've only had one accident in my life and no traffic tickets in twenty-five years!

Every night Kite and I had to take a great big truck and go get the ice the REA needed for the next day. On the way was a huge bakery, whose pungent fragrances we always picked up blocks away. Stopping by one night, the baker gave us a sack of hamburger rolls that had just come out of the oven. The smell of that hot bun! It was the best stuff we ever ate. However, about ten minutes later we both felt like we had swallowed a bag of rocks. Never again.

One night I was walking down in the rail yard from the terminal to the little all-night cafe and had to cross about fifteen railroad tracks. Halfway over, something touched me on the shoulder and said, "Look out behind you!"

I turned around just in time to see an empty box car that was silently but speedily coming toward me. I jumped clear just in time. It had broken loose from the rest of the cars and was on a happy holiday, heading down through the yard! Since I saw no one else, I was certain that the warning came from my guardian angel. I believe my angel has followed me closely all my life, including the afternoon when Jack and I, as small boys, went fishing with brother Frank, who pulled me out of Cedar Creek when I almost drowned; the night I almost bled to death in the Macon hospital when I was thirteen; that cold, rainy night when the guy who stole my wallet brought it back because he saw Jesus' picture in it; the time that I took my tour group to see the Dead Sea Scrolls museum in Israel, slipped on the wet stone steps, fell and badly broke my thumb, passed out—no pulse, no blood pressure, turned blue. When Allene got to me she thought I was dead. In tears, she began to pray in the Spirit and then screamed for help. Two medics ran to me from the emergency room of the large Hadassa Hospital that was only fifty yards away. When I came to, five physicians and four nurses were leaning over me. They saved my life. Only an angel could have put that fall and the hospital so close together that day. And, no fooling, those Jewish doctors in Israel are the world's best. Since the thumb was broken all the way back, it had to be set by an orthopedic surgeon, then another surgeon had to put about seven stitches in it.

As he was getting the needle and thread ready, I didn't see any hypo to deaden it, so I said, " Aren't you going to deaden that first?"

He growled back, "But of cose. After all, ve are not barrbarrians!"

I covered my laugh.

I could go on for pages with these miracles—but here I'll relate just one more. In the summer of 1970, I took twenty-four people around the world. We stopped for two nights in Fiji. The second day we had an all-day cookout on Tai Island about twenty-five miles off Fiji. Our small craft dropped anchor at Tai, about one hundred feet from shore. I quickly changed into my swimsuit, got the captain's permission to swim ashore, and while my group looked on, I leaped from the boat and grabbed the anchor rope. But the wind pulled me off, and I dropped into the rough sea. I began frantically trying to reach the shore, but the wind was moving against me, swiftly taking me to the end of the small island. I tried to touch bottom several times, with no luck. Then I saw this tall, solid black "Fuzzy-wuzzy" standing knee-deep in the sea, fifty feet from me, who in a deep bass voice, kept saying, over and over, "WALLCOME, WALLCOME!" I was sure that was the only English he knew, but I yelled at him anyway.

"Help! Help! I'm drowning! Ugh, ugh, can't hold on much longer!!"

My entire group was shouting, "Hey, you there, help our fearless leader! Can't you see he's drowning?"

He kept saying, "Wallcome, Wallcome," while he looked straight ahead, holding a long spear. Then just as I was starting to swallow the sea, a voice spoke to me, "Stop fighting the flow. Turn over and float on your back."

When I did, I relaxed and drifted to the tip of the island, headed out to sea! Suddenly, I put my feet down and touched bottom! Walking to shore was hard against the wind, but I made it. The Fuzzy-wuzzy just glanced at me and smiled, showing a big mouth full of white teeth. As I turned and waved to the group, a shout of joy went up from the boat. I learned a great lesson that day from my angel: "Don't fight it—GO WITH THE FLOW!"

Just days before Christmas 1945, the troops who had been in the Army four years or more were being released in large numbers, including most of my payroll section. Sgt. Kite had chosen to remain on active duty and was shipped out in early January to Japan. He asked me to take him to the Atlanta train station, where his mom and dad joined me in telling him good-bye. The four of us held hands as I said a prayer for his safe journey. We were all wiping away the tears as the train pulled out. I did not imagine that I would never see him again. After I left Atlanta and just before I left home for college, I called his dad to chat. I got a great shock when he told me that Kite was riding with a pilot friend in a fighter plane over the Sea of Japan when they evidently crashed into the sea and were killed, for no trace of them or the plane was ever found. His dad and I had a good cry. I promised him that I would come by to see them soon.

In early January, Captain Follette came back to my desk, sat down and crossed his long bony legs. I knew something was up when he slowly lit a cigarette, cocked his head to the side and began squinting one eye at me through a cloud of smoke. Although he had a full set of false teeth, he only wore them when higher brass was around.

He resembled an old lady as his flabby lips pressed down on his cigarette, which remained in his mouth as he spoke. "Sgt. Pippin, we're proud of you and your work. I've some good news and a proposition for you. I have just learned that you are scheduled to be discharged on February 14."

"You are kidding me!"

"Nope, I can show you the orders. Now calm down. Here's my deal. If you will stay with me for a few months and help me shut down this joint, I'll promote you to staff sergeant."

I said, while trying not to smile, "Sir, thanks for the offer. I've really enjoyed working for you. I'd love to stay and help, but there's just no way. I'm dying to get out of here and go home. I plan to enter college in the fall."

"All right, then," he continued, as he took a long drag from his cigarette, "I'm gonna sweeten the pot. I'll cut orders right now promoting you to tech sergeant if you will stay just two months, do a small payroll for the cadre and help me close her down. I have no one else to turn to."

"Sir, I am truly honored and flattered by your offer. I probably will regret this decision for the rest of my life, but, Sir, I can't do it. Have you thought of Miss Smith? I'm sure that Marie'll be glad to come in and pull you out. She'll be a whole lot cheaper for the Army than paying me. Do you want me to call her for you?"

Marie was only to glad to do it. Follette was so elated that he gave me two days off to get cleared, packed and ready to leave Fort Mac. Of course, it was hard to leave Marie. She got off and spent the entire time with me. We had been going steady for the past six months. She made me promise that she could come visit me at St. Simon's before I left for college.

So, on a cold gray morning, the fourteenth of February, 1946, after three years, three months and fifteen days, I was honorably discharged from the Army. The sergeant asked if anyone in ranks wanted to join the reserves. No one spoke. After we fell out, I went up to him and asked what was the deal.

When I found out that I would keep my years of service and my rank, I said, "Sign me up. I never want to be back in this man's Army again as a private."

So that day I became a member of the United States Army Reserve, a decision that shaped my future for the better in so many ways.

Months earlier I had gone to see my first cousin, Arthur Pippin Jackson, who owned the Chrysler-Plymouth dealership in East Point, near the base. He was tall, had straight black hair and was very handsome. I placed an order with him for a 1946 four-door Plymouth sedan, loaded. Though there was a long waiting list for any new car in those days, he told me he would give me the first one that came in! Veterans had first choice. Well, just imagine, two days before my release, he called to tell me that my car was in! Oh, what a miracle!

As soon as I was discharged, I drove over in my '38 Buick, and there sat that shining beauty in the driveway, waiting for me, ready to go. It was light tan and full of chrome. Arthur took my '38 Buick in trade, so I went in and sat down in his plush office. After a brief chat and a cup of coffee, I gave him a check for thirteen hundred dollars, and the car was mine. I loaded my gear out of the Buick, and after I kissed the old girl good-bye and glad-handed everybody, I hopped in and was on my way to St. Simon's and home. As I pulled out, I glanced up in my rearview mirror, and there was Arthur, several salesmen and a mechanic standing there waving good-bye to me.

This was truly a miracle day. The sun broke out, the birds were singing, and the smell of spring and honeysuckle mingled with the scent of that new Plymouth gave me a rare thrill. That morning, I had the same keen feeling of love for God and His beautiful world that I had on those days of fasting with J.C. I drove slowly through Hapeville and on out of the city limits. This took only a short time because the population of Atlanta in 1946 was only about three hundred thousand. (Now it's almost four million!) Before I knew it, I was out in the beautiful countryside of north Georgia, cruising along on the road to Macon.

Then, I just happened to glance down at my gauges and noticed the engine temperature was running hot, almost into the red! I pulled over immediately, stopped, cut the engine and found myself in front of an unpainted, framed house.

As I got out and raised the hood, an old man in overalls came out and asked, "Kin ah hep ya, sonny?"

We discovered that the radiator was empty. He got water, and after filling it up, we heard water leaking under the engine. I groaned, thinking I had a faulty water pump, or worse, but he stooped down and saw that it was only the little pet-cock that had been left open. They had "dreened" the radiator last night, and when they filled it this morning, they forgot to close the pet-cock! I could have ruined my new engine. But the old man said it sounded fine, so I thanked him (and God), and never mentioned this to Arthur.

Back out on the road, I regained my high spirits. The Army was behind me; the world and my future lay ahead. I cannot describe the sudden rush of freedom that overwhelmed me. No uniform, no restrictions, no deadlines, no need for three-day passes—but also no Marie and no Kite.

As I breezed along on that wonderful morning, my mind raced back over the highlights of those years: I thought of my first year at Lawson and Anne Puryear; of ASTP, the Yankee food, the Fathers and the Jewish girls; of meeting Ruzensky and being AWOL at Grant; of J.C. Lovett, the dayroom, and the fasting; of the miracle transfer to Lawson; of that good time of fellowship with Jack; of the angel that saved Jack and me during the hurricane; of the sweet fragrant Anne and the soft landing she gave me; then of all those days and nights of fun with friends like Kite and my darling Marie.

When I stopped for coffee and a sandwich south of Macon, I could not help but pause and thank God for the many blessings I had received while in the Army. The misery and the loneliness of those years had been sprinkled with many happy times that brought me closer to the person I really was. I felt that my tour on active duty had matured me because I learned so many good lessons in the virtues and in duty, honor and country. I surely was not the same person I had been over three years earlier. I had just turned twenty-four on January 19, paid cash for a new car, still had money in the bank, Christ Jesus in my heart and a wonderful family at home waiting for me. But most of all, I knew what I was going to do with my life; "who could ask for anything more!" I patted the steering wheel as I hummed the tune…Daaa da, dot dot, da da daaa daaa!

I would have been even more elated had I known then that in the next few months I would meet the gorgeous brunette who would finally become my wife, enroll in college and there meet a great man of God who was going to play a large part in the direction that the rest of my life would take.

❊ 14 ❊

Found Her on the Beach, But She Swam Away

I again got my old familiar welcome when I smelled the crisp salt air as I neared St. Simon's. The trip over on the old causeway with its panorama of marshes, rivers and the bright blue Atlantic Ocean to the southeast told me that I was home again. And the feeling was exhilarating! The rattle of the narrow wooden bridges brought back Krista and so many other memories to me. I was in constant prayer as I drove over that long bridge, remembering the night Jack and I almost lost our lives when it whipped and swayed, ready to come apart in the force of the hurricane.

It was late afternoon when I pulled into the carport in back of the house. Mama saw me and came running out to get the first hug. Papa called Jack and Sam and said just two words: "He's here!"

I ran in and hugged my sweet Papa's neck real good. Mama asked if I had eaten. I hugged her again and said, "I have, but you can make us a fresh pot of your great drip coffee."

As we sat the cups down, I heard screaming and fast running. Sam bounded in through the back door, Jack right behind her, carrying Daniel Jackson Pippin II on his right hip. I thought I was being attacked by wild animals. Sam squeezed me hard, twice! Then Jack hugged me with both arms for the first time in years! Then baby Danny put out his arms to me and climbed up into my lap. I guess he thought that now he had two daddies since I looked so much like Jack.

But then Sam came over and said to Danny, "Danny! This is your uncle James, say hello to your uncle James!"

He said, "Helwo, unkie Jam."

Mama poured us more coffee, and our talk "covered the waterfront," often all of us, except Papa, talking at the same time. They heard me out first, after which Jack brought me up to date on the store and his medical progress. Then the subject turned again to some of my Army experiences and what I had planned for my future.

Papa finally got a word in edgewise, saying he had phoned George and that he would come by there as soon as he closed the shoe shop. Almost at that instant, he arrived, hopped out of the car and bounded in the front door. Although I was two inches taller, I was kinda skinny, so he picked me up and wheeled me around like he and Frank used to do when Jack and I were kids. Of course, as soon as George came, he just had to go out and see my new Plymouth. This was the first new car he had seen in about six years.

I noticed that his eyes bulged, and his mouth watered, so I said, "George, thou shalt not covet thy brother's car!"

We both laughed and as we went back into the house, with our arms around each other's shoulder, he whispered, "Man, I can hardly wait to drive that beauty!"

Now with George there, the heaviest coffee drinker in the family, Mama had to put on a fresh pot, and it was more coffee for everyone.

I suppose this calls for a few words about all this coffee. The Pippins, going back to Papa's grandfather and beyond, kept fresh coffee on the stove almost all day. Papa's daddy, Thomas Clayton, from whom I get my middle name, and Papa's mother, Susan, were heavy coffee drinkers, as were all of Papa's brothers. Papa used to chuckle and say that all that coffee finally brought on his mother's death. She was eighty-nine!

My generation was introduced to coffee at an early age. Mama baked biscuits almost every night and at breakfast would take the ones left over from supper, split them and toast them golden brown in the oven of her old wood cook stove. The four halves were then placed on a saucer, sprinkled with sugar, and two tablespoons of strong hot coffee were poured on each. That crisp biscuit with sugar and coffee is a special treat, the taste of which I cannot adequately describe, nor can it be duplicated. I used to fix them for our three girls, and even now, Allene and I often have them that way for a simple dessert. Patient reader, I also know that this is not a cookbook! But what we eat today is so much less appealing than what we loved as kids "in the good ole days" that I just had to share this little treat with you. To the Pippin family, coffee time was almost a sacrament.

Allene and I have enjoyed espresso, cappuccino, as well as breakfast coffee in Taipei, Tokyo, Bangkok and many cities in Europe and the Middle East. We found some of the best in Israel. In the South, the midmorning and midafternoon coffee breaks are as common as tea time in England and throughout the old British empire. Allene and I have enjoyed high tea and coffee from the Caledonia Hotel in Edinburgh, Scotland, to the Peninsular Hotel in Hong Kong, the Lido in Beijing and all the way down under to the Hilton in Sydney.

Even so, with her simple old drip pot, Mama could turn out a cup that can't be beat. Right now, as I write this, I so wish I could hear her step down the hall and call out in her sweet voice, "James, come on, Son, the coffee's ready!"

The first few months I was at home were a major adjustment. At first, I could not go to sleep on the new soft innerspring bed, so I folded a quilt and slept on the floor. It took awhile before I was able to sleep late, always waking up about 6 A.M. The food at home was a little different, but the coffee was superb. Believe it or not, in a few days, I was sorely missing the Army, my friends, my Marie and my payroll section. I even wondered why in the world I was so eager to get out! Follette would have let me go home for two weeks and just imagine, I would have left the army a tech sergeant for giving him just two short months! But God knew why I did not need that rank. You will too, later.

When you have been in the Army for three and a half years, after the first few days with the family, your unconscious mind tells you that your leave is up and it's time for you to get back into uniform. But, thank God, the feeling didn't last long. But I only needed to spend a short time in the store to see that this life was not for me. Besides, Jack, Sam and Ed did not need me. Jack and I were still half-owners, but I knew the slow business couldn't afford me on the payroll. Anyway, I was restless to get out of there and head west.

But one night George and his wife, Vera, invited me to have supper with them. During our visit George offered me a job in the new wholesale leather company he had recently started. I accepted, since college didn't begin until September. This was the beginning of his plan to try to get me to change my mind about the ministry and come into business with him. The next few weeks found me in his shoe shop, first working the front, then later on weekdays going out on the road calling on his retail shops all over south Georgia. He and I spent Saturdays cleaning the shop, talking about the war days and drinking lots of coffee next door at the cafe. When I worked the route each week, George let me drive his brand-new 1946 Chrysler New Yorker, a shiny black coupe. Like my '38 Buick, it had a trunk as long as the hood. He had had it only about ten days, and it was his pride and joy.

Found Her on the Beach, But She Swam Away

On an afternoon in early July while I was working Savannah, it dawned on me that Krista and John lived there. So I looked up their address and drove out to the house. When I pulled up in front, lo and behold, Krista was painting some wooden swans on the lawn and did not see me. She was as slim, shapely and as beautiful as ever, wearing white short-shorts, a pink halter and thongs. She stood up, turned around and saw me getting out of the car. Dropping the brush she was holding, she just stood there, as if she had seen a ghost.

I said, "Don't you speak to old friends?"

Then she let out a squeal and ran to the car. She gave me a hug and said, punctuated with laughter, "I just knew that something special was going to happen to me today."

She did not believe it could be me. Then she grabbed my hand and pulled me into the house. I sat at the kitchen table while she served us iced tea. We sat chatting and sipping our tea for an hour that seemed like ten minutes. Remembering my days of loving Krista was much more painful for me than for her since she was happily married. Honest, now, I did not kiss her or hold her. Soon, she walked me out to the car, said a few words of farewell, and I was off.

Just to show you how very good God is, in only a few weeks after this visit, I met a girl on the beach who would fill my heart so full of joy that I had no time to miss Krista ever again. Hallelujah! That was the last time I saw Krista until almost forty years later when Allene and I were holding a meeting at Beaches Chapel near Jacksonville Beach. Krista and John then lived on St. John's River just over the bay from Jacksonville. One afternoon we invited her and John to join us for coffee at The Sea Turtle, which was right at the ocean.

As we walked in, I rudely asked her how old she was. She said, "James, that's the second time you have asked that; you know very well how old I am. If you ask me one more time, I'm going back out and wait in the car."

That was so sudden and so clever that we all laughed, she the loudest. We had a good visit over several cups and over several decades of our lives. That night they attended the meeting where I preached and Allene sang. We gave them some of our tapes and albums and in a few days, we received a very good letter of thanks from them.

One Friday afternoon in early August, as I was heading back home after calling on shops in southwest Georgia, I was caught in a rain storm on a slick asphalt road. I entered a sharp curve near

A MIRACLE A MINUTE

Boston, Georgia at about forty miles per hour, lost control of the car and flipped it over on its side into a ditch. I was not injured, but the whole right side of George's precious New Yorker was mashed in a bit. The tow truck pulled me back up on the road and raised the front fender off of the right tire so I could drive on into Boston.

When I called George and told him what happened, he said words of great comfort to me, "It's OK, Brother James. Don't worry about the car. I thank God you're not hurt. Just bring her on in."

After I got a bite to eat, I drove straight to his house. As I pulled in, I was thankful that it was too dark for him to see the damage until morning. I found out that night just how much Brother George really loved me. He never chewed me out, nor was he the least bit cross with me. Even so, that was the end of my career as a salesman calling on shoe shops. He didn't pull me off the road, I guess I just wasn't cut out to do that. I was so glad that the insurance company took care of the accident, except for the small deductible. The Chrysler body shop gave his car back to him in two weeks as good as it was the day he bought it.

In the days ahead, George and I talked long and more seriously. He still had hopes that I would join him in his wholesale leather business, even offering me a salary and 49 percent of the net profit.

Then one afternoon sitting at the counter over at the Cafe, with misty eyes, he said, "Brother James, I give up. I won't try any longer to change your plans to serve the Lord. You know, without me saying so, how very proud I am of you for sticking to your decision. I will miss you being with me, but I promise I will assist you in every way I can to get your education. Maybe you can work for me again during your summers, that is, if you'll promise not to wreck my car again!"

I turned, held up my hand and said, "I promise on my word of honor."

As I reached to shake his hand, we laughed and both almost fell off the cafe stools. That little visit showed me how great he was and caused me to love him even more.

After Brother Frank was discharged from the army in 1945, he was soon called to be the pastor of the 3,000-member Community Christian Church in Kansas City, Missouri. He phoned me in the middle of July and asked me to come out to see him to discuss my plans for college. I drove up to Jesup, had lunch with Belle and Stanton, and then caught the "Kansas City Special" there for the fast overnight trip. It was good to spend some time with Frank, Ozelle and my pretty niece, Julia. We all had a great time together. One night, after much discussion about where I would enroll, we selected Phillips University in Enid, Oklahoma, as our first choice. The next afternoon in his study, Frank picked up the phone and called Dr. Stephen J. England, the dean, to ask if it was too late for me to enroll for the fall semester. He replied that even though the College of the Bible was already filled, they surely ought to be able to squeeze in one more for Frank Johnson Pippin's little brother and would make a place for me. After Frank and I both thanked the dean, he hung up, gave me a big wink, shook my hand and said, "You're in!"

On my last night, back at the manse, we chatted until very late about the ministry, but of all his advice while there, I was most shocked when he said, "Brother James, you may think this strange, but my final and most important advice to you is this: Stay out of the ministry if you possibly can. Because if you can stay out, this will prove you should never have come into it in the first place."

Since I was there over a Sunday, he introduced me to the packed congregation and had me read the scriptures and bring the pastoral prayer during the morning worship service. But I was shocked when he asked me to speak to the youth in Bonfil's Chapel that night. I whipped up some notes but wasn't ready, so I went up and did the best I could. Frank sat on the back row and said that he would critique it, whatever that meant. Well, I found out in his study after everyone had left.

He began, "James, Son, you did good with your subject and your close. But, you are going into the min-*is*-try, not the men-stry. You must never leave coins or your car keys in your pockets as you speak. You constantly were playing with first one and then the other. And Son, the tongue is the ugliest part of the human body, so do your best to keep it out of sight and always in your mouth. You resembled a snapping turtle, sticking your tongue out to moisten your lips every few words." Here, he mimicked me by sticking out his tongue every few seconds in a sentence he said to me.

He continued, "Now here is the way a singer, actor, and hopefully a preacher moistens the lips. You put the bottom lip in your mouth and then the upper lip in your mouth, in this manner. It is done quickly and quite unnoticeably if you don't do it too often. And last, you said Sunday morning that you were happy to bring the past-TOE-rall prayer, the word is PAST-o-ral. Only illiterate or uneducated preachers call it what you did."

I should have been more able to take this criticism, since I had been chewed out worse by growling sergeants. But it was quiet a shock for this to be coming from Brother Frank. I sat there with my head down. When I had the courage to glance up at him, he leaned back in his chair and let out a howl of laughter—even though I had no idea why he was laughing that loud, I decided to join him. He wasn't kidding one bit in what he said, but he really thought I would be able to take it better.

He still chuckled as he said, "Brother James, I am getting you ready for those professors at Phillip's who are going to chew you up and spit you out. Don't worry, you will weather-in. Soon you can sit or stand there and take the strongest criticism from the best of them like a pro."

It was one of the best lessons he ever taught me. Most ministers are not able to take criticism in any way. Years later, when I heard graduates from seminary make all kinds of grammatical and punctuation errors, I would sit there and ask, "How in the world did this person get out of seminary doing or saying what she/he just did or said."

But Frank helped to save me. Later, in one of our undergraduate classes on preaching, whenever the student would say "Uh," the whole class would loudly say, *Uh!!* If the class heard the rattle of coins or keys, someone in the back of the room with a bucket half full of rocks would produce quite a clatter, so loud that the speaker would suddenly give a start and stop! You can be certain these speakers or any of the rest of us never repeated these bad habits.

On the way to Frank's car and to coffee, I mumbled to myself, "So, this is the way colleges teach us to be preachers." I took a giant leap into the world of reality that day.

Frank continued, as if he had read my mind, "In the military, you expected this, but in civilian life? And even more, in a Christian college?! You bet, lil brother, it's a jungle out there, and if you get out with your heart, your brain and your life intact, you are God blessed."

All this just made me more determined to get in the kitchen, take the heat and stay in the ministry no matter what. I made a vow that no one or no thing would ever run me out of the min-*is*-try.

I cannot fully describe what a rewarding relationship Frank and I had. He was so very proud that his baby brother was going to follow his steps into full-time service for Christ. Frank, George, Jack and I were always very close. But as I grew to an adult, their love, support and pride in me and my devotion to the Lord made the four of us even closer. I don't mean that I loved them more that I did Ray and Fred or the girls, Sister (Myrtle), Mary or Annabelle. Only that the four of us boys spent much more time together as we grew up and afterward. However, I must say that Frank did more to shape my life and ministry than any of the others. My times with Frank were always a deeply enriching and memorable event. This visit was no exception. In a few days, I was back home and anxious to wrap things up so I could finally head to Oklahoma, enroll and get ready to take anything they dished out!

Late that July, I got the idea that since I was leaving for college in a few weeks, I should sell my half of the store to Jack. Reluctantly, he agreed, so we met with Papa and tried to set a fair price. Jack did not have much money, but the store was making a profit and he was drawing a sizable disability pension. When we bought the store, there were three framed cottages that came with the deal. Papa suggested Jack give me the cottages and $2,500.00 cash for my half. We shook on it; Jack got a loan, wrote me a check, deeded the cottages to me and the deal was "signed and sealed."

I spent the next two weeks painting and cleaning up the three frame cottages. Then Dan Cowart, known to everyone as "Mighty Fine," who owned most of the lots and cottages in Glenn Haven, offered me $7,500.00 cash for all three of them. When he asked me what I thought of the offer, I said, "Mighty fine!" I put the money in the bank and with what Jack gave me, I had over ten thousand dollars, which was a large sum in those days, especially for a young man. I have regretted all these years that I didn't offer Mama and Papa some of this money. It never even occurred to me. How callous and unfeeling are most children. Once when I mentioned this to them, Papa told me that they would not have taken a cent of it. They wanted me to use it in getting my college degrees. However, I have tried to be more understanding with my three girls, since I realized what blessings I missed by not being more loving and helpful to my beloved parents.

I was glad that my college education would not be a burden to Papa and Mama, since Papa had such a small retirement income. All veterans had the GI Bill, which paid for tuition, books and a check of over one hundred dollars a month for expenses. That check was more per month than Papa ever made during his many years of retirement. I received these benefits for a total of five and a half years. I and millions of other veterans saw this as a valuable gift provided by a grateful nation for our years of military service. What a boost to our standard of living it would have been if Uncle Sam would have listened to Lincoln and in binding up the nation's wounds would have included the widow and the orphan of those who never came home. But that was then—20/20 hindsight.

A MIRACLE A MINUTE

Now all of my time was spent getting packed for the trip to Enid, Oklahoma. I was very excited about entering college to prepare for the ministry. The six months since I had left the Army had gone by so fast that the time for my departure came before I was ready. Although school did not start until the tenth of September, I needed to arrive early to find a place to stay, take all the entrance tests and enroll for the fall term. The number of veterans entering college was so large that Phillips was hard pressed to find room for all of us. I was disappointed to learn that because of limited parking, freshmen were not allowed to bring a vehicle to the campus. Although this was difficult for me, it was for the best. I did not really need it, and Mama would now have a way to get to church. She never learned to drive, so someone had to take her. I was glad that I could leave it for her and Papa, really a small gift in return for all they had done for Jack and me, including running the store while we were in the service. Had it not been for Mama, Papa and Ed, Jack and I would have lost the store and lost a total of more than twenty thousand dollars. Mama especially worked hard and went without to save the store for us. She never received a penny in salary during all of those years, taking only the few groceries that she and Papa needed.

Leaving this time was so much easier than when I entered the Army. Jack and Sam now owned the store, and Sam, Jack, Vera and George would share in looking after Mama and Papa. Since I had been home for such a short time, Mama was not ready for me to go.

I put my arms around her that morning and said, "Mama, Jack and I can never thank you and Papa enough for everything, including running the store for us. I will always regret, though, that I did not write to you more often. I will try to do better. You were so good to write me even if I did not answer. All three of us were strengthened knowing you prayed every day and night; I truly appreciate your many prayers for me. Just think, sweet Mama, you and Pa have prayed two of your boys into the ministry. God loves you very much. Keep on praying for us. You will wear a crown full of jewels in His kingdom for all you did for all of us and for Papa."

Those years in the store and in the Army seemed to fade more and more as my mind turned toward the west, to college and to the future. I gave it little thought then, but later the fact moved in on me that this time I was leaving home for good, never to return except for short visits. I now see that day I left home as one of the watersheds of my life. But before I left, something exciting occurred that was a vital part of that watershed. I truly believe what happened next was directed by the Lord. I think you will agree.

It all came about like this: The last week of August I conducted a week's preaching mission for the little Glenn Haven Baptist Church, which met in a remodeled frame house near our home and just across the wide, sandy street from where Krista used to live. Years ago, on rainy afternoons, she and I had skated back and forth on the porch of that old frame building.

I spent most of each day praying, studying and sharing with Mama, Papa, Jack and Sam what I was going to preach each night. The services were all well attended. The meeting was to end on Saturday night, the last day of August. Since I had to leave for Enid on Sunday morning, that Saturday afternoon, feeling a bit restless and a little bored, I drove down to visit with Vera and George. They lived in a large home that was only one block from the beach.

Soon after I arrived, I realized that this beautiful day was my last opportunity to take a swim in the ocean until next summer. After we visited awhile, I changed into a swimsuit, grabbed a towel and walked to the beach. Since I had lived on the Island for ten years, I was right at home as I stood looking at the glistening white sand that stretched for miles in both directions. The sky was filled with seagulls, which came so close that I felt they were my friends. The tide was high and the sky a brilliant blue, dappled here and there with white puffy clouds that were slowly moving west.

As I waded out into the ocean, I turned and saw three girls up on the beach lying in the sun. I swam south toward the pier so I could walk back by them and check them out. I walked as close as I dared, to see if they were pretty and if they would speak. They were all cute, but they had their eyes covered and never even knew I was around. I walked back past them twice, each time coming a little closer but losing my courage to go up to them and say hello. On my last pass, I got close enough to hear the brunette laughing and talking. But I crept away, looked back, took a deep sigh and gave up.

On the way back to the house, feeling a bit weak and low, I had a little chat with Jesus, "Lord, why am I so shy and afraid? Why don't I have the courage to boldly burst in and speak to girls I've never met? After all, what could I lose, and now, drat it, I have probably missed meeting a pretty girl. Never mind, Lord, I think I'd rather be a little shy than so bold I'd drive them all away. But, it's OK, I'll try to relax and leave all this up to You."

But God was not quite finished with directing my steps. He picked the time to the second as to where I needed to be that day.

A MIRACLE A MINUTE

Back at George and Vera's, I showered and dressed. Since George had gone over to the shop, I decided to drive over to see him. So, I jumped into my new Plymouth and headed for Brunswick.

After about a half mile, I looked up and saw three girls standing off on the grass trying to hitch a ride. Hitchhiking was popular in those days and very safe. All of a sudden, I realized that these were the same girls I had seen earlier on the beach. As I neared, all three of them began to jump, yell and wave, while throwing up a thumb at me. Of course, I pulled over. In a flash, they were in the car, all talking at the same time, thanking me for stopping. The long-legged blond hopped up in front. After some idle chatter and giving our names, they told me they had just graduated from Glynn Academy. I told them that I had also graduated from there, but it was centuries ago. Glancing around at the two in the back, I saw that one was a pretty brunette with very large brown eyes.

She asked me, "What are you doing on the island?"

I answered, kinda smart-like, "I live here, but I am also doing something."

"Oh? What?"

"I am going to college to study to be a preacher—leaving tomorrow. But tonight, I am preaching the closing sermon of a meeting I have been conducting at the Glenn Haven Baptist Church. Why don't you three girls come back over tonight and get saved?"

They all cackled out loud. I said that I would be glad to take them home. The blond up front said that would not be necessary, but she would show me where to stop that was just a block from her house. So, a few minutes later, at her direction, I pulled over and stopped to let them out.

As they were walking away, I said, "Say, girls, I sure hope to see you at the Glenn Haven Baptist Church tonight at 7:30."

They made no response but did thank me for the ride. While I drove on into town, I said to myself, "I'll probably never see any of them again."

That night arrived, and I was ready for my last service. The place was packed with people, including Mama and Papa. Just as I came to the middle of my sermon, the back door opened and down the aisle walked two of the girls I had taken to Brunswick. All eyes followed them as they took the only two vacant seats, which put them on the front row, about three feet from the podium where I stood. I was delighted that they actually responded to my invitation. When I glanced down though, I saw that one was the pretty brunette with the musical laughter and huge sparkling brown eyes. That took my mind a bit off the sermon. But when she looked up at me, smiled and I saw those cascades of glistening auburn hair falling down almost to her tiny waist, well—I lost it—literally!

I knocked my sermon notes off on the floor, and because I lacked the courage to pick them up, I just stood there, blushing. After I tried awhile to wing it on through the message, seeing that I was getting nowhere, I abruptly stopped and gave the invitation for people to accept Jesus. No one moved, so I stammered out the number of the closing hymn and went over to the center aisle. I stood only two feet away from her, so close that I got a slight whiff of a heavenly fragrance. Holding her hymn book high, and glancing at me now and then, she belted out the words of the hymn in a terrific voice so beautiful that it sent chills through me. Everyone stopped singing so they could listen.

After my closing prayer, "Mighty Fine," who was the chairman of the board and the church's biggest giver, came forward and said some words of praise about me. He then received an offering to help pay my expenses to Enid. "Mighty Fine" then announced that all were invited to stay for some of his famous homemade lemonade and cake out on the lawn. I breathed a deep sigh of relief, thanking a kind God that the service was over. Most of the people stayed, including the beautiful girl and her friend. I walked over to them and told them how glad I was that they came. The pretty one then came up close to me and said that her name was Allene Hall and that she was leaving in a few days to attend Wesleyan Conservatory of Music in Macon. That was the second time I heard her speak. Her voice had a quality hard to describe, uniquely different from any I had ever heard. There on that lovely evening, while standing under the ancient live oaks, a cool breeze swaying the Spanish moss, for a fleeting moment we looked deep into each other's eyes, and I created a delightful memory. I had the strange feeling that I'd known her for a long time.

Then she opened her purse and gave me a penny postcard with her name and address on it, saying in that voice with a charming southern accent, "Now, Mr. Pippin, you won't have any excuse not to drop me a line."

I took the card and warmly shook her hand, and then I walked them to her car to say good-bye. As they drove away, I stood there, ignoring everyone around me, watching her wave her pretty arm at me out the window until she turned the corner. When the car disappeared from sight, I had the feeling that we would some day meet again. The fact that I had seen her on the beach, and then they were there on the road waiting for a ride, and then they actually came to the service—I knew all this was definitely some more of God! Just imagine, if I had driven by only minutes earlier or later, I would have missed them. My drive to town at just that precise moment and the fact that I took them home, thus bringing her into my life, led to our marriage. Later, I knew that all this was a startling miracle. But this pretty girl was not easy to catch…it took four years.

I felt good as I left the little church that night. This was the first time that I had preached every night for a whole week. I could feel the love of these people who had known me for ten years. After Mama, Papa and I got home, I sat in my bedroom and looked again at her postcard. She was still in my thoughts as I cut off the light and went to bed.

I whispered a prayer, "If we are ever to meet again, dear Lord, I know You will arrange it."

Sunday morning I tackled the many things I had to do to get ready to leave. As I was putting the last items in the big trunk that Mama gave me, she came in carrying four beautiful quilts that were stacked in her arms. She noticed the surprise on my face, smiled and said that she had a few "quilting parties" while we were in the Army and had made four each for Jack and me. I put them in the trunk, turned, took her in my arms and gave her a big hug and kiss.

"With all your work in the house and at the store, Mama, how on earth could you have found time for this?"

She answered, "It was a pleasant break from the store. Besides, love always finds time."

She had given me a lot of help in packing that week, walking around misty-eyed most of the time. She knew I had to go, but it made her sad. I shared her feelings. As we grow up, we often long to be a child again and want to be held in our mother's arms. But now, with my going, Mama had finally seen all of her children leave the nest, and she sent them all off with love, tears, prayers and four quilts! She reminded me that I was the last.

To break the mood, I said, "Mama, you know and I know that I'm your favorite child. I know you love me the most. Why don't you just admit it and be done with it!"

"Now, James, don't you start that again. You know very well that I love all nine of you the same."

We laughed, and I said as I hugged her, "Sure, Mama, sure."

Found Her on the Beach, But She Swam Away

Ed Fennel came over early to give me a hand and go to the station with George and me. He grabbed my two suitcases while George and I lugged the trunk out and placed it in the car. Papa was not able and Mama preferred not to come to the station with us. She wanted to say her good-bye at the house. Although this departure was not the same as when I left for the Army, it was still hard. For the first time, George and Ed treated me like a grownup. I guess they thought that the Army had matured me. As they put my stuff on the train, I noticed the look on George's face that confirmed what he had said earlier…he wished he were also twenty-four and could hop on board with me.

As the train pulled out, I was waving good-bye not only to them, but also saying farewell to the Golden Isles of Georgia, a paradise that had been my home for ten wonderful years. I don't know what I thought college was going to be like, but waiting up ahead was a shock for which even three and a half years in the Army had not fully prepared me.

Mama & Papa on their wedding day—1900

Mamma & Papa with Myrtle, Frank & Ray—1904

School picture, Round Oak Georgia, —1930 (Jack, James Front Row, far right)

James Pippin,
Age 16 — 1938

Arlene Hall, Age 12
(So beautiful & sweet !)

The House I grew up in,
St. Simon's — 1937-46

— 14 getting over an 18
th siege of an accident on
t knee — 1936

Me & my three sisters — 1940

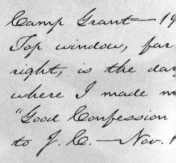

Camp Grant — 19
Top window, far
right, is the day
where I made m
"Good Confession
to J. C. — Nov. 1

Allene, age 16 — 1944
(she's wearing the wings
of a U.S. Navy Pilot!
Sorry, Lt.!)

Camp Grant — 194

Camp Grant — 1944

J. C. Lovett — 1944

C J.C. in front of our
"little house. in the field"
1944

Here are the Six Pippin Brothers: only
time all are seen in a Pix together.
(Front Row: Ray, Fred & Frank. Back Row: George,
Jack & James Pippin —1944

My good ole roommate,
Bob Book & me —1948

"Hot Stuff!"
My new 1950 C(
"Rocket V8."

Bathing Beauties — 1946
(Allene is 2nd from the right)

The one cent postcard Allene gave me. (I lost it, but it reappeared ten years later!)

The picture of Allene in N.Y.C. I carried in my wallet for years — 1951

THIS SIDE OF CARD IS FOR ADDRESS

Allene Hall
1923 Norwich St.
Brunswick, Ga.

Radio City Music Hall — 1951

Mama & Papa Pipp
on their 50th
Anniversary (Las
photo taken of
them)—
Sept 18, 1950

Frank at
"Ten Acres" with
my new Olds in the
background—1950

Front of old Cam
Creek Primitive
Baptist Church
where Brother
Williamson preache
"Peter do you love
me?" & wore Papa
seersucker suit!
— 1928

Three "Pippin
preacher brothers,"
James, George &
Frank—1951

Julia, Frank's Daughter
& Allene—1951

Our wedding day—
May 5th, 1951

Photo taken of [...]
by Billy — 195[...]

Two proud grads
— June, 1953

At Ozelle's
funeral From
left: Ray,
Myrtle, Fran[...]
Annabell &
George (I'm [...]
the back row[...]

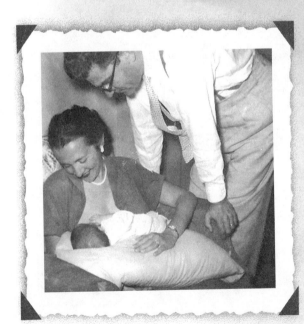

Allene Nu[...]
Janet — 19[...]

First Christian Church
FALLS CHURCH, VIRGINIA

Me, Allene & her mom.
(Allene, age 29)
— 1957

After church at
Falls Church Va,
August, 1960

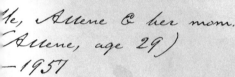

Capital Area
Christian Church
Convention: Me,
Charlie Bayer,
Bill Hogevoll &
Chester Barnett.
All impacted my
life! — 1957

Me, Janet &
Anne, "Our
Babies" —
1958

Our first trip to the *Holy Land* "The Trip of a Lifetime" — 1960

Miami Church Convention. Aunt Al across from Frank —1961

Maj. James Pippin with his 1961 280SE —May 1962

Arlene singing at the
Art Opera Theater
—1963

Our last Sunday
at Falls Church,
Virginia—Feb, 1964

Our New Home in
Oklahoma City
—1964

This is the
church in
Oklahoma City
that I served
—1964-1972

Church of Tomorrow

❊ 15 ❊

Allene Turns Me Down;
Enter Oral

The train ride from Brunswick to Enid, Oklahoma, seemed
short because I brought along a very interesting book titled
Roads to Knowledge. It briefly covered the major fields of study
included in the bachelor's degree and gave me a overview of the path
I was going to take for the next four years. I arrived at Enid in the late
afternoon. Two porters on the train helped me unload my luggage.
When the train pulled out, I looked around for a taxi, but I didn't see
one. Worse than that, there was not a living person in sight.

Then, all of a sudden, a tall, handsome man came around the
corner of the depot, shouting, "Hello, my name is A. C. Cuppy. I am
a graduate student at Phillips. I guess the person I was supposed to
meet missed the train. Here, let me help you with those. I'll give you
a lift to the campus."

I thought he was an angel, but he was at least a miracle! I expressed
my thanks, saying that he was a godsend. On the ride out to the
campus he shared with me what to expect these first few weeks and
even this first year. He pulled up to the registrar's building and told
me to sign in there and find out where I was to stay. In a few minutes I
was back in his car, directing him to the home of Roscoe Babcock,
only a block from the campus. Roscoe descended from the attic of his
house and gave us a hand in getting all my gear up those steep stairs. I
said "thanks much" to A. C., and he said, "Don't mention it!" and left.

I had to share the long narrow attic room with Roscoe. He said
that my bed was on the right and his on the left. They were separated
about six feet. He then led me downstairs to the only bathroom,
telling me on the way that his mother and a single sister lived down
there. He handed me a card that listed the times when I could use the
bath! After I had supper at the school snack shop, I discovered as I

unpacked and got ready for bed that the only place you could stand up in the attic was in the middle of the room. When I got in bed, I could reach up and touch the slanting ceiling that was only two feet away from my face.

The next morning I arose, shaved, dressed, had breakfast in the school cafeteria and began my first day of seven years of college. The beautiful but very windy morning was spent enrolling in the College of the Bible and taking the battery of entrance tests. After lunch, I was handed my schedule for the first semester. My dear Lord, it was worse than basic training and almost as bad as the regimen of Providence College.

Two years of Greek were mandatory for the AB degree. "No Greek, No degree!" So my first class in college was Greek, Monday through Friday at 7:00 A.M.! The first day of class the room was full, so I took a seat on the window sill. Instructor Sheldon Shirts, a graduate student and teaching fellow, assured me that there would be plenty of seats in three days because 20 percent of the class would fail his first test and be dropped. Just as he predicted, he gave the test, 20 percent failed, and I got a seat.

That Greek class is not easy to describe. I hated it…a lot, but I disliked the teacher more. At that ungodly hour of the morning, his voice sounded like he was talking under water, like he had not even had a cup of coffee, much less breakfast. I could tell that he probably didn't even drink coffee! (You know, one of those!) Swallowing those Greek lectures was much like taking Mama's castor oil, plain and right out of the bottle. Even worse, it was like having to take it every day. Although his assignments took two or three hours of preparation each night, I had no thought of quitting. I set my jaw, bit the bullet and almost lost my religion before I got those two years behind me. After Greek, all the other courses were a snap. Those first two semesters were like two years at Camp Grant—out in the field—on maneuvers—all in the dead of winter. Taking Greek was the same as drinking eight glasses of water a day. If you didn't drink any that first day, you'd have sixteen to gulp down the second day. Miss three days of homework, and you'd be outta there.

I got so sick of trying to do four hours of homework each night on translation and grammar that I had a chat with Mr. Shirts after class one day. I put him on notice that I only wanted to make a C-minus in his Greek class. I wanted him to notify me if I got up to a C so I could lighten up. After he grinned and shook his head, I asked him if he would give me a C-minus if I aced all of his vocabulary tests. He gave us fifty words in Greek during every class, and we had to give their meaning in English. He agreed but told me that I could not ace them all. Now, it wasn't easy; I could only miss two words and still get an A. I boned up on the meaning of the Greek words and aced all of those tests. I still know the meaning of hundreds of Greek words today because of that deal I made with Mr. Shirts (now Dr. Shirts). It also gave me more time to study for my other classes. I do believe that first year was the hardest year of all of my years in college. I could see that I was in for a very long haul.

But, thank God, things brightened up during the second semester. It happened the day I sat down on the front row in Mrs. Hale's psychology class. Next to me sat a tall, muscular, good-looking guy with straight black hair, a large jaw, high cheekbones and a mouth full of shiny white teeth.

I turned to him before class started and said, "My name is James Pippin, what's yours?"

"Oral."

"Oral? That your first name or your last name?"

I had never heard that name before. I thought his last name might be "Hygiene."

He said, "My last name is Roberts, and don't make fun of my name, pal. My mama named me Oral because it was prophesied that I was to be an oracle for God, called to preach the gospel of Jesus Christ and to bring His healing power to my generation."

Wow! Was that a mouthful! Oral Roberts. That name meant absolutely nothing to me. You see, he and I both were nobodies in those days.

Oral then said, "Pippin, what are *you* doing up here?" He said it as if I shouldn't even *be* in college. That shows what a great impression I made on *him*.

I told him, "I am up here trying to find God."

He turned, placed his hand on my arm and whispered, "I've got God. What do you want from God?"

I replied, "I am looking for the Holy Spirit."

He said, "Praise God, I've got the Holy Ghost. Let's go to my church and pray."

"Now, wait just a minute, Oral. After class let's go get a cup of coffee and talk this thing over," was my answer.

I highly suspected that when he wanted to drop everything and go pray that he was a "Penney-costial" of whom I was taught to be afraid.

However, after class, at his insistence, we were on our way to his church. As we drove up, sure enough there it was on a big sign: "The Enid Pentecostal Holiness Church. Oral Roberts, Pastor."

Even my experience with J.C. Lovett and the Nazarenes could never prepare me for this. We went in, and he led me straight to the prayer room, which must have been a converted bathroom because when he and I got in there the room was full. Then he looked at me, smiled, slipped down out of his chair and knelt beside me. He put one hand on my knee and one up in the air, just like J.C. Lovett. I became real jumpy. I just knew that any minute he was going to break out into that holiness jibber-jabber and scare me flat to death. We were taught as children that these people were called "Holy Rollers" because they would fall down in the sawdust and roll. They were even known to froth at the mouth. We were also warned that if we got any of that froth on us we would catch leprosy.

So I said, my voice trembling, "Oral, please sit back up here in the chair and listen. I have a piece of good advice for you."

He smiled, shook his head and came back up into his chair.

"Now, I want you to pay attention, Oral. You need to separate yourself from these Holiness, tongue-talkin', folks. If you don't, you and your wife are surely going to starve. You'll wind up in a little bitty church in the poor part of town and have to pass the offering plate around twice just to buy yall's lunch on Sunday."

He countered, glancing quickly around the room, "Naw, you're so wrong, Pippin. I'm dropping out after this year and going to Tulsa."

"Oral, whatever, pray tell, is in Tulsa? Stay here with me and let's get us two or three college degrees and go out and make a name for ourselves."

He retorted, "Look, pal, my mind's made up. Say, Pippin, I feel led to ask you to come with me, be my platform man, help me with my ministry."

I didn't know a thing about building platforms, so I turned him down.

Whenever I give my testimony, I usually say at this point, "You know what? Oral would not listen to me. He went on off to Tulsa, but I stayed in school, got my college degrees and went out and made a name for myself. I never heard very much about *him* after that. Does anybody here know anything about what happened to this Oral Roberts fellow?"

Of course, this always brings a good laugh. Not at Oral, but at this foolish author. For everyone knows that he became the preacher who started a worldwide healing ministry when there were few, if any, who had the faith or the courage to do this in those days.

Although I avoided letting him "pray me into the Holy Ghost" that day, what a great time Oral and I always had together. When our teacher, Mrs. Hale, was sick or out of town speaking, she would turn her class over to Oral and me. We'd take turns or team teach and believe me, we kept that entire class in an uproar. But they learned a lot and we all had a ball in the process. I wish you could have been there. No one would dare be absent. Prof. Hale must have been a Christian or a "crazy pagan" to turn that class over to us two preachers!...And she was gone quite a lot.

Oral was not only very intelligent, but he was also clever and right down to earth funny. He always introduced *me* to folks as the funniest man on earth. And, O my soul, was Oral one dynamic speaker?! From the first day I met him in class, we enjoyed each other immensely. He and I became real buddies. He was the best preacher I ever heard, except for, maybe, my brother Frank! We all missed him and Evelyn after they left for Tulsa.

Often when I am in the audience where he is preaching, he will have Allene and me stand and say among other things, "Dr. James Pippin here is the only person who can vouch that I was ever in a college classroom."

I probably passed up the chance of a lifetime when I turned him down and did not join his ministry. Then I would really have made a name for myself, right?!

Later, Oral and Evelyn and Allene and I became close friends, and we have remained so through these past fifty years. Yes, Oral and Evelyn did go to Tulsa, and from there they not only went out to conduct healing crusades all over the world, but also the Lord directed him to return to Tulsa and build Oral Roberts University and the City of Faith, possibly the two greatest Christian institutions of higher learning and healing on this earth. And to think it all started one night in 1947 at the Education Building in the little town of Enid, Oklahoma! Just wait awhile, for we will surely return to Oral and Evelyn.

My first three years at Phillips were spent taking all the required courses such as Old and New Testament, English grammar and composition, ancient and modern history, speech, debate, homiletics, Christian education, psychology, geology and electives—advanced grammar, voice lessons and The Phillips Chorus. As an undergraduate,

I took about eighteen hours each semester and double-majored in psychology and history.

You will remember that I chose to join the U.S. Army Reserve when I was discharged in February, 1946. I was told to find a unit and become an active member within a year after I was settled in college. So, in the fall of 1947, I found a Reserve unit meeting at the armory in downtown Enid, the 325th Hospital Train that had served in World War II, with honors. I met with Colonel Mark Holcomb, the commandant, who was delighted to have me aboard. We met one night a week during the school term only, hearing lectures, seeing films that briefed us on the origin and operation of a hospital train. When my records were received by the unit, I found that I had been promoted to staff sergeant. Staff has one rocker beneath the three stripes of the buck. A few of the men from Phillips joined, some of whom had not served in World War II. Although we received no pay, we were given points toward retirement for each meeting attended, which also added to our time in service. Being in the unit gave us a refreshing change from campus life and kept our knowledge of the Army current.

The students attending the College of the Bible were given a two-week break at Christmas and Easter and had all summer off. One of the main events before the Christmas break was the annual presentation by the head of the drama department, Dr. O'Berg, of Dickens' *A Christmas Carol*. He always gave this masterpiece the morning before Christmas break. His performance was so outstanding that we all left the campus with a heart full of the glowing spirit of Christmas as we began our journey home immediately after he finished. Often it was snowing as we made our departure. I had never felt "peace, joy and good-will toward men" ever so strongly as I did on those pre-Christmas days at Phillips University.

After our finals in late May, we were dismissed for the three months of summer. I spent the first two summers at home searching for my dream girl, who had vanished. What caused me to lose touch and made my search so difficult was that I lost the penny postcard she gave me. And worse yet, for the life of me, I could not even remember her name. Nor could I find any help from other people who were there that night she came to church. Vera told me early that first summer to forget that other person. She wanted me to meet this lovely girl who was singing on the radio every weekday. She did not know her name. Anyway, I was not interested. Besides, she could never measure up to the lost girl of my dreams who had attended my meeting.

A MIRACLE A MINUTE

The second summer I was home, Vera started in on me again. I let her know in no uncertain terms that I would never be satisfied until I found my gorgeous brunette, the girl on the beach who was interested enough to attend my meeting and give me the postcard.

One day Vera got put out with me and said firmly, "Well, James, why don't you at least go over there to the radio station and find out who this girl is. I think I heard her introduced as Allene Hall. Go see her and forget that dream girl."

I replied, "Not a chance; that's a waste of time."

Well, I admit that after two long years, I was about ready to give up, feeling I had lost her and would never see her again. How many days had I thought of her and how many nights had I prayed for the Lord to help me find her? I dated several girls at college, but I kept contrasting them with her. I felt it was a miracle that our paths had crossed; feeling that God was in it. The beach, the ride to town and her coming to hear me preach—I kept on reminding God that it was not all by accident.

One afternoon, in late August, 1948, with only one week left before I had to return to Phillips, something unexpected happened while I was in Brunswick helping George box orders at his wholesale leather store. It was hot and I needed a break, so I walked next door to the Gulf filling station, got a cold Dr. Pepper and went outside to enjoy the cool breeze. I was leaning against the brick wall at the front of the station, watching the traffic go by and feeling very lonely. I finished the drink, turned and placed the empty bottle into the crate, and started to walk away. Just at that instant, I saw out of the corner of my eye a 1941 Ford convertible driving in for gas. There was a little girl about two years old standing up in the front seat.

The driver, a beautiful brunette, with huge brown eyes, stopped, leaned out the window and said, "Well, hello, Mr. Pippin. Remember me?"

Did I remember her? How could I ever forget her? But, O my Lord, I just could not remember her name. But that voice, that face, those eyes and that hair I could never forget. This was the miracle of miracles! I could hardly contain myself. I had known that someday I would find her, so I never gave up and God finally came through with an answer to my many prayers.

"You are the girl who came to my meeting two years ago! Do you know I have searched everywhere for you since that night? My, it is so good to see you again. I am so ashamed to admit that I lost your card."

"Yes, I am that girl. My name is Allene Hall and I am a voice major. I've had my own radio program all summer."

I whispered to myself, "Singing on the radio all summ—lovely girl—why, that's the very person that Vera—O my great good Lord!"

Then I quickly glanced over at the little girl standing beside her. Suddenly, a terrible sickness hit me in the pit of my stomach as the thought flashed into my mind, "Woe is me! She is already married and this is her child!"

My heart was in my throat when I asked, "Is this your little girl?"

"Oh no, this is my sister Lucille's child, Peggy. I am just taking her out for a little ride," she said.

I wanted to jump in the car and hug and kiss that little child a million times. I felt like jumping *over* the car and running around the station barking like a wild dog! But I quickly took control of myself.

While the station attendant filled her car with gas, I brought them Cokes.

Standing there, trembling, I blurted out, "I am leaving in a few days to return to school. Would you like to go out to dinner and a movie tonight? Maybe we could take up the conversation where we left off that night a couple of years ago!"

She smiled and said, "Well, I think maybe that can be arranged. Mama has a dinner planned tonight for the family, but we can still catch that movie. Why don't you drop by the house—about eight?"

Although my hand was trembling and sweaty, I shook hers and said, "That's a date! I'll see you at eight! Bye-bye, Allene Hall. Bye-bye, you precious miracle child, Peggy!"

After she pulled out, I ran back to the store, shouting to Vera and George, "Hey, you will not believe this! I have just found my dream girl. And, guess what…her name really is Allene Hall! I thought I would never see that girl again."

I hugged them both so hard you'd think I hadn't seen them for years. I was talking so fast they had to slow me down to understand what I was saying.

I said half laughing, half crying, "Vera, you have been right all this time! God was shouting at me through you and I would not listen. O praise the Lord, praise the Lord! He's been trying to answer my prayer for two years, and can you imagine, this stupid dummy would not listen."

I grabbed their hands and started dancing around the store in a circle like a crazy person. She, George and I laughed so hard our jaws ached.

A MIRACLE A MINUTE

As I left, I was still laughing and kept saying over and over going to my car, "Thank You, Jesus, thank You, Jesus. God is good, God is so good. God, You are so very good! Thank You, heavenly Father, for answering my prayer."

I had to slow down over and over on the way home because I was in such a hurry to get there and share it all with Mama and Papa. I wanted to get out at every stop light and crawl up on top of the car and shout to every person: "I have found my dream girl! I lost her for two long years. Her name is Allene Hall! And I'm in love! Allene Hall…and I'm in LUUUUVE!"

The tall pines were more stately, their fragrance more pleasant than I ever noticed. There at the junction of Fredericka Road and Sea Island Drive, I caught the exhilarating breeze from the sea, bringing with it a refreshing whiff of the ocean with its sweet smell of salt. I glanced to the side and looked deep into the woods filled with live oaks swaying in the breeze, and hanging from them, the ancient Spanish Moss looking like girls with lovely hair, waving their heads gently in the wind. I was in a new world created by love, and a love created by God!

As I got ready at the house for that movie date I had waited so long for, I had never showered so thoroughly, never shaved so closely, never brushed my teeth so hard. I'm sure it is no surprise to you that I was there a little before eight and met her mother, Lucille, and her dad, Henley. They operated the beautiful "Hall's Guest Home" on Gloucester Street. Her mother especially made me feel at home when she asked me all about myself. They already knew George and Papa several years earlier.

Before long, "Miss Allene, Miss Allene, the prettiest girl I'd ever seen" came down the stairs and stood at the entrance to the living room. Dressed in a short black skirt, a fitted white blouse, black hose and heels, she looked like Elizabeth Taylor.

In a warm, melodic voice she said, "I'm ready to go, Mr. Pippin."

Her mother graciously walked us to the door, then turned to me and said, "It's so nice meeting you, Mr. Pippin. We hope to see you again before you go back to college."

"Thank you, ma'am. I hope so, too. Goodnight to you, and to you, Mr. Hall."

In a moment, we were in the car on the way to—we didn't know where. We learned that the last show began at 7:45, so we decided to just ride around and maybe stop for a Coke. Also, I had to leave in five nights, so I made her promise that she would give me a date every night until I left. On those six summer evenings of joy, we talked of how we met, my preaching service and the lost postcard. We got around to talking about the highlights of our pasts. Each night we seemed to get closer together. I played my courting cards right and waited until the second date to kiss her goodnight. I was so much in love with her, but I wouldn't dare let her know, for fear that I'd chase her away. Those nights flew by, but on our last night I made her promise to come home for Christmas.

So the long summer was ended, and I had to return to Phillips, she to Wesleyan; we both were beginning our junior years. I discovered that I was completely smitten by this girl. She was everything I had ever hoped for, dreamed of and prayed for. I knew she was *the one*, but did she feel that way about me? I found out soon enough.

Back at Phillips, Allene and I kept in touch through occasional letters and phone calls. But she had never even hinted that she missed me, was fond of me or especially that she loved me.

"I'll be home for Christmas" could not come soon enough. That thrilling week we had several delightful dates. On my last night there, I took her to dinner, winding up at Fort Fredericka. There we parked facing the river, under a canopy of moss-covered oaks, watching the moon touch the horizon over the marshes to the west. She laid her pretty head on my shoulder. I lifted her face up to mine and gently kissed her, and then I did something very stupid and premature.

I took a deep sigh, got up my courage, and whispered, "Allene."
"Yes?"
"Allene, I love you."
Now why didn't I just stop right there? But no, I had to go and say, "Will you marry me?"

I could tell by the look in those tragic eyes that I had blown it! Yep, she turned me down. I put my head on the steering wheel and tried to hold back the tears. First, she just sat there looking at me with a look of confusion!

Finally, she put her hand on my arm and said, "James, please don't take this so hard. I like you very much, but I'm not interested in getting married right now. I've got to finish college, and after that I'd really like to pursue a singing career in New York City."

I said, "Oh, I understand all that. It's just that…I care for you. I'm sure that this is all kind of sudden and unexpected for you. But it's OK. I'm sure I'll live."

We both gave a little nervous chuckle. Since it was getting late, I drove back to her house. When I walked her to the door, she turned, came up close and warmly kissed me good-bye.

While still holding me, she said, "James, I'm very fond of you and sorry if I hurt you, but I have to put this matter of marriage on hold for a while. I cannot make anyone a good wife unless I get this singing career out of my system."

She then made me promise to keep in touch by letter and phone.

On my way home, I thought, "You were doing fine, Stupid! Why did you rush her and ruin it?"

Before I got home, I felt a little better, but I figured she was only letting me down easy. So I had some serious talking to do with Jesus about "this matter of marriage" as she put it. I reminded Him of all that had happened between us, which seemed like a miracle to me.

I closed the prayer with, "Lord, I know You know best. But as soon as You can, would You please tell me just what is going on: Am I losing my girl?"

The next morning I felt depressed as I left for Enid, but on the way there I decided that I must get on with my life. It helped my spirits when I picked up the three students in Birmingham who were riding back with me to Phillips. So I began the new year feeling better, with a new dedication to school and a resolution for the new year. Thinking of the positive, I reminded myself that I had finished Greek, gotten a larger place to stay at Mom Berg's house and just finished enrolling in some great courses. I was again with the Army Reserve, now as a staff sergeant. I was also cheered up when my roommate, Bob Book, and close friends, Bill Howland, Bob Fudge and Jim Spainhower, took me out to dinner on my birthday, January 19.

Later that night as I lay in my twin bed out in our small screened-in bedroom, I felt very much alone. Bob Book was already sound asleep, but sleep held no interest for me. I clasped my hands behind my head and stared up into the darkness. I decided it was time to have a real serious talk with the Lord.

I said, "Lord Jesus, since my request for a good woman to go with me in this calling has been put on hold, and it may be years or never that we get together, I need to do something to bring me closer to You. You know, Lord, I think I would really feel much happier if You would help me get a church that would give me a place to preach on Sunday. However, Lord, I know student churches are reserved for seniors and seminary students. I know this is going to take a miracle, since I am only a junior and winter is not the time when they assign churches. But even so, nothing is too hard for You, so I earnestly pray for You to step in and help me."

Then on Monday afternoon I got up my courage and made an appointment. I went trembling in to see Dean England to ask him, of all things, to find me a student church. I just knew he was going to tell me not to waste his time.

I was prepared for his answer, "I am sorry, Jim, but you are still a junior and anyways, there are no churches available."

In class, it was "Mr. Pippin," but in his office it was "Jim."

"Besides," he continued, "you know that we usually assign the churches in the fall."

I then pleaded my case, "I know that, Dean, but I am six years older than most of the other juniors, I have a car, two years of college behind me and with my business and army experience, I feel I am ready to preach. I've just got to preach somewhere. I'll take anything."

"Well, hmmm," he smiled and rubbed his chin. "It has just occurred to me that we do have this one little church over at Marland, near Ponca City. Now, it's been closed for years, so don't get your hopes up too much. The former members have been going in to First Church, Ponca, on Sundays. But I got word just the other day that if the right person came along, they might try to open it up again. I think you may be just what they need. If you decide you want to do this, I'll phone one of the elders and see if they want you to come over there and give it a try. You go and pray and think this over and…"

I almost rudely cut him off. I came to the edge of my chair and said, "Dean, I already prayed hard about this. I want to do it! I promise, you won't be sorry. I'll give it my best."

He smiled, and while he was nodding his head, I stood up, reached across his big, blond oak desk, shook his hand and bolted out of the office, walking on air.

On Wednesday morning Dean stopped me in the hall to tell me that he had called and, guess what, the church wanted me to come on over and start services *this coming Sunday!* I whispered, "Thank You, Lord, for answering my fervent prayer." Then Dean asked me to come with him to his office. He first told me that he had highly recommended me. I grinned broadly and thanked him. Then he gave me the names of two of the leading families, the Murrays and the Yates, told me how to get there and, sorry, but they could only pay me twenty dollars a week.

I smiled at him and said, "Aw, Sir, that's no problem; I'll go for nothing."

"No, no, no" he said as he stood, "they will appreciate you more, Jim, if they have to pay you."

That was not the first of the many lessons I was taught by our great and learned Dean England. He was almost always quite formal, but he had a heart of gold. I liked him even better when I found out that earlier in his life, not only had he been an infantry captain, but he also came very close to making the Army a career. He and I were much closer after that day in his office.

My ministry at the Marland Christian Church began on the last Sunday of January, 1949. On that Saturday morning, I had almost driven right through the town when I noticed that I was about to pass Marland altogether. A little boy on his bicycle told me how to get to the church. It was one block off the main road.

As I drove away, he yelled, "Hey feller, there's no one there, and you won't like it 'cause it's dirty and been closed for years."

Thanks, little friend, for that warm welcome to Marland!

Yes, the church was closed all right, and I did not like it. The ancient frame building was boarded up, and there were waist-high weeds all around it. I sighed deeply but thanked the Lord anyway. I managed to pry open the front door. I shouldn't have, because when I got a look inside, I wanted to get in my car and race back to Enid. But then I heard myself saying to Dean, "I'll take anything." From the middle of the room all that could be seen was the half inch of dust that covered the wooden pews, the chancel and the big pulpit in the center. A green, threadbare rug ran down the center aisle. So, this was my First Christian Church!

I sat down on the steps of the chancel on an old newspaper, placed my face in both hands and began to pray. Suddenly, I looked up and saw that the front door was being pushed open. A rather large man in overalls was slowly walking up the aisle. He was Buster Yates, owner of the only grocery store and filling station in town. He got me out of there and took me to his house. There he presented his wife Annie, who made us a much appreciated pot of coffee and a large glass of cool cistern water. After I got a thorough briefing, the best news he had for me was that most of the twenty adult members were scheduled to arrive soon to "help me" get the place ready for church in the morning. We finished our coffee, and he, Annie and I drove over to the church where I met ten of the members. We all hit that dirty old building like a tornado, and in a few hours, it was all done and ready for our first service. After I showered and went to supper with the crew, the Yates put to bed a very tired but very happy, young preacher.

Allene Turns Me Down; Enter Oral

Sunday morning they all showed up, plus their kids and a few relatives and friends. We had a great service. They had forgotten to tune the old upright piano, but they promised that it would be fixed before next Sunday.

That day began a ministry that lasted two years. It was a great blessing to me and was the first time I felt like a real preacher. Every Sunday after church, a group or a couple would take me in to Ponca for lunch. It was only fifteen miles away from the church.

On the way over there one Sunday, I looked out at the green fields of new wheat and asked them, "What are all those small dark green circles out there?"

They all just looked at each other and laughed. Reford Murray said he would tell me later.

In the men's room at the cafe, he explained, "Brother James, the cows feed on the new wheat and that is where they fertilized the wheat, with...you get the idea." I got it, but I was still red-faced over it!

Often, I was invited to have lunch in one of their homes. When I came over on Saturdays, I spent the night with one of the families, most often at Reford and Myrtle Murray's home. In the next few months, I called on almost every house in sight, so the attendance doubled. The church was kept clean, but it sure needed fixing up, badly.

Although I am not a Mason now, God used it then to great advantage. When they found out that I was a Master Mason, the men, who were almost all Masons, took me over to Guthrie and paid my way through the Scottish Rite, which advanced me to a 32nd degree Mason. (Since then, I have rejected Masonry completely and have renounced my affiliation with the Masons.) The women, not to be outdone, invited me to become a member of the Eastern Star. Later some of them may have regretted this. For when I saw the Masonic Hall, I noticed it was royally decorated with a new ceiling, beautiful carpet, new drapery and cushions in the oak pews. I couldn't be too elated because of the stark contrast between the Lodge and the sad shape our little church was in, inside and outside.

The next time we had a board meeting, I warmly but with some firmness, declared with a smile, that they seemed to think much more of the Masonic Hall than they did of God's house.

Then I clinched the matter by adding, "It is hard for me to come to church on Sunday after a Saturday night meeting of the Masons or the Eastern Star and see the drab place we have to worship God in. What do you good people think ought to be done about this?"

The very next weekend, I was surprised to come into the sanctuary and see that the entire place had been almost completely redone. They had taken up an offering at a special board meeting during the week and all pitched in, not only with the money for the materials, but they also donated all their labor and fixed it up almost as good as the Hall. Several of the men were painters, the hardware store contributed the paint, and in three days they painted the whole church inside and outside and put new plush, carpet down the aisle. And to surprise me, they did almost all of it in one week!

Man, the next Sunday I preached to that bunch of sweet people a better sermon than I ever thought I could. I even amazed myself. From that day, I knew I had me a real church and that little church had them a greatly inspired super-preacher! However, I am only too ready to give all the credit to Christ. It was their love for Him, more than their love for me, that brought that staggering "Miracle on Church Street" in little old Marland, Oklahoma. I believe that with a powerful God and a loving preacher, this kind of faith in action can be found in any church, anywhere, by anyone.

Frank's famous quote, which I often repeat came to mind, "Faith makes all things possible; love makes all things easy."

I wish I had the space to list all of their good names and all of the kind things they did for me. You will be thrilled to learn that later this little church continued to grow, and when my good friend Charles Bayer followed me there, he took the church to even higher levels of service. That church went from being a closed, abandoned building to one of the best student churches in Oklahoma, which included the beautiful sanctuary and more Sunday school rooms.

Phillips University's program of student churches, which were served mainly by seniors and students in the graduate seminary, greatly strengthened the total Christian Church in Oklahoma, Kansas and Texas. Along with this, all of the graduates, both men and women, became more effective ministers because of their service to the student churches. Those patient, loving people accepted us as we were—green and rough around the edges—and lovingly put up with our immaturity. At the very least, we learned what not to do or say, and that love can make all problems go away.

One night in the spring of 1949, I got a phone call from Jack saying that he needed me to come and stay with him a few days. Months earlier, he and Sam had sold the store at the Island and moved to Albany, Georgia, where he bought a combination shoe repair and hat cleaning shop. He had learned to repair shoes and clean and block hats, even with his injured left arm. He was a hardworking owner/manager and had some good help, so the shop, which was located downtown on busy Main Street, was doing very well. In south Georgia we all called Albany "All-benny." It was such a classy, little city that they gave it the nickname "Little New York," because a lot of the businesses there were owned by people from New York City.

As soon as I finished talking with Jack, I called George and learned that Jack had started drinking, a lot, and was talking about suicide. When Jack phoned me that night, he was sobbing as he shared his problems. Because of his heavy drinking, Sam had taken the two children and gone to her parents. He begged me to come to Albany to be with him and try to get Sam to come back home. I told him I'd be there the next afternoon.

I was excused from school, found a guest preacher for my church and was on a plane to Atlanta early the next morning. Jack met me, and I drove us back to Albany. He was in bad shape, he needed a bath and a shave, but I was most shocked when I discovered he was carrying around a loaded sawed-off shotgun on the back seat of his car, threatening to kill himself. I spent every moment right by his side, got him showered and shaved, went to eat with him, watched him at the shop when he was sober enough to be there, and slept in the same room with him at his house. When I managed to get the shotgun away from him the first night, I hid gun and the shells separately.

He sobered up in the next two days, so I called Sam. She told me that he had broken all of his promises over and over. I pled with her to give him just one more chance. He stayed sober the third day, so her daddy, who was Rev. Glenn, a dedicated Methodist missionary to China, drove her and the two children back to Albany. I spent my last night there with them and we all had a great time. Before we retired for the evening, I prayed with them, asking that all would be forgiven and all now would be okay. The next morning Jack, Sam and the two kids, Danny and Martha Ann, took me to Atlanta to catch my plane. Jack looked like a new person, and I prayed that he would stay straight.

When I arrived back in Enid that night, I called Sam, and everything there seemed all right. However, two months later I learned that Jack had started drinking again, so Sam told him that she was going to leave him for good.

Then one night about the last of May, after I had trudged home from the library in a downpour of rain and bounded up the stairs to my room, I heard the phone ringing. It was Brother George with bad news. Recently, on a Friday afternoon, Jack had left his shop and went next door to the barbershop to get a shave. He had been drinking all day, and as he was leaving the barbershop, he picked up a straight razor and hid it in his inside coat pocket. He went home and persuaded Sam to go for a ride so they could talk. He pulled over on a country road and stopped. He took her hand and told her how much he loved her; he said that if she left him, he was going to kill himself.

Then he took out the razor and told her that he was going to use the razor to do it. Well, Sam must have thought he was going to use it on her, so she tried to get out of the car and when Jack reached for her, the razor slightly nicked the side of her neck. She started screaming, jumped out of the car, ran down the road and was picked up by a couple passing by. The police found Jack and took him to jail. The charge: attempted murder!

George said that his trial was coming up the first week of June, and Mama, Papa, Sam and her family wanted Frank and me to be there for it. I drove home, then picked up Frank and Annabelle in Jesup, and we drove together to Albany. The next morning Frank testified on the witness stand that Jack was an Air Force first lieutenant who was wounded while he served in India. Frank said that after Jack had almost lost his left arm, he started drinking to ease the pain. He added that while Jack had recently confessed to being an alcoholic, Frank did not think that Jack had really planned to harm Sam. However, for the sake of Sam the children's safety and for Jack's own benefit, he asked the judge to give Jack a light sentence so he could stay away from alcohol and get his life straightened out.

The judge warmly agreed and reduced a higher sentence to five years in prison. Jack was sent to the Georgia State Penitentiary in Newnan. There, he soon won over the warden and the guards, was put in charge of the commissary, edited the prison newsletter, and was made a trustee. All of his brothers and sisters who lived in Georgia visited him frequently. Frank visited him twice, and I went several times that summer.

Once, on my way home from Phillips, I had three guys and a girl riding with me to help with the expenses. It was a low-cost way for them to get home, and I needed the company. We always drove straight through to save the cost of a motel. As we passed through Tupelo, Mississippi, we stopped for breakfast, and while they drank their second cup of coffee, I stepped next door to get a shave. I walked in and took a seat. The barber came over, threw the cape around my neck, slapped the lather on my face and grabbed his straight razor. He was going to shave me without "stropping" the razor or without putting a hot towel on and a second lather. As he leaned over to begin,

I smelled whiskey strong on his breath.

I raised up to get out of the chair and he pushed me back down, "shaying," "Get back down there, Shunny, I'm a gonna shave ya."

I responded, "That's what you think!"

I sprung out of the chair, dropping the cape as I ran into the street. A few doors away, I saw another shop and headed there with the shaving cream still on my face. Only one problem, I had to go by the coffee shop where my gang was. I ran by and glanced in just in time to see them all pointing at me, bent over with laughter. As I entered the shop, all the barbers looked at me, and they started laughing.

Then one of them said, "Come on in, Son, and have a seat; you are the third person today that's run in here from that shop—already lathered!" More laughter.

They explained that he was the shop owner and the town drunk. After I got the much-needed shave, I rounded up the gang. As we were on our way, I told my passengers what had happened. Of course, there was more laughter, all at my expense.

That night, I took a short detour out of Atlanta and went to Newnan to keep my appointment to see Jack. I left my riders on the square of downtown Newnan at about eleven o'clock. I got to the prison about an hour late, and there sat Jack in the kitchen, reading a book and waiting for me. The kitchen was outside the fence; no guards were present. I walked in, and he gave me a big hug. Looking over on the stove, I saw that he had a great big steak, with potatoes, biscuits, gravy and coffee all being kept hot for me. While I ate the delicious steak, washed the biscuits and gravy down with several cups of coffee, he began to talk.

He told me, tearfully, how much he loved and missed Sam and the kids. Then he spoke of the prison life and what all he did there. We had over an hour together. He looked great, had lost weight and had proven to be a model inmate. I suggested that he read *The Harvard Classics* while he was in there. He asked for me to get him a set and said he would read them all. I gave him strong encouragement, stressing that none of us believed that he intended to harm Sam. I also expressed how proud we all were of his outstanding record while he was there. We had a long prayer, and when I finally tore myself away, I left closer to Jack than ever before. He walked me to the car, hugged me and said he loved me. I said, "Ditto," and we both had a laugh, remembering Lawson. As I left, I glanced at the rearview mirror and Jack was standing there alone, waving. There was still no guard in sight. I fervently thanked the Lord that he was that trusted, knowing that this made his stay there much easier.

I arrived back at the square and saw that my riders were all slumped in a doorway, sound asleep. They wanted to know where in the world I'd been, so I told them I had visited with my sick brother. By the way, Jack's sentence was reduced to two years for good behavior, and he was released on one terrible condition—that he must never make any contact whatsoever with Sam or the children for the rest of his life. Although it broke his heart, he had no choice but to agree. He immediately entered law school at Mercer University in Macon. I am certain that Jack never got over losing beautiful Sam and those precious children.

When I got home the next summer, 1949, I learned that the First Christian Church in Brunswick was without a minister. I visited with one of the elders who got the board to call me as the interim summer minister. I was glad, especially since Allene was spending that summer in Atlanta singing with the Atlanta Pops Orchestra. So, I had the church to keep me busy day and night and all weekend. This helped me to think of the Lord's work and not so much of her.

I even went back to the place at the beach where I had first seen her. I thought of her each time I passed the road where I had stopped to give her and her friends a ride into town. I really longed for her, especially one afternoon when I strolled over to the little chapel where she had come to the service that night when I preached. I sat for awhile on the wooden steps of the little church and thought about how I got my first real good look at her that night she stood "right over there" when we had lemonade on the lawn.

I had that bittersweet feeling each time I passed the old filling station in Brunswick where I finally found her two years later. I have often thought that if I had gone back into the leather shop just a few seconds earlier, I would have missed her. You see, I believe that God wanted me to find her; I was sure that He wanted her to be with me in this ministry. I knew it—knew it—knew it! "Well, Lord, I guess I've got some time to wait and a wide valley to cross first."

I wandered around Brunswick and St. Simon's that summer like a lost puppy. But I was also serving the Lord, preaching and calling on the members and having coffee and tea with them at their homes and at the cafe. One lonely, rainy afternoon I sat all alone drinking coffee over in a corner of the cafe. Some guy waited on me; Cindy must have quit. I had not seen her in the past few weeks.

Then I started mumbling to myself: "No problem, I can carry on. I know it's just me and Jesus now. But my Lord, there she is up there in Atlanta rubbing shoulders with the elite and I can just see all those orchestra guys flirting with her, maybe even taking turns dancing with her.

"O my heartless lover, I can see you go dancing by in the arms of another, but it is I, I who love you...Hit don't matter to me...I don't care. Don't worry about me, I'll get along...Time is on my side...I get along without you very well...My fair lady. Just you wait and see...I hope you're satisfied, you rascal you! I'm gonna wash that girl right outta my hair...and besides, I have no time to think all that much—of the only girl I ever asked to marry me in my whole life and she turned me down! But that's OK. The good Lord will pull me through this...He has never let me down nor forsaken me yet. And, O yes, I must not forget, I am a preacher and I will not think about earthly things like perfumed, pretty girls with big brown eyes and long flowing auburn hair...Ohhh, lonesome me, one day at a time, sweet Jesus. I'll think about that tomorrow. Now, hold it a minute, she did write me a couple of letters that summer...buuut probably just to keep me on the string, I suspect."

Seriously though, I actually had a very good summer with the church folks. The sermons were fun to preach, and I hope they were helpful. As I look back now, it was the last time I got to spend that many leisurely, happy hours with Mama, Papa, George and Vera. My, the memories of those lazy, hazy, crazy days of summer and the nights lying in my bed feeling the cool breezes; that summer of clear moonlit nights filled with the loud sound of millions of chirping crickets, and of the evening laughter of children from the neighbor's houses nearby. Yes, that summer missing...missing Allene, and remembering those days at the house with Papa and Mama when we were all together in the long ago. I had no idea then that the family circle would soon be broken.

It happened on the Fourth of July, 1949. We got a phone call from Mary B. at the Macon Hospital telling us that her husband, our brother, Frederick Ridley Pippin, had just passed away of a heart attack. He was forty seven years old and the first member of our immediate family to go. Fred was also the first to be buried in our little cemetery plot at the Methodist Church in Round Oak. Since he and Frank were very close, Frank preached the service. Losing Fred was hard on us all. There was and has been no one quite like Fred. He was the tallest and the handsomest, with bright blue eyes that slightly bulged, straight salt and pepper hair and a million-dollar smile. But he was overweight, smoked and enjoyed his beer a bit too much. Frank had the stone masons engrave on Fred's head-stone those beautiful words from Shakespeare: "Goodnight, sweet Prince, and flights of angels tend thee to thy rest."

Losing Fred brought the entire Pippin family closer together.

About the last of July, George rode with me up to Savannah where I traded my '46 Plymouth for a green '49 Oldsmobile Rocket Coupe. It was a loaded demo, and it was one race horse. In fact, the transmission was named after "Whirlaway," the horse that had recently won the Kentucky Derby. Of course, George just had to drive it home. He fell so much in love with it that you would have thought it was his. It was so much more car than his slow, long, lumbering, heavy Chrysler New Yorker that I had wrecked a few summers before. But I never said things like that to George. Wow! Did I enjoy driving that beauty back to Phillips.

In September, 1949, I began my senior year at Phillips. It was a good, fun time. For many years, the First Christian Church in Oklahoma City had sponsored a preaching contest. Each year in the spring, the homiletics professor would select three seniors, each of whom was given fifteen minutes to preach his sermon. Dr. James Hempsted, the teacher, chose me as one of the three, along with Don Salman and John Johnson. We spoke at a Wednesday night dinner that was held in the dining room in the basement of the old church at 10th and Robinson. I invited the other two contestants to ride down with me. Although we were friends, winning meant a lot to us, so things were quiet and a little tense on the way down. I am sure each of us had picked what he considered to be the best sermon he had ever preached. Dressed to the nines, we three sat at the head table, shaking, picking at our food and completely oblivious of anything that was going on around us. Throughout the dinner, when someone would chat with us, we would silently nod and smile as if we could not speak a word of English. I think I drank five cups of coffee!

Then, before we knew it, the dreaded time came for us to preach. Thank God, I was chosen to go last. I paid rapt attention to what each of them said and what they did. They were so very good and their messages inspired me so, that I did not have a chance to review my notes. I had been very moved by their words. But I did notice that they were both a little shaky and strident, so uptight that John came up a little too fast and almost pushed over the podium.

I missed a little of the first part of his message because I could not shake the story about the new young preacher, who in his first sermon, chose the text, "Behold, I come." Forgetting what came next, he stepped back and attacked the podium again repeating those words, "Behold, I come!" The third time he came a bit too fast, and as he repeated the same words, he pushed over the podium. Well, he and that podium fell forward right out on to the sanctuary floor, and he half-landed into the lap of an old lady who was sitting close to the front in a wheel chair. Seeing that he scared her, he got up and, full of apologies, tried to console her.

But while straightening her hat, she looked up, smiled, and said loud enough for all to hear, "That's all right, Sonny; I should'a been prepared. You told me three times you was a'comin'!"

When I returned my attention to the sermon, our second contestant had up a full head of steam, getting ready to close. Earlier, while we were eating, I thought that I had picked out the three judges in the audience. I arrogantly figured that if I preached to them, I'd have a better chance of winning. But there was such deep meaning in the first two messages and such loud applause after both of them, that when my turn came, I forgot the judges. When John sat down, I said a prayer as I arose and went over to the podium. Since neither of them had included any humor *or* sadness, I thought that I should try to lighten things up a bit and get the crowd to laugh, but much more than that, to sincerely make what I said as real to them as I possibly could. I somehow sensed that these two preachers had set the tone that night for a deep spiritual experience with God, so I forgot about any tricks.

I started off with the story I related above…"Behold, I Come!," which brought only a few chuckles, then launched into my sermon titled "The Extravagant Love of God." After I introduced my subject, I said that I proposed to lift up God's great love as seen in three instances in the Bible. First, I said to them:

> Note the grief that God must surely have felt in His encounter with Israel through His prophet Hosea. When God confronted His people, Israel, who were stubbornly distracted by their care for the world and their hardness of heart toward Him, He cried out to the nation, "When Israel was a child, I loved him and called my son out of Egypt. I led them with cords of kindness and ropes of love. I removed their yokes and bent down and fed them." Then God speaks in deep love more directly to Israel, "How can I give you up, O Israel? I have changed my mind. I am deeply moved. I will not act on my anger for I am God and not man."

The Extravagant Love of God.

God was saying in so many words, "I would have gathered you to my heart with the golden cords of kindness and love, and you refused to come back to me" (Hos. 11:1–9). We see what tender affection our Father had toward Israel, even after they broke His heart—a heart that can still be broken tonight by our indifference, selfishness and our refusal to come back to Him when we stray.

Second, I call your attention to David.

Upon receiving the news that his son Absalom, whom he loved so dearly, was dead, David, a heartbroken father, went to his chambers and wept bitterly, refusing to eat. Absalom had been swept off his mule when his long hair was caught in the limbs of a tree as he rode underneath. David cried out in deepest anguish, "O my son Absalom, my son, my son! Would to God I had died for thee, O Absalom—my son—my son!" (See 2 Samuel 18.)

What an extravagant, all-consuming love this father had for a wayward son. Wayward sons and daughters can today, as in Bible times, completely break a heavenly and an earthly father's and mother's heart.

The Extravagant Love of God.

Third, the greatest love ever to come to this earth was mixed with the greatest sorrow in the tender heart of God's Son, Jesus Christ. In the closing days of His life, while riding on a donkey, He paused at the Mount of Olives and looked out over His beloved city, Jerusalem. He then bowed His head and wept. What deep love! What sadness! Jesus then said those poignant words that still ring down through the centuries to tug at the strings of our hearts tonight, "O, Jerusalem, Jerusalem. You who kill the prophets and stone to death those who are sent to you. How often would I have gathered your children together, even as a hen gathers her brood, *but—you—would—not.* Behold, your house is left unto you desolate. Therefore, I say unto you, you will not see me again until you say, 'Blessed is He who comes in the name of the Lord'" (Matt. 23:37–39, emphasis added).

Then the Spirit of God came over me so strongly that I was almost in tears as I summed up and moved to the close.

I continued,

Just as He did over Israel long ago: God still weeps over the nations who forget Him. Like David did, fathers today also weep over their sons and daughters, and today there are many fathers and sons who seldom express their love for each another. Yes, and Jesus still weeps over our cities tonight for the many who are poor, lonely and lost, and for those who will not turn back to Him from their sinful ways. God calls you and me to go out there and bring all of these to His Son, that we might all dwell together forever with Him in His eternal kingdom. Maybe some of you have not seen the face of Jesus for a long time. To you He is saying, "You will not see me again until you say, Blessed is He…" Will some of you answer our Father's call and reap the unspeakable joy the prodigal son had in returning to his father and experience the great joy of winning souls for His kingdom? We should be both comforted and encouraged to know that God's extravagant love is deeper than our greatest sin.

So we have seen that the prophet Hosea, David the king and Our Lord Jesus all remind us of this one thing: The Extravagant Love of God.

I will close with this. Mama used to say, "You children cry at what I laugh about, and laugh at what I cry about." I wonder if she knew that the Lord gave her that statement. I feel that is just what God is trying to say to each of us tonight, "My children, you laugh at what I cry about and cry at what I laugh about." We may cry at a Christian's funeral, but God is standing at the portals of heaven with His arms stretched wide filled with love and joy and laughter—yet we are weeping. Remember, it is His good pleasure to give us the kingdom (John 12:32). Some Christians laugh at another's misfortune, when we should be sharing that grief. Some of us cry when our intelligent children choose the ministry instead of medicine, when we should rejoice at the godly wisdom which that decision shows. It is indeed a wise person who knows what to laugh at and what to cry about.

After a brief prayer I sat down. There was no applause. At first I was a bit surprised by this, but I was actually glad. The entire audience was strangely quiet. The three of us glanced at each other with misty eyes and weak smiles. We sensed that our three voices, through the Holy Spirit, had spoken as one.

A MIRACLE A MINUTE

Well, all of a sudden I realized that I had clean forgotten about the judges, but more than that, I had forgotten that I was trying to win. I silently chided myself for my earlier selfishness. By this time even the audience seemed to have forgotten that this was a sermon contest. If there had been any acting earlier, it was all gone now. I felt that we all had been swept up into the love of an extravagant Father, into a much more vital experience than a sermon contest. The sweet hush over the room remained. I could keenly feel God's presence. No one stood to leave. We all found ourselves in the midst of a miracle. The realization broke like a bright light over the room: Our Lord had taken this contest into the palm of His loving hand and changed it into a worship service. I was tingling to my fingertips when I realized that the Holy Spirit had actually moved upon all three of our hearts to bring *one* message. I am sure that none of us wanted to claim any credit for what happened. Now I really had tears in my eyes. By this time, I did not care which one of us won. That night I think that we all learned that no one should ever try to take the credit for what God does through the Holy Spirit. I hoped that the elder in charge would not even proceed with announcing the winner. Although I was awarded the first place prize of $25.00, this had lost its importance. The second and third place awards were $15.00 and $10.00.

We stayed back and visited with those who remained, and we met the associate pastor, Dr. Don Sheridan, who had started these contests many years before. Unfortunately, we didn't get to see their famous senior minister, the Rev. Dr. William H. (Bill) Alexander, who was speaking that night in another city. I knew him well through my brother Frank because they were very close friends.

As we walked back to the car, I knew my comrades were as hungry as I was, so I invited them to go out for a bite to eat, on me. They accepted! Beginning that night, the three of us became good friends. At the restaurant and on the drive back to Enid, we had a grand old time of fellowship, laughing, talking and singing.

The amazing miracle about my first place prize was that just fourteen years later, almost to the day, I was called to become the senior pastor of that same large church that had sponsored our little preaching contest. By then it was 1964 and the church had dedicated the futuristic "Church of Tomorrow," a brand-new building at 36th and North Walker. I had experienced many changes since I had enrolled at Phillips. However, that next year, from May 1950 through May 1951, would be literally crammed with the most thrilling surprises yet and would set the course I would travel for the rest of my life.

❋ 16 ❋

A College Grad;
Frank's Summer Minister!

lthough my senior year had hardly begun, I was into everything. One night a week I was at the Army Reserve meeting.
Once a month, I attended the Zollars Literary Society. I was on the
Student Council, and that semester I was also holding the office of
president of the Gridiron Club, which was somewhat like a fraternity.
Also, my student church at Marland, although a bright part of my
life, took all of my weekends. You can imagine how all this reduced
the time I had left to study or write those many papers. Each time I
settled down at my desk, I would look at my watch and discover that I
was supposed to be at some meeting.

I learned a very important lesson that helped me in the years
ahead. I determined to spend my time on the most important things
and let the others go by. So, the very next day, I resigned from all
activities that were not essential to my education. I remained in the
Army Reserve and at my student church.

Why I had not done this a year or two earlier, I'll never know. But
at any rate, during my senior year, I really hit the books, spent more
time on my papers and earned much better grades. It finally dawned
upon me that I could have spent so much time in campus activities
that when I graduated, I would have found out too late that I had
missed what I really came to college to get: an education! Perhaps my
account of this lesson learned just in the nick of time will help some
student learn this lesson—don't cut everything out, just keep
extracurricular activities at a reasonable level.

One night four of us were headed to my car as we left a cafe in
downtown Enid. A boy carrying papers was actively trying to sell me
one.

I told him, "Sorry, Sonny, I don't have time for outside reading."

He shot back, "Well, why don't you take the paper home and read it inside!"

I was awarded the Bachelor of Arts degree the last of May, 1950. As a kind of graduation present to myself, I took my '49 Olds to the dealer in Enid and traded it in for a brand-new, pale blue 1950 Olds Rocket. The old green lady had served me well, but she was tired, had a lot of miles on her and needed new tires and some other repairs. But I didn't have to pay much difference because the old '49 beauty was really loaded, including leather. I knew later that it might have been better if I had fixed the old one up, for the new one was not the car the old one was.

That next Sunday morning, the last of May, when I rolled into the parking lot of my church in my new blue Olds, several of my leaders stared at me, wondering just who in the world this was.

They walked in with me, shaking their heads and grinning from ear to ear, while one of them mumbled, "Our young preacher has gone and bought himself another new car."

That day I preached my last sermon at Marland, and it was a time of both joy and sadness. I struggled through a service that came to an end too quickly. The joy came when the Board Chairman said some good things about me and the Lord, and then he took a special love offering to help send me on my way. The sadness was heavy when, on the front porch, I hugged, kissed and shed tears with each adult and child as they filed out one by one. Those good people were my first love in the work of the Lord. How can I ever forget how much they meant to me? Across the years, I have kept in touch with a few of them. I also had the sad privilege of conducting funerals for some of them years later when I was serving the church in Oklahoma City and even in the last few months with the death of Dee's husband, Kenny Spaulding.

Back in Enid, the Monday after graduating, I was busy packing for my trip home. But all morning Allene kept coming into my mind. We had not been in touch much during the past year. On an impulse, I stepped to the phone and called her home in Brunswick.

Her mother, Lucille, answered and said, "I'm sorry, James, but Allene is not here. I hope that this will not overly upset you, but in these past several months, she has gotten a bit too interested in John, a young man in Macon, who is trying to marry her. She has just graduated, and I am afraid that he will give her a ring in a week or two. I hope you'll be glad to know that I am going to do everything I can to break this plan up."

"Am I glad? You can bet your bottom dollar on that, Lucille."

A College Grad; Frank's Summer Minister!

She chuckled and continued, "I knew you'd feel that way. But don't worry, I have persuaded her voice teacher, Professor Zorin, and his wife, Vera, to leave immediately and take Allene to New York City with them on their way to Connecticut. I feel certain that this John would have interfered with Allene's plans to study in New York and continue her career in voice."

I told her, "Oh, I agree, Lucille. If that happened, then all your hopes and dreams for her, and all the money and time you've invested in her education, would go down the drain. You are a very wise and loving mother. Please tell Allene that I called and that I still love her. I'll be home in a few days and will come and visit with you, if that's OK."

"I'll be very glad to see you, Son. Please do keep in touch with Allene; she is still very fond of you. By the time you get here, I'll have her address and phone number."

I said, "Give my regards to Henley. See you soon. God bless you."

I hung up and stood there thinking about this strange romance I was supposed to be having with this girl. It had been in and out, off and on, up and down and hot and cold for the past two years. I was about ready to completely give up on her again.

I thought to myself, *If it is to be, God will bring her to me.*

That afternoon I had just finished packing my car for the trip home when the phone rang. I just knew that Lucille had been in touch with Allene and talked her into calling me.

But no, instead it was Brother Frank saying, "Son, I think you'd better sit down for this. The minister I had scheduled to preach for me while I go on vacation is ill and cannot come. I know it is very short notice, but would you come and be my summer minister?"

I had a hard time getting the words out, but I said in a shrill voice, "Do you really mean it? You know the answer is a great big—*yes!* I will be delighted to do it. Do you realize what a great honor this is, Brother Frank? Are you sure I can do this? You know that I will just love…"

He replied, "Just calm down, Son; you're talking too much and too fast. Would I be asking you if I thought you couldn't do it? What do you say?"

"OK, OK, I accept. I will be on my way as soon as I call and tell Papa and Mama that I'm not coming home," I blurted.

"Don't bother, l'il brother. I've already talked to them, and they are tickled pink about it. Just get in that racing car of yours and come on up here! We'll be waiting for you at Ten Acres."

A MIRACLE A MINUTE

I hung up the phone, grabbed my suitcase and several sermon files, and in minutes I was on my way. On the drive up I had lots of time to think, to talk to myself and to talk with God. It occurred to me that this was more than a surprise—it was a shocking miracle, mainly because Brother Frank had always invited the most outstanding preachers or college presidents in the nation to serve during the six weeks while he was on vacation. He told me later that Jim Brown, a brilliant "pulpiteer" who had also graduated from Phillips, and I were the only two who could keep the offerings from falling during the summer! Of course, he was quick to stress that finances were not the main reason why he chose us!

As my new Olds quickly clicked off the miles, cruising "North with the Night," I began to get a little weary so I stopped for a bite to eat. Inside, as I sipped my coffee, I began to feel a bit anxious. That famous church with a large staff and over 3,000 members was a tremendous challenge to a young preacher. But I was determined not to let Frank down. Since I was his baby brother, somehow I felt I had to top all of the others who had preceded me. I would much rather have had him closer by to advise me, but he, Ozelle and Julia always left town, usually spending this time in Colorado or Minnesota. He very rarely ever checked back for a report, so I would really be on my own. However, I knew this would bring me closer to the Lord, to the staff and to the church leaders. Suddenly, all of my fright was gone.

When I got back in the car, I repeated over and over, "I can do all things through Christ who strengthens me." (See Philippians 4:13.)

The moon was shining so brightly that when I cut the lights for a few seconds, I could still see the road ahead like a shining ribbon, a silver river winding up the long hill that lay ahead. The scene seemed right out of another world. Then I received an unexpected blessing. I turned on the radio right in the middle of a broadcast of a sermon by Dr. Fulton J. Sheen, a popular Catholic priest who had millions of listeners. At the close, he always gave a final sentence to sum up his subject. That night, in his clear deep voice, he closed with these words: "We are not saints, not because we cannot be; we are not saints because we do not want to be."

These words staggered me with both a sadness and a challenge. I couldn't shake them, so in the next hour I wrote a sermon in my mind, and I put it on paper during the next few days. I preached this sermon at Community that summer. I chose the title: "We Are Not Saints." I think it is one of my best.

A College Grad; Frank's Summer Minister!

All the lights were on when I pulled in at "Ten Acres" a little before midnight. Frank, Ozelle and Julia were waiting with hugs and laughter. I had a plate of delicious food in front of me in a flash. Julia, now a teenager, sat with me while I ate. She was and is a pretty girl, with red hair and big brown eyes. One summer when she was only twelve she read all the volumes of *The World Book*; she is a very intelligent person indeed.

Later, while Frank I were alone in the den chatting, he assured me that God would make the summer more of a joy than a burden. Frank was a night person, often doing his best writing and sermon preparation from midnight to 2:00 A.M. His article in the weekly church paper was titled "Thoughts in the Night." One of his five books is a collection of the best of these. He often slept until ten o'clock, arriving at his study about eleven. However, he could get more done in two hours than most of us can in eight. I was glad that I had this time with him before he left town.

After breakfast we joined in a circle of prayer, and then they left for their trip to Colorado. I followed them back to Kansas City, where they headed west on I-70, and I drove on to their spacious manse and moved in. It was Thursday, the fifth of June.

That first Sunday almost two thousand people attended the two services, about eight hundred in the first and the second was filled to capacity at twelve hundred! Even though I had conducted several revivals, nothing could begin to compare with serving as Frank's summer minister. Some speakers will not admit it, but the larger the crowd, the more inspired most speakers are to do their best—and also to seek God's help to prepare to preach and to challenge many persons to walk with Christ.

Community Church was filled with great Christian people, warm, friendly, cheerful and intelligent. They stayed right with me on every word and would laugh at the slightest bit of humor. Then the efficient and competent staff stretched my mind and talents to the limit. They were all so helpful, especially Paul Tanner, Frank's former barber who was now the business manager. He drove me on hospital calls and often took me to lunch. Paul's daily advice helped me immensely and taught me a lot of common sense that kept me out of a whole lot of trouble. The famous architect, Frank Lloyd Wright, designed the church so that the inside of the futuristic stucco building somewhat resembled the catacombs in Rome. The sanctuary was constructed so that the speaker felt very close to all of the worshipers, including those in the balcony.

A MIRACLE A MINUTE

In less than five years, Brother Frank had built a super church, filled with outstanding people, and had selected a fine-tuned and efficient staff. He had surrounded himself with outstanding lay leaders, both men and women. They all displayed enthusiasm and joy as they functioned together as a highly trained team. I think I learned more in those six weeks about how to serve a big church than I had in four years of college. My days were spent working with staff, editing the weekly church paper and worship bulletin, conducting funerals, weddings, baptisms and making hospital calls. The evenings were filled with meetings, fellowship in the people's homes and sermon preparation.

I believe those six sermons were the best I had ever preached. As I stood up there each Sunday looking into the faces of that beautiful congregation, I felt that they literally pulled those sermons out of me. I had always used humor, but these folks thrilled and challenged me so that I kept them laughing half the time; then at the height of their laughter, I would drive home a vital teaching of Jesus Christ. During the coffee hour that was held at the back of the church after the services, I was surrounded by so many people with words of thanks that I felt like I was Dr. Frank Pippin, Dr. Peale and Billy Graham all wrapped into one!

Whenever they would say that the sermon was good or I was great, I would always respond, "Thank you, dear friend, but God is good and Jesus is great. I give all the credit to Christ, for without Him I would be nothing, still back in Georgia cutting meat and pumping gasoline."

Of course, there is nothing wrong with working in a store; I did it for many years.

The weeks sped by so fast that I was shocked that Monday morning when the phone rang in the study. It was Frank, saying in that great voice of his, "Hello there, Brother James, I'm back. Take a break, Son. Come on over to the drug store and join Brother Paul and me for coffee."

If you ever heard Frank say "hello there," you'd never forget it. And one could recognize his voice in the middle of Beijing, China. I took a great sigh of relief, dropped everything and almost ran across Main Street. As I entered, Frank gave me a big hug as he and Paul Tanner stood up. I sat down to the best cup of coffee I'd had since he left.

As I looked at Frank sitting there, almost glowing with his deep tan, in clean creased pants and shirt, I said, "Man, you really look fresh and rested, Brother Frank. Boy, am I glad you're back. Before I say another word though, I gotta tell you what an outstanding guy you got in this Paul. I couldn't have made it without his support."

Frank smiled, and as we sipped our coffee, he said, "Paul here is one main reason that I could leave town and know all would be well. But listen, you disgustingly young and good-looking, hardworking preacher-boy; from what I hear, I do believe you will go far in the ministry. Seriously, I am very pleased at the job you have done. Many good reports from the staff and members have already come to me about your preaching and your work."

Paul finally got a word in and told Frank, "Brother Frank, this guy moved so fast these past six weeks, I could hardly keep up with him! Say, Brother James, you are planning to leave right away, aren't you? I need a rest!"

That got a good laugh. You can imagine how this all made me feel. Frank then strongly urged me to stick around for a few days longer, but I was ready to be on my way because I was a little tired and was looking forward to going home and getting some rest myself.

That afternoon I packed and got the manse in good order, leaving it about as clean as I had found it. The next morning I changed the sheets on my bed, left the key under the mat, called Frank to say good-bye and was on my way.

I had twelve hundred miles of road stretching out ahead of me. The speed limit was seventy, but my cruising speed was eighty if the road was good. In 1950, most of the U.S. highways were two-lane concrete, often with a four-inch dropoff at the edge. If it was raining and you happened to drift a bit to the right, you would drop off into mud. Then if that did happen and you were not particularly careful, you would flip the car over trying to get back on the road! There were no lines, so you had to give your full attention to driving and could not relax or pull off the road. Along with that, there were no rest stops and few if any cafes, but there sure were a lot of railroad crossings. In the small towns, you had better watch those speed limits, or you'd wind up down at the jail paying a big fine to the sheriff—in cash. There were very few good motels, called "tourist courts," that had naked light bulbs hanging down in the middle of the room. I stayed that night in a clean hotel in Tupelo, Mississippi.

After breakfast I was back on the road. It was such a bright and refreshing morning that I burst into song, quoted Scripture and praised God for the blessings of the summer morning. I went back in my mind through all four years of college. That second day of the trip passed by so quickly that I could hardly believe the sign that read, "Brunswick City Limits." I drove over on the causeway to the Island just at sunset, and the scene before me never looked so good. I believe I was even happier to be home this time than I had been when I got out of the Army.

What a pleasure it was just to relax and chat with Mama and Papa, and then enjoy a great supper prepared by my favorite cook. After supper Papa told me how proud he was that I was the second one in the family who had graduated from college. He mentioned how well Jack was doing, making straight A's at Mercer and had not touched a drop of alcohol since he was released from prison. This made me very happy.

I said, "You show 'em, Brother Jack. I knew you could do it!"

Then Papa smiled and said he had saved the best for last; George had come by the house a few weeks ago and said, "Papa, it looks like you are going to have three boys in the ministry. James would not join me in my business, so I am going to join him and Frank in theirs! I'm entering Mercer in a few weeks."

Papa laughed and said to me, "We were so happy when George told us, we both stood and gave him a big hug. Mama pulled her apron up over her face and began to cry and laugh at the same time! George has moved his leather business to Eastman, enrolled in Mercer and started studying to become a minister!! Now we've got three preachers and one lawyer in the family, so we'll have no trouble getting saved and buried and having a lawyer to keep us all out of jail!" Pa had a keen sense of humor; he just didn't use it enough.

I was glad the summer was nearly over. Although Allene and I had not been in touch that much the past few months because she was all infatuated with this John fellow, the Island just was not the same without her. Lucille won and had gotten her out of the state the week after she graduated in June. Now she was away from John and caught up in the life of an artist in New York City. It was also sad to realize that Jack and Sam were divorced and good that George had actually moved Vera, the boys and his business near Macon at Eastman, where he served a student church on weekends! Yes, he had actually decided to become a minister. So many changes! But a shocking change for me was just ahead.

It began when the phone rang and Colonel Holcomb, Commander of the 325th Hospital Train, notified me that because the Korean War was going so badly, they needed our hospital train. Our reserve unit was being called to active duty! I was ordered to report to the armory in Enid on 3 September to ship out to The Presidio, San Francisco. Me? Called back into the Army? Hard to believe, but true.

I phoned Frank, told him the news and asked him to drive me to Enid. After packing light and saying some fast farewells, I drove to Kansas City. I arrived the last Saturday in August. Brother Frank was shocked, but he made me feel better when, like George, he confided to me that he wished he was going on active duty with me. After an inspiring Sunday morning service and a quick lunch, Frank and I left for Enid. There, we loaded all my belongings into the back seat of my Olds and filled the trunk with all of my books. He didn't mind the fast trip down and back, mainly because he was elated that I had asked him to keep my car while I was gone.

My feelings were strange that night as I stood in front of the Berg house and watched Frank drive off to Kansas City in my new Olds, loaded with almost everything I owned in the world. It was actually easier to say good-bye to him than to part with my brand-new car! When and how I got it back is a small miracle in itself.

✣ 17 ✣

Angela, Charlie Brown, the Moon and New York City

Early Monday morning after a restless night, Bob Book took me to the Armory and actually hugged me tight as he told me good-bye. I had tears in my eyes as I fell in with the other members of the unit. After we were issued our gear and had eaten a box lunch, we were marched to the station, where the train was waiting to carry us to San Francisco. Before we boarded, the unit was dismissed so that the families and friends who were waiting could wish us all farewell. Since there was no one left to say good-bye to me, I picked up my heavy duffel bag and boarded the train. After I selected a comfortable seat in the middle of the car, I sat there feeling kind of sad while I looked at all those men embracing their families, wives and sweethearts.

I glanced down at my duffel bag and, said to myself, "James Clayton Pippin, what in the world are you doing? Dropping out of school to go off to Korea, not knowing when or if you'll ever come back."

Then I got real with myself and continued, "But I am in the Reserve—not only to get pay and points, but I am 'the U.S. Army in Reserve,' ready to be called up to active duty when needed by my country."

While deep in these thoughts, the men came aboard, and it was a moment or two before I realized that the train was moving and we were on our way.

It took three days and nights for us to get to Los Angles. The journey was filled with a lot of dozing and many boxed meals. In LA we were bused to an armory where we took a shower and got a good night's sleep. The next day, in fresh uniforms, we were taken on a tour of Universal Studios. Here and there I saw several movie stars, but looked in vain for Clark Gable.

Helen, Charlie Brown, the Moon and New York City

The unit arrived at the Presidio, San Francisco, the eighth of September. Our barracks were near the shore of the Bay, in full view of the Golden Gate Bridge. At sunset that modern wonder of a bridge looked like a blazing, multicolored strand of beads. I drifted off to sleep while I watched the blinking lights of Alcatraz and listened to the moans, sighs and shrill whistles of the buoys out in the Bay. These sounds bothered me at first, but after a few nights they became a lullaby that put me to sleep.

We were assigned to Letterman Army Hospital, a part of the Presidio, and the next day we went to the railyards for a tour of the hospital train. Major Ross selected me to be the mess sergeant of the train, then put me in charge of my barracks and gave me a private room at the head of the stairs. Our winter green uniform never changed year 'round because the weather was always so cool and heavenly. I got used to the fog and rain that paid us a visit almost weekly. After a few days of getting settled in, we were taken on a tour of the Presidio. I had never seen an Army post so absolutely beautiful: the bright blue skies filled with seagulls, the white stucco buildings with red tile roofs, the lush green lawns where baby rabbits were often seen, the manicured yards, the hundreds of palm trees playfully swaying in a breeze coming up from the Pacific and the fresh scented smell of flowers. All of this convinced me that I was in the middle of a kind of paradise—off somewhere in a brand-new world.

One afternoon four of us drove out to the famous restaurant called Cliff House. We were seated by a large picture window, and when I turned and first saw the Pacific Ocean, the waves of that massive sea breaking on huge rocks just beneath our table, a great thrill shot through me. I gazed almost spellbound, as far as my eye could see, at that mammoth body of water. I simply cannot find the words to describe it. Even though I was raised very near the Atlantic Ocean, I was overwhelmed that afternoon with a mixture of awe and peace that no scene on earth had ever brought me. I suddenly realized why Magellan named that great ocean "The Pacific;" for me that day it truly was the Sea of Peace. The four of us were finally able to take our eyes off of the view long enough to enjoy one of the best dinners I ever had. To put it mildly, the Presidio was good duty, indeed!

The next morning the whole unit was divided up and sent to various service schools to prepare to go to Korea. I had casually told someone on the trip out that I used to cut meat in a store where I was half-owner. This fact must have reached the commander, Maj. Ross, because he put me with fourteen others who were being sent

215

to the Sixth Army Food Service School. The fourteen others were to be trained as cooks and bakers, and I was to become a mess sergeant. My group was put in one of the large, permanent stone barracks that were built in World War I.

Here again, somehow they got the word, because I was made barracks sergeant. The school was six weeks of misery. Each morning, except on Sunday, we had to report to a large unit mess at 5:30 A.M. After lunch I attended classes to learn all the duties of running a messhall. I was selected for the choice duty of serving in the Officers' Open Mess during the last two weeks of the school. As certificates were given to us on Graduation Day, all the men of the five training buildings fell out in separate groups. The training commander called out my name... front and center. I was given a special "citation of leadership" for having the best kept barracks out of the five. Somehow, all of this failed to bring any real excitement into my life.

However, things became a lot brighter a few days after I was assigned to the Letterman Army Hospital Mess as assistant mess sergeant. About twice a week the food service dietitian came by to check out the mess. *She* was a tall, slender, pretty, red-headed first lieutenant. Bypassing the head mess sergeant one day, she came straight over to me and asked me to show her around the messhall. The next time she came she asked me to have coffee with her over in a far corner. Female officers are not supposed to fraternize with the enlisted men, so she could only visit with me on duty.

She said her name was Angela Barefoot. She was from Pittsburgh. She had lovely bright, blue eyes and a sweet voice that was tinted with a Yankee dialect. At the close of our "staff meeting" she asked me if I was married. When I said no, she invited me to meet her for a late lunch that coming Saturday at a place that was in walking distance from the base. I did just that, and that night we wound up downtown having dinner and dancing at the Top of the Saint Francis. Since I had recently learned that Allene, my pretty, faithful sweetheart was dating two Italians and one Jewish guy in New York City, Angela's attention was all the more welcomed. So, we dated often and developed a great friendship.

Then one night two weeks later, she had me over to her apartment for dinner. Afterward, while we sat on the sofa having coffee, she put her coffee down, leaned over close to me, put her arms around me and— "Wal, she upped and kissed me."

Down home we would say, "She laid one on me!" She cut the kiss short, just long enough to whisper, I love you, and then she continued the big long kiss. Imagine this, the very next moment, she asked me to marry her! Somehow, there were distant recollections in my mind of this scene of a guy under an old oak tree who kissed this girl, told her that he loved her and then asked her to marry him! I blew it then and Angela blew it there.

After the long and very pleasant kiss, I tenderly unwound myself from her sweet lips, her delicately perfumed body and all of her other endearing young charms, and said, "Angela, I think I need to tell you about Allene."

When I finished this saga, she expressed disappointment and not a little anger. She finally said, "James, to me this sounds awfully like an 'iffy' relationship that you need to get out of. Besides, does she have a well-paying career skill that will put you through seminary? Does your 'Broadway Baby' have six thousand dollars in the bank to buy you a new Cadillac for your wedding present? What do you think of that?"

I started grinning and said, "Angela, you are fabulous! You know that I like you very much, and you can tell that I'm both flattered and honored to have a beautiful girl like you in love with me. But...you know, I think you might be right. I guess I do need to force Allene to make a decision about me."

She agreed, "Now you are talking sense. Since you have ten days leave coming up for Christmas, on your way home, why don't you fly to New York, see her and get it over with?"

I said, "Yeah, on my way home! That sounds like a very good idea. I'll just do that!"

I finished my coffee, did not resist the one more sweet kiss at the door, left her apartment, went straight to a phone on base and called Allene. She seemed thrilled, saying that she couldn't believe that I was actually coming to see her. After a few warm words, she promised that she would write me a good long letter that night. I hung up, went bounding up the stairs to my room and wrote *her* a "good, long letter," saying in part that I was looking forward to my visit with delight.

In two days, I received Allene's very long, special delivery letter with some of her sweet words. She had added instructions for me to get a cab when I arrived and come to the Woodward Hotel. From there I could walk just around the corner to her place at 157 West 57th Street. I fell asleep that night fervently praying that this was the Lord's will and all would work out in line with His plan for my life. I was in love with Allene, but she did not share my feelings. At the same time, I was very fond of Angela, who seemed to be deeply in love with me. So this trip could clear the air, end my confusion and might even determine whether Allene would ever come with me on my life's journey.

The afternoon before the day my leave started, Angela phoned the messhall and told me to bring my suitcase to her apartment after duty hours. I thought, "O my God, I sure hope she is not planning to ask me to spend the night!"

When I arrived she pulled open the door and gave me a warm welcome. Then as she walked away, I noticed that she was wearing white "short shorts," pink high heels and a starched pink shirt, the tails of which she had tied in a knot under her full bosoms. I sat on the sofa, and when she brought my coffee, she slowly stooped over to hand it to me. Then she pursed her lips and barely touched mine as I got the full display! I sipped the coffee while my eyes followed her around the room as she began to unpack my bag. She starched and ironed my shirts, pressed my trousers and ties, and then folded and placed everything neatly back into my suitcase, all the time chattering nonstop. She then stood in the middle of the room with her feet wide apart and her blue eyes blazing, pointed her index finger straight at me and started giving me a hot lecture.

Then like a lawyer she summed up, "Now, James Pippin, you've got to promise me that while you are there you will not even mention my name. If she knows about us, she will be all over you with more of her promises."

As she waved her thumb toward her chest, she continued, "Listen, we girls know each other. She's been keeping you in the side pocket all these years, maybe even waiting to get a better offer or more likely stalling, until her career skyrockets, and then my dear one, she'll drop you *like that*"—she loudly snapped her long fingers—"and you'll never hear from her again."

She then cooled down a bit, and we had chicken salad sandwiches followed with cherry pie, ice cream and coffee. After a few more of her sweet words of instruction and encouragement, she came over to the sofa, stood there, and reaching down, removed her shoes one by one; they clicked as they fell to the hardwood floor. Then she sat on my lap, leaned over, placed her head on my shoulder and gently kissed me on the neck. O Lord...I closed my eyes...I did not know how I should respond to her, I did not even know what to do with my hands...I was certain that if I touched her anywhere, I would explode! After a fleeting moment, I gently had her stand up, took her into my arms and held her close. As I got to the door she embraced me and tenderly kissed me.

Then with her sweet breath close to my lips, she whispered, "Sweetheart, you can leave your bag here because I have borrowed my boss's car, and I am going to take you to the airport early in the morning." Then she pressed me against the door with her warm body!

Whew! I took a deep sigh, turned and almost stumbled down the few steps to the street. As I walked slowly back to my room that night I could still sense her body with its heavenly fragrance and sensuous warmth. O my Lord! In my confusion, man, I knew I'd better get started with some really strong prayers.

"Dear Jesus, what on earth am I to do? Angela is so pretty, sexy and sweet, and she loves me so much. Lord!!...if I could only feel more like that about her there would be no decision to make."

I continued praying after I went to bed. When I told the Lord that it all just had to be left in His hands, I drifted off to sleep.

I arrived at Angela's place the next morning just as the sun was rising. If you have ever seen just one sunrise over San Francisco Bay, it will stay with you forever. As I stood on the steep sidewalk taking in the grand scene, she walked out and handed me my suitcase. We got in the car and drove toward the airport. We were both quiet all the way there. She walked me to the gate and with a kiss for luck, I was on my way. I turned at the entrance of the mammoth TWA Constellation to wave, then quickly went to a window to watch her slowly go inside and disappear. I had mixed feelings of sadness and anticipation. But this trip turned out to be a journey of firsts.

My first long airplane trip nonstop from San Francisco to New York City took about six hours. This was December, 1950, and that plane was the world's finest. The entire flight was a thrill. The pilot taxied to the end of the long runway, revved up those four Pratt and Whitney's and we roared off. After we were airborne, although I was in coach, my slightest wish to the lovely stewardess seemed an instant command; I figured it was partly the well-fitted "Class A" uniform that we had to wear to get the low military fare. A fabulous breakfast and lunch were served in flight, my first time to dine aloft. Almost before I knew it, we were descending over New York. From my window seat I looked down on the nation's largest city, another breathtaking first. What with that dazzling sunrise over San Francisco Bay that morning and now this view from aloft of the sun setting over across the Hudson River from Manhattan...Well, it was almost too much for one day.

A MIRACLE A MINUTE

We landed at LaGuardia Airport, and since I had only the one small bag, I went straight to the street and hailed a Checker cab. On the way to the Woodward, the cabby pointed out Allene's apartment building. She lived right across the street from Carnegie Hall. I paid the fare, tipped the driver, walked briskly into the small lobby, registered, went to my room and immediately called Allene.

I said, "Hi, Sweetheart, this is James."

She let out a scream that ended with, "James, I can't believe you're here!"

"I am here, and I am at the hotel and dying to see you."

"Well, come right on over. I just happen to be between shows at the Music Hall, so we'll have a little time to visit before my next show."

I freshened up, brushed my teeth, combed my hair and walked the short distance to the front door of her apartment building. As I rang the bell, an old and pleasant looking elevator man came, opened the door and with a big smile and a thick Brooklyn accent, said, "I'll bet you a dollar to a doughnut you are James Pippin."

I smiled.

When he opened the door on the fourth floor, there stood Allene at the elevator, all hugs and giggles. She wore black slacks, a well-fitted beige blouse, black hose and heels. Her beautiful, auburn hair was all tied up on top of her head.

She led me in by the hand and introduced me to her roommate, Maude Jackson. Maude, who was in her forties, was single, intelligent and seemed very fond of Allene. Like many New Yorkers, Maude was born, raised, went to school and worked in Manhattan. She had never been off the Island and had never even been up the Empire State building. After a brief chat, she excused herself and went to her bedroom.

Since I had a late lunch on the plane, Allene had me sit in the living room while she served us each a cup of very good coffee. She asked me all about the trip, and then told me the plans for the evening. Her last show for the day at Radio City Music Hall was to begin in about an hour; she had reserved a complementary front row center seat for me. So after we chatted nonstop for a while, we finished our coffee, told Maude goodnight and walked the few blocks to the theater. On the way there she told me that after the show we had reservations for dinner at the Green Room of the Astor Hotel. After we hugged tight at the stage door, I walked around and entered the theater.

Helen, Charlie Brown, the Moon and New York City

The lobby was the largest and most beautiful I had ever seen. The large glistening chandelier, the wide curved stairway, the colors all so tasteful, and the columns that were covered with gold—in a word, breathtaking. The total impact just made me want to stand there and stare. I really had little desire to enter the theater. Soon a cute usher took me to my seat where I then turned and took in the sweeping panorama of the largest and most awesome movie theater in the world.

But it was so much more than just a movie theater. As I took my seat, my attention was riveted to my left where a great pipe organ slowly came out of the wall, with Dick Liebert at the console, and he filled the theater with a resounding show tune. After the organ numbers, the large orchestra gradually came into view as it rose up out of the pit until it was only a few feet from my seat. From then until the end of the show there was never a dull moment.

The curtain went up, the orchestra began to play, and the stage was suddenly filled with a stunning Christmas scene, illuminated by millions of lights. Then six sleds with two beautiful girls in each came gliding across the stage, being pushed through mounds of "snow" by the guys in the chorus. As they stopped in the center, the girls in dazzling outfits with short white skirts stood up in the sleds and in a blaze of light, jumped into the arms of the guys. Then all twenty-four of them, hand in hand, singing to the lively tune, "Sleigh Ride," divided, half of them moving out on one side of the stage and half on the other, proceeding out about fifty feet to the sides near the walls. It was then that I first caught sight of Allene. Of course, she was the prettiest of all the girls. I felt that I could almost reach up and touch her. After some delightful Christmas songs and tunes, the curtain closed on this scene.

Then, in front of the curtain, ten black guys in black tights, slowly climbed up on each other and made a high pyramid while they juggled pins that were spewing fire! I grabbed the armrests of my seat, praying that none of them would fall. Next, the curtain reopened and the orchestra whipped up a lively jitterbug number while the guys and gals in the chorus came out in bobby socks, short skirts and loafers and started dancing a kind of swing. Then a couple went center stage and cut loose doing the real jitterbug, and lo and behold, it was Allene and one of the guys. She told me later that she was the only girl in the chorus who knew how to jitterbug. Boy, did they "strut their stuff." He threw her up over his head, swung her down through his legs, balanced her on both hips and closed by spinning her like a top! When he and Allene came up front stage and bowed, the crowd burst forth in applause. She said they gave her five dollars a week extra for doing that jitterbug!

The stage was immediately cleared, and out came the "Corps de Ballet" all in white. They filled the stage with such beauty and grace that I found tears in my eyes. Next the stage was full of dogs, ponies and breathtaking magic. Then a comic stood in front of the curtain and began fighting with the mike cord. His antics kept the entire crowd howling nonstop with laughter. I laughed so much that my face literally ached and I felt like my sides would split. All the while, the comic never said one word. Finally, he was so hopelessly tied up in the cord that two ushers had to come out and remove him from the stage, mike cord, mike and all!

As the laughter faded, the lights slowly went dim, the curtain opened and a hush came over the audience. Spotlights shone on a nativity scene while the orchestra played and the choral ensemble sang "Silent Night." Then "Mary" and "Joseph" placed a live "baby Jesus" into the manger. Standing around were animals, shepherds and wise men. Then the ensemble sang the enchanting "O Holy Night." I was tingling all over. But wait, if you can stand it, there's one more scene!

The final curtain opened and the Rockettes burst out in sparkling white tights with short red skirts and filled the stage with some real fancy dancing. They all seemed to be the same height and the same size as they danced in perfect time. Then after their thrilling dancing, they filled the entire stage and ended with that precision high kick that made them world-famous. As the final curtain closed, the audience suddenly stood to their feet and gave the show a deafening applause that continued for minutes. I took several deep sighs and was sad it was all over. I had just seen what many feel is the best show in the USA! It was my first "spectacular extravaganza!"

I went backstage, found Allene and immediately began sputtering about how great the show was, how proud I was of her...so happy that I was there...so glad she was a part of that wonderful show. I was still chattering even while she took me on a quick tour of the place. The living and working area of the company that put on the show included a dormitory where the entire group often stayed during winter storms and snows, a cafeteria, a dispensary, dressing rooms, and several rehearsal halls. "They shore did take good care of them pretty girls." The Rockettes and ballet beauties were everywhere, smiling and winking at me.

Helen, Charlie Brown, the Moon and New York City

Back at the stage door exit, Allene grabbed my hand and said, "Let's go eat! I'm starved."

We half-walked, half-ran the short distance to the Astor. The streets were jammed with traffic, mainly with taxicabs that were constantly blowing their horns. The noise was deafening. You walk with the lights, strictly following the "walk" and "don't walk" signals—no jay walking. Some comic once said that the only two kinds of pedestrians in Manhattan are "the quick and the dead." I believed it! As we were seated at our table, we oohed and aahed with delight at the beautiful Christmas decorations.

Our waiter came over with the wine list, and before he or I could even speak, Allene said, "No wine, thank you."

I almost said, "Speak for yourself." I thought, *You know, it's Christmas! We've both had a long, hard day and all.*

But to be respectful, I smiled weakly and said, "None for me either."

I figured she also wanted wine, but was trying to make a good impression on me since I was a preacher. I suddenly recalled that she had been dating two Italians and I knew how much they loved wine. Well, no matter. Oh me! I tried to relax as I sipped my water.

We had a very good dinner and much interesting talk. She said that she was keeping very busy, worked as a dental assistant for two months when she arrived, was singing every Sunday morning as a paid member of the Brick Presbyterian Choir, was auditioning for some of the big Broadway shows and occasionally appeared on radio and WOR-TV. Mr. Zorin had placed her with Alfredo Gondolphi, a former Metropolitan Opera tenor, for a weekly voice lesson. Not long after she had arrived, she auditioned for the Choral Ensemble at Radio City Music Hall against scores of pretty girls, all with trained voices…and she got the job. During the holiday seasons she had to do five shows a day while at the same time rehearsing for the new show. She was really so busy it made me tired just to hear her tell about it.

After relating all this, she wanted to know about how I got called back on active duty. In the middle of my story, the orchestra began to play and she reached over for my hand and said, "Come on, let's dance!"

During the second tune, I told her what a good dancer she was. She laughed and told me that I was not so bad myself. Later, after we had a cup of cappuccino and dessert, she suggested that we go back to her apartment.

When we got there, I sat on the love seat by the window while she tuned in some soft music on the radio. Then she disappeared into the kitchen. I guessed that Maude had retired because her bedroom door was closed. Then Allene came out with Cokes for us, and sat way over on the other end of the love seat. I was puzzled by this, but quickly started telling her again how thrilled I was with the show and that dance she did. She sat with one foot tucked beneath her, and as she slowly swung the other to the music, I looked at her and realized anew what a strikingly beautiful girl she was. The sweet, soft music, her beauty and our wonderful evening together, all made me begin to feel a little amorous. After we chatted for awhile, she seemed quite nervous when I reached for her hand in an attempt to pull her a little closer to me. She put both feet on the floor and instead of moving over, she stood up and walked quickly toward the kitchen. On the way she cut the music off and said that she didn't want to disturb Maude.

I sat there wondering what on earth had come over this girl. Here I had flown all the way across the country to see her, and now she was hiding in the kitchen. Suddenly I looked up and here she came in holding a cold, greasy, drumstick in one hand and a large napkin in the other—and this after that great dinner we just had. She sat down resuming the same position and proceeded to eat the chicken while remaining absolutely quiet.

I was so stunned I could think of nothing to say, so I sat there staring at the floor. There was absolute silence in the room, for how long I can't remember. I heard the noise of the traffic down on 57th Street, and a loud police siren blared somewhere in the distance.

Finally, I stood up and managed to get the words out of my mouth, "Well," I mumbled as I stretched, "I think I'd better be going. You've had a long day, and I could use some sleep."

With a startled look, she quickly wiped her mouth, put the napkin and the drumstick on the coffee table and followed me to the door. I opened it, turned and said in a voice filled with sorrow and anger, "Well, since I'll be leaving early in the morning, I suppose this is good-bye. If you should ever care to contact me again, you can call me collect at my home. They will know where to find me."

She dropped her head looking very dismayed and forlorn, put out her beautiful little hand and said in a shaky voice, "James, I am so sorry; I wish you wouldn't go. Thanks for coming to see me...I thought that you were...and thanks for the wonderful evening."

Without so much as a small hug, or even a greasy little kiss, I turned and closed the door. A feeling swept over me that once and for all I was closing the door on a sad and hopeless chapter in my life. I stood there in the dark for a while, then reached for the exit door and walked the four flights to the lobby. On my way back to the hotel, I could neither speak nor think. I felt very small and of no importance as I slowly walked the streets of Manhattan, one of the largest cities in the world, on that cold December night. The traffic was much less heavy now. I felt as though someone had just pulled the switch on my life and left me standing in the dark. I was reminded of what Abraham Lincoln said after he lost an election. When asked how it felt, he said, "It hurts too much to laugh and I'm too old to cry."

Back in my room, I undressed, crawled into bed and was about to turn off the light when Angela Barefoot's face came vividly before me. I sat up and called her.

She answered the phone with sobs and little chuckles, and said, "Hello, my sweet darling. No, you didn't wake me, I've been waiting for your call. Does this mean that you have some good news for me!"

I knew what she wanted to hear, but I couldn't say the words. I must admit I didn't feel very romantic toward anyone at that moment.

I answered, "Well, I can say that this has not been the best day of my life. Things didn't turn out very well. But I want to tell you about the visit when we are more rested and relaxed. I'm leaving in the morning for home and looking forward to spending some time with Papa and Mama. I will call you tomorrow night after you and I get some sleep. Please don't worry, and thanks for all you have done for me. God bless you."

"That's fine, dear, I understand. I'll be praying you'll have a safe trip home. Merry Christmas, James; I love you. Please hurry back to me."

I prayed silently, "Why, why O Lord, are these two beautiful girls in my life? Please help!"

After a restless night I arose, shaved, showered, dressed, checked out and hailed a cab to the airport. Within an hour I was aloft and on my way to Savannah and St. Simon's.

On the plane, between naps and a meal, my mind was filled with confusion; my heart was very heavy as I tried to sort it all out. The clear message I got from Allene was that it was all over between us. But even so, I could not let Angela jump to the conclusion that I was going to race back out there and start plans for our marriage. I was very fond of her and flattered at her devotion to me, but I simply was not that deeply in love with her.

A sort of peace began to fill my heart when I remembered that I

could turn this whole situation over to the Lord, the heartbreak of
how Allene and I parted and the fact that I didn't know what to do
about Angela—whom I certainly did not want to hurt. So, with the
roar of the plane engines as background, I spent a long time doing
some very heavy thinking and praying.

Since I had to change planes that afternoon in Savannah, I called
home and asked Papa to have Ed Fennel meet me at the St. Simon's
airport. Papa found him, and there Ed was at the gate with a big
"Hullo." O my dear Lord, was it good to back on the Island. At the
house, I ran in to greet Mama and Papa. Ed put my bag down and
said that he had to hurry back to work. I asked him to come by
tomorrow.

You guessed it. Mama came in with a fresh cup of her famous drip
coffee and a big smile on her face. When I asked what the smile was
all about, she said, "Well, you received a collect phone call a little
while ago from Allene in New York. She wants you to call her the
moment you arrive."

"O me! Her collect call, so soon?"

Later, when Mama called Papa to come to supper, I sat over in his
big chair and placed a person to person call to Allene at her apartment. She answered the phone, choking back the tears, then slowly
began to get it all out, "James?"

"Yes, Allene?"

"James, I am so very sorry for the way I acted when you were here.
I would give anything to be able to go back over those precious few
hours. I simply cannot believe that I was so cold and so rude. I guess I
thought you were going to stay longer. I admit I was a bit nervous.
Please try to find it in your heart to forgive me. You were so handsome in your uniform, and had flown all that way to see me. I could
just kick myself. Boy, you should have heard how Maude chewed me
out royally for being so absolutely heartless! Would you give me just
one more chance to show you how fond I am of you? Please talk to
me; tell me you don't hate me. James? James! Are you there?"

"Yes, Allene, I am still here."

"Well, I am going to go sit right down and write you a long, long
letter. I promise I will never treat you that way again. Should I send
the letter to your home or to your Army address?"

"I am leaving here to go back to the Presidio probably tomorrow.
So send it on out there. Since I have a lot of thinking to do and
because I would like to see some of the country, I have decided to
take an express-through bus back to San Francisco. That trip takes

five days, so in order to get back on time, I should leave here day after tomorrow at the latest."

"James, you'll never know how I resisted running after you when you left. I wanted so to call you at the hotel. But I knew that you were exhausted, and so was I. James, will you please let me hear the words I'm dying to hear? I hardly slept a wink last night. We have known each other so long; please don't tell me it's all over for us."

I said, "Allene, you know I have loved you even before that day I found you again at the filling station. I just can't take any more of this hot and cold, in and out, up and down, off and on romance. I came to see you because I love you. You know I forgive you, so stop crying and cheer up. It's not the end of the world. We were both tired, and you were under quite a strain last night. Besides, you probably thought I would be there two or three days. And I would have been, had you invited me to do so. I'll have some time to think and pray on the trip back west. I promise to call you as soon as I get there."

She responded, "O James, you will never know how happy those words have made me. I don't want to hang up, but this is costing you loads and besides, I'm almost late for the last show at the Music Hall. So, I'll say good-bye, my dear, and God bless your sweet heart."

"God bless you, too. I really am happy that you called. Let's just both pray that we can find God's will for each of us." This was my answer for now.

I hung up, moved onto the sofa and sat in quietness as my mind went back over the events of the past two days. Later, Papa finished supper, and he and Mama rejoined me. I briefly told them about my trip to see Allene and what happened in New York. They listened closely and were glad it all turned out the way it did. Papa mentioned how good I looked in my uniform. He then reached over and rubbed my staff sergeant stripes as he gave me a wink and a big smile. Mama asked if I knew how long I'd be in the Army this time.

I said, "Well, Ma, if the rumors I heard before I left are true, we are not going to Korea. Since they have "O" gauge tracks over there, we can't use our hospital train. I sure don't want to spend a year or more in the Army as a mess sergeant. I feel that I should try to get out, go back to Phillips and get my seminary degree. Then maybe if the Army still needs me, they might call me back in as a chaplain. But it really doesn't look like there's much hope of getting out. Major Ross will probably fight it tooth and nail. But let's trust God that on my return He will see fit to bring about what's best for the Army and for me."

Mama said, "I think that finishing college is more in line with God's will for your life, Son. We will be praying day and night that it's also His will for you to get out—real soon."

I slept in the next morning. After breakfast, I called Angela and told her my plans. She couldn't wait to see me. She even wanted to wire me the money to fly. But she understood when I explained that I needed that time alone. After the call, I went in and asked Papa how I might get to Jacksonville, explaining that I could get an *express-through* bus from there to San Francisco. He said that he would ask Mr. Cherry to take me.

Although Mama waited on me constantly, I was still restless and a bit lonely. Jack, Sam, George and Vera were not there; we had sold the store; Krista was married and my old buddy, Doyle Baldwin, was out on the road painting signs for Texaco. "Oh, lonesome me!"

The next morning after we said good-bye, Mr. Cherry took me to downtown Jacksonville where I caught a big express bus with a sign on the front that read, "San Francisco." When we all boarded, every seat was taken. Then began that five-day, five-night, coast-to-coast trip with stops only in the large cities. At each of the stops we deboarded for about forty-five minutes. This gave us the chance to freshen up and have a meal. What an experience it was for me to see all of those large, often very beautiful cities, some by day and others by night, on our way to those downtown bus stations. Since I had to travel in uniform, I would usually take my plate and ask to join a couple who was not on our bus. This way I got to meet and chat with many interesting people with all their different dialects, stories, and attitudes toward life and the Korean War.

After the first day, most of us got to know each other, so we began to tell stories, sing songs and play cards. Sleeping was no trouble, but often during those nights, I leaned my chair back and gazed up at the heavens. As I looked up at the myriad of stars, I spent a long time in thought and prayer. I often quoted scriptures that I knew by heart like, "The heavens declare the glory of God, and the earth shows forth His handiwork" (Ps. 19:1). Other scriptures I reflected on included Psalm 23, 1 Corinthians 13 and the Lord's Prayer.

As I sat there one night, it occurred to me that in the last three months I had gone to the West Coast from Enid on a train, had taken a plane from San Francisco to New York City and now was covering the length of the nation from east to west on a bus! But when I looked back later on all of that traveling I did in such a short period of time, I remembered the bus trip as being the most rewarding. Seeing the country from the federal highways (there were no interstates then), going through so many small towns and having five days with no decisions to make, no orders to take, and no work to do—well, it was a mixed blessing indeed. And besides all that, I had loads of time to think, and I did more praying than I had ever done before in five days. This all helped to get my mind off myself and my troubles.

I learned a great lesson on that trip. I had a chat with the Lord about "troubles." I knew almost everyone had lots of them. Troubles, what do we mortals do about these ever-present troubles? Almost in a flash I got His clear direction, and I have had much less trouble with troubles since then. While I sat on a bus with everyone asleep but me and the driver, somewhere way out west in the middle of the night, gazing at those millions of stars, I got His simple answer.

It was this: I must go over them one by one and turn each of them completely and finally over to Him! Then a word of Scripture came to me loud and clear: "Cast all your cares upon Me, for I care for you" (1 Pet. 5:7).

So, I immediately began to release all of those troubles one by one over to Him: I needed to get out of the Army; I wanted to get back into college; the confusion and concern about Angela; and was Allene really the one to travel this journey with me. I even wound up naming everyone in my family, beginning with Mama and Papa, then Ray, and Fred whom we had lost the year before, in 1949. I also named Myrtle, Frank, George, Mary, Belle and Jack, lifting each one up, turning them over to God, and asking that He take over their lives and bless them. Practically all of them had real problems in their lives, intimate troubles which they shared with me every time I was with them.

As I turned each of these troubles, mine and theirs, over to the Lord, a sense of peace and security came over me. My own care, worry, doubt, concern and fear all began to leave me, and my mind and heart were instead filled with a great sense of freedom. I must have fallen asleep because when I awoke, the sun was just beginning to rise. I was completely refreshed and felt that the new day brought a deeper meaning to life and a more personal relationship with the Lord. This practice of "turning it all over" to God has followed me to this day. That revelation from Jesus alone was worth the trip on that bus. The last two days went by so fast that before most of us seemed ready, we were pulling into the bus station at San Francisco. After we all embraced and said warm words of farewell, I took a cab out to the Presidio.

The first thing I spied in my room was a letter on my bed from Allene. Since it was too late for supper that evening, I shoved the letter in my pocket and read it while I ate a hamburger at the NCO club close to my barracks. That gorgeous girl said the letter would be sweet, and boy, it was sweet indeed. Not only sweet in words but each page carried the slight hint of heavenly fragrance. It was so warm, personal and intimate that I got the message that she was finally serious about us. So I rejoiced that God was already beginning to give me answers to all those "troubles" I had cast upon Him.

I had a date with Angela the very next night. She never looked more lovely. She hugged me so tight that I could hardly breathe. We sat and she listened with deep interest as I told her about the trip to New York, Allene's coldness, her collect call and her long letter. Angela was quiet and had very little to say. I ended by telling her my plans to try to get out of the Army, go back to Phillips and finish my education. She was not comfortable with all of this, but agreed that I should try to get into seminary. She then took both of my hands and stated that this decision to leave the Army need not have anything to do with our relationship. She seemed sure that Allene would grow cold again. She laughed when I told her that I was going to see the chaplain. She asked if things had really gotten that bad!

For years it had been an old Army joke that a soldier only went to see the chaplain as the very last resort. Most NCOs in the Army had very little sympathy and no patience for your tough personal problems. I could hear the old familiar line, "Oh, Pippin, so you are going to see the chaplain?! Don't forget to take your TS card so the 'Chappy' can punch it for you!" TS meant "tough s...(you know what)"

One clever chaplain printed his TS card with a large T and a small h-e...and a large S with a small a-v-i-o-r. Hence, when you first glanced at the card you only saw the big TS, but when you looked closely you saw the two words The Savior! After you finished your session with him, he would actually punch the card and hand it to you. It had his name on one side and scriptures on the other.

I told Angela I knew getting out was going to be tough, yes, tough enough to go see the chaplain. When I said that I was going to need all the help that was available from heaven and earth to get out of "this man's Army," she agreed and promised to pray hard for me. I was at the place where I really needed for God to give me a huge miracle since it almost takes an act of Congress to get out of the Army. So as I left Angela that night, I embraced her and thanked her for offering to join me in prayer. I added that God would surely find a way. I mentioned that Mama was also praying day and night for this to happen.

After lights out that night I pled fervently with the Lord to bring the possible out of this seemingly impossible situation. Even though there's nothing all that wrong with being a career mess sergeant, I just felt that God seemed to agree that my time would be much better spent getting further college training to better serve Him. But how to get tough old Major Ross to see it God's way? It almost seemed useless to try.

Because I had always kept fairly close to the chaplain, I had a different attitude about seeing him. The next day was Sunday, so I attended services at the beautiful Presidio Chapel. The chaplain who preached was Lt. Colonel Charlie Brown, the Deputy Sixth Army Chaplain. His sermon was very good and very brief—about twelve minutes! As I left that morning, I asked if I could come see him tomorrow.

He answered, "You bet, Sergeant. Let's make it about ten in the morning. But give me a hint as to why you need to see me so I can give it some thought."

I told him I was recently called in as a reservist and was now a mess sergeant. I explained to him that I had the BA degree in religion, and since it didn't seem that my unit was going anywhere, I wanted to get out and go to seminary so I could get my graduate degree and even possibly come back in as a chaplain.

He smiled, grabbed my hand and said, "Hey man, I agree! OK, Pippin, I will check the regs (regulations) and all the ramifications of this thing and see what I can come up with. See you at ten."

That was the first time I ever heard the words *regs* and *ramifications*. When the secretary admitted me into the chaplain's office the next morning, he had stacks of army "regs" all over his desk. Chaplain Brown was a short, stocky man, with wire-rimmed glasses, black hair parted in the middle, a small black mustache and a thick Kansas accent.

When I entered, he jumped up and said with great excitement, "Pippin, I believe I've got it! Here look what I found. Read this and weep for joy, my boy. Listen, *'All enlisted personnel, who were called to active duty with their unit should have applied for deferment at that time.'* You see, the regs used the phrase *should have*, not *must have!*"

A MIRACLE A MINUTE

He punched the big book with his finger and continued, "My fair-haired lad, I am going to spring you out of this man's Army on that one word! All you need is a good reason, and you've got that! Sit right there while I call my good friend Col. George Gordon, the G-1, Chief of Personnel."

After Chaplain Brown told Col. Gordon the entire story and read the regs to him, citing the book, page and paragraph, Chaplain Brown paused and then said, "Do you mean if I send this request across your desk right now for Sgt. Pippin's release you'll sign it?...Super, Sir! I'll have the paperwork on your desk pronto!"

He then turned to me and said, "We got it, me boy! Just stay right there a few more minutes, *Reverend* Pippin, while I get this request for your release typed up."

I was in such shock, I could not move. In about twenty minutes he came back, papers in hand and with a big grin on his face said, "Come on, Sergeant, let's go over yonder and take this to Col. Gordon—he is on the first floor of that building right there across the street. He said he'd have your orders cut in just minutes after we get there."

I was shaking with excitement as we entered Col. Gordon's office. He was so gracious you would have thought I was his son. When his gorgeous secretary came in and handed him my orders, he smiled broadly and handed them to me. I almost broke my arm saluting him. He said to have my hospital commander, Major Ross, call him if there was any problem. After I thanked the colonel, the chaplain and I left.

Out on the sidewalk Chaplain Brown vigorously shook my hand and said, "Pack your bags, Pippin, you're out of the Army! Go tell your commander, then you can leave immediately."

I couldn't find the words to fully thank Chaplain Brown. Because I knew that the Lord had sent me in to see him, I couldn't seem to stop repeating to myself, "Thank You, Jesus." Little did I know that our paths would cross many times in the years ahead and he and I would become close friends.

All the way back to my barracks, I continued to give praise and thanks to an all-powerful and all-loving God for that chaplain. I then packed my duffel bag and walked over to headquarters (the head shed). Before I walked in, I paused at the door and prayed a fervent prayer for the Lord to calm me down and walk through this with me.

After I got First Sergeant Sullivan's okay, I went in to see the Old

Man to ask for his approval. I was shaking as I entered. I felt sure that he would do his best to stop me. Well, when I told him what had happened, he sprung up out of his chair, flew into a rage, stomped, almost swallowed his cigar and yelled so loud at me that the First ran in to see if I was actually attacking the man!

Major Ross thundered, "You are very sadly mistaken indeed, Sgt. Pippin, if you think that I am going to just sit idly by and let you get away with going behind my back and over my head to try and get out of my unit. I let you do this, and every man here will be digging up phony ways to go home. You just go forget it." He waved his hand for me to leave.

I very softly said, "Sir, Col. George Gordon, G-1 Personnel, has already cut my orders and wants the major to phone him right away."

He growled as he snatched up the phone, pointed his finger at me with the wet cigar in his hand, his face as red as a beet.

He loudly said, "Preacher, I'm gonna show you that you cannot pull a stunt like this and get away with it. I'm gonna give that colonel a piece of my mind. The very idea of him messing with my men. You just stand there and listen."

Sergeant Sullivan stood near the door, all the while slowly shaking his head at Maj. Ross, who paid no attention to him. When he grabbed the phone and slammed it down in the middle of his desk, I feared he'd break his big finger or rip the dial off the phone. I had actually stopped breathing.

"Col. Gordon, Major Ross, Commandant, 325 Hospital Train Unit. I want you to rescind those orders on SSgt Pippin right now... Sir?...Oh....Yes, Sir, I know who I'm talking to...Yes, Colonel Sir...I'm listening...Yes, Sir, undivided attention... Regs?...Oh...I see...back to schoo...Col...Yes. Sir...Oh, no Sir, no need to mention that, I would never think of standing in the way. You are exactly right, Sir, no need to make a big fuss about this...I agree 150 percent...that in this special case...we should do exactly as you say. Oh, yes Sir, don't worry Sir, he's outta here right now. Oh, no Sir, never again, Sir!"

Major Ross slammed down the phone, then proceeded around the desk, came over to me, pointed his cigar stained finger in my face, and said, "Sarge, no one must ever know that this man went to see that dangerous chaplain. My God, he is probably smart enough to find ways to get my entire unit out of the Army! Now listen, both of you. The Colonel has ordered us to forget the entire matter. OK, Pippin, I was told to apologize, but God help you if you ever do become a chaplain, you'd jolly well better pray that I'm never your commander again. Now I want you outta my unit and off this post immediately! And hey, you," the major walked up closer with his cigar finger almost touching my nose, began shouting, and as his voice turned shrill, he concluded, "Don't you dare talk to a soul, do you understand? You keep that big mouth of yours SHUT 'til you are off this post…DO YOU READ ME?!!! If you ignore my order, so help me God, I will strip those stripes off your sleeve and get the Sergeant here to go find you and shoot you!!"

I popped to and said, with a wide grin, "Yes Sir! Major Ross, Sir!! I fully do understand. But, Sir. I want to apologi…"

He rigidly pointed his finger, his cigar and his big red nose toward the door and yelled, *"Get outta here!"*

"Sir, I am outta here!"

As I left, I stopped to shake hands with a smiling first sergeant, who whispered to me, "So long, Pippin, proud of you, get back into school and good luck!"

I was so ecstatic, I almost hugged the sergeant's neck. I sped to my barracks and started praising the Lord again for using Chaplain Brown to get me out of the Army. Can you believe that all of this happened in less than two hours! I asked for a miracle, and O my sweet Jesus, did I get a whopper!! Just prayers of faith *and a very smart chaplain* made it a reality. Also, something big had to happen 'cause Mama was praying! The good Lord always seemed to set great store by Mama's prayers. I was reminded of the time when the Lord changed my orders and sent me to Lawson. I got my bag and cleared the post, but before I could leave for Enid the next morning, I kept what I thought was my last date with a certain pretty girl. Name? Angela Barefoot.

Yes! Praise God, I was out of the Army. It was January 13, 1951.

❋ 18 ❋

What a Woman!

Since the second semester at Phillips was to begin on January 20, there was no time to lose. Just before I left the base to see Angela that afternoon, I got a letter from Brother Frank. While I sipped coffee with Angela, I removed my shoes and gently put my feet up on her coffee table. I then handed her the letter and asked her to open it and read it to me. Frank had been selected as the "Christian Challenge Week" speaker at Phillips University, beginning the twenty-fifth of January. He would speak twice a day for a week, each morning in chapel at 10:30 A.M. and each night at an all-campus meeting at 7:30 P.M.

When Angela finished the letter, she looked up and asked, "James, would it be OK if I come to Enid to hear Frank?"

I said coolly, "You can't be serious!"

She just smiled and shrugged her shoulders. But on the way to the airport the next morning, she said, "Guess what? I have arranged to take a week's leave. Would you please check with Frank and see if it is OK for me to come?"

I didn't want to give her any encouragement, so I answered, "Angela, I really don't think that this would be quite proper."

Still, as she grabbed me and kissed me good-bye, her last words were, "See you in Oklahoma in a few days." And I knew she would.

I walked to the plane, waved and said laughing, "Oh, sure, you bet. Bye-bye, and let's keep in touch."

I looked back at her just in time to see her stick out her tongue at me!

On the plane, I kept wondering what in the world I was going to do with this pretty girl. I had felt certain all along that she would come to Enid. Since the only decent hotel there was the Youngblood, where Frank was likely to stay, I could see her in that hotel, up bright and early, eating breakfast with Frank and trying to wiggle her way into the Pippin family. I chuckled and said to myself, "What a woman! That girl is quite a character!"

She was so outgoing, intelligent and sweet, I knew Frank would be flattered to have her company. But my mind and heart were so involved with Allene that I was sure Angela felt I had no intention of getting serious with her. But she was no quitter.

I changed planes in Dallas, got a Braniff Airways DC-3 to Enid and arrived about midafternoon. As I walked away from the plane and the pilot cut the engines, I stopped in my tracks. That sound, that smell, brought a vivid mental flashback to the many times when I had heard those DC-3s at Lawson. I couldn't shake the memory of all those wounded men and women being off-loaded; some were groaning, and others were crying and laughing at the same time because they were so glad to be back on Georgia soil near their homes.

I took a deep sigh, went on to baggage and then went out to the street to hail a cab. I asked to be taken to the Berg house, and I prayed on the way there that I would have no trouble finding a room. As the driver dropped me off, Bob Book walked out on his way to the library. He dropped his books, I dropped my bag. Then we laughed and hugged until we were both in tears. He couldn't believe I was out of the Army and back at Phillips.

As he wiped his eyes, he told me, "Pip, can you believe that some of the professors and students thought you had quit the ministry. When one of your professors heard that you were going back into the Army, he said, 'Well, that's the last we'll ever see of Jim Pippin. He has abandoned the ministry for the Army. Believe me, he'll never return!'" Wishful thinking!

But Bob so believed I'd be back that he had Mom Berg hold my room for that semester. As we walked toward the door he told me that my old room was waiting upstairs and he'd be glad to have me as a roommate again.

The next day I enrolled in seminary for second semester, then went in to see the "student bishop" to ask if there were any churches open. He had one small one at Comanche, Oklahoma. I took it, but waited until after Christian Challenge Week to get started.

I had only been back in my room for a minute when Angela called to tell me that she had found Frank's number and called him. She said he was delighted that she could come and had reserved her a room, and get this, it was adjoining his room at the Youngblood! He failed to mention to her that before I got serious about any girl, he had to check her out. Now this had always been and was a fact. Almost as if I were his son, Frank always had to meet all of my girlfriends. I guess in all my years at Phillips, I ran about five girls past him. He usually had nicknames for them like "Little Chalk," a girl whose legs were small, white and straight like pieces of chalk. Another he called "Stringbean," for she was kind of erect and skinny. The last one he called "Toad Frog" because she had no neck! So, he invited Angela to Enid, not only to have a pretty girl around, but to look her over and pick her brain to see if she might be right for me.

Angela told me Frank said that since I would be there for some of the meals that week and then staying in the evenings to chat, he wanted her room next to his—so we could all be together more.

O my Lord, I thought. Then I asked her if she and Frank had any bright ideas about how we were going to pull all of this off. *He* couldn't walk into the meetings with her, and *I* didn't dare, because if I did walk in with her, those students would be all over me thinking she was my fiancée. Plus, they would just know (assume, that is) I was staying down there in the room with her. Gossip would flood the campus. Then Dean would call me in and probably kick me out of school. I certainly didn't want to have to do all of that explaining to anyone.

Well, she came back with, "Not to worry, no big deal; I will get a cab and enter the chapel alone. James, would you please just relax and stop worrying about what people will think!"

Oh, yeah, I thought, *fine thing for you to say.* But I did just that. I relaxed and decided to go along with their little scheme.

Frank drove up in my '50 Olds late Sunday afternoon. He picked me up at the Berg house, and I drove him downtown to the Youngblood, where he checked into one of their largest rooms. I was very glad to get my car back, but I was shocked when I looked at the odometer. That sneaky little rascal, he had garaged his car and driven mine every day for almost five months and put almost twenty thousand miles on it! I never let him know I knew about it though. It didn't matter to me because he had always been so liberal with me.

Now, the plot thickens…

Angela arrived on Sunday evening and checked in to the room next door to Frank, who was tickled pink. He had not heard that Allene and I had made up, so here he was at his famous matchmaking game again. But he was right about having Angela come, because beginning with that first night when he met Angela, the three of us started having a great time together. It was a most delightful week. Angela put her best barefoot forward (please excuse that awful pun). Of course, this was no task for her to do, including wearing some of her most beautiful clothes—short dresses, sexy hose and heels—each evening. Since she was a first lieutenant dietitian in the U. S. Army, Frank, who was a retired lieutenant colonel, had a hundred Army jokes and stories to tell her. She hung on his every word and laughed at all of his jokes. He also gave each of us copies of his latest book. He personalized them with his autograph and a thoughtful note. He was very impressed with Angela, to say the least. She was quite a challenge for him…in many ways. Old Frank was beside himself!

So, when the meetings began on Monday morning, she was rolling in high gear with her secret little plan. Since we couldn't be seen together in the dining room, I would drop by to have breakfast with Frank and Angela in Frank's room, then I would take him to the Phillip's Chapel in time for the ten-thirty morning service. Angela always came to the meetings by cab, crept in and walked to the back of the chapel—often sitting right next to me! After the service, I stood up and introduced myself to her, acting as if I had never seen her before.

Many of my friends, both boys and girls, kept asking me, "Who was that pretty blond? She is so charming!"

I would answer, "I agree with you fully; she is beautiful." As my friends walked off, I always had this little sheepish grin on my face. As a matter of fact, I wore it all week.

I was never more proud of Brother Frank. He was at his very best at both the morning and the evening services. He had lunch each day with some of his good friends at the university, but he always wanted me to come down and have a sandwich and coffee with him in his room at about five in the afternoon. After the services, he saved his evenings for Angela and me. We would dine at one of the two best restaurants in town, or he would have us over to his room and order up a gourmet dinner for all of us.

On the last night, Frank preached that great message "Come Before Winter," based on a sermon that had been preached years earlier by Clarence E. McCartney. The aged apostle Paul, in 2 Timothy 4:14, requested for Timothy to bring him his cloak, his books and above all the parchments and to "do your best to come before winter." Frank took that topic and soared with it, in prose, electric; in poetry, devastating; closing his sermon with such intensity and packed meaning that I wished he'd never stop. Then he said these final words and sat down: "If you are going to come at all, come to Christ before winter has turned your heart cold, and age has turned your head white."

This was one of Frank's best. Dr. McCartney's sermon on this subject was so great that his congregation insisted he preach it once a year, and he did so for many years. Imagine that happening today!

That night as he spoke, we were often on the edge of our seats while Frank led us up unto the hills, way above the timberline where the air was thin and our minds and our bodies seemed to float, and all the while, he had us laughing and crying. Many people felt that Frank was one of the top ten preachers in the nation. The *Kansas City Star* showed that they agreed by putting a brief version of his Sunday sermons on the front page, full left column, every Monday morning for several years.

Frank also did not "suffer fools lightly." In a joint student meeting that was held over in the women's dorm after the evening service, a smart young man asked Frank a rather complicated question about the law and the church. Frank saw through the situation immediately and answered, "Sir, have you read *Beverage's Life of John Marshall?* No? Well, go look it up, the answer is in there." (Sure, but in which one of the five volumes?!!) The entire group exploded with laughter.

So the week of great preaching was over too soon, but what a blessing it seemed to be to all the students and faculty who attended, and especially to Angela and me. Frank asked me to drive him back to Kansas City and spend the weekend with him. I had finally told him that Allene and I were back together. Since we could not get Angela a flight out of Oklahoma City, Frank and I took her to Wichita, where she was to catch a nonstop flight to San Francisco. It helped that Frank walked with us to the gate. It was so difficult for me to say good-bye; she had been such a sweet lady and a dear friend. Since I had tried to keep things kinda cooled down that week, I think she knew that this might be a final farewell.

Holding hands, she and I walked a little closer to the plane, where fighting back tears, I took her tenderly into my arms, gave her a tight hug and a long kiss. Then I watched her as she walked up the steps and into the plane. She did not turn around to wave. When Frank and I got back to the car, we waited to watch her plane take off. It flew directly over our heads. Frank got in the car, but I stood there for a moment and watched the lights of her plane wink out into the night. I sobbed, sighed deeply, took out my handkerchief, wiped my tears, blew my nose and then got in the car and drove off.

Frank turned to me and said, "Son, I really believe that Angela is the finest of your girlfriends I have met so far."

I only nodded; no words would come. As we drove on into the night, I wondered, *Are marriages really made in heaven? Why do we know so little about the human emotions and so little about what makes us fall in love with one and not another.* I have often thought that there were several persons on earth with whom I could have fallen in love and lived happily ever after. I suppose that it all depends on place and time and a certain person being in our immediate environment. I looked at Frank who was now dozing, and concluded that all this was a bit too much for my feeble brain and sad heart to figure out. Anyway, I missed Angela already and would have liked to have kept her as one of my...dearest friends. Oh well!

After that night, Angela and I talked a couple of times on the phone. Each time I tried my best to explain the dilemma, telling her that because of my longtime feelings for Allene, I could not right now think of marrying anyone else. With a sad heart, I told her how fond I was of her. I also expressed my thanks for all we had shared and all she had done. When I asked if we could please keep in touch, she gave no answer...but quietly placed the receiver in the cradle. After that night in Wichita, we never saw each other again. Why does it have to hurt so bad?

I had only been at the little church in Comanche for a few weeks when Frank asked me to be his weekend assistant. I saw this as a great opportunity to advance my knowledge and experience. So, beginning in late March, I began driving up there every weekend.

Allene and I wrote each other often during the next few weeks. We also talked on the phone frequently. One afternoon, I went to the campus bookstore, bought her a nice New Testament and had it gift wrapped with a card inside that read, "I miss you and love you more every day. Sweetheart, why don't you transfer all that talent from the stage to the church chancel?"

Her next letter ignored that suggestion.

During my next weekend at Frank's church, he told me that since Brother Jack had been released early from prison, he had been doing great at Mercer University. He said he had been talking and writing to Gertrude Evans during the last few months. She was an attractive, slender blond with blue eyes and was—as Allene would quote that line from a movie—"your usual nightmare." She was one of Frank's active members who had been divorced years earlier. Lo and behold, Frank then said that Jack was coming to meet her and he thought they just might be thinking of marriage. It must have been those sweet letters in his beautiful handwriting because when Jack arrived it was love at first sight and they decided to get married the following weekend!

All of a sudden, I had an explosive idea. Since I was going to drive Jack and Gertrude to Brunswick and Macon after the wedding, I took the long-shot chance of my life. I phoned Allene and suggested that she take a few days off and come to Kansas City that weekend for Jack's wedding and ride to Brunswick with us. I offered to wire her the money for her ticket if she would come. I was trembling, so sure she'd turn me down.

Her answer? "Wow, James, you sure do know how to sweep a girl off her feet. Let me call you back in about an hour."

I sat by the phone waiting, and in less than an hour she called and said, "James, I have never done anything like this in my life. This is crazy! But I'm coming! Wire the money! I'll be on the first plane out of here in the morning."

I did, and she did! Frank and I met her that Friday afternoon at the old airport just across the river from downtown Kansas City. He and I waited for her at the gate. The moment Frank saw her coming, he noticed her pretty face with those huge brown eyes, all that lovely auburn hair, that shapely figure, and how she carried herself in the tailored suit she wore.

His face lit up like a neon sign and he turned to me and said, *"Son, by God, this is the one; she's TOPS!"*

Allene ran and leaped into my arms, then gave Frank a big bear hug. From that day until he died, Frank never called Allene by any other name than "TOPS."

As we drove to "Ten Acres," Allene told us, in that uniquely sparkling voice of hers, a little about what she had been doing in New York and how she was able to leave on such short notice. At "Ten Acres," Jack and Gertrude joined us for dinner. That evening comes back so clearly now in my mind. After dinner, we all sat around the mammoth fireplace, its flames flickering across our faces, as we chatted until the wee hours of that night of nights in the long ago. Julia, their pretty, brilliant, teenage redhead, spent the evening smiling, winking at me and letting out a giggle now and then. She was totally amused at her two romantic uncles, but really impressed by the two beautifully different girls that were in the room that night.

I went to bed, but I was too excited to sleep. I had taken Allene to her room, had a prayer with her and a goodnight kiss, tucked her in and then come to bed. I was tingling all over with excitement. Just imagine, my girl was in one bedroom, Jack's in another; and he and I were on cots in the den, staring up into the darkness, unable to believe all of this was happening. If you had told me one week earlier that this was how things would be, I would have said, "Never in a million years." But by now, you and I know that with God, time is no problem. Talk about a miracle a minute! That coming week was crammed with them. Life is so wonderful when one is in love!

After breakfast, Frank took Allene and me into town so she could see the church. Jack drove Gertrude back to her apartment and went on to the parsonage. Allene was very impressed with Brother Frank and the church. After he showed us around that unique structure, we wound up in his large, new plush study. He served us fresh coffee from his coffee bar.

Then Allene went over to the phone and called her mother. When Allene said, "Mama, I'm in Kansas City," Lucille yelled "WHAT!" so loudly that we heard her clear across the room. Allene tried to explain the whole thing, but then when she said she was with me, Lucille settled down and things seemed better. When Frank got on the line and assured her all was fine, that really made it OK. Allene told her about Jack's wedding and that we would be home late Monday night.

Then the three of us were off to the Union Station Restaurant at the beautiful, old train terminal for some super coffee and an unforgettable lunch. Frank kept Allene talking the whole time, showing keen interest in all she had been doing.

Frank had a sneaky little trick he used whenever several of us Pippins ate out together. Since he usually picked up the bill, he had us order first. To go easy on him, we usually ordered one of the lesser priced items on the menu. Then, when the waiter had taken all of our orders and finally came to him to take his, Frank would order one of the most expensive items on the menu. Then several of us would speak up in unison, "Waiter, please give me what he ord...," but Frank would break in with a broad smile and smugly announce, "Sorry, guys, you have already placed your orders; you cannot change them now!"

We would glance at each other and let out a big groan, "Foiled again."

When I told this story to Allene, she and Frank got a great laugh out of it. However, he did not pull this little trick that day because he wanted us to have the very best.

As soon as we were seated, he said to me, "Now, Brother James, you two order whatever you want from the left side of the menu, and remember, your money is no good in Kansas City!"

After I grew up and had a good income, I would usually pay, or he and I would split the bill. Most of our brothers and sisters and even some of our close friends seemed to know that he or I would pick up the tab. But when we were with a group of our "freeloadin' family," he or I often pulled his sneaky little trick! But it was just a game. Frank, Jack, George and I were always glad to treat, and we thanked a loving God who blessed us so that we could do this.

Sunday morning at Community Christian Church was a time to remember: two packed services with the great old hymns, good music and a stirring anthem. Jack, Gertrude, Allene and I sat front row and center. Frank asked Jack and Gertrude to stand for an introduction and told the church about the wedding that afternoon. Then after some complimentary words about Jack, he looked at Gertrude and told her how much everyone was going to miss her. Before the service, Frank had asked me to read the scriptures and bring the PASToral prayer. As I went up to the pulpit, the church broke into applause. I was delighted that they were glad to see me again. I glanced behind me and saw that Frank was applauding as loudly as anyone.

Just before he began his sermon, he called Allene up to the pulpit, introduced her, told them she was my girlfriend, fresh from New York City, where she was pursuing a career in voice. After the congregation gave her a hand, he asked if she would sing the Lord's Prayer for us. He had tipped off the organist, Gladys Cranston, who hit a chord and she and Allene together filled that house with a touch of glory.

When Allene finished, the congregation stood and gave the Lord and her a hearty applause. I don't believe there was a dry eye in the place. When she came back down and sat beside me, I was so moved I felt like "melting and flowing down the isle!" I put my arm around her, took her hand and gave her a wink and a hug. Jack and Gertrude also whispered their love and approval. I wondered if life could ever be this great again! You can imagine how her solo and the church's response caused Brother Frank and me both to burst with pride. Of course, after all this, he had no trouble preaching a super great sermon. At the close of the service, Frank reminded the people of Jack and Gertrude's wedding that afternoon, and then asked all four of us to go with him to the foyer and greet the congregation as they left. Many people just had to hug Allene as if they were welcoming her into the family. She was so gracious to everyone. Her bright, tragic eyes showed me that she was beside herself, sparkling with joy at being there and so surprised that Frank had asked her to sing. From that day until he retired, we claimed Community Christian as our home church and Brother Frank as our pastor.

It was a beautiful wedding in Bonfil's Chapel that Sunday afternoon. The church members filled the place. Allene sang the familiar song "Because" and Gertrude was a picture of charm and beauty. She wore a tailored beige suit with matching shoes and blouse. At the reception, Frank and I gave her a hug and a kiss and told her how glad we were to have her in the Pippin family. In the midst of a shower of rice and farewells, Frank, Ozelle and Julia walked the four of us out to my Olds. After Frank's usual circle of prayer, we were off on our long trip to Brunswick. He, Ozelle and Julia stood waving until we were out of sight. Jack and I shared the driving, so I got to spend a lot of time with Allene in the back seat. Since she was too shy in their presence and in broad daylight for us to smooch much, we just held hands and gazed into each others eyes…and waited for it to get dark!

We drove all that afternoon and all that night. There was no use in stopping at a motel because none of us could have slept a wink! I was driving the morning we got to Tupelo, Mississippi. I knew just the place to stop. As we drove into the city, I told them about the drunk who tried to shave me. Then I pulled in and parked in front of the restaurant that was a few doors down from that barbershop. To save time, we sat at the counter on stools and ordered breakfast. As Allene and I touched our coffee cups together, I wondered how anyone could be so beautiful after a sleepless night. Jack and Gertrude were deep in conversation when Allene suddenly turned to me and out of a clear blue sky, said, *"Well, Mr. Pippin, just when would you like to get married?"*

Well…my dear Lord! I almost fell off the stool. She had just said the very words I thought would never come out of that pretty mouth of hers—and when they finally came, it scared me to death.

I thought of the time I saw a little dog being chased by a big one. When the little one stopped and turned, the big one wheeled around and ran for his life! I had been chasing this girl for years, trying to get her to say she would marry me, and now here she was actually doing the proposing! I do not remember my answer. Neither does she. I also don't recall what I ate, or if I ate.

When we got back on the road with Jack driving, she took my hand, turned "those cool and limped brown eyes" on me, her face covered with this great big grin, and said, "Well, my dear, I finally just upped and said it! What do you think?"

A hundred things were going through my head as I responded, "Now Allene! Are you sure? What about New York, your job at Radio City, your singing career, your voice teacher, the choir…does your mother know…and just when did you decide you wanted to marry me?"

After a pause, she started to talk, first slowly and quietly, and then more and more rapidly until I was having trouble following her.

"James, I've been wanting to marry you all along and wouldn't admit it! Look, if you are ready to get married, so am I. *Of course*, my mother doesn't know. I just decided this morning! I am not going back to New York. Maude can ship me all that stuff. Remember that sweet note you sent me in the Bible, telling me that I should transfer my talent from the stage to the chancel? Well, that started me to thinking and praying about my future. Then your asking me out of the blue to come to Kansas City, your wonderful brother Frank, his great church service, his asking me to sing, Jack and Gertrude's lovely wedding, getting to know you as you really are, knowing the long time you've been in love with me…and how long you have waited for me…I simply just…caved in. Guess what? I even thought of grabbing you by the hand and marching up there after Frank finished with Jack and Gertrude, and saying, 'Brother Frank, do it again for James and me!!'"

Here she let out a loud cackle, and the other two "love birds" in the front seat joined in.

She continued, "While I've been with you this weekend, I've come to realize that this is where I am supposed to be and supposed to stay. In a few words, James, I also want to be a member of the Pippin family. I want to become Mrs. James Clayton Pippin. That's all I know to say."

I just sat there smiling. I thought of Gable's words about Scarlet in *Gone With the Wind*. He smiled, shook his head as she drove off in the buggy, and said, "WHAT A WOMAN!"

I said to the newlyweds in the front seat, "You know, this here's one gutsy little girl. What do you all think?"

Gertrude answered, "Aaat's right, Brother James, but she's gonna have to have lots o'guts to put up with you, boy!"

Then Allene jumped in saying, as she hit me on the shoulder, "Wait a minute! Is there something about you that I don't know, 'Bruuther James'?"

To which I answered, "A lot, my little chick-a-dee, a lot!"

A MIRACLE A MINUTE

After Allene socked me again and laughed, I pulled her close to me and said, "I'm just kidding, Sweetie!!"

Then Gertrude chimed in with, "To tell you the truth, Allene, I have also wanted to get into the Pippin family, but Jack here was the only one left!"

Now Jack remarked, "Well, thanks a lot!"

The car was suddenly filled with laughter. I hugged Allene tight and Gertrude jumped over and threw her arms around Jack, almost causing us to leave the road. Then when they were not looking, Allene fell over with her head in my lap and I tenderly kissed the future Mrs. James Pippin.

She sort of startled me when she put her hand on the back of my neck, pulled me down close and said, "Sweetie, could you give me just one more like that?"

I could feel her lips moving against mine as she whispered, "As they say in the movies, 'once more...with feeling!'"

In the middle of her kiss, the car seemed to be floating above the clouds. O my good Lord! I felt like ET and Elliot on that bicycle, soaring off into the sky! All of this...and the nearest cold shower was a thousand miles away!

Allene sat back up, and the new Olds purred along clicking off the miles. We both gradually began to get drowsy. As I slipped my arm around her, her head slowly fell over on my shoulder and we both drifted off to sleep. The next thing I knew, Jack was shaking me, saying that it was time for coffee and lunch.

For the rest of the trip, Jack and Gertrude did most of the talking, and all the while, Allene and I were smiling, grunting, nodding and stealing a kiss now and then, hardly hearing a word they said.

We pulled into the driveway of Allene's home Monday afternoon, twelve hundred miles and twenty-four hours later. She and I led the way into the house, Jack and Gertrude following close behind. Allene's mama and daddy were elated to see her and all of us. Then over coffee and hot buttered biscuits in the kitchen, Allene brought them up to date on what was going on and how all this had come about. This was all OK with Lucille since she had loved me long before Allene did. After getting up my courage, I turned to her dad and meekly asked if I could have his daughter's hand in marriage.

Henley answered, "This suits me."

Lucille shot back in a flash with, "That reminds me, Henley, you're going to need a new suit for the wedding." That brought a laugh from all of us.

I said, mainly to Henley, "Thanks, Mr. Hall, I'll do my best to make her a good husband. But after that pun from Lucille, do you think you can stand one more joker in the family?"

Jack smiled and reminded us that we needed to get going since we all could use some sleep. So after handshakes and hugs with my future parents-in-law and several tight hugs and kisses with Allene out by the car, she and I tore ourselves apart. Then Jack, Gertrude and I went on over to our house on St. Simon's.

Mama and Papa listened to all the "rapid and revoltin' developmunts" with their eyes and mouths wide open. We three sat there with Cheshire cat grins covering our faces. They just fell in love with Gertrude right off the bat. Mama jumped up to go and start supper, and Gertrude went in to help. So Papa, Jack and I had a chance to have a private chat, a pleasure we had not had in years.

The next morning I drove over to Brunswick and had breakfast with Allene, after which we went to Cunningham's Jewelry to pick out her rings. While Allene was in another part of the store, I whispered to Mr. Cunningham to tell her that the ring wouldn't be ready until tomorrow. I wanted to pick it up later that day and surprise her that night. When we got back to her house, Lucille told us that Jack had called from the Island, saying that Belle wanted us to come up there to their house in Jesup for supper. So I left Allene at home to get ready. Before I went to the Island to pick up Jack and Gertrude, I dropped by Cunningham's to get Allene's ring.

Within the hour, the four of us were on the road to Jesup, just forty miles north, with my sweet lady by my side. Halfway there, I stopped the car and asked Jack and Gertrude to get out and give us a minute alone.

I told Allene I had a surprise for her. Then I pulled out the ring and placed it on her finger, kissed her and said, "Now, you are mine, all mine forever. We are officially engaged!"

She held up her beautiful hand and gazed at the ring, and as tears filled her eyes, she threw her arms around me, hugged me tight and covered my face with kisses.

My sister Belle and her husband, Stanton, were elated to see us. Stanton Lee was handsome enough to be in the movies. He had straight black hair, deep blue, sparkling eyes and a pencil mustache. He favored Sean Connery, my favorite James Bond. Stanton and Belle were dying to get caught up on all the news, which Jack and I gladly took turns telling. Then we all sat down to one of Belle's special country suppers: a large plate of pork chops, biscuits and gravy, fresh garden "wugetables," lots of coffee, and for dessert, a double serving of banana pudding. Thank God I'm a country boy! Belle, Jack and I had grown up together and were very close, so we had many stories to share with Allene, Gertrude and Stanton. We three blushed a lot, but we had some good laughs.

Then Belle said, "I cannot believe that both of my baby brothers are sitting here, one just married and the other soon to be, and are marrying two of the most beautiful and finest looking girls I've ever met. You guys not only know how to pick 'em, but you don't waste any time doing it either!"

I glanced at Allene and said, "Belle, if you only knew how long it has taken me to get this girl to say she wanted to marry me!"

Later we all stood up, exchanged hugs and had a circle of prayer. Then after words of thanks for the evening and the dinner, we said goodnight and were on our way back to Brunswick.

Vera and George had the four of us over for supper the next night for some more great southern cooking. Their three boys, Tom, Bob and Johnny, were made to eat in the kitchen, or there might not have been enough to go around! Just kidding, guys! I do believe those growing kids were hollow from head to foot, but they were so handsome and such fun. I was close to them because years earlier, I often had to baby-sit them.

During supper, I reminded Vera that she was the one who had tried to put Allene and me together two years before the Lord made it happen. George kept going on about how in the world could these two pretty girls, Allene and Gertrude, marry two such plain and ugly Pippins. Actually, he and Vera were delighted at how things had turned out for both of us. Vera said she could not believe that all this had happened so fast.

I responded, "Well, it's hard for Jack and me to realize it, too. But we give all the credit to Christ because all of this is just more of His special miracles."

Gertrude and Jack said, almost in unison, "That is so very true."

We hated to break away, but it was getting late, and since Jack had to return to Mercer University the next morning and I had to head back to Phillips, we said good-bye to George, Vera and the boys. They walked us out to the car, and just as we got in, Vera said that she and George wanted to have our rehearsal supper at their house. Allene and I were overjoyed and said how wonderful that was of them. We had not set the date yet, but promised to tell them as soon as we knew. That night I realized, more than ever before, what wonderful families Allene and I had. After we dropped Jack and Gertrude off at the house, I drove Allene home. I was misty-eyed all the way back to her house, but had a feeling of joy that I cannot describe.

That next morning was the hardest. Jack, Gerturde and I had breakfast with Papa and Mama. Since I would be returning for the wedding soon, it was so much easier to leave them. But it was not so easy when I had to part with Allene. She even wanted to ride to Macon with us and get the bus back, but I talked her out of that. I gently pushed her against the car, hugged her tight, looked her straight in the eye and kissed her so hard it hurt. I could not say another word, so I quickly got in the car and I drove off with Jack and Gertrude.

At Jack's place in Macon, I helped them unpack. Then I freshened up, had a sandwich and was on my way to Oklahoma. I think it was the longest, loneliest trip I have ever made. I kept reaching over for Allene in the seat. It's strange how two people could become so strongly attached in so short a time. I missed her from the first moment we parted. The next afternoon I arrived at the Berg house tired, hungry and lonely.

My roommate, Bob Book, immediately told me that Allene had called, so I phoned her back. She had called her pastor at First Presbyterian and told him that she had chosen Sunday afternoon, May 6, 3:30 P.M. as the day and time for our wedding. He said this was fine with him. Allene and I both wanted Frank to do our service, so I checked with him, and he was delighted. When I called Allene back, we officially set the date. She said she would order the invitations the next day.

Before we hung up, she spoke words that she had said very few times to me in the past, "I love you, dear one, and I miss you more every day."

Then she added, "Oh, guess what! I have been asked to give a farewell concert to a large group over at the Cloister Hotel on Sea Island. I want to do my very best, so please start praying for me. I'll tell you more about it later. Are you missing me? You're not messing around out there with any of your old girlfriends, are you? You'd better not, or I'll come out there and scratch their eyes out. Seriously though, pray for the time to fly 'til we are together forever. I can't wait!"

I assured her that I sorely missed her, only had eyes for her and would be praying that all would go well at the concert. We wrote almost every day, and my phone bill that month would have paid off half the national debt. But it was more than worth it. Those wonderful and intimate calls helped the time go by so much faster.

One afternoon about two weeks later, Allene called. In a shaky voice she said, "Sweetheart, you are going to get a special delivery letter from me in the morning. You've got to promise me *that you will not open it.* Please, you must not open or read that letter. Do you promise?"

"Of course, Honey. What's going on?"

"Nothing. Everything is OK now. Don't worry, I'll tell you all about it tomorrow night."

She would not even give me a hint as to what the letter was about. I promised her that I would honor her wish, but I was on pins and needles wondering what was up.

The next morning at about eight o'clock Bob Book walked in and handed me the letter. As he gave it to me he chuckled and said, "Here's a special delivery letter for you, Pip. She's backed out!"

As soon as he left, I went to the bathroom and fought the strong temptation to open it. I then tore the letter up into small pieces and flushed it down the drain. As I did this, I wondered just what in the world was in that letter. Believe me, I spent a very long day praying and waiting for her call.

That night after supper, she phoned and told me the whole story.

"As you know," she began, "I was asked by the Cloister Hotel to have this concert as a Sunday afternoon feature for all of their guests. Well, at that concert, which was also attended by many of my friends and classmates, the room was packed and I evidently did well. Then this lovely lady, one of the guests at the hotel, came up afterwards to tell me what a grand voice I had. She was an older lady, covered with furs and diamonds.

"She came up close, took me by both hands and said, 'A gift, my dear girl, that's what you have, a great gift! One of the best voices I've ever heard and believe me, I've heard quite a few. Now, I'm going to make you an offer tonight that you cannot turn down. I want to send you to Italy to study for a year. I have connections there. I will cover all of your expenses. But meet me in the lobby after you have finished greeting your guests, and we'll talk about the details.'

"James, I was absolutely swept off my feet. Everyone told me that I could not turn that offer down. Only Mama had reservations about it, saying that if I accepted the offer I would have to postpone the wedding. So I sat down yesterday morning and wrote you that letter, telling you the story and asking you if you would agree to put the wedding off for a year. As soon as I dropped it at the post office, I was torn to pieces with doubts and confusion. I regretted that I had decided to go and that I had the heart to do this to you and put it all in a letter. Then I thought, how could I even think of asking you to wait another year after you had already waited so long. Well, I was so distraught, I cried all afternoon. When Mama came to my room, I told her that I really needed prayer and I just had to go and find a pastor to pray with me about this."

She continued, "Well, the only praying man of God I could think of was Dr. Webster, the pastor of the First Baptist Church here in Brunswick. Mama and I made an appointment and met him in his study. There I explained my serious dilemma. I told him that I had to have the Lord's direction on this. Believe it or not, all three of us got down on our knees, and he prayed the most wonderfully devout prayer I have ever heard. We stood up, and as he showed us out, he said he was confident that I would do the right thing. As we left his study, I knew in a flash what I was going to do. As soon as we got to the house, I called the lady and with many tears I thanked her and told her why I felt that I must turn down her great offer."

Allene continued to explain, "As soon as I hung up with her, I called and told you not to read the letter. James, I am so thankful that you did not read that letter. I know that you didn't because you would have called the instant you read it and told me to forget the wedding, forget you and forget about us forever and ever. As the poet said, 'Cancel all our vows!' Right?"

I answered, "Yes, I tremble to think that you are right. No, I did not read it, Sweetheart. I thank God that your call came before the letter did! But listen to this. As Bob handed it to me, he laughed and said, 'Pip, here is a special delivery letter for you. She's backed out!'"

She said, shrill and loud, "You have got to be kidding!"

I said, "No, I'm not!"

Then we both began to laugh. But her laughter quickly turned to sobs. Before we hung up, I assured her that everything was OK; and I was really fine. After hearing that, she was a very happy lady.

(I have wondered a thousand times why Allene didn't tell the dear lady that she would be glad to go if she could take her new husband with her! I could have studied "abroad" for a year, but none of us thought of that at the time. I just know that the woman would have joyfully given that to us for a wedding present.)

But, I wasn't about to give her the chance to receive another such offer, so I got Dean England to let me off early. I arrived home on the third of May, and I hardly let her out of my sight until Saturday. That afternoon I met Frank at the airport and took him to George's. Allene's only sister Cille was going to be matron of honor, so she and Jimmy arrived on Friday. After Frank performed a smooth rehearsal Saturday night, we had a great rehearsal supper at Vera and George's house.

Sunday morning, after breakfast, Mama and Papa wanted to know all about how Allene was led to leave New York and how she had decided to marry me. While we were chatting, Mama also told me how glad she was that our prayers and that chaplain got me out of the Army and back into college. Papa was delighted about my plans to finish my graduate degree. He was also happy about the reports he had heard about my ministry at Community. Mama reminded me of the good visit she had when she went out there to see Frank. It was a special blessing just to sit with them and have a good chat. She also told me they were sorry they could not come to the wedding.

On Sunday afternoon I showered, shaved closer than ever, and dressed to the hilt in my new, tailored, white suit. After having a time of prayer with Papa and Mama, I was at George's by about 2:00 P.M. He was going to be my best man and was also dressed in solid white. Then the Rev. Dr. Frank Johnson Pippin suddenly appeared in his all white suit, all ready to go "tie the knot." I told them we looked like the "Three Stooges!"

At a quarter to three, George, Frank and I got in my Olds and headed for the church. Vera and the boys were coming a bit later. All three of us were sitting in the front seat, George was driving and I was in the middle. About halfway over on the causeway, we heard a siren behind us. Sure enough, a policeman pulled us over. But when he saw how we three brothers were dressed and heard where we were going, he slapped his book shut, jumped on his motorcycle and yelled, "Follow me!" He then raced us directly to the church! The policeman knew George, and the editor of *The Brunswick News* knew Frank. So somehow the story of these three brothers who were caught speeding on the causeway on the way to their baby brother's wedding and then were escorted to the wedding by the cop made the *Associated Press* and was published Monday morning in thousands of papers all over the nation. *The Kansas City Star* even got a picture of the three of us and put the story on the front page.

All eyes were on us as we came roaring up to the front of the church, led by the cop, with his motorcycle siren blazing! Well, after we got settled down, the wedding started on time and went great, except the photographer's camera broke (no kidding) and we got only a few pictures. Jack and Gertrude, Belle and Stanton, and Sister and Johnny B. were all there. So were Allene's parents and her brothers, George and Bobby, and their wives Tellie and Jo. Allene and I went to the front door of the church to greet all of the guests as they left.

Brother Frank was the last one to come through the line. We were in tears as he hugged and kissed us good-bye. He said another prayer for our future, then Allene and I walked him to Brother George's car. George was waiting to take him to Jesup, where he would catch the "Kansas City Special" for an overnight ride back to Kansas City. The railroad had given Frank a "white pass," so these many trips to Georgia were free.

One of George and Vera's wedding gifts to us was a night in the bridal suite overlooking the ocean at the King and Prince Hotel. After we said our farewells to all the family, my bride and I escaped to the quietness of our room, where fruit and champagne were waiting.

While Allene was in the bathroom, changing "into something more comfortable," I changed into the silk pajamas she had given me. Then I went to the bathroom door and said in a rather low voice, "Allene Pippin, I'm getting lonely out here. Whatever you do, please don't come out of there holding a big, greasy, chicken drumstick!"

She jerked the door open so fast it startled me. She marched out, stood right up in my face and said, "James Pippin, I really do believe that you will never forget about that dumb drumstick, will you, will you?!"

As she said this, she began to pound me on the chest and push me toward the bed. Then, in a laughing voice, she kept repeating, "Will you, will you, will you!"

As we fell across the bed, she whispered, her lips touching mine, "Mr. Pippin, I promise you that after this night, you will never again think of that drumstick!"

I laughed and said, "Just a minute, young lady, let's start this marriage on the right track. Come on, let's get down here by the bed on our knees and pray."

She laughed nervously, but slipped off the bed and joined me. After a short prayer, while still on our knees, we turned toward each other and hugged, and then I put my hands on the back of her long hair and said, "Honeymoon Hug!"

A MIRACLE A MINUTE

All through our fifty years of marriage, whenever we pray on our knees, I take her in my arms, put one hand on her hair and repeat those words.

Much later that night, I lay there watching the gentle sea breeze move the curtains around as I listened to the waves of the Atlantic Ocean break on the beach just below our window. Then I felt her hand on mine.

She whispered, "You asleep?"

"You kidding? I've never been more awake. What do you say, we go over and wake up Vera and George?"

"Now, *you* are kidding. At this time of the night? It must be four-thirty in the morning!"

"Naaah...Come on let's go do it."

George was at the door in a jiffy, smiling and saying, "Come on in, Mr. and Mrs. Pippin and don't mind the time; Buck and I had to get up at five anyway." George had called Vera "Buck" for years, but no one but the two of them ever knew why.

When Vera appeared, we went to the kitchen and the four of us drank two full pots of coffee. We talked and laughed until past dawn. The sun was just rising as Allene and I got back to our room. Soon we were devouring the full breakfast I ordered up to our suite. After a long nap we were up, packed and on our way to the house to let Mama and Papa see their new daughter-in-law. They were so proud and happy for both of us. We did not stay very long, so after I led them in a prayer, Allene and I were soon back in the car and on our way to Enid.

School would be out in only three more weeks. On the long drive west to Phillips, we reflected on the days and nights that had passed since she had shown up at the Kansas City airport. So many surprises, so many blessings, so many miracles. Now comes our first fight to balance off all this sweetness and light!

❧ 19 ❧

A Great Prayer Secret

After we arrived at Phillips, Paul Gary, the student liaison, found us an apartment upstairs in an old frame house. It was a real shock for Allene to be taken away from an artist's life in noisy New York City. She had been taken off "The Great White Way," the breathtaking stage at Radio City Music Hall, and shoved into a dreary, old attic in the small, barren, flat town of Enid. And even worse, we were in Oklahoma where there were few trees, no water in the rivers except when it rained real hard and a thirty-mile-per-hour dusty wind blowing most of the time.

A few nights later she was laboring away in this attic, typing a term paper for me that was due the next morning. Then suddenly she stopped, put both her hands on her hips, leaned back and let out a groan.

I went over and asked her, "What's the matter, Honey?"

"I've got an awful stomachache," she replied.

I quickly got out a couple of tablets and told her, "I'm sorry, Sweetie. Here, take these and chew them up slowly. That will stop it in a few minutes."

"No! I don't want to," she announced.

I then said, "Now, Allene, take them and eat them!"

She loudly retorted, "*No, no, no!*"

As I turned and walk away mumbling something about how bull-headed she was, like a shot out of a rifle, here came a hair brush speeding through the air that bounced off the side of my head. I wheeled around in shock, to find her sitting there with her face in her hands. Then she started bawling.

I went over, pulled her up, folded her in my arms and kissed all the tears away. I gently reminded her that in only a few days we would be out of that dark old attic forever and back in Kansas City, serving again as Frank's summer minister. While sniffling and wiping her tears, she looked up at me with red eyes, slightly smiled and said, "I'm so sorry, sweetheart. This has not been a very good day, but could you please give me some help on the typing?"

"You know I will. Anyway, this is the last darned old paper for the semester. I'll finish it."

She sobbed, smiled broadly and let out a weak "whoopee," and then gave me a big hug. I took her into the kitchen, sat her down, massaged her neck and shoulders and served us up two steaming cups of hot chocolate. Then she was as good as new.

The week before we left for Kansas City, Paul Gary called and said that the Hunter Christian Church was sending a committee in to interview for a student pastor to begin there in September. Hunter Christian was one of the largest student churches Phillips had to offer. When he asked me to be one of five to go in for the interview, I was elated. On the day we were called in, I noticed that the candidates were the top students, including John Johnson, who had also been chosen for that sermon contest a few years ago. John was a tall, good-looking, brilliant, straight-A superman. He was "everybody's darling," so the rest of us were almost sure he was "Paul's Pick." I was a little depressed and nervous because I was the last to go in. Even though I wanted to get the church and felt that Allene and I could do a good job, I just as much wanted the Lord to help the committee pick the right person. So after they had finished interviewing me, I stood, extended my hands and asked if they minded if I led them in prayer. They all jumped up and grabbed hands, and I prayed a short but sincere prayer expressing that the Lord knew they needed a good preacher. I asked Him to guide their decision so that they would choose the very one that would meet their needs. Before I left, I warmly shook their hands and said "God bless you" to each of them.

Later that afternoon, Paul called and told me, "Well, Jim, you lucky guy, you got the church."

We thanked the Lord for this decision. That next fall, after Allene and I had served the Hunter church a few weeks, the lady member of the committee who interviewed us that spring took us aside and said, "We were told by a university official that any one of the men would be fine, with the exception of Jim Pippin. He felt that we ought to know that you were kicked out of the chaplaincy for drinking. However, we checked and found out that you were not a chaplain but a mess sergeant, and that you were not kicked out for drinking but honorably discharged in order to get into seminary. Our committee all agreed that you were our choice because you were the only one who led us in prayer. We decided that we'd rather have a man of prayer who maybe drank a little than a teetotaler who was not deeply spiritual."

We laughed, and then I told her that their decision reminded me of a story of the man who said, "If I were drowning, I'd much rather have a drunk to come along who could swim than a priest who couldn't!"

After the semester was over, we drove to Kansas City in high spirits. We were out of that attic for good, were going to serve Community Christian, live in a grand house and had that great student church to come back to in the fall. We drove straight to the parsonage, and after a quick check of the house, we brought all our stuff in, shared a pot of coffee and took a much-needed nap. I had to meet Frank at the church the next morning.

Frank, Ozelle and Julia had moved to "Ten Acres" a few weeks earlier, so he drove in the twenty miles every day. We had a great time working together until the three of them left on about the tenth of July for a vacation in Colorado. They would return after Labor Day weekend, so I would again be at the helm as Frank's summer minister for almost two months.

Soon after they left, Allene and I drove down on Main Street to the Olds dealer and traded for a brand-new 1952, Super 88, four-door sedan! It was her belated wedding present. Cost: $3200.00!! It was a beauty, and we enjoyed it for many years.

Serving Community Church was much more exciting than the previous summer because now I had a lovely, talented and deeply spiritual (if a little hot-tempered) wife there to support me. She joined the choir and was asked to bring a special solo every other Sunday, just before I preached. This was our first experience to serve in worship as a team. It was the beginning of a ministry in which we would share Christ in hundreds of meetings to thousands of people for many years. Each evening before we retired, we had about an hour of devotions. Because she was with me, I felt that I was more accepted by the church members and able to minister to the congregation in and out of the pulpit with much greater effectiveness. I must tell you, I was amazed at how much a solo by her could inspire me to preach like I did that summer.

The summer attendance at church and youth meetings was thrilling. Many families and individuals were added to the membership of the church, and yes, the offerings each Sunday more than kept pace with what they had been the previous summer. As usual, much of my time was spent visiting members and new mothers in the hospitals, performing weddings and conducting funerals and baptismal services. Jerry, Madge, Gladys and James, the head custodian, again made my time there go much more smoothly.

Allene was a Presbyterian, and like all new converts in that denomination, she had only been sprinkled. At that time many Christian churches believed that everyone should be completely immersed in water. I thought that she should be baptized before we went to Hunter because I just knew one day some little old man would come up and say to her, "Mrs. Pippin, I understand that you were a Presbyterian before you were married to Rev. Pippin. Have you been baptized by immersion yet?"

I wondered how I was going to handle this delicate matter. I knew she didn't need to be immersed to be saved, but church doctrine and all, you know. Then one Sunday afternoon, I was down in the water, conducting a service of baptism in Bonfil's chapel. Six teenagers were lined up on the stairs, ready to descend at my call. After the last one walked out the other side, I turned to say a closing prayer. But then I glanced up to my left and saw this beautiful girl standing there in a white robe, waiting for my call. Tears came to my eyes as I reached out my hand to receive her.

Allene came down into the water, those tragic eyes like saucers locked on mine as I gave the words of preparation, "Allene Hall Pippin, upon your reaffirmation of faith in Jesus Christ as your Savior and Lord, I now baptize you in the name of the Father, the Son and the Holy Spirit, amen."

I then placed a handkerchief over her mouth and nose, and with my other hand on her back, I slowly let her down under the water. As she came up, the water almost perfectly parted her beautiful long hair in the middle, so that she looked like an angel. When she walked up the stairs, I turned to face the congregation and paused while they rose to give her a rousing applause of welcome into the Christian Church. Although she had decided a week earlier that she was going to do this, she had sworn everyone to secrecy. She knew that this would make me very happy. That day I loved her more than ever, since she was now a "Christian!" Ha-ha!

While we were in Kansas City, Papa phoned to say that Mama was going to need surgery. He asked if we could plan to come home as soon as we finished our duties there. We kept in touch with them regularly, learning the last week in August that Mama had surgery and a large tumor was found growing around the appendix. It had spread to the abdominal wall and could not be removed. The doctors gave her only months to live. This news came to the family as a great shock, more so since Mama was only sixty-eight years old. Next to our last Sunday at Community, I shared this news with the congregation and requested their prayers. The chairman of the board came forward and led us in a moving prayer, filled with genuine concern.

We knew their love for us was deep and tender, but on this Sunday Allene's solo and my sermon seemed to have touched their hearts more deeply than any other I had preached all summer. Community Christian was filled with such loving people. At the close of the service, I told them that we loved them all so much that we wished our arms were long enough and strong enough to reach out into the audience and embrace them all at the same time—real tight. I gave them the signal to stand, but I was so near weeping I was unable to lead the closing prayer. So as I stood there, the choir sang the choral benediction after which the congregation left the sanctuary in silence.

On our last Sunday, I kept my message light and brought in a lot of humor. We planned to leave right after the service. I was barely able to get the words out, but I requested that they be kind to our hearts and stay in their seats during the organ postlude so we could slip out the back door and be on our way. We will never forget that moment when, just before we left, Allene and I quickly turned and saw them all sitting there with their heads bowed.

As we drove out of town, we were both silent for a long time. Then Allene commented that Brother Frank was so blessed to have such a fine congregation, but they were also blessed to have a great man like Brother Frank as their preacher. I agreed with a soft "Amen!" Frank, Ozelle and Julia were not coming back to town until that Wednesday, but we thought we really needed to be home with Mama.

We stopped overnight in Memphis, then later ate in Tupelo at our little restaurant. We even sat on the same stools where Allene proposed to me. Then we went three doors down to get me a shave from a sober barber! Allene was such a good driver that we traded off about every two hours. That new Olds made the trip a sweet delight. We arrived at her home rested and glad to see everybody.

Mama and Papa were much comforted that we came. Mama was still in bed but looked well and was gaining strength. They wanted to hear all about our time at Frank's church, so we told them a little bit about it each day. A very nice lady was living in with them, and Dr. Greer came to see Mama regularly. During those precious few days we were there, Allene and I went in twice during the day to read Scripture and have prayer with Mama. At night, when she was ready to cut the light out, I would go in alone and chat and pray with her. Papa bowed his head in the living room close by and said a loud "Amen" after each prayer.

We wanted to stay longer, but because school was starting in a few days, we said our sad farewells. Papa came in and joined us as we had a prayer around Mama's bed. I leaned over and told Mama how much I loved her. I also told her again how much I appreciated everything she had done for us, especially all of the hard work she and Ed did to keep the store going while Jack and I were in the service. Then I lightly kissed her on the lips and told her that I would be praying for her every day. It was so hard for us to leave that morning and difficult for them to see us go, but they seemed to understand.

On our way out, we went by to see Vera and then on over to Brunswick to have a brief visit with Allene's folks. Of course, George was waiting at the leather shop to buy us a cup of coffee at the old Brunswick Cafe. He comforted me as much as possible and assured us that we were not to worry; he and Vera would watch out after Mama's every need. My heart was warmed by the realization of how much closer we all had become, especially since it seemed that we were going to lose Mama. As we sipped coffee, he reminded us that Belle and Stanton, Jack and Gertrude, Sister and Shirley, and Mary from Michigan had all either been there recently or were coming soon to see Mama and Papa. It was always delightful to visit with George. He sat on the middle stool, Allene and I on either side. We had several cups of coffee each and many laughs. As we left, George paid the bill; it was fifteen cents for all that coffee—including all the cream and sugar that George used!

We drove on to Macon to see Gertrude and Jack. He had recently graduated "cum laude" from Mercer University, and then opened an office on Cherry Street, with Gertrude as his legal secretary and office manager. She had worked at the Federal Reserve in Kansas City for many years and was a great asset to the law firm.

While we were visiting in Macon, we spent one night with Dr. and Mrs. Zorin, thus giving Allene and him the rare joy of a couple of voice lessons. Everyone knew that Allene was Mr. Zorin's pet, and, of course, he had a fatherly crush on her. After a tremendous

A Great Prayer Secret

dinner of Russian food, we retired to the living room and were captivated by the story of how Prof. Vladimir Zorin, a white Russian, escaped being murdered by the Red Police. He also told us about the loss of freedom that accompanied Russia's inexorable slide into Communism. He gave me the main points to watch for that would alert us if our own nation started moving toward Socialism or Communism. I led in a prayer, then Allene and I retired. After a good night's sleep and a tempting breakfast, we were on our way to Memphis and on to Enid to begin my second year of graduate studies. The Zorins remained close to us, coming later to Oklahoma City to see us a few times before they retired to Florida.

Back in Enid, it was good to get enrolled, find a better place to stay and start a very busy new fall semester. Allene taught music at three schools, and upon my insistence, entered the master's program at Phillips while I was getting my graduate degree. This required that she go to class every Thursday night and Saturday morning for two school years.

We will always remember our first weekend at the Hunter Christian Church. The church was full, Allene shook the rafters with a great solo, and I followed it with a challenging message. These weekends gave us a refreshing break from her teaching and from my classes at the seminary. Those wonderful people took us in as their son and daughter and, as it was at Marland, every Sunday after church we had dinner in the home of one of the members. They even gave us a locker at the town freezer. Once a month a few assigned members went by and left a few chickens, steaks, chops, sausages, bacon and sometimes even pheasant and venison! Our church attendance often ran two hundred and more on Sunday morning. I visited every home within an eight-mile radius, knew all the members and the children by name and baptized thirty-six people on our first Easter there! This was more than the previous minister had baptized in the seven years he was there. Maybe I seem to be bragging, but I give the credit to Christ Jesus for giving me such a love for those people. That love is what challenged me to baptize as many of them as I could during the two years we were there. Allene also helped make it all come to pass. She not only went visiting with me, but also complemented my ministry in other ways including being a choir member, teaching the youth and singing a solo almost every Sunday.

Beginning that fall, since I was now married, I cut out some (not all) of my foolishness, studied harder, made higher grades and got so much more out of my classes. My stock shot up when the students and professors met Allene. They all liked her, including even some of my old girl friends. I think a few professors got a "crush" on her, especially Dean England, Dean Shirley and Dr. Ralph Wilburn. Remember the song, "A pretty girl is like a melody?" Well, it is probably trite to say it, but Allene can light up a room, not only by singing but by just walking in. God sent her into my life at precisely the right time, for I was going to need her positive and cheerful outlook, steady faith and love more than ever in the next few weeks. Ever since we had left for our return to Enid, we talked to Mama and Papa often. Within about two weeks, we were told that Mama was in great pain and failing fast.

Mama passed away March 21, 1952. The night Allene and I arrived at the funeral home in Brunswick, a huge spring moon was just rising over the marshes, and perched up in the top of a tall pine near the entrance was a mockingbird, singing sweet and loud. As we walked up the steps and into the home, my mind raced back across the years to the time when we were children. Often when the mockers sang at night in the trees around our house at Round Oak, Mama would gather us all out on the front porch after supper. Sitting quietly, we would listen to the beautiful songs of the mockingbirds until it was time to go in and take our baths. Then she tucked us into bed, had us say our prayers, and after a big hug, a kiss and a "good night, sleep tight, hope the bed bugs don't bite," she'd walk out carrying the old kerosene lamp and leave us in the dark.

When any of us was sick, she would get up often during the night and come in to be sure we were resting well. Now the Old Lamp Lighter, the Lord, the Light of the World, had tucked her in for the last time, but He did not say "goodnight," but rather "good morning!" He will also watch over her until we meet again and never leave her in the dark. As we walked back to the car, I was convinced that the Lord placed that mockingbird up there to sing over the place where Mama's body lay. That angelic little bird was still singing her heart out as we drove away.

Mama was buried in the Round Oak cemetery on the twenty-third of March. Frank conducted the service, and the entire family was there—all except Papa, who was not able to travel, and Fred, who had died in 1949. Although we were glad Mama had been liberated from her body of pain, none of us ever stopped missing her. She and Papa had celebrated their fiftieth wedding anniversary only a few months earlier; they were so very close all those years. Just six weeks later, Papa died—of loneliness and a broken heart, I was sure. The family gathered again at the old Sunshine Methodist Church at Round Oak for the service, then placed Papa beside Mama and Brother Fred under a large oak tree in our little plot. We noticed that Brother Frank had put the perfect epitaph on Mama's grave-stone: "Her candle goeth not out by night" (Prov. 31:18).

I am now overwhelmed with gratitude and sadness as I have just read again those words of scripture, which have caused my mind to race back across the many years I watched a loving mother going at night from room to room carrying her kerosene lamp in our little frame house in Round Oak, down by the railroad track. Now she, Papa and Fred were united in the kingdom where there is no night.

The family slowly walked away from the cemetery, and we got into our cars for the ride back to Macon. I suddenly realized for the first time in my life that I had lost my home. Until that day I could always go back home to see Mama and Papa. I was shaken by the reality that I could never again go back home. If my mother and father were still living, I would call them, write to them, go to see them much more often than I had done, and tell them over and over how much I loved them. Alas, I learned that precious lesson far too late.

I might be miles away and it may be years later, but in springtime I can still vividly see the brilliant midnight moon making a dappled pattern of shadows across those faded headstones where lies all that is left of the two persons who meant the world to me. Although I am sure they are in God's eternal care, I miss them as though they departed only yesterday. So very often, as I do tonight, I hear as clearly as though I were back there, that sweet and faithful mocking-bird singing her little heart out in the top of the old oak tree.

None of us would have ever suspected it then, but very soon there would be another dearly loved one placed there, breaking again my freshly broken heart. And I now remember the moonlit nights years ago, which fell across his face by the window near the silver river. Soon shadows would fall across his place next to Fred in that same small plot...but this part of the story must wait a little while...for I cannot go there tonight.

My call to active duty at the Presidio in 1950 had caused me to miss an entire semester of graduate school. However, when I checked my transcript, I noticed that to graduate with my class I only needed nine more credit hours. I could get six credits in summer school at Union Theological Seminary in New York City, and three more credits at Phillips in August, which would give me the total of nine. Dean England was pleased to learn of my plan and said he would transfer those six credits from Union. I whispered a prayer of thanksgiving to the Lord that those months spent in the Army would not prevent me from graduating with my class.

So Allene and I spent six weeks of the summer of 1952 in New York City. We stayed with Maude, who was delighted to have us. It was really a fun time. Allene visited with some of the friends she made there earlier, including Gondolfi, her former teacher. The classes I attended in the morning gave me the rare privilege of sitting at the feet of some of the nation's most notable professors, like Paul Scherer, Herbert May and Dr. Muilenberg. I also took an advanced course in speech at Columbia University, which was just across the street from Union. The professor of the that speech class helped me enormously, including getting rid of my southern "nasal twang."

Then on Sundays, we were blessed by the sermons of the great pulpit giants: Harry Emerson Fosdick, Ralph W. Sockman, Norman Vincent Peale, James T. Cleland and George A. Buttrick. Each Sunday afternoon Allene planned some other interesting things we could do together. We went up the Empire State Building, saw the stage show at Radio City Music Hall, attended the Metropolitan Opera, saw some of the best Broadway plays and visited several museums.

Allene got a morning job with Compton's Pictured Encyclopedia as assistant secretary to the New York manager. He was so swept away by her charm and so impressed by her descriptions of me, that one afternoon he called me in and had me sit in a big, red, leather chair right in front of him. He told me that anyone who sat in that chair would be challenged to make a most important decision. After we chatted for awhile, he offered me the job of manager at the company's biggest region in Rochester. I declined, saying that I had already made a more important decision—that of being an ambassador for Christ, the greatest Man who ever lived! He laughed and told me that he was a former clergyman and, as if he hadn't heard a word I said, he offered me an annual salary of $30,000 with benefits, including three months of training. In those days, professors and members of the U.S. Congress got only $25,000!

So that was a staggering salary for anyone, anytime; but it was a colossal one for a student preacher in 1952, probably equivalent to $300,000 in 2001 dollars. But you know, in all of my years in the ministry, I never for a moment regretted turning that offer down. It was a great honor and a greater opportunity, but I had a strong feeling that all that money and responsibility could steal my heart from God and cause me to forsake His calling. I often think of what Jesus said to the multitudes: "What will it profit a man if he gains the whole world, and loses his own soul? Or what will a man give in exchange for his soul?" (Mark 8:36–37).

What with the beautiful, old campus of Union Seminary, the Riverside Church just west, with Julliard School of Music across the street north, and Columbia University just east across Broadway, I felt that I was in the midst of an awesome academic heaven.

After New York, we came back to Phillips and during August of that long, hot summer, I had the opportunity of studying the Book of Hebrews in Greek with the aged Dr. Marshall, former Dean of Phillips Seminary. I believe this was the last course he taught. I wondered how one summer could be so rich.

Now, as I write and look back across all those years of school, college and seminary and through the fifty years of ministry, a great cloud of faces flashes before me. Faces—faces, so many precious faces—of Mama and Papa, of all my brothers and sisters and their spouses, and of all my dedicated teachers, professors, preachers and the members of the churches we served, many of whom have now gone to their eternal reward, all leaving in their path unspeakable gifts we received, gifts of which I am not worthy and for which I can never pay. A feeling of overwhelming gratitude to God who placed all those faces into Allene's and my life brings me to my knees at an altar of thanksgiving. I am shaken with tears, tears of deep sadness but greater joy—sadness because they are gone, joy because of who they were and what they gave me of themselves, and unspeakable joy knowing that they are all still alive in the Lord, in my memory and in the memory of thousands of others. My heart overflows anew with a love for all of them, a love so strong it could never be put into words, although I spoke with the tongues of angels, as the apostle Paul said. (See 1 Corinthians 13.)

That last year at Phillips and at Hunter was also a very happy time. We were so involved and active. It went by so fast we could hardly believe it was time for us to graduate. Allene looked stunning in her cap, gown and stole. But when we lined up to get the diplomas, she was way ahead of me!

I thought I would have some fun since we were just standing around waiting for the program to start, so I ran up to her, acted real mad, got right up in her face and said, "Allene, what in the Sam Hill are you doing way up here? Listen, you part-time, off-campus student, I spent three years, in residence, to get my bachelor of divinity, and you went only one morning and one night a week for two years and got your master's. Why are you ahead of me in line? It's just not fair!"

All of a sudden I felt a hand on my shoulder. It was Dean Stephen J. England! He came up, took me by the arm and said, "Mr. Pippin, would you please calm down and get back there where you belong?"

As I dropped my head and slowly walked away, I heard about fifty graduates laughing, laughter that was being led by Allene and the dean!

Thirteen years after she and I graduated, Phillips University awarded me the honorary doctor of divinity degree, and as far as I was concerned, it was "earned," not honorary. So when the elders of the First Christian Church in Oklahoma City gathered around me at that Wednesday night dinner, in May, 1966, to conduct the meaningful and solemn service of placing their gift of a beautiful doctoral robe and stole upon my grateful shoulders, I looked down at Allene and with a big grin, gave her a wink that shouted, "You never dreamed that all our work through all those years would bring me a degree higher than yours and make you the wife of a doctor, did you, Sweetie?"

But seriously, the members were as pleased as we were that night, and as they stood to applaud, I called for Allene to join me on the platform. This brought a resounding response from all of them, showing deep love for both of us. She and I will never forget that night when at the early age of forty-four, I became the Reverend Doctor James Clayton Pippin. Even though great numbers of people have called me Dr. Pippin across these many years, Allene's admiration, respect and love mean more to me than all the words of praise I have received from others.

So that this part will not get too stuffy, let me add that I am sure you have already concluded that I am a very humble person. No, wait. As a matter of fact they gave me a medal for my humility, but they took it away from me because I insisted on wearing it. Every now and then in our chat together, I feel you and I need a break, just to take a deep breath and a sigh and have someone say something stupid so we can throw back our heads and have a good laugh. Matter of fact, I think our lives ought to be filled with more love and laughter, with a lilt in our step and a twinkle in our eye. Sure, we should always take God and life seriously, but we must never take ourselves too seriously. The great apostle Paul said in Romans 12:3, "I bid everyone among you not to think of himself more highly than he ought to think," and he finished the thought in verse 10 with "in honor, preferring one another" (paraphrased).

A Great Prayer Secret

The best joke is the one we tell on ourselves. And if anyone tells a joke on you, remember that people joke about those whom they admire and love. I heard my friend Norman Grubb, who died recently at ninety-six, say, "The only people who are serious are those who are not sure."

Someone has said, "The far left socialist liberal 'egg heads' can never be completely happy because they're always worried that someone, somewhere, just might be having a little fun."

I have finally learned to relax, express love and try to spread a little humor around...get someone to laugh; and like Mama used to sing, "Brighten the corner where you are." There are too many of us who live in dark corners and are so void of humor that no one wants to be around us. In life's journey we should be serious, but never solemn. I have not always had this attitude toward life. I was kind of solemn and a bit arrogant when I was a sophomore. And like so many young preacher-students at that stage, I was so heavenly minded I was no earthly good. By the way, *sophomore* in Greek is *sophos-moros*, meaning "wise moron!" Brother Frank would remind me of that line from Zhivago, "Your attitude has been noticed, you know."

When I was a sophomore, he told me, "Brother James, why don't you grow up, come on out and join the human race? Because if you don't, Son, one of these days life is going to snatch you out of your dark, stuffy corner, bring you out in the bright sunlight, and slap the he...—(that solemn attitude) out of you!!"

I think his instructions (including his explosive remarks) and his influence has done me more good than all the degrees, the track record of good deeds, lectures I have sat through, Scripture read and prayers said, all the sermons preached and goals reached put together. Frank helped me to be happier, less worried and less uptight. He kept reminding me that 95 percent of the things we worry about never happen—and that I should be more concerned with what I think of myself than what others think of me.

I remember how our Lord Jesus said (my paraphrase), "Don't be anxious; rejoice. I am come that you might have joy and that your joy may be full; that you might have life abundant. Consider My deep love; how I care for the sparrows of the air and the lilies of the field. Relax, they neither toil nor spin, yet your heavenly Father cares for them. You are of much more value than many sparrows. Rejoice, be glad. It is your Father's good pleasure to give you the kingdom. I give you a joy that the world cannot give nor take away!" (See Luke 12:22–32.)

A MIRACLE A MINUTE

I really believe this is what the gospel is all about. It's about *love, laughter, peace* and *joy*, about *God*—and *MIRACLES*. It's about LOVE, for *all* persons, because God is gender-blind and colorblind; LAUGHTER, mainly at ourselves because we bring most of our problems on ourselves through our stupid, selfish decisions; PEACE, because we don't have to fight to win and it's OK to lose now and then—anyway, the battle is the Lord's; JOY, remembering Him who is the only source of true and lasting joy. (Lincoln said, "All of us are about as happy as we make up our minds to be.") GOD, because His existence does not depend upon our belief in His existence, and because God is a Spirit and God loves each of us; and MIRACLES, because our very existence in time and space is a staggering miracle, and we do not have to believe in miracles for them to happen.

I recently heard Martha Williamson, the originator and a producer of the weekly TV show *Touched by an Angel,* say to an agnostic interviewer on *Sixty Minutes*, "God loves you; get over it!"

I started really living the day I stopped fighting God, life and people, and began to enjoy God, life and people as my friends. God is just that good, just that unpredictable and just that extravagant! Contrary to the widespread belief of some religious people, God is no respecter of persons. He lets His rain fall and His sun shine on the good and the evil. This is true mainly because if His rain and sun, His blessings, came only to the good, all of us would strive desperately to be good. If being good paid off instantly, even the Mafia would be good. Well, does it pay to be good? The really good never ask that question. But the greatest shock Frank ever gave me was when he said, "Brother James, don't forget that God is interested in something besides religion."

I like the story of the old lady who years ago marched through the streets of London with a torch in one hand and a bucket of water in the other. To those who asked what on earth was she doing, she said, "I am going to burn up heaven with my torch, and put out the fires of hell with my bucket, so people will then be good for nothing." We laugh, but most of us are still trying to be good *so that* something…so that we can get into heaven or to stay out of hell. I just realized that I have been preaching again! Are you surprised that I waited this long in the book to preach a little?

Well now…After graduation, Allene and I went from the mountain top of achievement to one of our deepest valleys of rejection. It was not very funny at the time, but it thrills me now to share a secret we learned about prayer. Months before graduation, most of the seminarians were being called to full-time church positions. However, by the end of May, I was the only seminary grad who had not received a call to a church. So we began to get depressed and a bit worried. We said fervent prayers day and night for the Lord to open a door.

As the days slowly crawled by like months, we were even reluctant to be seen because of the usual remark, "What are you and Allene doing still on campus, Jim? We figured you two would be the first to be called."

Thanks—a lot!

These words caused us to get more serious and pray harder. At first, our prayers were of a general nature. Then we thought we should get down to basics, get specific and "storm heaven" with such prayers as, "Dear Lord, here both of us are with all this education, experience, talent, ability and dedication, and yet no one wants us. Father, there is a church out there that needs us. We know that You know where it is, and You know where we are. Could You, please Sir, just put us together?"

But even with all of our praying, no one called, and after checking our mail box every day, I would walk in and sing to Allene, "No letter today." What we needed was a big miracle. But we tried not to fret. So one night we began to praise and thank Him for what we knew He was going to do. I was reminded again of the time I prayed so hard to be sent back to Lawson instead of Ft. Lewis. This night Allene and I found ourselves shedding tears as we thanked Him for what He was already doing. It was while we were sweating and crying that our Father let us get to the place where He could teach us the most important secret we had ever learned about prayer.

We finally relaxed and prayed like this to God:

"Father, if it is what You want, we would be perfectly satisfied to spend the entire summer and even the next year serving You right here in Enid; we would go door to door, even street preach. All we want is to be in Your presence and do exactly what You want us to do. If we don't get a church, we know simply that it is not Your will for us to have one right now."

Then we relaxed and forgot about it. When we really left it all with Him—stopped struggling, whining, sweating and begging, all of a sudden, a great peace and contentment came into our hearts. We just flat turned the entire situation over to Him and remembered that "the battle is the Lord's." That night Allene and I chatted into the wee hours about how we could serve God and the churches right there in Enid! We turned over and had the best night's sleep we'd had in months.

And guess what? The very next day God moved! Finding a church came so quickly and from such an unexpected source, we were sure that our new attitude had been heard and God was ready to give us that miracle. It still thrills me to tell how God did it all by Himself. We just stood back and watched; we were simply witnesses.

That next morning was a dreary, rainy day. I was on my way to check the mail at the post office when I ran into old "Pop" Kirtley. He was a retired preacher, still working every day even in his eighties, and was always seen shuffling around the campus delivering university mail. I really wanted to avoid him that day, thinking, "I've got other things to do. Just what can this old retired, 'out of touch preacher' do to help me?"

But I took a sigh and stopped to speak with him anyway. He started his usual chatter, saying, "I am very surprised to learn, Jim, that you and Allene have not found a church. By the way, I want to tell you about my son Edwin."

Those were familiar words, for he was always talking about his famous son Edwin Kirtley to any student who would listen.

He continued, "You know, Jim, my Edwin is a very close friend of your brother Frank. Well, Ed is a chaplain with the rank of colonel, and is right now stationed at the Pentagon in Washington, DC."

Shifting from foot to foot I thought, *For goodness sake, Pop, it's misting rain and I've gotta get to the post office. Please spare me this old story about your son.*

By now I was only half-listening. Then just as I was about ready to slap him on the shoulder and say, "Gotta go, ole friend," he quickly put a hand on my arm and continued, "Jim, you and Allene don't have a church yet, right? Well, six months ago my son Edwin was called as the founding interim minister of a small group of about one hundred twenty-five, which has started The First Christian Church in the Falls Church, Virginia area. Though he has been with them only a few months, their number has grown to almost two hundred, and they have moved into a school that has a large auditorium and many classrooms."

He continued, "You see, Jim, I've just learned that Edwin has to leave the States very soon to become the head of all Army chaplains in Europe. So he told me just the other day that he has to find the church a full-time minister right away. Ed has everybody praying and looking hard for a minister. However, after several weeks they have made no progress. Listen, Jim, do you think you and Allene would be interested in going up there and taking over that little church?"

Now Pop had my full attention! Tears filled my eyes as our dear Lord instantly transformed this old, tired, nobody preacher into a bright and blinding angel, sent to me directly from His presence. I no longer noticed it was raining. I hung upon his every word. I was now sobbing uncontrollably.

Pop Kirtley then continued, "If you're interested, I'll be glad to phone my son today and tell him all about you and Allene."

Interested? I heartily shook his hand and tearfully told him, "Oh my dear Lord, Pop, we surely are interested. Allene and I have been praying day and night that we might find a church. But last night, we decided to quit worrying about getting a church and just turn it all over to Him, even if He wanted us to stay in Enid, Oklahoma forever!"

Now, fasten your seat belt, because the Lord is about to start moving really fast. Pop phoned Ed that very afternoon. Ed phoned Frank, who gave him a glowing, if somewhat gilded, report that his baby brother and that beautiful, gifted wife of his had a shining record of solid leadership at Phillips University, and also at two student churches. But more than that, he capped it off by telling Ed that we had done a super job as summer minister and wife, for two years at his three thousand member church. So! In view of all this, he said that he was absolutely sure that James and Allene Pippin were the very persons Ed and the church were looking for.

When Chaplain Kirtley phoned to see if we were available, we had a long chat. Man, were we available! That very night he called a special board meeting, repeated Brother Frank's glowing recommendation, related his phone interview with us, and then urged the board to vote to ask Allene and me to come and be interviewed. The next day we received a telegram telling us that the board had unanimously voted to call us to come and preach so the congregation could take a look at us and vote on the board's recommendation.

On the morning of the third day after the occasion of my chat with Old Pop Kirtley, God had lifted Allene and me up out of a lonely, miserable valley, secured that interview for us, packed us up, led us out of Enid in our 1952 Olds, and escorted us all the way to Falls Church, Virginia. If either of us ever had the smallest doubt about whether our God was a God of miracles, that doubt was absolutely all gone then. Here is a brief review of the secret to answered prayer we learned which we believe caused God to move:

A MIRACLE A MINUTE

First: In complete faith we had to turn the need entirely over to God.

Next: We ceased to be anxious, and we let God know that it was His will we wanted, not a church, and that we were completely willing to serve Him in that little town of Enid forever.

Third: We never prejudged whom God might use to answer our fervent prayer.

Fourth: "Be ye kind to old, retired, unimportant preachers, for you never know when you might be entertaining an angel unaware!" (See Hebrews 3:2.)

And fifth: We must always give great and continual PRAISE to God for answering the prayer and for all His blessings to us.

This was our greatest lesson about prayer. It has blessed us throughout our lives with so many answers.

Just how exciting a miracle this call really was and all the super things God was getting ready to do in that "little" church in Falls Church will further witness to the supernatural way He still hears and answers prayer. He still makes Himself known to all who seek to know His will and who have faith and patience in His goodness. This kind of faith waits for God to act in His own way and on His own time table. With this vital lesson behind us and the fertile field of opportunity in the Capital Area waiting before us, amazing things were about to happen!

❧ 20 ❧

Falls Church, Here We Come!

*A*llene and I pulled into Falls Church with a loaded Olds, bulging eyes and rubber necks. As we checked out our new environment on this beautiful afternoon, the first week of June, 1953, the tempo and excitement of our young lives were at their highest. Falls Church is joined to Arlington, Virginia, and is a part of the "bedroom" of Washington, DC. What a thrilling surprise! We thought we were going to a small town in Northern Virginia, never suspecting that we would be only twenty minutes from the Lincoln Memorial and fifteen minutes from the Pentagon. We were right in the thick of the life of our nation's capital.

We were told to go first to Frank and Ruth Busbee's house for a brief visit. He was chairman of the board and she was the choir director. They made us feel right at home. Frank asked me to join him out in the front yard, while Ruth and Allene went to get some coffee ready. Does God really have a sense of humor? Well, tell me in a moment after you see how a simple chair in the home of a chairman and a choir director brought a great young titan down a few notches.

Frank seated me in a high back, folding chair that had a canvas bottom. Just as I reached up to get my coffee from Ruth's hand, the bottom of my chair split in two and dropped me on the ground. Then the chair folded over me and I was sort of trapped in it. Ruth grabbed my coffee and Frank jumped up to help me, but he and Allene were paralyzed because they were doubled over, laughing so hard, they were in tears. Poor Ruth was as white as a sheet. There I was on the ground locked in the chair and no one seemed able to do anything but laugh. Finally, when Ruth and Frank each grabbed a hand to pull me up, the chair came up with me. As I stood bent over, still stuck in the chair, Allene ran around in back of me to try to pull the chair away from me. Well, the chair first stuck and then came loose so fast that Allene fell backward on the ground, the chair now on top of her! They disengaged her from the thing, and when we all got our breath and stopped laughing, the coffee was cold. But sweet Ruth soon came out with a fresh pot.

As we finally sat to enjoy our coffee, none of us would dare look the other in the eye, for whenever we did we all started laughing again. What a way for a sharp seminary grad and a talented southern songbird to begin serving their first church. As you can imagine, this story of my fall from grace was told and retold across the years that we were there. Until this day, I have never again come anywhere near a canvas-backed chair.

Frank Busbee took us over to meet Bob and Jean Gates, with whom we stayed two weeks while we waited for our apartment to be made ready. Bob and Jean and their three kids, Bob, Henry and Jenny, waited on us constantly, fixed sandwiches and meals or took us out to eat. Bob got a few days off from his job at FAA, drove us around to visit some of the church leaders, and showed us the northern Virginia area. During those summer, rainy afternoons, while Jean and Allene went out to visit some of the women, I sat in the middle of the living room floor and played Monopoly for hours with those three precious kids. I became their hero and still am until this very day…I hope.

Chaplain (Col.) Edwin and Edna Mae Kirtley were super people, just as Brother Frank had said they were. On that first Sunday, the auditorium at McKinley School was almost full. Ed introduced us to the congregation, Allene sang a magnificent solo, and I got up and preached my heart out. Afterwards, Allene and I were dismissed to the kitchen where fresh coffee was waiting. After about twenty minutes, we were called back in and told that upon the recommendation of the official board, the congregation had voted unanimously to give me a call to become their first full-time minister. The congregation all stood and gave us a resounding applause.

The next Sunday Ed preached his farewell sermon. He had been there for six months and the church had grown under his fine leadership. Ed and Edna Mae treated us like we were family. They passed their love and admiration for Brother Frank on to Allene and me. We will never forget the deep love and support that the Kirtleys and their four fine boys Kendall, John, Stephen and Paul have given us through the years.

About the last week in June, we moved into our Willston apartment, which had two bedrooms and a furnished kitchen. Since Ed and Edna Mae were to be gone to Europe for three years, they asked us to keep all of their furniture. So our apartment was royally furnished, including a piano and a large television set, the first one we had ever watched. I am sure you have already sensed that our coming and their leaving was timed by the Lord. But this was only the beginning of many miracles that filled those years at First Christian, Falls Church, Virginia.

But first let me pause for this:

Remember when I mentioned the two most important books that impacted my life? They were the Bible and *Think and Grow Rich*, by Napoleon Hill. I used the principles in Hill's famous book to grow the church and to build the first two units of the church. The "Rich" in the title means much more than money. Hill's principles have been stated by many people in many books and in many different words, but all have more or less the same steps that will result in the reality of your plan, dream or desire.

Let me list for you in my own words the eight steps one must take to reach any worthy goal. All eight of these steps must be permeated with a white-hot, burning desire to have as a reality what you want to accomplish. (I mixed prayer with all of these.)

1. First, you must know exactly what you want. Then hold ever in your thoughts the specific goal you plan to reach. Do not be vague; you must be able to actually see the finished plan.

2. State plainly what you are willing to do to achieve the goal. You have to give something *to get what you want.* No free lunch!

3. Set the date, down to the month and the year you plan to finish the goal, the exact date it will become a turnkey reality.

4. Develop an actual plan, blueprint, that you will faithfully follow to achieve your goal. Break it down in months and years; first things first; set all action in priority. START the plan; put it into action the day you have finished these eight steps. Do not hesitate to begin.

5. Write out all of the above: what you want or the goal you will achieve, the month and year that you will reach your goal, list what specifically you will give, things you will do or time you will spend daily and weekly to bring your goal into reality. Then clearly write down the entire plan; what

will be done, the methods that will be used to produce the finished product.

6.　You now must read every word of your plan, or all of the above, at least twice each day. When you arise in the morning, before you utter a word to anyone; and let these be the last words you say before you go to sleep; also try to find time to read this during the day.

7.　Each time you read the above, fix clearly in your imagination the object of your plan; emotionally desire to see it as if it were already a reality.

8.　*Finally, never, ever think of quitting. Burn your boats at the beach and burn the bridges as you cross them!* You cannot lose if you don't quit!

Now these steps can be applied to money you desire to have in your possession; a building or project you want to finish; goals for yourself, your family and your employees; or the physical, financial or spiritual life into which you want to grow deeper or higher. But do yourself a favor and get the book! It is readily available. I now state a power that I cannot explain: "As soon as Life (God) is sure you know exactly what you want and Life (God) is absolutely convinced that you will never quit but will continue toward your goal until you have it, Life (the Lord) then gives it to you in a very short period of time." But be sure your goal is worth your life, because in the getting of it you just might have to give it your life.

Having a beautifully furnished apartment made it easier to start a ministry, even though there was no church building, no office, and no secretary. We could only use the school building on Sundays and two evenings during the week. All the young church owned was a beautiful but valuable four and one-half-acre lot located at 120 Leesburg Pike, near Seven Corners, and *it* wasn't paid for. My first office was in the basement of Frank and Ruth's home. I soon moved it to the attic of the home of the Dorothy and Jim Shepherd. Dotty Shepherd was the daughter of our leading elder, Claude Slusher, and his wife, Ruth, who were leaders in the church and in the Capital Area. Dotty became my first part-time secretary. That first week, she began doing the worship bulletin and helped me start a weekly church paper.

My mornings were filled with office work, letter writing and talking to members on the phone. My afternoons were busy with hospital calls, calls in the homes of visitors and members, and frequent meetings over coffee with some of the church leaders at their places of business. Then that summer after dinner, Allene and I would often make short visits to two or three families. Beginning in the fall of 1953, Allene taught fifth grade in an Arlington school—and was she glad she had that master's degree!

Every Sunday our church attendance grew. There were about thirty people in Ruth's choir, and Allene sang twice a month. About sixty families regularly attended, including a large number of children and teenagers. Soon that school building was literally crawling with excited people, and every seat was taken for the church service. Now I had to face our first real problem.

The building committee was very active indeed, meeting weekly. But at each meeting we talked about all the things that needed to be done to get into our first building. Often we got into disagreements about what the building was to look like, whether we would build the sanctuary or the education building first, and how we would raise the needed funds. We got tangled up in all these matters, often all of us talking at the same time. Those first few weeks revealed to me just how much I didn't learn in college and seminary. I desperately needed a course in how to get along with and organize a bunch of strong leaders to build a church.

One night after a most frustrating meeting, I went to the apartment and had Allene make us some coffee. As we sat down to chat, I sighed and told her I really needed help. I shared with her how we seemed unable to make any progress in that building committee. I told her that we just had to pray for our Lord to help me solve this problem. We prayed, and just as I opened my eyes, I glanced at the mail on the table and started casually flipping through a church furniture magazine. There in the centerfold was an article titled, "How to Organize a Church Building Committee!"

Well, praise God! The first paragraph described our situation to a tee. As I read the next few sentences, our first building was born. The writer advised that we have a building department, divided into three committees. One group was to deal with the architecture, the second to guide the construction and the third to secure the finances. Why didn't *I* think of this? The article went on to stress that these three should meet on different nights so the pastor could attend each meeting. The genius of the article included the suggestion that each person should be assigned to the committee where he or she would be best able to give good advice.

So, that night and the next day, Frank Busbee, the chairman of the committee, and I selected the people who would form each committee. The five members on the construction group were in the electrical, plumbing, carpentry or heating and air conditioning businesses—one of them was actually the head of a construction crew. For the finance committee, we chose a stock broker, a banker, an insurance salesman and two high-income people, including one woman. Finally, the third group would focus on architecture. The people we selected for this committee had fine homes, and one of them had recently built a new home. Two of them were women, one dabbled in painting and the other had a flair for interior decorating.

Yes, you guessed it. We made great progress in these separate groups, and within just a few weeks the full building department was ready to submit a proposal to the board and then to the congregation, requesting to move forward on the first stage: the completion of the education building!

But at the board meeting, the building department had to face the question about which we should build first, the sanctuary or the education building. The majority wanted to immediately build a sanctuary that would only seat about three hundred fifty people. I almost fell out of my chair because this would only expand our capacity by about a hundred. We were already running close to two hundred fifty on some Sundays. After hearing this, I whispered a prayer, rose to my feet, reached down into my best powers of "it seems to me" persuasion, and asked to be recognized by the board. I suggested that the children and young adults should be provided for first so the church could grow faster, and a fellowship hall on the upper floor could serve as our temporary sanctuary.

Then I put my foot in my mouth. I said that when we project our past rate of growth over the next two or three years, constructing the education building first would be the best choice because then we would have more time to plan a sanctuary that would seat a thousand people!

Well...I have never heard so much laughter from a church board. As they laughed, some of their faces showed pain and utter disbelief. Most of them thought that I had lost my mind. But I noticed quite a few were smiling and nodding their heads at me. After everyone settled down a bit, I said, "Well, if we don't dream big, big things will never happen." When the majority began to laugh again, I chuckled and asked the chairman if we could be adjourned. Without waiting for Frank to reply, almost everybody got up and scooted out! Then a few of the board members came over and encouraged me to stay (hang) in there; they were with me all the way. You can imagine how all of this disbelief increased my determination to a white-hot desire to reach or exceed the dream of my foolish heart. One week later at a called board meeting, I noticed that some of their faces were still covered with smiles. But the majority agreed that, since the Sunday school was the foundation of the church, we should start with the education building. This was a major victory for the future of the church.

The challenges continued at the next finance committee meeting. They all looked quite sad when they told me that they had tried all funding sources, both locally and with our denomination's board of church extension, and had hit a stone wall in trying to secure a loan to begin construction. Well, I knew that we could not remain in that elementary school much longer, so I started praying that God would increase my faith and confidence to get us a miracle loan. *This was a definite step in my plan.* That night Allene and I prayed, saying that this was God's battle and asking for the Lord Jesus to open up a way. *No obstacle could stop me in achieving my goal.*

The next afternoon, I dressed up, got my presentation together and started praying about where I should go to ask for a loan. I seemed to be directed to the Clarendon Bank and Trust, which was then a relatively small bank near Key Bridge on the Arlington side. When I walked in, I was able to get an appointment with the president right away, so I met with him in his office. My presentation included the present size of the membership; projections of income and budgets; church goals and programs, both local and worldwide; estimated church growth; and lastly, a sketch of what the education building would look like. The president listened patiently to all of this. Then he asked me how much we would need to erect the building.

When I responded, "About fifty thousand dollars," he smiled and said, "Mr. Pippin, this bank has never made a loan that large, and besides we don't loan money to churches."

I replied, "Sir, maybe the Lord wants ours to be the first church your bank helps to build. Also, you might consider starting a church loan department because there is going to be a lot of church construction in the next few years. If the bank wishes, we could have several well-to-do families sign the note. I can guarantee you, Sir, that you will never regret this loan. I promise you that we will pay it off faster than the schedule."

He smiled, rose to his feet and walked me to the door. Just as I turned to leave, although I felt sorely defeated, I told him that I was sure that I would see him again.

A MIRACLE A MINUTE

He then said, with a chuckle, "You know, young man, somehow all of a sudden, I feel good about this. I can't promise you anything, but let me take it up with the committee and get back with your church in a day or two. And by the way, if you ever decide to leave the ministry, I'd like to give you a good job in my bank." He then gave me a big wink.

We both laughed and shook hands, and I was off.

Three nights later several of our leaders and I were sitting in a school room where we were meeting with the president and two vice presidents from the Clarendon Bank! After about an hour, several pots of fresh coffee and some homemade brownies and cookies, the president arose and said, "On the basis of your information and your minister's comments, we are going to make you an immediate loan of fifty-five thousand dollars on a ten-year note at 5 percent interest."

We all stared at each other with amazement. I sat there with a silly smile on my face, thanking and praising our "Great God of Miracles!" Frank Busbee promised to take the bank's offer to the board. Then we all stood and almost shook the hands off of those three beautiful men from the bank.

As the president was leaving the room, he turned and said with a wide smile, "And hang on to that young preacher, because if he leaves, we'll call your note!"

We all had a good laugh at that. But as soon as they left the building, man, we all started jumping around, laughing, dancing around the room hugging each other like children. I assured the group that it was really the Lord and the fine impression they just made that clinched the deal—much more so than "that young preacher." You can imagine what a great service we had the next Sunday and what a super sermon on faith I preached. The members could hardly believe how quickly things were moving along. We chose an architect, let out the contract for bids and started construction within a few days.

Allene was required to stop teaching by the fifth month because *she was going to become a mother!* She got more beautiful each day and I got more proud! On August 20, 1954, she gave birth to our first child, a girl, whom we named Janet Diane Pippin. She was just about the most beautiful baby I ever saw. While Allene was at Arlington Hospital, the church helped me move into the new home we had bought at 1305 Normandy Lane in Broyhill Park, Falls Church. In addition to our *new* congregation, we had a *new* home filled with practically *new* furniture, and now Allene came in carrying our *new* baby Janet! And very soon we would have a *new* education building. Remember what God promised? "Behold, I make all things *new!*" (Rev. 21:5).

Each Sunday in the weeks ahead we had a large number of visitors at the church services, and a few of us called on them. Many of them then became members, so the attendance and the membership increased monthly.

The beautiful education building was dedicated on November 20, 1955, almost to the month called for in my plan. The Rev. Dr. Frank Johnson Pippin preached the dedication sermon. He fell in love with the congregation and they with him. He was also very proud of his "Timothy" in the faith and of "Tops," his Timothy's gorgeous wife. We sat up late the three nights he was there and enjoyed our usual long chats that covered past and present. Frank also stressed how very glad he was that his dear friend, Colonel Ed Kirtley, asked the church to call us. His pride in Allene and me was evident. The fellowship hall seated over three hundred in folding chairs, had a divided chancel with lectern and pulpit, room for the choir and organ, and at center back, a baptistry. In just a few months, we had to start holding two services on Sunday mornings.

Now comes a luncheon that further changed my life. One afternoon a few weeks after the dedication of the new building, Wilbur Hogevoll, the minister of the First Christian Church in Alexandria, phoned me. Allene and I had recently been invited to his home for dinner. We were impressed with him and his wife. Now, he was calling and asking me to meet him for lunch. Bill Hogevoll was a tall, slender man with a little white mustache who had the habit of clearing his throat frequently. He was a veteran of World War II and was now in the Army Reserve as a lieutenant colonel, chaplain. He took me to Howard Johnson's, where we found a table over in a corner.

After we ordered and the waitress brought more coffee, he said, "Jim, your time is running out if you plan to become a reserve chaplain."

I answered, "Bill, I think I am too old to get a commission."

But he corrected me, "No, your four years of active duty come off your age. There will be no problem if you act fast."

I was elated because, as you recall, I had always wanted to come back into the Army Reserve as a chaplain.

The next day he slammed a stack of forms on my desk and told me, "Get on the ball, pronto, and fill these out...very carefully, my boy!"

He promised to do what he could to get me before the proper Army board as soon as I had completed the forms. When I looked the forms over, I held in my hands reams and reams of paper covering every phase of my life and waiting to be filled out—in triplicate.

When I yelled for help, Bill teased me, saying, "Brother James, don't worry; if you have the intelligence to fill out all those forms, they'll give you the commission!"

So I continued working every day and into the night. About a week later, in a weak voice, I called and told him that I had finished. I then took them over to the Pentagon to the Office of the Chief of Chaplains. There a major looked them over and sent them on to the proper Reserve board, which would review my application forms and make or decline the recommendation that I be commissioned. In 1956, soon after we dedicated the education building, I passed muster and was commissioned as a first lieutenant, chaplain.

On May 29, 1956, we welcomed into our little family our second child, another beautiful girl, Anne Elizabeth, who, like Janet, was born at Arlington Hospital. When the nurse handed her to me, I noticed that she had her two little bitty fingers stuck into her little bitty mouth. I just knew that she had also done that before she was born. Now baby Janet had a sister to watch over and later to help raise.

About this time, Allene developed an annoying little habit. Holding one of the girls on her hip, she started following me to the door each morning as I was leaving for the church. After giving me a big hug and kiss, she would always ask me two questions: When would I be back so she could use the car, and could she please have a little money?

After several weeks of this, I sat down one morning on my way out and said to her, "My dear Allene, I went by the bank recently and fixed it so you can write checks. I am also going to buy me a 1957 Volkswagen tomorrow. I've had to wait two months for it. Now, my sweet lovely, you can have the Olds for your very own and can pay for anything you have the courage to buy with those checks."

She gave me a big smile and one of her best hugs and kisses ever. Never again did we have that little hassle at the door that started my day—my good Lord, why didn't I think of the checks and the car months earlier? We have always laughed about that. Even once and awhile now, as I leave to go teach, I ask her if she will need the car and if she has any money. Although she says "no, and yes," she still gives me that hug and kiss like before, but often it is now a pat on the arm and a little peck on the cheek! Of course, since then she has always had her own car and access to *all* the money.

One Sunday in the summer of 1957, just as I stood to begin the sermon, I looked up the aisle and here came Jack, Gertrude and little Martha Ann II. They had arrived from Macon too late the night before to phone us, so they stayed in a motel near the church. Well, I was swept off my feet with pride and joy that they were there. I was actually shaking when I called them up front to introduce them to the congregation. Wouldn't you know that this was the Sunday that I had to leave immediately after the sermon to go to Bethany Beach to be the camp leader for a weeklong camp for the young people of the region. I had the only keys to the buildings and had to hurry over there to let them all in.

But worse yet, Allene had left with the girls and gone home to Georgia for two weeks. So after church, I took the keys to the house off my ring, handed them to Jack and asked a deacon to lead them out to the house. I just barely had time to have a quick cup of coffee with them in the church kitchen. I so wished that they had phoned me. I would have ask them to come a week later, but that's kinda how Jack did things. He wanted to surprise us. They spent the night in our home and left on Monday. Since I had two weeks off after the camp, I drove to Macon on my way to Brunswick and stayed a night with them. I asked them to come to St. Simon's with me, but they couldn't.

Later in the winter of 1957, I attended Chaplain Basic at Ft. Slocum, New York, located on an island in Long Island Sound just off the coast at New Rochelle. The fort was reached by ferry. I was there for six weeks, returning to Falls Church on weekends to preach. And who do you suppose was the Commandant of the Chaplain School? None other than one full Colonel, Chaplain Charlie Brown, the former Deputy Sixth Army Chaplain at the Presidio, who got me out of the Army and into seminary! He took me in as a son, so very proud that I was now a Reserve chaplain. We often went fishing off the pier and returned to his elegant quarters where his lovely wife, Ava, served us martinis and dinner.

Soon after finishing basic, I was assigned to the 354th General Hospital, which met over in Washington, DC. Since I was filling a captain slot, I received that rank after one year. For two weeks in the summer of 1958, our unit was sent to Indiantown Gap, Pennsylvania. While standing in ranks one morning my name was called. I was ordered to the Office of the Commander.

In his office, Col. VanMater, gave me the tragic news. My dear brother Jack had taken his own life that morning at 5:30 A.M. The colonel expressed his deep regret, then had me rushed to the airstrip where an Army plane was waiting to fly me to a small airport in Falls Church, only three blocks from my house. The colonel also phoned Allene, who was waiting when I landed. She related through tears the sad details of Jack's passing.

In just a few days, I experienced the greatest grief of my life up to that time. You will recall that following two years in prison, Jack attended Mercer University, graduating *cum laude* with a degree in criminal law. He was editor of *The Law Review*, a teaching fellow and also passed the Georgia bar exam during his last semester. With Gertrude's able support, he quickly built a large practice with his offices in downtown Macon. Jack always came to court, dressed to the nines, fully prepared, and often even without a briefcase. In recent cases for five of his clients he had gotten the death sentence for first-degree murder reduced to life, which gave them a chance for parole in ten to fifteen years.

During his fifth year of practice, he started having a drink or two in the morning after breakfast before he went to court. Because of his great intelligence, speaking ability and trial skills, he rarely lost a case. This made some of the other lawyers jealous and angry. Because of his record of cases won and his ability to call up out of his memory precedent after precedent that applied to his case, he became in much demand for criminal cases. But the judges loved him because he never wasted their time on trifles. So it seems that his opponents were just waiting to catch him in a breach of ethics or something so they could can him.

Their chance was not long coming. Jack settled a small estate for a family of seven adults in the loss of their mother. They were each to receive nine hundred dollars. He gave six of them a check earlier in the week for their share. The seventh arrived the Friday afternoon Jack and his wife and their new daughter, pretty little Martha Ann II, were leaving town for a vacation. Gertrude had already gone home with the checkbook. The man just had to have the money, for he said he was also leaving town that afternoon. Could Jack please—please—give him his money. At this point Jack made the mistake that cost him his life. He went to the safe and brought the person nine one-hundred-dollar bills. In his haste, Jack did not have the man sign a receipt stating that he had received the money. When Jack returned from vacation, the man showed up with a lawyer, asking Jack for his money. The man swore that Jack never gave him his share. The lawyer, of course, took his client's side, and a phony charge of fraud for the nine hundred dollars was entered against Jack. In the next few days, three of the attorneys, who were his archenemies, hauled him before the Review Committee of five, which included a couple of judges. The vote was three to two to recommend that Jack be barred from practice for one year. The Judicial Review Board voted by a one-vote majority to approve their recommendation.

Jack's shock, grief and anger could not be assuaged. He was an ex-convict and was certain that he would never be allowed to practice law in Georgia again. And after his wife and child, the law was his very life. He went home that evening a broken man, began drinking, and took some pills to help cover his pain. The next morning, Gertrude was able to get him into the Macon Hospital Psychiatric Ward, placing him under the care of a noted psychiatrist. Three days later Jack acted so normal he persuaded his doctor to let him go home. Back home, after dinner, he used alcohol and drugs to put himself to sleep. Jack awoke the next morning at 5:25, went out to the garage, took a .38 pistol and with one shot behind his right ear, ended his life. To me, it was like the "shot heard around the world."

Since we had the two small children, Allene could not come with me to the funeral in Macon. When I arrived at Hart's Mortuary, which was housed in an old remodeled southern home, I was comforted to see that all the members of the family were already there. The family, including Gertrude and Martha Ann, were glad to see me. I stooped down to hug and kiss Martha Ann. I just had to go through the cute little routine I had heard her and her beloved daddy do so many times when she was a younger child. Martha Ann would climb up into Jack's lap, and he would look at her and say, "You know what?"

She would brighten up and answer, "What!"

"That's what!"

"What's what?"

"That's what!!"

"Oh!"

Then Jack would hug her and shake her, and they would both have a good laugh. Martha Ann never tired of this cute little chat with her beloved daddy. But today, at the funeral home, she could not find the courage to even smile. I picked her up in my arms and held her tight.

We were all thankful that both Mama and Papa had gone to be with the Lord earlier and were spared this deep sorrow. After I was greeted by my brothers and sisters and their spouses, I asked to be allowed to view Brother Jack alone. The manager, Joe Childs, who

was our first cousin, escorted me to an upstairs room where Jack was.
I still remember the creaking of those old stairs as we ascended. Joe
let me in and left, closing the door behind him.

I stood in absolute silence. I turned and looked and saw a scene that
not only broke my heart, but also one that I shall never, never forget.
The room was filled with flowers. Joe had placed Jack in a beautiful
bed, two large pillows under his head, his glasses in one hand and in
the other an open Bible. His head was slightly turned and he looked as
if he had just fallen off to sleep. How I prayed that this were true and
that in a moment he would open those big, brown eyes and speak to
me. Near the head of the bed was an arrangement of two dozen long
red roses, Jack's favorite flower. The roses reminded me of the dozen
he sent Allene the day before our wedding. I went to the side of the
bed, fell on my knees and began to weep sorely and to speak with
trembling voice some strong words to Jack:

> Jack, O Jack, my dearest brother Jack, why did you do this?
> Why did you end your precious life this way? I loved you
> so much, I depended so much on you. We all did. Jack, this
> family will never be the same without you, you should
> have known this. O my brother—how often I have fer-
> vently prayed for you, that you would find peace in your
> heart and mind, and health and happiness. I so wish that
> you had found the great faith in our Lord Jesus Christ that
> you said I had years ago. Then maybe this would not have
> happened. I wish my faith was strong enough right now, so
> strong that I could lay hands on your body and in the
> mighty name of Jesus, raise you up from this untimely,
> unnecessary death. O Father, would You do that for me
> and the family? I ask You now, O my sweet Lord, glorify
> Your great Name, please give him back to us, bring him
> back to life and let us go back downstairs together.

At this point, I lay my head on the bed close to his body, my hand on
his, and wept bitterly. When I was able to compose myself, I arose and
walked out of the room. On the way back down those creaking stairs, I
knew for the first time the terrible finality of death. His death was all
the more staggering a blow because it was so premature and so
absolutely foolish. Jack was only 38. I joined the others, and soon we all
went out to my sister Myrtle's home for a much-needed cup of coffee
and later, supper.

Now, on the lighter side, I will briefly describe what the Pippin custom was whenever we attended a funeral of a member of the immediate family. After Mama and Papa died, about the only time we got together was at a family funeral. The day before the service we would visit the body and get our weeping over as we hugged each other in the viewing room. Then the evening before we attended the service the next day, we would have supper together at one of our homes. We would sit around and relate the impressive and often hilarious things we remembered about the deceased.

This was our practice, beginning with the death of Fred, then Mama and Papa and now Jack, who was the fourth to go. If it was in summer, the windows of our house in St. Simon's were open, and the neighbors for blocks could hear the laughter that filled the night air for several hours. We were all Christians, believing that "blessed are the dead who die in the Lord from now on... that they may rest from their labors, and their works follow them" (Rev. 14:13). So we refreshed and comforted one another with all the fine and funny things that graced the life of whoever had just left "for the Larger Life," as Frank always said. Even though we were criticized for this, we continued it through the deaths of all of the family, except Sister and Ray, who were the last to go and there was no one else around who felt like laughing but me.

We believed that a funeral or memorial service should be a celebration, not primarily a time for weeping. Therefore, there were few or no tears at the service, and we did not have a grand display of loud weeping, having to be pulled away from the casket just before it was closed. I am not implying that the show of strong emotion at a funeral is wrong, for I have wept many times at the close of the casket, even for friends and loved ones for whom I conducted a service. I know that all families are not the same, neither is any service like another. That was just our way of trying to witness to a strong belief in life eternal, that the deceased was not there, but rather was with the Lord.

The next morning, Brother Frank did Jack's service, and aware that many of those present were troubled about the suicide, comforted us with these closing words, "Our Lord God would never condemn anyone to hell for an act done in an instant, when one is ill. Our merciful and loving Father, as any loving father here, would choose to see the whole life and the total good that life had done. I am confident that our dearly beloved brother, husband, and father, Daniel Jackson Pippin, believed that Jesus Christ is the Son of God and his Savior, and I firmly believe that today Jack is with his Lord in the kingdom."

He then finished the moving message with an inspiring statement on the joys of immortality, closing with a deeply meaningful prayer.

After the service in Macon, we took the old familiar ride to Round Oak, where we put Jack's body to rest beside Mama's under the large oak in the little cemetery. After everyone else had left, the immediate family had a quiet chat while sitting in the cool shade of the oak tree. Then George, Mary and Belle drove Frank and me to the Atlanta airport, where we had supper together. Later, we saw Frank off to Kansas City. Then they walked me to the gate to catch my plane back to Philadelphia and to summer camp, where I had another week to go. Because the past two weeks had been very difficult, I was glad when my chaplain friend, John Harris, and I pulled up into the driveway at my home in Falls Church.

The loss of my dear brother Jack left me not only sad, grieved and lonely, but more than all of this, I was burdened with a feeling of the sheer waste of his early death. I feel his death was partly brought on by the professional jealousy and anger of other lawyers, some of whom were probably glad the courts were rid of Jack. There is a hatred that often comes from some of one's colleagues, regardless of the field one is in, sometimes brought on by the great intelligence or great wealth of the person despised, and when these are combined in one's legal opponent against whom a trial lawyer cannot often win—then there is a white-hot desire to be rid of such a person, who will never be missed, and one who goes to the grave unloved and unmourned by some of his "colleagues."

Given by the Lord a brilliant mind and a poet's heart, Jack's keen abilities in many areas were strikingly unique. In only five years, he had acquired many acres of land, on which the sale of the lumber alone would have made him wealthy. The whole family depended on him for so many things, but Annabelle was the most grieved. She and Jack were four years apart and shared so many of those intimate and often secret things that many of us share when growing up. That love between Jack and Belle deepened through the years. Belle was devastated and deeply depressed because of his death. Next to Belle, I stood closest to Jack; she, Jack and I dearly loved each other and knew so many things about each other that no one else ever knew.

I am certain that you have had a member of your family, or maybe some close friend, whom you found it almost impossible to get to really know. His or her life was filled with so much pain, suffering and unfulfilled aspirations—feelings so deep, their thoughts on a plane so much higher than our ability to understand or their ability to express. They seem to be set apart in a world all of their own. Often seemingly too large for their environment, they are easily bored, but yet possessed of a capacity to love so much greater than the chance of ever finding that special one on whom to pour all that love. So they furtively clutch onto someone who often cannot possibly comprehend the depths of such a life or a love and can seldom ever rise to the capacity of fully appreciating that life, or worse, of returning such love.

So the poured out affection is rejected or misunderstood, and the result is a heart that has a broken place down deep somewhere, a wound that no person on earth or anything else, save God alone, can come close to mending. There are so few who can ever make such a person really happy or hold that person's interest or love for very long—rarely for a lifetime. This limited interest span often moves from personal relationships over into the person's career, where almost no challenge from friend nor foe is found; one finds few if any opportunities to build friendships that are deeply intimate or long lived. Such a person can seldom find a spouse, friend or colleague in whom there is no competition, resentment or jealousy, so that the two can find adequate time to develop a profound respect and a growing love for one another. Such a person was our dear Brother Jack.

When Jack entered the courtroom, he was so brilliantly prepared that few judges and almost no lawyers ever came close to giving him a challenge. He rarely raised his voice, seldom got overly excited or spoke very long. He always forced his opponents into long fevered responses to his short points. Jack was also a serious student of Abraham Lincoln, who studied and thought long and hard until he found what he called the "nub" of a case, that fact on which the entire case rested. Lincoln would then focus on that and nothing else.

For instance, Lincoln once had a client, a large railroad company, which was being sued by the Mississippi boatmen. The boatmen were trying to keep the railroad from building a bridge across the river. The courtroom was packed in favor of the boatmen, and even the judge didn't give the railroad much of a chance. So "Abe" had his work cut out for him. But he won the case with this simple statement, "One would think that the railroad would have just as much right to go across a river as the boats have to go up and down it."

Ah yes, and did the judge love that stellar example of brilliance! Ole "Honest Abe" was one of a kind. And so was Daniel Jackson Pippin.

A MIRACLE A MINUTE

Frank was much this way in his personal life and in his calling as a minister. In some measure this is also true in the lives of our three daughters, Janet, Anne and Beverly—especially Janet. Often a great intellect and high efficiency in a life can be a curse as often it is as a blessing. Around these kinds of people, life is seldom dull. Evidence of this unique perception often comes out in the most unexpected situations. When one of Frank's girlfriends wanted him to take her to a movie, he answered, "Movies are attended by a bunch of dull Peeping Toms who pay money to sit there and watch others have a good time. Let's instead go out and make our own movie!"

One often either hates these people or loves them, but no one can ever forget them. They leave one with no middle ground. But when one such leaves us, no one else can ever fill that empty place. In a rare radio interview, I heard Carl Sandburg read his famous poem on Lincoln, which contained these two lines on Lincoln's tragic death:

> He went down with a great shout upon the hills,
> And left an open place against the sky.

Our dear brother Jack left a large lonesome place in all our hearts that neither time, circumstance, any person nor any event can ever completely fill. I look forward to my reunion with Brother Jack and the rest of my family in the kingdom of God. Because he was so utterly unique, I miss Jack the most.

In the months just ahead, Allene and I experienced two of the greatest events in our ministry. We dedicated our new sanctuary, and then took what turned out to be the trip of a lifetime!

✼ 21 ✼

The Trip of a Lifetime!

We could not imagine what a profound impression the dedication of our beautiful new sanctuary would make upon Allene and me, our church and on the entire region. It had been under construction for about six months. The two buildings blended perfectly, mainly because we had the same architect and builder; and we were even able to match the brick perfectly.

So, on Sunday afternoon, December 18, 1959, the Rev. Dr. J. Warren Hastings, minister of our National City Christian Church, preached a moving dedication sermon titled, "What Mean These Stones?" Since all of the Capital Area Christian churches were invited, the sanctuary, balcony and parlor were packed with over eight hundred people.

At the close of a gala reception for members and friends, Dr. Hastings got our attention, lifted a cup of punch and said, with his million-dollar smile and a chuckle, "Brother James Clayton and Allene, we toast you and this congregation for what you have been able to accomplish here in only six short years. Next to National City Church, yours is the brightest light in the Capital Area!" His toast gave us a good laugh, and we all heartily applauded this great man of God.

Allene and I and the whole congregation were elated at what the good Lord had brought about in these few years of our ministry there. We thanked the Lord that the education building and the sanctuary had been started and finished almost to the month according to our TAGR (think and grow rich) master plan. Since we had gone back to one service, the next Sunday the lower floor of the sanctuary was full. Now our growth both in numbers and in depth of Christian commitment continued at a faster pace. Since we had finished and dedicated the beautiful church building, our emphasis turned next to the task of growing a more effective church within the building. It is easy to raise the funds and inspire the people to erect the buildings. However, it is often much more difficult to edify and build up the "living stones," the people, the men, women, boys and girls, into strong servants of the Lord. In the immediate years ahead, all of our effort was toward reaching this—our new goal.

But the new year, 1960, was filled with excitement, including that "Trip of a Lifetime" for Allene and me. She and I are delighted to have you go along with us! The next World Convention of Christian Churches was set for August, 1960, in Edinburgh, Scotland. Dr. Jesse Bader, Executive Secretary of the convention, asked me to be the Capital Area chairman. If I got twenty people to go, I would get a free round-trip plane ticket. I signed up forty. Since I had to pay Allene's way, the church gave us fifteen hundred dollars. Counting the thousand I had saved, that gave us a total of twenty-five hundred dollars. We would leave Janet and Anne with a German Christian girl, Erna Kaiser, for the three weeks we would be away.

It was a happy day indeed that afternoon when Allene and I walked into Brother Frank's room at the Waldorf Astoria. He rushed to hug "Tops." As he was on his way over to hug me, I pulled out of my coat pocket twenty-five hundred dollars in travelers checks and, with a shout, threw them toward the ceiling of the room. There were ten folders of two hundred fifty dollars each. Frank suddenly broke off his planned hug, hit the floor and crawled around grabbing all ten folders. I watched him as he grinned with fiendish glee and stuffed the checks into the pockets of his fancy hotel robe. It was only after he ordered up a scotch and soda for himself and a pot of fresh coffee for Allene and me that he realized he could not cash a single one of those traveler's checks. So he threw them over on his bed, one by one, all the while groaning and wiping fake tears from his eyes. What a character! What an actor! Frank actually did a lot of acting in college. In fact, he gained some local fame as Peter in the play "The Rock" for several Easter seasons at Eastside Christian Church, Tulsa.

This trip abroad began the first real vacation Allene and I ever had. We flew in a huge DC-9, four-engine prop plane, from New York to Shannon, Ireland, where we were bused to Edinburgh. We stayed in a nice private home for bed and breakfast, but Frank got a room in the fancy Caledonian Hotel in downtown Edinburgh. The convention was fabulous. There were thousands of people there from all over the world, including members of the Church of Christ, the Independent Christian Church, and our Christian Church (Disciples of Christ.)

Frank gave one of the keynote sermons, and Allene sang a solo at two of the services.

The final Sunday I was guest preacher and Allene sang a solo at the Fairmilehead Church of Scotland. On Saturday afternoon, I called the clerk (Clark) to find the location of the church, and he told me it was out a certain street with which I was familiar. Frank, Allene and I had been out on that street Friday night to a very old and famous bar. We heard that they served Glenlivet scotch there out of large kegs. The bar is called "Canny Mans," pronounced "Connie Mahns." In the bitter cold winters for many years, the hack drivers would run in there for a pint of beer and a jigger of scotch. As they tossed the whiskey and chuck-a-lucked the beer, the bartender would yell out to them, "Canny Man, Canny," meaning "Easy, easy, man, slow down!" So the name Canny Man's Bar, also known for its scotch, one of the best and most expensive in the world.

When the clerk started having trouble directing me to the church, I broke in and said, "I know that street, Sir; is it anywhere near "Canny Man's"?

He laughed and exclaimed loudly, "Ah! So you know Canny Man's?" When I told him that we were there last night, he was a different person. He gleefully said, "Well, Sir, the church is just in the next block!"

Sunday morning, as the clerk met us at the door of the ancient gothic structure, he was overly warm and friendly. Scottish gentlemen love their scotch, so we were welcomed as members of the club! To some of the other leading men, he kept saying quietly, as he smiled, "The preacher knows Canny Man's!" To that, they all nodded and smiled broadly.

Then he proceeded to turn the entire service over to me. I figured that he would lead the service, and I would only preach. Then as I stepped out to the pulpit seat, I realized that he had failed to give me the hymn numbers! I did not know a single hymn, and I could not even find them in the book! So I mouthed the Lord's Prayer and the 23rd Psalm during every hymn and no one caught on. They seemed blessed by Allene's solo, but as soon as I started talking, they all began to glance at each other and smile. I'm sure they were amused by my Georgia accent, just as we were by their Scottish brogue. They didn't get a single one of my jokes, but while I was preaching, they were very quiet and listened to every word. After church, the clerk and his lovely wife took Allene and me to lunch at a superb restaurant on Princes Street. As we parted, he gave me an envelope containing twenty-five dollars in crisp new pound notes. I was sure it was not a "love offering," but I really had not expected anything at all.

All of Scotland is a paradise, but Edinburgh is the pearl: Princes Street, the Castle, the small, well-kept gardens, the flower clock run by water, the afternoon tea, the superb restaurant food, climaxed by the world's most tempting desserts. The real delight was all those wonderful Scottish people, who are proud of James Bond (Sean Connery) who was born there. The week was an event we will long remember. I kept looking for Bond all over town, but no luck.

After the convention, Frank, Allene and I took the tour and cruise up on the Lochs of Scotland. This is one of the most beautiful places in the world. No, we didn't see the Loch Ness Monster. While we waited for our bus back to Edinburgh, we sat in a little hotel cafe that had large picture windows overlooking one of the beautiful lakes. Frank ordered a service of high tea. Over delicious tea, scones, finger snacks and sweets, Frank, being so inspired by the scene at twilight, began to quote poetry from Burns, Keats and Shelly, finishing off with several of his own poems. I took movies on the boat and at the cafe, which brought a little bit of Scotland back home for us to savor.

Frank got his plane to New York the same day Allene and I went down to London by overnight train. Our small bedrooms were numbers 17 and 18, ordered by me, thinking they would be together in the middle of the sleeper. Instead, each was at opposite ends of the car, right over the wheels! It was needless to complain because the train was full. As we slowly rolled into London the next morning, tea and scones were served to our rooms. We went directly to the dealer and took delivery of a 1960 VW. Before we left, I hired the assistant manager to drive us out of London and on the road to Brighton. I was terrified of that drive on the left side of the London streets. Outside the city limits when I took the wheel, it became a five-lane road, which was bad enough, but thank the Lord, we made it fine.

We visited the little church where Frederick W. Robertson preached in the 1850s and got to chat with the organist, who was a handsome man wearing a plaid suit and a wide handlebar mustache. When he took us to coffee, he gave me two books on Robertson and a portrait of this famous preacher. From Brighton, which is a lovely resort right on the channel, we continued on to Dover and at sunset, we spent the night at a quaint little inn where we fell asleep with the "squaking" of hundreds of seagulls in our ears.

The next morning we took the large ferry over the English Channel to Calais. It was a beautiful morning and, unlike on that fatal June 6, 1944, when thousands of our troops hit the shore, the channel was calm. As we neared the coast of France, someone on board pointed out to us all five of the beaches that our Allies used in the D Day invasion. It is hard to describe the impact that scene made upon me. Anyone who remembers that day and crosses that channel cannot do so with dry eyes. U.S. casualties alone those first few days on and after D Day were the highest we have ever suffered in any war. What I heard Winston Churchill say on radio about the Royal Air Force can also be said about our troops who gave their lives on those beaches and in the hedgerows: "Never in the field of human conflict was so much owed by so many to so few!"

From Calais, we drove the new VW to Brussels and Luxembourg, but now on the *right* side of the road! Every August the Germans celebrate "Fahshing," so just about everyone was drinking beer, including all the waiters and waitresses. It was as though the entire Fatherland was a veritable Hoffbrau House! We continued on through Germany to Kaiserslautern, where Ramstein Airbase was located. We were delighted to see our hosts Col. and Mrs. Philip Long. Phil, a senior pilot in the Air Force, had been the choir director at our church in Falls Church when he was stationed at the Pentagon before being sent to Germany. The son of a devout minister, Phil was about forty-eight, had his hair cut close and almost always wore, when off duty, a fancy sport shirt and fitted wool trousers. His wife, Lucille, was slender, attractive and had short brunette hair and deep brown eyes. She wore beige shorts, a tailored white shirt and jeweled white sandals on her pretty feet.

As Lucille served us fresh coffee and a good bratwurst on German bread, Phil discussed our trip to the Passion Play. He and I made a deal that we would go halves on the cost of taking Dean England with us to the world-famous Play in Oberammergau. Our beloved Dean arrived the next day from Paris, and we all piled into Phil's new VW bus for the drive to the play. Even though Phil drove at top speed through the German countryside on a two-lane road, we all said our prayers and sang halfway through the night on the way there. Dean was so very glad to be with us. He felt right at home since three of us had been students at Phillips.

This quaint, little town where the play has been shown every ten years for centuries is cradled in a valley with mountains on all sides. When the killer Black Plague hit Europe in the early 1600s, the whole town of Oberammergau gathered in a prayer service, where they vowed to God that if He would spare their town from the plague, they would present the story of Christ's last seven days on earth every ten years until His return. Not one soul contracted the pandemic plague! That is how we got the famous and blessed "Passion Play." It first ran only during Lent, but has been expanded to run for about four months in the summer every ten years and takes almost all day. The players are local people from the little village. The major characters often play the same part all their adult lives. Once there was a man who played Jesus for over forty years. A beautiful room, great food, a glorious play and the exciting fellowship all made it a joyful and inspiring two days. Allene and I have taken groups to the play in 1960, 1970 and 1980. However, in the summer of 1990, we were in China and did not go.

After the play, we drove Dean to the Frankfurt airport where we told him farewell with tears and embraces, then waved good-bye at the gate as he boarded his plane for the States. The four of us returned to Phil's apartment on base. The next morning, Lucille had to pull the three of us apart so she could serve breakfast. There could never be enough time to talk about all the fun we had with Phil, water-skiing, watching his movies, and the years we spent together at Phillips University. Nobody needed rocking that night; we all fell asleep as soon as we hit the bed.

Monday morning after breakfast, I looked at Allene and asked her if she would like to go to the Holy Land. She was shocked at the idea but delighted. They all thought that I had lost my mind. Phil then revealed that he had planned to take us in his VW bus on a trip over the Alps to Milan. Allene and I jumped up and hugged them both, exclaiming, "Oh, how wonderful of you to want to do that with us."

I countered with the idea of our going on to Israel and meeting them in Milan. Phil laughed and said, "Just how do you plan to do that, Chaplain?"

I said, "Well—let's see. Do you happen to have a travel guide here for Italy?"

He got it and handed it to me with a big grin on his face.

"OK," I murmured as I leaned forward with my finger on the page, "here is a five-star hotel near downtown Milan, not too far from the airport. Allene and I will spend Tuesday, Wednesday and Thursday nights in Israel. Friday morning we can fly to Beirut and on to Rome and Milan, and meet you in the lobby of—this hotel— say about 4:00 P.M.?"

Phil burst out with laughter, "Only a crazy captain would come up with such a wild idea. But you're on, Chappie! Allene, help Marco

The Trip of a Lifetime!

Polo get your gear together and we'll be off to the Frankfurt airport!"

Thinking that we had to travel as light as possible, I suggested that we pack in our flight bags for the three nights in Israel. We asked Phil to bring our luggage with them to Milan.

With a look of shock still on their faces, Phil and Lucille rushed us to the airport. He said, with a chuckle, "James, do you have reservations for a plane out of Frankfurt or a hotel in Israel?"

I shook my head no.

He continued, "I have often flown Air Force jets by the seat of my pants, but this is a bit ridiculous. Knowing you though, I've no doubt you'll make it."

Because we had no reservations, I'll admit that I was a little nervous as we walked up to the British Overseas Air ticket counter in Frankfurt and I handed the agent my new American Express card. Phil and Lucille waited back a few feet, Phil with a smirk on his face, arms folded, while he patted his foot. They didn't want the airline personnel to think that they knew us!

After I told the pretty "Fraulein" ticket agent where we wanted to go, I turned and smiled broadly at Phil. The clever girl got the picture, looked at Phil and said loudly to me, "Sir, you are in luck! I have just two seats left on our flight to Beirut that departs in thirty minutes. Here are your tickets; you may board now."

I smiled at Phil, who now was shaking his head in utter disbelief. Before Allene and I went to the gate, I ran over and hugged and kissed Lucille, hit Phil on the shoulder and turned to board. Then, just as we entered the boarding ramp, I yelled at them, "See you guys in Milan."

So we flew out of Frankfurt that morning, on a BOAC "Caravel" nonstop to Beirut, Lebanon! Food was great, service super. A Pakistani man, who we met on the plane, had been taught about Christ and was saved through American missionaries in Arabia. Then at Beirut customs, this Pakistani man saved *us* from having our tickets confiscated and being detained for days. They asked me where I was going and in my haste, I foolishly told the customs officer we were going to Israel. I momentarily forgot that the Lebanese were at war with Israel! No one was allowed to go to the Jewish part of Jerusalem from Lebanon. The officer jumped up and, with a loud and angry voice, demanded our passports and plane tickets.

Just at that moment our Pakistani friend, who had now changed into an "angel," stepped up quickly and said in their language, "My friend here is from the States and he is very mistaken. He and his beautiful wife are not going to Israel at all. They are rather going by car to Damascus, Amman, continuing to Jerusalem Jordan, then coming back here to Beirut and flying to Rome."

The officers all smiled broadly, handed back our passports, and told us we were free to go. We three could not get out of there fast enough. Our "angel" shared a cab with us, and as we pulled away, he told us what he had said to those custom officers. I thanked him warmly, but he just waved his hand and recommended we stay at the new Federal Hotel near the sea in Roc (new) Beirut. He assisted us with our check-in, then accepted my invitation to stay for dinner. At the close of a very exciting and busy day, Allene and I finally got to bed. After prayers of thanks for the miracles of the day, we drifted off to sleep, with the room filled with a cool, salty breeze and a background of the sound of breaking waves coming from off the Mediterranean.

We were stabbed awake at 6:00 A.M. by the unbearable heat. The water in the shower was too hot to use even on the cold side. After a light breakfast, we got a cab to Martyr's Square, right in the middle of downtown Beirut. It was even hotter there! The square was filled with cabs; all drivers blowing their horns and shouting strange sounds at the other drivers. The sidewalks were wall-to-wall with vendors. Hundreds of men, women and children were hurrying somewhere, all carrying on their shoulders or on top of their heads firewood, meats, chickens, breads and even live pigs squealing bloody murder. I glanced at Allene, who had been holding me tightly around the waist. I could tell by her shaking she was about ready at any moment to bolt and run for her life.

Against all of this bedlam, I kept trying to find someone who spoke English, hoping to locate a tour company. I had no luck. Even the police spoke no English. As we walked on around the steaming, teaming square, I glanced up and saw a sign on the top of a small building that read, "Terra Sancta." In a flash I grabbed Allene's hand and as we ran toward the building, I yelled, "Come on, Babe, the Lord is with us; that sign means 'Holy Land.'"

Sure enough, it was a tour office. We climbed the stairs and entered the office, which was filled with fans, all running at top speed. Immediately, a small boy walked in with coffee and scones, and with great authority, motioned for us to "sit." In a few minutes a short, bald, very fat man walked in, with a big cigar in his mouth, wearing shorts and a T shirt. He asked in good English what he could do for us.

Now, before I left the States, I had secretly checked with American Express, told them of my plans and asked them how much money should I set aside for this trip. They told me between eight hundred fifty and one thousand dollars.

The tour agent pulled up an old wicker chair, sat down and wheezed out, "Now, how can I help you?"

I told him that I wanted a good car, a driver and a guide—to take us to Damascus, Amman and on to Jerusalem Jordan; along with that I wanted a good hotel for three nights, all meals, tips and entrance fees to sacred sights. Then we must be brought back here to Beirut.

The owner took out a greasy little notebook, and with his huge hand, pulled a stubby pencil from his pocket, and wet it with his mouth. He began to scribble and mumble.

After a few minutes, he looked a me and said, "How does three hundred fifty dollars strike you?"

I answered, "What? Sir, you don't understand...what I want are a *good...*"

"Yes, yes, I know...", he mumbled."

Then he frowned, looked at his figures, squirmed and said, "OK, OK. Hummmm...What about two hundred eighty-five dollars?"

I smiled broadly and told him, "Let's make it 300 dollars. But be sure that all I told you, a good car, a..."

He broke in and kept saying, over and over, "Yes, yes, sure, sure, my dear friends, just leave everything to me; you will have *the trip of a lifetime.*"

The boy ran for more Turkish coffee and pastry while I signed the travelers checks and gave them to the agent. A little later, I glanced down to the street, where a young driver and an old man were standing by a shiny new Mercedes motioning for us to come on down! The engine was running and the windows were up, which meant we had air-conditioning! The agent picked up both our carry-on bags, and while he held Allene by the elbow, he walked us down the stairs and introduced us to our driver and guide. He handed the guide a brown paper package and then gave him detailed instructions in Arabic. As we were boarding the car, the agent shook my hand and I palmed him a crisp new twenty-dollar bill. He bowed and grinned, saying, "Thank you, bye-bye, thank you, bye-bye." Allene and I waved farewell as we sped away from the square—and its heat, strange smells and deafening noise. In a few minutes we were out of the hot, busy city and on the beautiful road to Damascus.

Just for fun, I turned to Allene and whispered, "You know, Honey, what if they turn off the road up here, go down an alley, stop and

A MIRACLE A MINUTE

knock us in the head, rob us, leave us on the street and then turn around and go back to the tour office?"

She grabbed me, her eyes a big as saucers, and said, "You've got to be kidding…You *are* joking, aren't you?"

I assured her I was.

Paul Afiff, our old guide, had a head full of bushy white hair, shiny white teeth and bright blue eyes. He wore a clean, starched white shirt, khakis, expensive sandals and no socks. He told us he was reared in a Catholic orphanage. He spoke seven languages, including German, French and very good English. The driver, Abdul, was short and dark, and mumbled strange sounds to Paul all day. The winding, narrow road was taking us farther and farther up into the mountains. Suddenly it was so nice and cool that I asked him to cut the air. At the top of the mountain range, he pulled over and stopped at a little store. Paul went in. The laughter of children playing near made us a tinge homesick for our girls. A large, white rooster perched on a little house in a garden was crowing his red head off. Paul returned with something in a large sack. As Abdul pulled away, Paul turned in the seat and handed us two large bottles of white Jordanian wine.

He then said, "Pastor, you and your lovely wife must not drink the water, but you'll find this to be the best wine you ever tasted."

I tried to pay him, but he said, "No, no, it's included. Besides all four bottles, two for us and two for you, only cost one U.S. dollar!"

Later, in Damascus, where we lunched at a sidewalk cafe, we found that Paul had told the truth about the wine. Paul and Abdul never took their meals at our table, but ate from a different menu, out of sight in the servant's dining room. From the cafe, we went to the "street called straight." In Bible times, it was a wide street, several miles long, running from the northeast to the southwest through the city. On this street, we stopped in a shop of one of his friends.

While we sat at coffee, Paul told us all about the apostle Paul's visit to Damascus. He concluded, saying, "The name of the city, 'Damas,' means blood, and 'Scuss' means mound; 'Mound of Blood,' in memory of the first murder in the Bible. Cain slew Able not too far from where we are sitting."

I was amazed! You can't find that meaning of "Damascus" in any commentary I've ever seen in the U.S.; they all say "meaning unknown." I took his word for it. We wanted to ship something back home, so Allene bought a large wood and leather camel seat, which we still have in our clubroom today. Anything you buy in the Middle

The Trip of a Lifetime!

East and have shipped home, you will receive; you can count on it.

On the outskirts of Damascus, we stopped and Paul showed us a building that had a big window up on the third floor with a rope hanging out of it. He said this was where Paul's Christian friends let him down in a basket in the middle of the night and thus saved his life. Of course, we knew this happened, but wondered whether this was the building.

He mentioned that much of the road on which we traveled on to Amman was built by the Romans. As we sped along he pointed his old, gnarled hand out the window to an ancient, vine-covered ruin out in a field, and said, "There is the famous Arch of Hadrian; real name, Publius Hadrianus, who was emperor of Rome from 117 to 138 A.D."

All during our tour, Paul would give long and detailed stories about every important place, sculpture or famous person. We stopped for a delicious lunch in Amman, then continued on to the old city of Jerusalem, where we checked into a beautiful hotel. Paul came to our table at dinner, telling us to dress casually in the morning, to wear walking shoes and be in the lobby at 8:00 A.M., ready for a thrilling day of sightseeing in the old city.

He smiled broadly, showing all of his white teeth, and raised his hands and said with a flair, "Tomorrow, we shall be walking in the steps of Jesus."

For the next two days, Paul gave us the royal tour of the city and Bethlehem. One afternoon, he took us down twenty feet below street level and showed us some wide marble stairs that were hollowed out from years of wear and a narrow cobbled street that ran under a solid wall.

"Here," he said, "is the only place in Jerusalem you can actually walk where Jesus walked. That Friday, the day Jesus was killed, He actually walked down these stairs, and on that street. Our Lord could have touched that column there to steady Himself as He carried His cross to Golgotha."

He told us that the city streets in Jesus' time were twenty to thirty feet beneath the streets we walk on today. Allene and I thrilled at the thought of actually standing where Jesus stood in Jerusalem. We then sat on the bottom step, took off our shoes and socks and placed our bare feet on the street. In my imagination, I saw our precious Lord, crowned with thorns, His body covered with His blood from the lashings, carrying His heavy cross down those stairs. I sobbed and whispered a prayer. I leaned over, kissed the step and the stones of the street, then went over and tightly embraced the ancient column that Jesus may have touched. We couldn't hold back the tears. Paul was also moved.

Even on the shores of Galilee, one cannot know for sure whether one is walking exactly where He walked, maybe in the ruins of the synagogue at Capernaum. We have been to the Holy Land many times since then, but we have never had a guide who knew where that place was in Jerusalem. It is sad, indeed, to think that maybe it was destroyed in new construction.

That afternoon we went to Bethlehem, and there Paul pointed out a cave where he said Jesus was actually born. Then we descended to the basement of the Church of the Nativity, built over where the stable was located. There we saw an eternal flame, where it is said His cradle rested. Out to the back of the church, he led us through a large grape harbor to the hut of an old Coptic priest. Paul introduced us to Father Manuell, who spoke Aramaic to Paul but English to us.

Paul had to leave for a while, so the priest asked us to stay and have a little wine. He had deep blue eyes, a white beard and hair and wore the habit of a Coptic priest—a black robe, white sash and black sandals. There at sunset, in that sacred place, as we sipped wine that he had made from the grapes in the arbor around us, he told us that this was the same kind of wine Jesus poured for His disciples in the upper room and most likely from this same arbor! Allene and I both had already felt Christ's presence, but when the priest said that, we were tingling all over. While he went inside, our attention was attracted to the many strange but beautiful birds that flitted here and there. Down the hill toward the Shepherd's Fields, two dogs barked and the cool breeze was heavy with the fragrance of the ripe grapes, all covered with brown paper, hanging in the arbor.

Soon, the old priest came out with a tray of bread he had baked, poured us a little more wine and conducted a communion service. At my request he spoke in Aramaic the words Jesus used during the Last Supper. We felt an even closer presence of our Lord as we took the cup and the loaf. The three of us "remembered him in the breaking of the bread and in the partaking of the cup." Just imagine, this deeply spiritual experience right near the place where He was born. A little later, as we bade the old cleric good evening, he embraced us both, placed his hand on our head and gave us a blessing and the holy kiss. I told Allene that his blessing placed us in "apostolic succession" since his blessing goes back through all the hands all the way back to Peter.

Paul was waiting with the car at the front of the church. On the way back to Jerusalem, we were all very quiet. Allene began softly singing "O Little Town of Bethlehem." Paul, Abdul and I joined in, and led by the Spirit, we had vespers, a time of worship of the Father and of "Little Baby Jesus." We also stopped and saw Rachel's tomb, which overlooks the beautiful Shepherd's Fields. I'm sure that you share with us the presence of the Holy Spirit as I describe how the gospels came alive there in that precious old city at twilight time.

Thursday morning just as we finished breakfast, we were already regretting the fact that our time was running out. But when Paul came over to our table he had some good news. He gave us tickets he had bought for us to fly back to Beirut on Air Jordan, thus avoiding an entire day of driving. This gave us extra time on our last day to visit Jericho, where we drank water from Elijah's fountain; and Qumran, where the Dead Sea scrolls were found. We went swimming in the Dead Sea and had lunch at Hebron. Although I have led many groups to Europe and the Holy Land since then, this, my first visit, was the very best.

At the airport, early on Friday morning, Allene and I said our farewells to Paul Affif and Abdul. I generously tipped them both, then Paul presented Allene with a gorgeous necklace. As we all hugged, I told them what a great blessing the trip had been. After the four of us joined hands for prayer, we boarded the old DC-3. On a semi-dirt runway, we took off with the roar of those engines in our ears as we left old Jerusalem behind and were on our way to Beirut.

In Beirut, we changed to another BOAC "Caravel" for our flight back to Rome. We had lunch at the Rome airport, then got a plane to Milan, arriving there about 3 P.M. Since we had no checked luggage, we stepped out to the street and caught a cab for the short ride to our rendezvous hotel. We walked into the large and impressive lobby, took a seat there and ordered coffee and sandwiches. We were just finishing when Phil and Lucille came sweeping through the doors at exactly 4:00 P.M.! They walked over with Phil laughingly saying, "I do not believe this! Pippin, I simply do not believe that you two are sitting here so cool, calm and collected and having coffee."

When I told him that we had only been there for about thirty minutes, he was amazed. All our spirits were high as we climbed aboard the VW bus.

As Phil was driving us away, he was muttering something about, "God must be smiling on that chaplain."

Then Lucille turned and said, "Phil, don't you know a miracle when you see one? This all has just got to be the hand of God."

A MIRACLE A MINUTE

I answered, "A big amen to that, Sister. But you know, I think we are going to have to get that husband of yours saved!"

In the small lobby of the pension in Milan that Phil had reserved for us, we met a couple who were there on holiday from Berlin. They told us that the hot spot in Milan was a club that had the only man-made beach in northern Italy. They were going there that night and asked us to join them. We agreed.

At the club we sat down at a table that was out in the open and right by the lake. Multicolored lights were strung all around, and a large band was playing great, romantic, dance music. On the dance floor were well-dressed, handsome men, dancing the cha-cha with pretty girls in beautiful, short, flared skirts, which rose farther as they twirled. Allene and I just had to get out there and show off. When we came back to our seats, I bragged to them about how Allene used to be a jit-terbug star at Radio City Music Hall. We had great fun the entire evening. It was the first time I ever danced with a Fraulein. We man-aged to do the two-step quite nicely. A little later, while I was dancing with Allene, I broke in on a couple, and the handsome man and the gorgeous girl were very delighted. My partner spoke English well. Some of those pretty girls favored Allene! Remember, Allene looks both Italian and Jewish! I wish we could have stayed there a week!

The next morning we went to an outdoor cafe for breakfast. While we ate, we suddenly heard this male tenor voice coming from a balcony two buildings over. He was belting out the first line of "Rudolpho's Aria" from the opera "La Bohéme." Allene stood up and sang the next line in Italian, then he excitingly came back with his part and they sang the whole duet together. When they finished, all the people in the café (including all the waiters and even the cooks) stood and gave Allene a rousing applause! One of the waiters came over and bowing, told Allene, "Madam, you should come to Italy, be a big star in our world-famous Milan Opera House."

Of course, Allene just had to tell him how she had been offered a year of study there, but chose to marry this preacher instead. Then the Italian waiters had a big laugh and painful looks on their faces that said, "Why, you silly girl!"

We kept waiting for the mystery tenor to show up, but he never came. After breakfast, we visited the beautiful, world-famous, Milan Opera House. Allene could not resist the urge to stand on that famous stage.

I told her, "Sweetheart, go ahead and sing 'Vissi Darte' so you can tell people you sang a solo in the Milan Opera House!"

The Trip of a Lifetime!

She laughed loudly, which resounded all over the house, and said, "Oh sure, you foolish man! But I wonder how many ambitious singers have done that!"

I reminded her to "judge not, lest she be judged." I have always regretted that I did not insist that Allene sing an aria in that famous place.

We were awestruck by the grandeur and size of the Milan Cathedral, for it is Gothic architecture at its highest. Just out the towering front doors and to the right is the little room where Leonardo da Vinci painted his renowned "The Last Supper." The hushed silence was broken only by the click and flash of several cameras. I got a 35mm slide that turned out really good. In the last few years, that famous painting has been completely restored to its original brilliance.

After having breakfast in the small but pleasingly clean dining room, we four bade farewell to our new Berlin friends and to beautiful Milan. We then began our motor trip up the Po River Valley, heading for the Alps. About nine o'clock that night we stopped high in the mountains to have supper. We were served the best spaghetti I had ever eaten. We got rooms in an inn that was above the restaurant. As Allene and I retired, we discovered that our large mattress was filled with straw. Lying there in the dark, I kept hearing in my mind the song "Miranda," which is accented by loud castanets. Allene had sung it in several of her church benefit concerts. I sang a few lines of it. "Do you remember an inn, Miranda? Do you remember an inn? And the fleas in the high Pyrenees...!"

I sure prayed that there were no fleas in our mattress. I leaned over and whispered to Allene, "My dear, do you realize that this song you have sung for many church concerts is all about a guy who took this chick, Miranda, on a whirlwind fling and shacked up with her in a flea-infested inn in the Pyrenees mountains?"

She mumbled, "Oh, shut up and go to sleep."

I just had to chuckle. About the time I stopped, she started laughing.

Our drive the next day took us through some of the most inspiring scenery in Europe. A motor trip through this part of the world is something everyone should do at least once. We ended up in Paris, where before the time of the birth of Christ the Seine River flowed by a small fishing village. It was our first visit to this enchanting city. For three days and nights, we saw many of the famous sights in the city of lights, including the show at the Lido, lunch in the Eiffel Tower on the way down and two hours in the

A MIRACLE A MINUTE

Cathedral of Notre Dame. We could have lived in the Louvre. We also walked up and down "The Chomps," military lingo for the Champs-Elysees.

We will always remember fondly our very first visit to Paris and that quaint little hotel where we spent the last night of our trip; it was only a short block down from the Arc de Triomphe. The sun was just rising over a cool, quiet Paris when Phil and Lucille took us to Orly, the Paris airport, for our KLM Airline flight to New York City. Parting with them was hard since we had shared so many exciting things together. It was a bittersweet farewell.

Allene and I slept almost the entire plane trip. Upon arrival in New York, we had lunch at the airport, and then within about two hours we boarded a plane to Washington, DC. On this flight our trip was coming to a close, so we began to look back across these past three weeks, feeling blessed by the Lord. We went over all the days and the nights to remind ourselves of the fact that God's hand had been upon us all the way.

We recounted the spiritual uplift of the World Convention; the beautiful city of Edinburgh, with its castle, Princess Street, its flower clock, and especially its fine restaurants with their heavenly desserts; preaching and singing in a Church of Scotland; the trip up on the "Lochs" with Brother Frank; the train ride to London; the purchase of a new 1960 VW; the trip to Brighton, Dover, Calais and the Netherlands; the thrill of the Passion Play with Dean England, Phil and Lucille; the last two seats on the plane to Beirut; the Pakistani "angel" who saved us at customs and got us a hotel; finding the "Terra Sancta" tour company in the midst of the heat and bedlam of Martyr's Square in old Beirut; the low cost of that glorious tour, with its fine car and its outstanding guide and driver; the tour of Damascus, Amman, and Old Jerusalem; the Bethlehem blessing with the old Coptic priest; the no-hassle plane connections at Beirut and Rome; the amazing on-time rendezvous with Phil and Lucille at the hotel; the restful and inspiring ride through the Alps; then on to Paris, the jewel of France with all of its never-to-be-forgotten beauty; and finally the good food and service on KLM Airlines to New York.

On that brief flight to Washington, with all of the miracles of the trip still fresh in our minds, Allene and I joined hands and thanked God for every minute of it. He is a good God and a good Father, that is for sure. It is great to travel abroad, and Allene and I had the time of our lives; but it is always a greater thrill to come back home, to the greatest nation in the world with its flag of freedom, and back to our house and to our precious girls. As we pulled into the driveway, our daughters Janet and Anne ran down the walkway and leaped into our arms. Erna Kaiser stood nearby, waiting for her hug. She told us that the girls were beginning to think we were never coming home. During the next few days the girls kept demanding that we tell them every single detail of our journey. But first they had to tell us everything that had happened to them while we were gone.

The next Sunday morning the sanctuary was packed. Allene and I shared many of the highlights of our tour in a sort of travelogue, which was in itself a spiritual experience. We were interrupted several times with laughter, and we noticed that there were often tears in their eyes. At the coffee after church they were all so loving we knew that these were our people and that they had actually missed us.

In the challenging and busy days ahead, all of the church members were more and more thrilled with our beautiful new sanctuary, the increasing number of new members, and the rapid growth of the church school. The great love of all of the people who seemed so glad to have us home really warmed our hearts. There was no way I could predict that in the next few months the Soviets would put up a wall, the president would call up the Reserve and I would be plucked *back into the military!*

❋ 22 ❋

Called to
"The Church of Tomorrow"

The spring of 1961 brought tensions that mounted between the United States and Soviet Russia. Many thought that we were close to World War III, especially after the Soviets put up the Berlin Wall. All of Washington was real jittery, so much so that Secretary of Defense Robert McNamara called up the Army Reserve. The Pentagon dubbed it "The Berlin Crisis." Army general hospitals were in great demand, and yep, they called my 354th General Hospital to active duty. I received a leave of absence from the church, and in August 1961, I found myself back in the Army at Ft. Meade, Maryland, just about an hour from Falls Church. Since no one knew how long the crisis would last, Rev. Ewart Wyle was called by the board to serve as interim minister. Allene and the girls remained active in the church.

Chaplain (Captain) John Harris and I opened the chapel in our area at beautiful Ft. Meade and carried on a program of service to the unit, which had about sixty nurses, forty medical doctors and a large group of enlisted men and women. After two weeks of settling in, we spent a month in the field, much like the eighteen days at Camp Grant, but the duty was easier now since I was not only a captain but a chaplain. When the field duty was over, we officers and most of the enlisted personnel were able to go home on weekends to be with our families. John and I, of course, had to conduct a service in the chapel each Sunday morning, but the drive up there was no problem. The post chaplain, Col. Hale, had monthly meetings, so we got to know all of the active duty chaplains in Third Army. Also, the Army Chaplain Board was located there, giving John and me the opportunity to get to know the eight senior Army chaplains who were on the board.

Called to "The Church of Tomorrow"

The highlight of that time was the birth of our third daughter, Beverly Allene, on June 21, 1962. Just like the other two, she was a beauty, with a head full of red hair and, in a few weeks, green eyes. But Beverly (the medical bills, that is) only cost us about seven dollars because she was an "Army baby" born at the base hospital at Ft. Belvoir, near Falls Church.

That year of active duty had its challenges and also its good points. I had the experience of serving on active duty as a chaplain and captain, and when the unit was released in August, 1962, I was promoted to major. The year away from the church was like a sabbatical. I got a rest from the heavy load of my duties both in the local church and in the Capital Area Regional program. But probably the best of all was the fact that the church had a year's rest from me! I was glad when the time came for me to be back with them and back home full time with the family. While I had been on active duty, Allene stayed close to the people and the activities of the church; she had sung in the choir and had briefed me regularly on the church's progress and decisions that were being made. Rev. Wyle did a good job, but he was happy to leave and take a congregation of his own. Soon I was back into the routine, and the church continued to make solid progress.

A year later, our unit served the two weeks of summer duty in our old area at Ft. Meade. One afternoon Chaplain John Harris and I were sitting on the front steps of our chapel just at sunset. All of a sudden I seemed to be able to see into the future. I turned to him and said, "John, I have a strong feeling that this next year will bring a great change to me and my family. I don't have the details clearly, but I don't believe we will be in the Washington area much longer."

In late November, 1963, since Brother Frank had lost his wife, I called and asked him to come for a visit with us and speak on Sunday for our church. His dear wife, Ozelle, had died a year earlier from colon cancer. I drove my 1961 Mercedes to the funeral. On the way I stopped in Pittsburgh, picked up George, who was serving a church there, and he and I drove on turnpikes all the way to Kansas City. George fell in love with that car, and I had to fight him to get to drive it at all on the entire trip. It was hard for us to say farewell to Ozelle for she was dearly loved by all of the family and also by the members of Community Church. Julia, their only daughter, was sorely grieved. She and her beloved mother had been very close. So when Frank came to see us that November, we tried our best to comfort him and talked much of Ozelle and Julia.

A MIRACLE A MINUTE

One Friday afternoon while Frank was still visiting with us, I was alone in my study when Mary May, our secretary, brought in the mail. In it was a letter from the First Christian Church, Oklahoma City, asking if I would be interested in becoming their minister. This great church was one of our denomination's largest, with a membership of thirty-six hundred and four awesome buildings, including a dazzling futuristic sanctuary that would seat two thousand people.

As I was reading the letter and about to reach for the phone to call Allene with the good news, the study door burst open and Frank came rushing in, out of breath. He was weeping. As he sat down, he put both hands up to his face and said, "Brother James…on the way back from the Capitol…we heard on the radio…that President Kennedy…has been shot in Dallas…he is dead."

I answered with stark disbelief, "Frank, surely you're joking. I cannot believe this!!"

As he shook his head and continued to sob, I placed my face in my hands, leaned down on my desk and wept. Mary came when she heard the weeping, and when Frank told her what had happened, she fell onto the sofa and also began to weep. This went on for a few minutes, and then the phone rang; Allene was on the line sobbing loudly and asking if I'd heard the news.

That afternoon, Friday, November 22, 1963, about 2:00 P.M., Eastern time, President Kennedy was pronounced dead—killed by an assassin's bullet. The nation and the entire world were thrown into a valley of deep mourning. All Americans stayed in front of the TV for many hours through the sad days and nights that led up to the funeral.

When Frank composed himself and after Mary left the room, I handed him the letter I had been reading.

He sobbed, "Son, please, I don't want to read anything right now."

I smiled and said, "You will when you see what it is!"

He wiped his eyes, blew his nose and took the letter. Suddenly his face changed to a big smile, and he cleared his throat and said, "My good Lord, Son! This is the opportunity of a lifetime! You must immediately accept. This is a great challenge!"

After talking at length with Allene and Frank that night, I phoned the chairman of the committee the next day and said that I was interested in the call.

Frank wanted to stay for the Kennedy funeral, but felt the urgency to return to his church to help his people with their grief. Since he loved to ride the train, I took him to the Washington terminal.

As we embraced farewell, he said, with shaky voice, "These are perilous days, my brother. Be strong so you can do your best to comfort Tops and the girls, and also the members of your parish."

Allene, Janet, Anne and I went to Arlington Cemetery for the President's interment. Thousands of people were there, so like Zacchaeus, I climbed a nearby tree and watched from a distance of only fifty feet as President John F. Kennedy's body was laid to rest. Before the nation even partially recovered from JFK's assassination, we had to suffer the loss of Bobby Kennedy and the murder of Dr. Martin Luther King, Jr. Investigations are still underway, trying to find the truth about what led to the deaths of these great men. The American people may never know the real truth about the deaths of any of them.

In December, without our knowing it, the church in Oklahoma City sent two people to visit one of our Sunday services to hear me preach. Then in late January, upon their invitation, we flew out there. I spoke and Allene sang to a packed dining room at a Wednesday night dinner. Later that evening, we met with the Pulpit Committee and certain selected leaders of the church. I had to answer many questions about all phases of my ministry and my doctrine. I had a few questions for them as well, mainly if I had the full authority of a senior minister to call an entire staff of my own. Yes, was their answer, so I felt very good about the visit.

We left on Thursday and flew to Kansas City to preach and sing on Sunday for Brother Frank at Community Christian. After Allene and I finished greeting all those loving folks, Frank took us to the airport and to lunch. On the way to the gate, he told us how very proud he was of us, then he reminded me again that I simply could not turn down the offer to be called to one of the five largest churches in our denomination. He told me later that after we left, he called Dr. Eugene S. Briggs, chairman of the committee, to speak for me and found out from Dr. Briggs that the church was about ready to give me a call. Dr. Briggs' son, Bill, who was a member of National City Christian Church, Washington, DC, also gave his strong support to me.

The recommendation of the Pulpit Search Committee to give me a call to become their senior minister went first to the board of elders, then to the official board, and then to a meeting of the church congregation. Dr. Briggs phoned me the last Sunday in February and gave me the news. The church had given me a vote to become their minister. He requested that I be on payroll beginning the fifteenth of March so we could be there for Palm Sunday and Easter services. I asked Dr. Briggs if the vote was unanimous. He said that there was a group of about twenty persons who voted "no" because they wanted the associate minister to have the position. But when he told the people that under no circumstances would I accept the offer unless the call was unanimous, after a little discussion, those twenty people yielded and gave me the unanimous vote. The reason I include this detail will be made clear when I tell you what happened in the months that followed.

It was very hard to leave the church in Falls Church. It was our first pastorate after seminary, plus we had served there for almost eleven years and had led the congregation in a program of continued growth and effectiveness that included a church plant with an education building and a large beautiful sanctuary that seated seven hundred fifty people. By March of 1964, the membership had grown to over eleven hundred. But my leaving was made even more difficult by the fact that we could only give the church a three-week notice of our departure. Along with that, Allene and I had made many dear friends among the ministers, their wives and the members of all of the churches in the area because during those eleven years I had been very active in the Capital Area, including serving as chair of the regional board of the Capital Area Christian Churches and also as president of the annual convention for two terms.

In addition to all this, there was the fact that we were not only very close to the nation's capital, but only a short ride on the train to New York City. Allene and I went there for a few days about twice a year to see the shows and eat in some of the world's best restaurants. Also, Allene had many friends in the Arlington Opera Workshop where she had sung a major role, and I was close to the Pentagon, where I got to know and visit with many of the senior chaplains, including Charlie Brown, who was then a two-star general and the chief of chaplains. He and his wife, Ava, paid us a visit a few weeks before we left. He strongly urged me to accept the call to Oklahoma City. However, the closer we came to the date of departure, the more we trembled inside…wondering if we had made the right decision.

After much prayer and being told by the local church leaders that the church could not stand in the way of this opportunity, we began to do all the things that had to be done before we could leave. The list included selling our home on Normandy Lane, which we bought in 1953 for $17,500 and sold in 1964 for the low price of $26,000. Runaway inflation hit that area beginning in 1970 and as I write, that house sells for over $300,000. I have asked myself a million times, "Why didn't you rent the thing, you dummy?!"

Called to "The Church of Tomorrow"

Since I was going to become one of the top ten ministers in our denomination, I had to get ready for the part. I already had a 1963 Mercedes 280-SE, bought from a Peruvian diplomat, but now I also bought a 1962 Cadillac Fleetwood Brougham De'Elegance. I topped all this off by going over to Lewis & Thos. Saltz, a very high-priced men's clothing store in Washington, and walking out with some very expensive suits, including a morning wear outfit with a long coat and striped trousers, complete with a black Homburg hat! So, after Allene did all she had to do and the girls said good-bye to their friends, all was done. O, how I dreaded that farewell sermon. Allene managed to get through her solo, but I could not keep back the tears as I preached. Then, we five had to suffer through a farewell reception.

Allene, the girls and I pulled out of Falls Church on March 11, 1964 and headed west to Oklahoma City. Janet was ten; Anne, eight; and Beverly was only twenty-two months old. We were soon to find out that this was God's will for us, because had we not taken the church, I would not have met Lovenia James who almost drove me crazy trying to get the Holy Spirit into me. And you probably would not be reading this book. It is going to be difficult to describe this very unique church, its many splendored buildings and its star-studded members! But I will give it a try!

Two days later we drove up in front of George Swisher's home in the Lakehurst subdivision of Oklahoma City, and out walked George and Jenny Swisher, Bill Wilson, the chairman of the board, and his lovely wife, Roine. They leaned back and laughed when they saw us pull in, driving a '62 Cadillac towing a '63 Mercedes! They told me later that after seeing this, they had immediately suspected that they had probably hired a "character" for their new minister. We stayed for two weeks with the wonderful Swishers in their large elegant home, complete with swimming pool, five bedrooms and four baths. We remained there until the church could rent a temporary house for us. Then five months later, in August, we purchased a beautiful home. It was in Lakehurst on Chapel Hill Road, only two blocks north of the Swishers' house.

This was not the first time I had ever seen the church I was to serve. In fact, in the fall of 1962, I had conducted a week's preaching mission for the University Place Christian Church in Enid, Oklahoma. After the meeting, Wanda Kennedy, the soloist, took me the eighty miles south to Oklahoma City to catch my plane back to Washington. We arrived in the night, but she insisted that we drive by so she could show me the grounds and buildings of her church—the First Christian Church, Oklahoma City, which a year or so earlier had called a new minister after the tragic and sudden death of Rev. W. H. (Bill) Alexander.

After she had shown me all of the buildings, Wanda turned to me and made the startling statement, "James Clayton Pippin, you are going to be the next minister of my church."

I said, "Sure, Sure," and actually never gave it another thought. But I have always believed that Wanda got those words of prophecy from the Lord.

Although Allene and I had been taken on a fast tour of the entire facility in February, as we drove onto the church grounds with the Swishers that morning, it somehow looked different to me—much larger. The awesome grandeur of the church buildings and grounds is not easy to describe. The first construction on the forty acres of land, formerly the Edgemere Golf and Country Club, was a thirty-five-hundred-seat amphitheater that was dedicated in August of 1947. Here, Sunday evening services were held every spring and summer until the sanctuary was built. A brave new program of New York style entertainment, called "Twilight Time," was offered on Friday nights in the "theater under the stars." It drew big crowds and heap-big criticism! But Rev. Alexander, then the popular pastor, and his forward-looking church were used to criticism. It began years before, when the youth center of the old church at 10th and Robinson offered for the first time in the nation, as far as I know, church dancing classes and even held dances for the youth on Friday and Saturday nights!

Rev. Alexander often got the question, "Preacher Bill, just what do you think about the youth dancing in the house of God?"

He answered, "I don't think about it. But I do believe that it is a whole lot better to have our young people dancing in the church than roaming the streets at night, getting into all sorts of trouble."

On December 23, 1956, the sanctuary, the four-story education building, the Jewel Box Theater and the bell tower were dedicated by thirty-six hundred proud members and many guests from the city and the nation during a week of outstanding speakers and music. The sanctuary, where two thousand people comfortably worship in beautiful red theater chairs, is a futuristic-style, sparkling white dome that resembles half of a mammoth egg sticking out of the ground. Adjacent to the dome is the very tall, white carillon (bell) tower. This white spire and the dome caused some to call this "The Egg and I" church. Just west, connected to the dome is a round four-story education building with gleaming silver fins that deflect the sunlight. Joined by a breezeway farther west is "The Jewel Box," a rose-colored theater in the round built to resemble a jewel or music box. On the far east side of the forty acres and across a little creek stands the large youth center, which was dedicated later and includes classrooms and a full-sized basketball court.

The longtime minister, W. H. (Bill) Alexander, had the vision for this entire facility. He was a tall, red-headed, handsome, blue-eyed, broad-shouldered, nationally known and very colorful pulpiteer. He called his grand dream "The Church of Tomorrow." Bill was the most loving and most loved of any minister the church ever had. One of a kind, he is impossible to fully describe or evaluate. Warm, unpredictable, exciting and hilariously funny, he held the people who came each Sunday morning in the palm of his hand. Wherever Bill was, there was never a dull moment, that's for sure. When someone was in his presence, both in person and in church, that was the place to be at that moment, because nothing of importance could possibly be happening anywhere else in the world. For years, he was one of the nation's top featured after-dinner speakers, bringing in annually over fifty thousand dollars in personal income. In those years this was a small fortune. But his salary at the church was never more than fifteen thousand dollars.

One year Bill switched parties and ran for the Senate as a Republican against Mike Monroney. Since Bill knew just about everybody in the state, he gave Monroney the run of his career. On Election Day, Bill lost, but he received more votes than any other Oklahoma Republican had received in a run for the Senate before. He narrowly missed becoming a senator.

Bill and my brother Frank were very close friends. I came to know and admire Bill through Frank. The first time I ever heard Bill speak was at the East Side Christian Church in Tulsa. This is the church that Frank started "from the first person and the first brick up." Bill preached the dedication sermon for the new sanctuary, and I was on the front row. He was great! He used no notes, and was all over the place, right up in the faces of all of us, seemingly, at the same time! He was the first preacher I ever knew who could leave the chancel and walk all around, and because what he was saying was so captivatingly amazing, no one ever noticed that he was not behind the pulpit.

No matter how long he spoke, it was not long enough. I am not exaggerating one bit. If you ever heard him, you would agree that W. H. (Bill) Alexander was one of a kind, and for me, no one before and no one after could ever measure up to his radiant and all-consuming personality. When he chatted with me that day long ago in his study at Tenth and Robinson, he made me feel like I was the only person in the world.

How often I have heard Frank say, "I strongly recommended my longtime friend Bill Alexander to the First Church in Oklahoma City when he was a very young man years ago. And when I came out of the Army in 1945, he recommended me to the Community Church in Kansas City. His letter had a lot to do with my getting the church."

During the week of dedication, this beautifully unique church was featured in many newspapers around the country. The picture plus an article about the church were picked up then by *The World Book* encyclopedia and carried in its Modern Architecture section for several years. There were so many visitors from all over the nation that guides were furnished each Sunday to take them on a tour of the premises. Bill started this years before any other church did. That courtesy was still needed when I arrived there in 1964.

However, in the midst of all this beauty, publicity, celebration, great and growing church programs and some of the best sermons in the nation, the unbelievable happened: The church, the city, the state and much of the nation were greatly shocked and deeply grieved when only about four years after the dedication, Dr. Alexander and his wife, Mary Louise were instantly killed in a plane crash near Hershey, Pennsylvania, on April 3, 1960. Bill's family, the church members, and countless close friends would never fully recover from this tragedy. At Bill's funeral service, the sanctuary was not only packed, but it also took every room in the church to handle the huge overflow crowds.

Rev. Donald M. Sheridan, the dearly loved associate, took the helm for about six months until Dr. Walter MacGowan was called as minister in November, 1960. He served the church for about three years, with Rev. Sheridan as his associate. Rev. William K. Herod, who had been on the staff for several years, was called to serve as associate minister when the church was saddened by Rev. Sheridan's passing. When they had served there together, Bill Alexander had been the preacher, but everyone knew that Rev. Sheridan was the pastor. The position Don Sheridan left on that staff could never be filled by anyone. Next to Bill, he was the most loved person who ever served the church. Also, the faithful, hard-working Bill Herod was then appointed the interim minister until I walked in on March 15, 1964.

How can Allene and I ever forget or fully describe the feelings, the thoughts and happy experiences that filled the first months after I was called as senior minister of the First Christian Church of Oklahoma City? Of all the churches in our denomination, this pulpit was one of the top five in the nation and was desired by so many of our leading ministers. Letters of congratulation came from many of them and also from my classmates and friends.

My first Sunday was Palm Sunday, 1964. Jenny and George Swisher served us a hearty breakfast. After Allene dressed the girls in their pretty new outfits, she wore her finest and I donned my new morning wear outfit, complete with gray vest and gray tie. Then Janet, Ann, Beverly, Allene and I climbed into George's new Cadillac, and off we went. George said I looked more like a senator, or even the president, than I did a preacher. Bill Wilson, who had been the master of ceremonies at the dinner when we came to the church in January, and his gracious wife, Roine, were waiting in the study where we all gathered in a circle, and Bill led us in prayer. Bill, Roine and Allene also took the girls to their classes and introduced them to their new teachers. Then Bill and Roine escorted Allene into the sanctuary.

Everyone else had left the room, so I was left in the study alone. I went into the little prayer room that was just out my study door and fell on my knees. I can remember that prayer almost word for word:

> "Father God, in the precious name of your Son, Jesus Christ, if anything good happens in this first worship service and in my first sermon, You are going to have to do it. Anoint me with your Holy Spirit that I might bring peace, excitement, understanding and love to these Your people. I give You all the credit, in the name of Christ Jesus."

When I finished the prayer I knew that I was no longer alone.

My first sermon, "The Greatness of God," was one I had preached before, but as I stepped up to the pulpit that Palm Sunday, I knew that in their minds I could never fully measure up to the stature of their late, great Preacher Bill. So I prayed that I would simply be myself. Just as the congregation had packed the dining room back in January, they turned out in droves to see and hear their new senior minister and his charming wife, Allene. She came up to the lectern and sang a brilliant solo and well...I think I did OK.

Even with all those prayers that morning, I was still a bit uncomfortable, especially at the coffee hour, where I felt sort of like a piece of Swiss cheese, thinking that all eyes were boring holes through me. Our two girls stood around, wearing silly grins as they each stuck out a limp hand for all to shake. But I began to relax when I suddenly realized that these were some the most understanding and loving persons we had ever met. Their genuine Oklahoma warmth put us all at ease.

So after that first Sunday, we were "off and running" as pastor and first lady of this great church. The next Sunday was Easter, and we had over thirty-three hundred people in three services. I was officially installed the first Sunday after Easter in an impressive service, where many church dignitaries and other local ministers took part. Bill Wilson presented me as the candidate. Also present were Rev. Joe Shackford of St. Luke's Methodist; Dr. J. Daniel Joyce, dean of my seminary; and our beloved dean, Stephen J. England, Ph. D., who gave the charge. The prayer of installation was given by The Rev. James Clark (Jim) Brown, one of our greatest preachers and Brother Frank's second favorite summer minister! After a solo by Allene and a stirring anthem, Dr. Frank Johnson Pippin gave a moving sermon titled, "The Problem and Power of Preaching Today."

I was so proud and happy that Brother Frank could be a part of this great occasion. After the Sunday service, Mrs. Bob (Vi) Angerman and her hard-working committee hosted a lovely reception in the huge dining room for our family and guests. The rest of the day we rested a little, and then Brother Frank took us to dinner. He would have to be returning to Kansas City the very next morning. After I took Frank to the airport, I walked in on Monday morning, and the full staff of over thirty people held a welcoming coffee for me. The staff included five ordained positions: a director of children's education, director of youth, an associate minister, a minister of music and a business administrator. The church also had two secretaries, a chief engineer, four custodians, a dietitian and three full-time cooks. Since we held a core staff meeting each Tuesday morning and a full staff meeting once a month, I got to know personally all of the staff members as competent, friendly and dedicated Christians.

It was my good fortune to inherit Pastor Bill's exceptionally brilliant, personal secretary, Miss Vera W. Stovell. Vera was also one of a kind. I could not have made it through those years as pastor without her. She opened and sorted my mail, ran our personal checkbook, made my coffee, took all of my dictation and even rehearsed all of my weddings! Also, during long afternoons over coffee in my study, she clued me in on much of the information (and maybe even a little gossip) about the membership, the church facility, the program, the protocol and what was expected of the pastor. Vera screened my calls and shielded me from certain individuals she thought should not be taking up my time. Super-efficient and experienced, she took accurate dictation, was a very fast typist, a perfect speller and knew her grammar. Bill Wilson, the chairman of the board, told me to always remember, "James, everything that goes on around this church has to be VERA-FIED…by Vera!"

Of course, she did all of the above and more for her Pastor Bill, whom she almost worshiped. But, didn't almost everybody?! No joke.

Vera was a fixed monument, having served on the staff for many years. She was very slender, pretty and to top off all that, no one ever found out how old she was. Always "dressed to the nines," a phrase she used so often, she looked about forty-five; but we could not find out whether she was fifty, sixty or seventy. She would not go with me on a tour to Europe or the Holy Land because she knew I would have to see her passport. But she went to New York City at least once a year with her boyfriend, and when they pulled up in front of a Broadway theater in his white Rolls Royce convertible, everyone stared, thinking they were seeing a movie star. And, you know, she was really a star in her own right. She surely looked and dressed the part. When she departed this life not long ago, I know that she made quite a stir as she swept through the gates of heaven. I bet you that she demanded that there be no birth date placed on her head stone! God rest her sweet soul!

But my, my, I could write a long paragraph about most of the people on that large staff. Like the short, handsome, efficient business manager, Ralph W. Chaney, who longed to be six-foot-four so he could swagger around the church as did his favorite buddy, Pastor Bill. Those early morning chats with good ole, hardworking Ralph in his office didn't hurt me a bit, either. Allene and I were dancing at the Moose Club a few years ago, and there sweeping across the floor, smiling and winking, was Ralph and his pretty new wife. He and Vera were quite the team at the church, and what an asset to me and to that church they were.

Then there was Alvin Griffin, the little black boy whom Preacher Bill had brought in off the street. He was immediately adopted by the staff as their own child. Sweet little Alvin made the church his home, and on cold winter nights he slept in the furnace room. He was a very good hand around the church, was loved by all and grew up to be the head custodian. When I ran into him at the mall recently, we fondly embraced and chatted awhile. He hasn't changed a bit in all these years.

Rev. William Herod, the associate minister, worked with me for a few months, then became an Episcopal priest serving at the large All Souls Church in Oklahoma City. He had a warm Christian spirit and held no regrets about not becoming the senior minister. On his last day, he came in to see me. We had a long coffee chat. As he stood to leave, I expressed my thanks for all he had done to strengthen the church while he was there.

When we got to the door, I mentioned that I was concerned because I was not filling the sanctuary on Sunday mornings. He then said to me, "James, you've been having twelve to fourteen hundred. During Bill's last year, he had an average of about fifteen hundred. So cheer up, you have no reason for concern."

I was almost sure that Pastor Bill had more than that. However, his kind words broke all barriers between us, and that day we became better friends.

His boss, Father Robert Shaw, told me later that Bill was doing a super job at All Souls and added, with a broad smile, "You know, Pippin, you Christians make good Episcopalians!"

As I look back now, I realize that no one could ever really "follow" Bill Alexander, mainly because of the leadership style he established during his last ten years there, a style few senior ministers could follow today. I will share with you the pleasure and the pain, the terror and the triumph, of being the senior minister of that church. I am persuaded that I was called of God to that pulpit, and I gave the job all that I had, trying to make the impossible possible. Christ anointed me with a blessing so great that it transformed all the pain into joy, all the terror into confidence and all the tears into a healing balm. In those early wonder-filled days—my cup ran over!

❋ 23 ❋

We Flee to Bavaria

The official board of the church consisted of twenty elders, about thirty-five deaconesses and over one hundred fifty deacons. The board alone was larger than many of our churches. This large official board made me feel that I had several bosses. My glorious honeymoon lasted about six months, months crowded with a very busy schedule. I had to get to know and direct the staff and the leaders who made up the board, call on the members of the church in fifteen hundred homes, visit about twenty persons in the hospitals twice each week, conduct an average of three funerals each week, perform about that many weddings, attend the Wednesday night dinners and speak at many of them. Then added to all of this were the meetings with the elders, the deacons and the deaconesses, meetings of the finance committee, the official board, the administrative council, all twelve departments, many of the committees down under the departments, the core staff, the full staff and the several adult Sunday school classes. Furthermore, there were the frequent requests for counseling.

One Saturday afternoon, I realized that because of all of the above, plus much that I've left out, I had very little time to prepare Sunday's sermon. Very often, I had to spend all day Saturday at the study grinding out a new message. Many nights I would come home after 10:00 P.M. and fall into bed, exhausted. Then Sunday morning, I would arise and start all over again. Well, most of the honor, the dignity, the pride and joy of the whole thing began quickly to fade away. One Monday morning I sat down in my study, and it suddenly dawned upon me that I had wound up with a very difficult job filled with an impossible load of hard work. Since the majority of these meetings were at night, Allene and the girls saw less and less of me. I seriously wondered if this was really what Jesus intended His shepherds to do and His church to be.

Although I had an associate and a youth minister, a director of Christian education and even some of the elders who offered to pick up some of this load, most of the members expected me to be at almost every meeting. Though I sent all five of my staff out to call in the hospitals, the members would say that no one called because the preacher didn't come. Later, some of them would pause as they left the church service, turn to me, wag their finger and say, "I was sick in the hospital, Preacher, and you did not come to see me."

Nothing I could say seemed to do any good. At the close of that first year, I began to wonder how long I could endure that heavy load. Most of the leaders and the members never seemed to realize that they all got two days off from their jobs—Saturday and Sunday. Most were working only about forty hours each week while I was putting in eighty to ninety hours. I couldn't rest on their days off, for those were my hardest. What response do you think the vast majority of the members would have if any minister insisted on taking Monday and Tuesday, or any two days, off?

Now, with deep and sincere respect and in a kind and loving way, let me say that Rev. Alexander, the senior minister, was in a very different situation because he was not there all of the time. And it wasn't long before he began to get some criticism from a few of the leaders and members who felt that he was a part-time pastor. Remember, Bill was popular around the nation and in great demand as a speaker, which meant that he was gone most of the week and often returned to the city on Saturday afternoon or evening. He would preach a great sermon Sunday morning and visit with everyone at the coffee hour after church. After a quick lunch, he would call on every member who was in one of the four hospitals in town and on most of the critically ill and shut-ins. He had important meetings with his leaders late Sunday afternoon. Then he almost always spoke to the young people on Sunday night, staying over to visit. Sometimes he would even go out to eat with them.

On Monday, he would rise early and meet with the large men's prayer Breakfast at 7:00 A.M. to speak a challenging message to them and to lead them in a time of prayer. After visiting with those who could stay back, Bill would go by the office, check briefly with the staff and write his article for the weekly church paper.

Often, he was in a hurry to catch a flight, so he would ask guest writers to fill in. Bill was able to work that heavy weekend schedule because he was free from the church all week. Sure, he had to fly from one city to the other every day or so, but this was easier than what a senior minister of his church had to do. Since on the road he spoke at night, he had much of the day to rest after he arrived at his new hotel. Also, he seldom spoke every night, giving him some days of complete rest. In the hotel, he could get room service and leisurely get ready for that night's speech, on which he spent no time at all since he knew it by heart!

And Bill loved this lifestyle. He was made for it. But we must never overlook how much help and inspiration he brought to thousands in his vast audiences. The main problem was some felt that serving a large church was incompatible with such a heavy schedule of speaking that took him out of town all week. No one loved Bill the less for this, but to be the senior minister of a very large church and to be gone that much meant that someone had to pick up the slack, the heavy load of the weekday and the many evening responsibilities.

One Monday morning in 1949, when I was in his church at 10th and Robinson for a convention, he called me into his office, and we had a warm visit. We talked much about my goals in life and also about his good friend, my brother Frank Johnson. As Bill walked me to the door with his arm around my shoulder, he asked me to write his article for that week's church paper! To me, that was a great honor.

Since Bill had to fly out that morning and I was running late for my flight back to Enid, Ralph took Bill and me to the airport. What a rare treat it was to sit and visit with him a bit longer. On my plane ride, as I began writing the article, we flew over the forty acres, the future location of his grand dream, the Church of Tomorrow, including the amphitheater. Just as this came into view, I was inspired to write the article, which I called "The American Spirit." Someone sent me a copy of the church paper that next week. Fifteen years later, when I became the minister of Bill's church, one of the first things I did was to dig up the issue of that paper in the library and read my article again. With great delight and not a little pride, I reprinted it in the next week's edition of the church paper, the one which also headlined my installation there as senior minister.

When Bill was out of town, the real load of the church's day-to-day operation rested upon other shoulders, mainly those of Rev. Don Sheridan and the rest of the full-time staff. Bill was most often spared the nitty-gritty, exasperating, often trite situations that needed immediate attention, those things that popped up and required an instant decision during the day, and the occasions during the night that required one of the staff to rush out to a home or the hospital to minister to the sick and dying. So, you can see why he tried his best to partly make up for his absence during the week by his very heavy schedule on Saturday afternoons, all day Sunday and early Monday mornings.

My good friend Howard Conatser, one of the greatest preachers I ever knew, served as minister of a large church in Dallas and had an almost identical schedule to Bill's. One time when I spoke for him, he confessed to me, "Brother James, my work load here at the church is so heavy and my out-of-town engagements are increasing so fast, my wife, Helen, and I often get on a plane on Monday and fly off somewhere, even if I don't have a place to speak. I just have to get out of this town; if I didn't, this large church would surely drive me crazy."

I have wondered if Bill was often tempted to say and do the same thing. I regret to say that Howard died of colon cancer at the early age of fifty-two. Although in his last days he said that he had no regrets, I feel the heavy work schedule, the constant stress in the church, eating on the road and always being on the run all converged to bring on his premature death.

To make matters worse, I, as the new preacher, came on board just as the congregation was preparing to celebrate the church's seventy-fifth anniversary, stressing long years of tradition in which patterns were established in the way things were done and by whom. Early on, I concluded that the church resembled a lovely old lady who was very much set in her ways. Because of the seventy-fifth birthday celebration, almost all of the church leaders' attention was toward the preparation for this event. The contrasts between the church I had left and the church I had come to were many, and these differences were the cause of most of the problems that were to occur. This fact did not really dawn on me until I was there long enough to want to change some things.

Late one rainy Saturday afternoon, after a hard day that ended with a long meeting of the anniversary committee, I went to my study, made myself a pot of coffee and sat alone on the sofa with my feet on the coffee table. Suddenly, I had an attack of loneliness, wishing I were back in Falls Church. My thoughts turned to how very different serving the church there in Oklahoma City was from the situation I found when Allene and I came to Falls Church. There were over two hundred members who greeted us when we arrived in 1953, fresh out of seminary. For over three years, we met in a rented school building. I was their first full-time minister with the honor of presiding over building the entire church facility. After my first year, they didn't resist change and new ways of doing the church's business. Most of my ideas were accepted. It seemed that everything I touched there turned to gold. I knew the names of all the adults and children. Before I left, I had begun to baptize the children whom I had dedicated as infants, and later to conduct the wedding ceremonies for the young adults whom I had baptized.

On the other hand, since I had not grown up with that huge Oklahoma City congregation, I knew only a few people intimately, and almost no one seemed to want to get to know me! They all seemed to be preoccupied, not only with the seventy-fifth anniversary preparations, but also very much with the past and how great things used to be when Bill was there.

Then one night I pulled quite a stunt at a board meeting! Much of my pent-up frustration, disgust and weariness were caused by Oklahoma City's lack in giving to missions work. I think it was evident to some people that Allene and I had already begun to sorely miss the people and the church in Falls Church and the members and ministers in the other churches in the Washington, D.C. area. We even felt that maybe we had made a mistake in coming. As I sat there, sipping my coffee, I remembered the first board meeting we held two months earlier, and I am sure that I took some of these feelings into that meeting. That night, the room was packed with over two hundred members of the board.

Well, near the end of the meeting, when the mission chairperson reported the total of the offering the church had given during the "Week of Compassion," the amount she reported was so much lower than we had given back at Falls Church that I almost fainted. I was about to explode as I went to the podium, asked the chair for the floor and told them, "Do you realize that eleven hundred members in Falls Church gave four times more than your thirty-six hundred members have given here? This will not do. Mr. Chairman, I am going to have to ask you to permit me to take up another offering here and now for world missions. I have no interest in being the pastor of a church that will send up to our national missions board such a puny little offering. This is a moment of truth for me, for this board and this church. Please, I do not want anyone to leave. As a matter of fact, I want four deacons to go to the two exits and let no one out. This offering is for all of us, or none of us. I challenge you men and women to reach into your purses and wallets and bring out those hundred dollar bills you've got folded down in there and drop them into the plate. Here is my hundred dollars. If we don't come up with an offering larger than the one we gave in Falls Church, I think that Allene and I'll just pack up and go on back up there—I hear that they are still looking for a preacher."

As I went back to my seat, no one moved and there was not a sound in the room. But wow, I had never seen so many hundred dollar bills pop up that fast in my life. When the ushers finished, I asked that the money be counted at the back of the room. Everyone sat motionless, including me! Then a deacon, waving a piece of paper up over his head, came running up to the chairperson, who looked at it and with a broad smile said, "We made it; we went way over the top of the amount we needed!"

A deafening applause followed, then a burst of laughter that served as a welcome relief for us all. You know, I had never done anything like that before, and I never did it again. I really felt that it was the Lord who led me to do it. That meeting and that offering set the pace for my entire ministry there.

However, the story of that incident went all over the state and nation. It seemed that each time someone repeated it, they expanded on what really happened, some even saying I pulled a pistol on them! I was told that one pastor in Texas said, "Those folks up there in Oklahoma City must have hired them a Hitler for a preacher."

All of the board and most of the members admired me for the stand I took that night. Now here I was, months later, about to be fired because I suggested that we remodel the woefully outdated chancel of the sanctuary. But before I could tackle that dangerous task, I needed to get away…far away!

We had accepted an invitation from the Army Chief of Chaplains, Major General Charlie Brown, to go to Europe, so in late February 1965, Allene and I were off to Germany. I was invited to be the retreat master at a two-week seminar for all of the Protestant chaplains in Europe, traveling in the status of a GS-18, which at the time was about the rank of a brigadier general. We flew to Frankfurt, where Chaplain and Mrs. Bill Lindsey met us and drove us through a winter wonderland across Germany to Bavaria and Berchtesgaden. The day was bright but bitterly cold. There was three feet of snow on the roofs of the quaint buildings. We were driven up the narrow, winding road to the General Walker Hotel, located just under the mountain where Hitler's summer home, the "Eagle Nest," had been located. We checked into the hotel and were assigned to a suite in which many of Hitler's generals had stayed while they waited for their turn to meet with the Fuhrer.

We Flee to Bavaria

We received the red carpet treatment as VIPs, and when we entered the dining room that Sunday night, all of the three hundred chaplains and their wives stood and gave us a round of applause. Our host, Chaplain (Colonel) John Wood, his wife, and Allene and I were seated by a roaring fire. A string ensemble provided background music to the chatter and laughter that filled the room. The dinner and the fellowship were outstanding. Chaplain Wood, the chief chaplain in Europe, welcomed everyone, introduced us and after speaking briefly, called on me to say a few words about what Allene and I planned to present during the next two weeks.

After the exciting dinner, Allene and I chatted with some of the chaplains and their wives. Later, we made friends with our waitress and asked her to bring a continental breakfast, including two pots of freshly brewed coffee and a pitcher of cream, to our room at seven o'clock each morning. Monday morning, she arrived at exactly seven and after my generous tip, was there every morning with a tray that was loaded down with all our hearts could desire. Twice when we came down early for dinner, she chatted with us in the dining room and briefly shared some of her problems. One night, we pulled her aside and prayed with her. She said that was the first time in her life anyone had ever done that. As we left the dining room one night, she handed us a note. Her kind words led us to believe that her heart had softened toward the Lord.

For two weeks, I conducted a series of morning lectures for the chaplains only, beginning at 9:00 A.M. with a thirty-minute break at 10:00 A.M. for coffee and rolls. The lectures resumed at 10:30 for an hour, at which time I asked for questions or comments. The morning sessions broke for lunch at noon. Every afternoon, we were free for tours or snow skiing until dinner at six. Then at eight, we conducted a worship service for chaplains and their wives; Allene sang two songs, and I preached about a thirty-minute sermon. The lectures covered points I felt would help the chaplains in their roles, and in the sermons, I called the couples to a deeper walk with Christ.

There was no Friday night service, so we were free until late Sunday night. Allene and I had already made plans for the weekend break, so on Friday we were driven to Salzburg after lunch, where we boarded the famous Orient Express to Vienna. Not only was this a world-famous train, but the scenery was also some of the most beautiful in all of Europe. The food on the train was superb, and the people were friendly and interesting. Vienna is lovely any time of the year, but in winter, the city had a charm all its own. We had a large room in a five-star hotel a few doors from the Hoffbrau house and right across the street from Saint Steven's Cathedral.

Friday and Saturday evening we attended the Statsopera and saw *La Bohéme* and *Carmen*. The opera house is one of the three most elegant in the world. During World War II, because of its value and beauty, it was one of the few buildings that was spared. For Allene, this experience was worth the entire trip to Germany. When we entered the opera house, we noticed that it was packed with distinguished looking people who were also the best-dressed men and women we'd ever seen. Friday night during the intermission in the grand lobby, we joined the group for refreshments. When our order came, I handed the waiter a ten-dollar bill. He could not accept U.S. dollars, and I had no Austrian money. Seeing our plight, a very handsome man came over, and as he handed the waiter the money, he said he would be honored if we would be his guests. As we thanked him, he introduced us to his charming wife, and we had a delightful conversation in perfect English. We ran into them again at the reception on Saturday night. This time we had local money, so we had the honor of returning their treat. A tour of greater Vienna on Saturday gave us a much deeper appreciation of that lovely old city, including the great men and women who once lived there. We yearned to stay there a month, but after breakfast on Sunday, we boarded the famous train back to Salzburg.

Monday morning started off with a bang and set the tone for the rest of the retreat. However, that afternoon led to a second bang that I'd have just as soon avoided. Chaplain (Col.) John Wood invited Allene and me to go out on the ski slopes with him. He was a slender, good-looking Lutheran and a "jump chaplain," a former member of the famous 101st Airborne division. Although we were experts at water skiing, we had never snow-skied before. Against Col. Wood's advice, I sped down from the high slope on the third day and fell, injuring the cartilage in my right knee. Bang! The doctor put a cast on the leg, and I went around during the entire second week on crutches! But this did not slow me down much. I had used crutches before.

The second week of the retreat went much smoother than the first. During the afternoons, we were driven around the area and had dinner two evenings with Chaplain Wood in quaint little taverns. We found that Bavaria and all of southern Germany are filled with enchanting and beautiful places—a part of Europe that is in a class all by itself. We had tea two afternoons in our hotel lobby where we chatted with the hotel manager, a handsome, erect German, who told us in detail about the hotel's fame during World War II. Then he took us to a room on the basement floor where Hitler's generals and high-ranking staff often had gathered in the evening for cocktails. He told us that Hitler did not drink alcohol in any form but would be served his favorite drink, strong fresh-brewed coffee with two lumps of chocolate sugar when he joined them there. The manager smiled, and said with a bit of sadness in his voice, "It was a time of conversation and much laughter—then we all got to shake hands with our dear—the Fuhrer."

He hastened to assure us that none of the German staff of the hotel was ever a Nazi. Actually, on the whole three-week trip, we did not run into a single person who would admit to ever being a Nazi.

The retreat ended Friday night with a formal banquet. Chaplain Wood gave an outstanding speech and said some very nice things about Allene's singing and my teaching and preaching. Saturday morning, we bade farewell to the chaplains, their wives and the hotel staff. Then our host chaplain took us on a breathtaking drive on the *autobahn* to West Berlin. Sunday morning, Allene and I had the great experience of singing and preaching in the Berlin Brigade Chapel. This was probably the most beautiful of all the military chapels in the world. It was built entirely of stone, including the floors. It seated almost a thousand people, and it was packed. Because many services, both Protestant and Roman Catholic, were conducted there on Sunday, my sermon was limited to twenty-two minutes. At a coffee reception in the large fellowship hall, we met some of the sharpest troops from all branches of our military. Later, we were taken to one of the finest restaurants in Berlin for lunch.

And my, oh my, the sparkling grandeur that was West Berlin. We were furnished a sedan and a young German guide who took us on an extensive tour. The Berlin Wall had been built by the Communists four years earlier, and we covered most of its length. Every fifty feet, there were heavily armed East German guards keeping watch, standing on the east side of the wall. No one would want to get in, but the guards were there to keep the imprisoned East Germans from getting out. If any of them attempted to do so, and many did, the guards were ordered to shoot them dead on sight. No private citizen was allowed to own a gun in East Germany, only the guards and the military. This law was not only in East Germany, but also in every Communist country in the world; no private ownership of guns.

At one location along the wall, there were stairs that led up to a wide platform where tourists could peer into East Berlin. The contrast was shocking. West Berlin was almost completely rebuilt, and many fine cars were on the newly paved streets. The shops were filled with lots of goods and shoppers, and the city cafes were crowded with happy people. They called a cafeteria a "Move and Pick." Each evening, the streets and the city were ablaze with lights. There was no curfew.

In stark contrast, on the East side, the streets were empty except for a few bicycles, motor scooters and maybe one truck noisily chugging along. There were no shops, few lights and very few pedestrians. Everywhere, it resembled the war-ravaged city it was in 1945. The twelve-foot wall was built in a straight line, across streets and even trolley-car tracks. In one place the wall was built across the front of a large church, just three feet from the front doors. All the churches were boarded up or were used as museums. Looking east was a window into the enslaved Communist world, while looking west was a beautiful window filled with free people living in a free world. The Soviets did not want their captives to see the beauty and prosperity of the West, so they were forbidden to come anywhere near the wall.

This stark contrast between slavery and poverty, freedom and plenty, saddened us. It took awhile to shake it off. This contrast should convince anyone who saw it that this is the kind of nation ours would be if the Socialists/Communists continue to advance their agenda. That form of government has never worked anywhere, but most liberals seem to believe that all they need is just one more chance to try it, and surely it will work—here. Not so, my moldy-breathed Muscovites!! It will never happen, that is, unless most of our registered voters decide to continue to stay away from the poles. The vote is about all we have left.

Our good guide showed us the new Berlin Opera House, which the Germans nicknamed "The Pregnant Oyster." Then we saw the rebuilt Cathedral, which they called "The Compact and Lipstick Church" because the type of architecture consisted of a tall octagonal glass spire that resembled a silver tube of lipstick and a small two-story entrance that looked like a woman's compact. The German people are famous for such clever responses to their people and surroundings.

From Berlin, we went to Paris for two sparkling nights and then to London, where we spent two frozen nights. Our hotel had only one small heater halfway up a wall. Our warm plane to New York left the next morning, and from there, we got on our plane to Chicago and back to Oklahoma City. A large crowd of people from our church met us at the gate. Mary Jo and Bob Douglas, who planned the reception, were holding up a big sign reading, "Welcome Home, Pippins—We Missed You!"

We Flee to Bavaria

After a few days of getting reacquainted with our sweet girls and getting some rest, I was back on the job, ready to take on the staggering task as senior pastor of our big new church. Vera and I had a full day of going through a tall stack of mail. Then the next morning, I faced the greatest challenge yet: my plan to remodel the chancel. But I didn't mention this hot potato until after we had the first Wednesday night dinner, where to an overflow crowd, we showed our many pictures and told them of the fine experiences we had on our trip to Germany. Their pride in our leadership was never higher. It was at the close of this meeting that I asked for a few minutes to present my plan to change the chancel. The room was quiet. The chair of the board closed with prayer and everyone left quietly.

It took time, many meetings with the leaders, a lot of prayer and some sweet talk, but we got the permission to redo the chancel. First, we removed the large plywood-looking, boxlike pulpit in the front middle. The plan called for a divided chancel, with the pulpit on the left and the lectern on the right, light blue carpeting on the chancel, and steps and a cushioned altar placed around the entire front. A tall cross rose between two towers that resembled the Notre Dame Cathedral. The eye was pulled to the communion table as the central statement of the entire setting. The total message of the chancel emphasized The Word Read, The Word Preached and The Word's Blood Shed, shown in the communion table and the large cross, with the bold message that Christ died for our sins. To set it all off, multicolored stone in panels about eight feet tall were placed to the sides at floor level. That old "Baptist Looking" chancel was where Bill Alexander used to preach, and it was a sacred place many of the members did not want touched. However, most of them thought the changed chancel was very beautiful indeed.

Some months later I was not so successful, however, when I suggested to the Department of Christian Education that we change the order and the methods of instruction in the Sunday morning adult classes. At Falls Church, the adult classes were conducted in a relaxed atmosphere, usually around tables. The hour contained lecture-discussion, using a marker board, an overhead projector and often some training films and audio tapes. The class freely asked questions and shared comments anytime. This approach fostered much spiritual growth among the members. After a short break, the members of the classes would fill the sanctuary for the worship service, which we all saw to be the climactic event of every Sunday morning. The boldest step at Falls Church was when we introduced a teacher-training program where teachers only taught six months, after which they would attend the training for six months, and then be assigned to a class.

But our seventy-five-year-old church in Oklahoma City had the ancient custom of a teacher having the same class for many years, and the format of the class had actually become a brief copy of the morning worship service. In each class, there was an opening prayer, several of their favorite songs, a scripture passage and then a longer prayer, followed by the recognition of birthdays and a class offering. Then the teacher would present a thirty-minute lesson, usually a straight lecture, with no discussion and no questions from the class. It was really a sermon. After a closing prayer, the class would remain in the room for coffee and fellowship. Many of the class members would then skip the morning worship service and smile as they "beat the Baptists to the cafeteria."

Since their needs for prayer, singing, teaching and a fellowship coffee had already been met, most of them saw little reason to go up into the sanctuary and sit through "the preacher's service," which to them was a longer repeat of what they just finished in their class, except for the communion. Often, the class songs were the old slow ones that brought back "precious memories." Plus they knew everybody by name, and some felt that their beloved teacher's lesson was often even better than the new preacher's sermon—and a whole lot shorter!

As a result of this practice, the attendance at the worship service was more and more drastically affected. When I caught on to what was happening, one Sunday morning I suddenly appeared out in front of the church and shocked them as they left. I darted here and there to see how many of their hands I could shake, telling them that they would be sorely missed in church. It did not go over very well. Back in the study, I sat looking at my sermon notes and began to sob as I thought of the many hours I had spent on that sermon. However, I was saddened even more because so many of our leading members did not join us for worship, communion and the warm fellowship after church in the dining room. I really did not know what the solution was to this disturbing problem. The more I looked at the way the church operated, the more I realized that these kinds of problems had been going on for a very long time. I saw those adult classes, especially the Solo Class, which I will mention later, as being just a bunch of little churches, filled with members, most of whom had no real interest in the total life or purpose of the body of Christ. I became more and more disenchanted with the whole situation.

We Flee to Bavaria

Sensing that I was feeling low, Ralph attempted to lift my spirits by taking me down to the old church at 10th and Robinson one Monday afternoon. There, he showed me a narrow concrete side-walk that ran from the back door of the old education building and around the back of the church to the parking lot. This was the exit route by which many of the class members made their secret escape.

Ralph then looked at me with that great big smile of his and said, "You see, Brother James, many of them also ran out on Brother Bill and Dr. MacGowan before you came! By the way, this walk here is named 'Highley's Highway' in honor of one of our best teachers."

Since Fred and Lorene Highley were our close friends and two of the church's strongest supporters, Ralph and I began to laugh. As the months passed, I did my best to get to know the teachers and the members of the classes better. I visited a different class every Sunday and prayed that they would gradually begin to stay for the worship service. I soon found most of them to be truly great Christians and lovable people who over the years had simply fallen into a bad habit.

However, I still had the strong feeling that the members needed to learn that the worship service should be the focus of all that happened in the life of the church during the week, especially on Sunday morn-ings. Also, because of the number and location of the buildings—with the youth and Solo classes meeting in the Youth Center clear across the creek—it was a Herculean task to get all these scattered classes to come as a group into the large sanctuary and worship as a church family. And there, I believe, I finally stumbled into a discovery—the real cause of the ancient problem was that the church really never was led to see itself as a *family*, with God as Father and Christ as Elder Brother! It consisted of many diverse individual groups that never found a common purpose, a *koinonia*, which made of them the body of Christ, a divine Fellowship and a force working together to do the will of God to those in need there and around the world.

As the minister, I saw the problem as more serious than this. The concept of a senior minister as the central leader of the total church, the body of Christ, was missing. You see, when trouble came from new ideas that were introduced by me, I had no strong group to back me up and fight for me. The teachers had their classes who were a solid block behind whatever that teacher wanted; the youth minister had a large group of the young people who dearly loved him, and you didn't dare touch him; the minister of music had the adult choir of fifty people and several other choirs, all of whom thought he hung the moon; and all of the above met weekly for fellowship, study, prayer or rehearsal. At

A MIRACLE A MINUTE

these meetings, they got to know and love the members of their group who, by the way, would give strong support to any program that their own leaders might put forth. The primary loyalty of each of these persons seemed to be to their leader and to the group to which they belonged—not to the church at large and certainly not to the senior minister. I also suspected that few, if any, of the teachers or staff leaders ever mentioned the importance of regular attendance in the morning worship service. This was evident when we saw that most of these adults and even the youth seemed to see little need or value in attending the Sunday morning worship service with any regularity. You must imagine the adverse effect this lack of unity had on both the senior minister and the total mission of the church.

But, and this is the rub, since the morning service had more people, less intimacy and no comments from the audience, the "poor" minister had no group with which he met weekly for intimate spiritual and personal fellowship. I lacked a large, loyal group which would become a solid, loving part of the church, ready to support me if any serious criticism came my way or if I had a new program I wanted to adopt. The Sunday school class members and the members in general usually gave their major loyalty to their teachers or the individual staff members with whom they worked. And here is the frightening possibility. Any one of these groups, especially if they were joined by another group, could make the life and work of the senior minister a hell on earth, and could even mount a campaign to have him fired! However, no such thing would ever cross their minds, and all would be filled with sweetness and light as long as the minister rocked along with the status quo. It was when I changed the way they did things or introduced a new and, as I saw it, a better way to get the work of Christ done in the church that I often ran headlong into a thick stone wall.

It seemed to me that the role of the senior pastor had eroded over the years so that I had little or no part in how the total church was operating—how the adult classes, the choir, the children, youth, and adult departments, or the elders', deacons' and deaconesses' boards were organized or how much they were growing spiritually, carrying out their functions. These were matters that they saw to be of no concern to the senior minister, and they sorely resented my intrusion. But this role as leader of the church was exactly what my formal education and years of experience in the previous churches prepared me to do. I seemed to hear most members say, "What do you think you are doing, Sir, and who do you think you are? Bill

334

never stuck his nose into our plans and certainly never tried to boss us the way you do."

They had gone for many years without anyone ever having the nerve to poke a nose into anything.

Now, the knife got twisted and rammed even deeper. Wouldn't you think that the senior minister should at least be seen as the leader of the Sunday morning church service? But even this erroneous notion faded away when one day in core staff meeting, I suggested to the minister of music that some of the hymns were a bit too fast. Because the congregation could not keep up, they simply stopped singing. Could he please slow them down a bit? He just smiled at me and flatly ignored the request. So a few Sundays later, right in the middle of one of his fastest hymns, I stopped the organist and the choir. I called the minister of music by name and asked him to kindly slow the tempo down just a bit so we all could follow along. Result? He set the tempo so slowly that all the congregation, the choir and even the staff began to chuckle. So I weakly laughed along with them. I really wanted to walk out or have them all stand for the benediction. But I changed my mind, threw up my arms and shouted loudly, "OK, OK, OK! You win. Go on back to your original tempo."

So, for the time being, that was the last time while that minister of music was there that I ever got into that. What everyone, even including some of the core staff members, seemed to be telling me was, "Hey, preacher, we'll run our classes, our departments and our shops the way we want to, we'll come to the sanctuary if and when we want to, we'll give what we want to, or we'll even go to the lake or the mountains all summer, if we choose. If you will please stay out of our business and just pull your own little red wagon and leave us to pull ours, everything will be okay."

This unspoken reality not only stunned me, but I also knew that none of this attitude had any place in any church of which Jesus Christ was the Head. I was determined that such attitude would *not* be allowed to continue in any church of which I was the minister. There was just so much of this I could take. Just as it was in the early months at Falls Church, there was a point beyond which I could tolerate no more. It was not a model that I learned in seminary, and not the way I learned to lead the congregation in Falls Church for eleven years. Although this was definitely the *modus operandi* here, I had great confidence in my ability to lead a church in the direction I believed Christ would have it go. But I was not sure I was interested in spending the years, the grief and the adrenaline that would be required to change this undisciplined, disorganized, goal-less group of people into what the body of Christ must be in order to change lives and the world.

I was so troubled about this problem, which included the staff, that I talked and prayed often with Allene about it. I decided that if I could not make the staff into a team with me as the team leader, I might either have to call an entire new staff or resign. When I came there, I requested and was given the right to call my own staff. But before I went through that excruciating pain, I wanted to get the counsel of a couple of my older minister friends. So, I arranged to have lunch with two older Disciple's pastors of our region.

After a great time together at lunch, we retired to a private room so we could chat. They listened warmly to my dilemma. Then one of them explained that my church was very unique. I heartily agreed and asked if either knew how the church got that way and what in heaven's name I could do about it, other than resigning or firing most all of the staff.

The older minister spoke first and said, "James Clayton, I think I know the core of the problem. Bill Alexander, from the very beginning, never wanted to interfere with or be entangled in any of these day-to-day operations. Then later, when he was more and more away from the church during the week, the planning of the worship service and the daily decisions were increasingly left to others—his able secretary, the minister of music, the associates, the staff and the church members who enjoyed doing all that themselves. They see your suggestions as an unwanted and unneeded intrusion. To them, you are the new kid on the block, poking your face into the operation of *their* church."

The other minister then added, "Brother James, I agree. But I'd advise you to do your best to work this out with the present staff first. Then if they resist becoming a team with you as the leader, replace them, but do this very slowly and prayerfully so that you don't make too many enemies in the church this early in your ministry."

This was indeed a good luncheon with two colleagues who both respected me and loved the church. After I went back to my study for a little while that afternoon, and then to the house later to chat with Allene, I felt so much better.

In the next few days, while I sat back feeling better but still a little unnecessary, some more irritants came.

Old Mrs. Stanford limped down the aisle just before the service started and finding some stranger in her seat, said, while she tapped the person on the shoulder with her cane, "Sonny, that's my seat. If you don't move this instant, I will crack you across the head with my cane!" The young man, seeing the raised cane, leaped out of the seat and ran from the sanctuary. He was never seen again.

Then there was the tall, skinny old deacon who sat on the front row to my right. Almost every Sunday, just as I spoke the first line of my sermon, he would whip out his handkerchief and very loudly blow his nose—both sides. But worse, when he finished about three snorts, he would then open his handkerchief and look at it! I wondered what in heaven's name he hoped to find in there, some little snakes? How would you like to try to preach after that?

Also, the pastoral load kept increasing. There were many new babies, sometimes two each week; then there were the weddings, almost three a week. One time I had five weddings in one day. Funerals? Yep, at least three per week. After a few months of this, with so many babies, weddings and funerals—I felt as if I were just hatching, matching and dispatching! This is what overload or burnout can do to you.

And there was so little response to my sermons. A nod was great approval and a smile was like a loud "Hallelujah!" As I got up to preach, I knew most of the congregation was praying for me because a few minutes after I started, they closed their eyes and bowed their heads. Then one Sunday, there was a lady on the aisle who started winking at me. Man, that set me on fire. Each time I made a good point, she'd wink; then I'd pour on more steam. I thought, *Thank You, Jesus, You've sent me a winker. O bless you, my little sister.* But when I went out into the foyer, I noticed that she was winking at everybody—she had lost control of her left eyelid, which kept dropping on her. So my high spirits hit the floor again.

Talk about boredom. The pews were packed with yawning and dozing folks. I was even bored—and I planned the service. After a while, I got bored with my own sermons. I felt that I was chairman of the bored! I often told them, "You folks must have checked your brains and your pocketbooks at the door. If you were to run your businesses like you want to run the church, you would all be bankrupt!"

About the only time my leading men would get really excited was when one of them sold five cars in a week or another sold a million in life insurance. Very few of them ever brought any excitement into their church lives. One morning, I was standing in the middle of two of my elders at the communion table and turned to the one on my right and asked him to give the prayer for the loaf. Well, he was so crouped up, all that came out was "...Ahh...Faaath...inheaaaa." I turned and asked him what was the matter. He whispered, "Pastor, I lost my voice at the football game yesterday, would you please do my prayer?"

O sure, I could picture him standing up on his seat, yelling: "Go Sooners, kill 'em! Kill 'em!...hold that line...hold that line... team...team...team!!!

Yet in church, I could not remember if even one weak little "Amen" had ever slipped from his lips.

But there was a bright spot of sorts now and then in the Sunday morning service. One hot Sunday in August, halfway through the sermon, out of the blue, the organ burst out—playing one note—toooooooooooooooooooooooooooooo—loud. Now, I mean, really loud. The organist stepped quickly to the console but could do nothing. I looked at the minister of music who shrugged his shoulders and lifted his palms in dismay. I then called for someone to get the engineer to shut the thing off. Louis Noe had to go down into the cellar and pull the main breaker switch to stop it. What a relief. But just as I got started preaching again, I realized that he had also shut off the air conditioner. So, that was all she wrote for that Sunday. I simply had them stand for the benediction!

One afternoon about a week later, a leading member came by my study and asked me what I planned to do about this strange class that met over in the youth center on Sunday morning. It was called "The Solo Club." He said that it was very famous and a very large class, and he wanted the name changed to "The Bible school class for single adults." As he talked on, he said, "That class is taught by a psychologist, and it is rumored that he will not let them bring a Bible to class, or even mention a scripture or a teaching of Jesus. And worse than all that, very few of the class, including the teacher, ever come over to the Sunday worship service. It seems to me as if they are just using our church for a place to meet. I think they give our church a bad name." Looking me in the eye, he concluded, "Preacher, either you change them, or I want you to go tell them to leave!"

As I sat there, with a startled look on my face, I remembered the story of the missionary to Africa who found that the chief of the village had thirty wives. The missionary told the chief that since he was now a Christian, he had to go tell all but one of those women to leave. The old chief looked sternly at the missionary, leaned back, smiled broadly and said, "Ummm, *you* go tell 'em!"

I wanted so badly to say to the troubled member, "Look it," to use a favorite phrase of Bill's, "my mama didn't raise any foolish children. I wouldn't touch that class with a ten-foot pole. Sir, *you* go tell 'em."

Instead, I asked if Bill Alexander or Dr. Mac or Don Sheridan knew about this situation.

He said, "Yes."

"What did they do about it?"

"Nothing."

Then, I smiled, stood up, reached to shake his hand and as I walked him to the door, told him in a serious tone, "My dear friend, I will look closely into this matter. Call me in a week or so and let's talk more about it." I never heard from him again.

I thought things were finally going to get a little better, but in the next few weeks, some of the members came by in twos and threes, urging me to lead the effort to get our congregation out of the National Council of Churches. They did not know that I also had been upset by some of the Council's social programs and was very angry when I learned that the Black Panthers had taken over their offices in New York. Instead of calling the police and getting them out, the Council's executives did not seem to care. They simply all went home and left them there. After several of our members came in to see me, I phoned one of them and offered to chair a meeting in the parlor to discuss this matter. I notified the outreach chairman, the board and the general membership about this. Then I got a call from a member who told me that these people were very conservative, and they were that bunch of about twenty who, on the first round, voted against my coming to Oklahoma City. You can believe that made me very interested in getting to know "that bunch" as best I could.

Well, at the meeting, much to their surprise, they discovered that I was on their side. After a little discussion, they found that I was also conservative both theologically and politically. We went through the proper channels, and then put it to a vote by the board and the congregation. It carried. We were out of the National and the World Council. This came as a shock to many of our own national leaders since they knew how solidly I was behind the national and world program of our denomination. Later they, and most of our local church members, were also confused when I, at the same time, supported some "liberal social causes," such as the integration of our churches. On the other hand, I was very much against busing our children all over the city. I saw this to be throwing the racial problem into the laps of our children and youth, while we adults copped out. I was for children going to schools in their own neighborhoods.

A MIRACLE A MINUTE

As I saw it, our great need then was for open housing, so the blacks and other minorities could live anywhere in the city and go to the school nearest their homes. For this to be possible, it meant I was for more minorities going up to higher paying positions and for equal pay for blacks and whites on the same job. But (ahh…fools rush in!) I actually went further than this. I pushed for the same pay for women and men on the same type job. I calmed down a bit, though, when I found a group who wanted me to run for Congress. I remembered that there was a serious group in Falls Church who felt the same about my being in Congress. Actually, I believe that we should have more clergy, both men and women, in the Congress and of course, more Christians in politics, and most of all, more Christians voting.

However, the peace I got from making friends with "this bunch of strange conservatives" was shallow and short-lived. I could not get used to this bunch of folks who were divided theologically, spiritually and politically. I was getting more and more disenchanted with the church locally and with my entire denomination as a whole.

So one Saturday night in November, I stopped right in the middle of preparing my sermon, slammed my Bible shut, cut all the lights out, slammed and locked the doors and went home.

After we tucked the girls in with prayers, I said to Allene, "Sweetheart, come into the dinette; we've got to talk!"

She could tell by the look on my face that this talk was going to be very serious. We had a short prayer, and then I reviewed for her my struggle to make a church out of this crowd, the mounting strain of the heavy schedule of pastoral duties, the little irritants and the struggle we had endured to make of them a *koinonia*, a deeper fellowship in the Holy Spirit within the body of Christ. I also pointed out how the church was taking me more and more away from the family. I paused, took a deep breath and said, "Allene, I think I've about had it. I have decided to quit!"

"Quit! Quit what? This church? The ministry? How will we make it? James, you just got started. We have not even been here two years."

I knew exactly what would be next. She tuned up for a real crying jag. The tears flowed as she continued, "I don't know how in heaven you figure we'll make it. This is what you know how to do best. And some of the folks around here seem to believe you can't do this very well. Sweetheart, this is not like you. You are not a quitter! Now, let's pray about this and—besides, Christmas is just around the corner, think of the girls, of Santa and all." She sniffled, wiped her eyes and nose and said, "Please, Honey, could we just wait 'til after Christmas? Pull-e-a-s-e!?"

I breathed a deep sigh and assured her that we would continue to pray and yes, I would wait until after the first of the year. Then I took her in my arms and prayed that God would give us His guidance and tell me what to do. I asked God to take this entire situation into His hands. Well, He did. And HOW! But not in any way that you or I would have ever dreamed!

✱ 24 ✱

Enter Lovenia!

That next Sunday morning I knew that the service would be a struggle. I was fully prepared to groan and grunt all the way through it. Then just as I was beginning the sermon, I looked over to my left, and down the aisle came this little old lady. She was about five feet high and almost that wide. All eyes were upon her as she took a seat a few rows from the front. She was a rather pretty lady who wore a large diamond broach in her colored hair and a fur stole. But something very strange was going on from the bottom of her nose to the bottom of her chin. She was wiggling her lips at me while whispering odd sounds. I thought maybe this poor woman had a tomato seed stuck under her plate or perhaps she had apoplexy of the upper lip. I said to myself, "That little lady really needs prayer."

Man, it was I who needed the prayer, devout prayer—to get through that service and the next few weeks.

Her name was Lovenia James. Her father, Rev. J. H. O. Smith, was one of the early ministers of the church. I didn't have to wonder very long about what was wrong with her. After church, she pushed me back against the stone wall of the foyer and spoke loudly enough for everyone around to hear. She said, "Preacher, I have a word from God for you!"

I answered, kind of prissily, "O, I love words from God. Pray tell me what He said."

"I will, Sonny, if you'll get that silly smile off your face. The Lord has revealed to me that you are going to get the baptism of the Holy Ghost and speak in tongues, or you're going to get fired."

With this oracle from God delivered, she whirled around and walked out of the church. This incident began a battle between Lovenia and me that increased in intensity almost weekly.

Enter Lovenia!

The next Sunday, I prayed she would be absent. But no, there she was sitting in the same seat, and she was there without fail every Sunday. I tried not to look at her, but each time I turned my head, my eyes did not cooperate. They were glued upon her face and mouth, which continued doing that lip thing. One Sunday, I was preaching away on material I'd gotten from the *Reader's Digest* and coming to the climax of the message as I began to quote from Francis Thompson's "Hound of Heaven:"

> "Down the labyrinthine ways, He sought me—chasing me down the nights and down the days—down the caverns of the centuries—"

That was about all she could stand. She rose, and shaking her big red Bible at me, yelled, "Preacher, could we please just get back into the Bible?"

But the sad thing was that I wasn't in the Bible in the first place. I saw absolutely no effect on the congregation of any of my sermons that were from the Bible. One morning, during the communion hymn, Lovenia started singing aloud in some strange foreign language. Then during the faster hymns, she would sway to and fro while clapping her hands. It got so bad that no one would sit anywhere near her. She was flat messing up my worship service and my sermons. Lovenia was bad enough in church, but she was really bad in the coffee hour after church. Here was one place I definitely did not want her. Those who attended the coffee reception were my best families, my fur coat and Cadillac people, my new members and young couples ready to be married. And oh my, did we drink a lot of coffee!

We drank coffee before Sunday school, during Sunday school around the tables, between Sunday school and church; the choir drank coffee out of a thermos during the sermon; and after church, we had the formal coffee in the large dining room where the coffee was poured out of solid silver. But, not to worry, it was OK; all that coffee was in the budget. Of course, I was expected to be there for the entire coffee thing. But by that time, I was a bit weary. You see, I arose early on Sunday and crammed down some eggs. Then Allene got the girls ready while I dressed in my "mourning" wear. When we arrived, I did a lot of hand shaking. I shook them into the church, I shook them down in the offering, I shook them up in the sermon; then I went out into the foyer after church and shook them out.

Walking into the main coffee hour, I began to do some more shaking. Then some lady, with a broad smile on her little old face, would come over to me with a cup of coffee in one hand and two little cookies on a plate in the other. Now you definitely needed an iron stomach here because the coffee had been made about seven that morning in a very large urn and was by now solid battery acid. After a while, my knees began to buckle, so I would sit down, with my coffee in one hand. If I planned to eat the cookies, I had to place the little plate on my left knee. About that time, Lovenia proceeded herself into the dining room. Actually, Lovenia proceeded herself everywhere she went; most of Lovenia arrived before the rest of her showed up. Just as my trembling hand reached for a cookie, she spied me, rushed up, grabbed my free hand, and as she shook it wildly, the coffee flew in one direction and the plate and cookies in the other.

O yes, Lovenia was there big time to take over this coffee hour in grand style and in general, to make herself completely obnoxious. If she ever walked up to me and asked how I felt, even if I ached from head to foot, I'd always say that I felt "fine!!" because weeks before, during the coffee hour, I answered that I had a pain in my left shoulder. She grabbed me with both hands, started speaking in something strange like, "Boka, docka, locker, mocker, socker." Then she slapped me across the forehead, drove my glasses back into my nose and gave me a hefty push so fast that I went down backwards to the floor. She stepped back, with one foot raised and one hand up in the air, and said so loud that all in the room could hear, "Praise God! Come look at the preacher, slain in the Spirit!"

I wasn't slain. She flat knocked me down. I sat there, gently pulled off my glasses and checked with my handkerchief to see if I was bleeding around the nose. I was so totally humiliated that as I got up, I finally decided one thing for sure: I hated this woman—a lot. That Sunday, I longed to own a hotel with a thousand rooms in it and to find Lovenia dead in every room. I thought that she had left, but no, she added insult to injury. As she was leaving that morning, she noticed that several of the men were having a cigarette with their coffee. She threaded her way quickly past all of them, pulled the cigarettes out of their hands and stuck them in their coffee cups. We could hear the sound of the cigarettes hitting the coffee! She then marched out, saying over her shoulder, "It ain't fit to smoke in the house of God. It just ain't fit!"

I almost lost it. If I had not had on that robe, I do believe I would have dashed across the dining room, made a flying leap and tackled her, hoping she would fall and bust her hard head wide open on one of the steel posts. On the way home that Sunday, I saw a man with this machine, feeding tree limbs into it. The limbs came out the other side in little chips. I did not want to buy the machine; I just wanted to rent it for about an hour, find Lovenia and feed her into that thing, limb by limb. What little Christianity I had left was going fast.

But, you have to get ready for this! She was always giving me tapes and books on the Holy Spirit and the gifts of the Spirit. Often after church, while I was in the foyer shaking them out, Lovenia would come up behind me and put tapes and little tracts in my back pocket. In an attempt to break her from this practice, I began wearing my robe. The next Sunday, I felt my robe being slowly raised from the back. I froze. Then I realized that Lovenia had just put a tape in my back pocket. In the heat of anger that swept over me, I thought of a plan that would give her the shock of her life. I know this is crazy and in no way Christian, but I thought, *"What would this wild and crazy woman have done if, as she pulled up my robe, she suddenly discovered that I had forgotten to wear pants that day! It would have served her right!"*

But knowing Lovenia, it would not have fazed her one bit; she would have simply tucked the tape neatly in at the top of my briefs!

Whenever I give my testimony, at this point the entire room explodes with laughter so loud and long that I often have great difficulty getting them to settle down so I can finish. Some have told me that as they laughed through the testimony, they seem to have shed much of their stress and tiredness. And of course, I am always blessed when the Lord uses me to bring this great release that replaces their burdens with His joy. Proverbs tells us that "a merry heart does good, like medicine" (Prov. 17:22).

The tempo now accelerates, and I have only a short way to go before I get out on the other side of this conflict with Lovenia. By this time, I had more than enough of this woman. So one Sunday when she came marching up to me in the foyer with this great grin on her face, I raised my hand, stopped her in her tracks and started shouting at her. All the people in the foyer moved back against the walls and there was complete silence. Then I yelled, "Loveniaaaa. I want you…to leave…me…alone!!! By the way, who is that behind you?"

"Why, it's Dr. Maxine Reiff, and she's got it!"

"Hummff! That figures. But I meant who is that behind Maxine?"

"Oh, it's her husband, Dr. Bill Reiff."

"Uh huh. Well Lovenia, has Dr. Reiff got it? Does he have this baptism in the Holy Ghost, and does he speak in those strange tongues?"

"No."

"No, he doesn't. Now, Lovenia James, I want you to listen carefully. You go work on this man with all of your cute little tricks and—*leave me alone, do you understand?* If Dr. Reiff 'gets it,' then you come back and maybe I'll listen to you. Until then, I demand that *you leave me alone.* Do you read me, Madame?"

While smiling, she took Maxine and Bill by the arm and marched out of the church. I let out a loud sigh, glanced sheepishly around at the people in the foyer, then made a quick departure.

I was certain that I was rid of Lovenia forever. For Dr. Reiff was a sane and honorable gentleman, a full colonel, Chief of Staff of the 75th Division, U.S. Army Reserve, a reputable doctor with a large practice, a leading elder, one of my closest friends and my personal physician. I knew that he would never have anything to do with any stark foolishness such as this.

When I arrived home, Allene and the girls had beaten me there. As they all laughed and hugged me, I said beaming triumphantly, "My dears, that's the last of our war with Lovenia. I saw you all standing over there while I was getting her told. I'm safe at last. My friend Bill Reiff will never submit to that crazy woman and her jibber-jabber."

Well—the very next Sunday, I thought, *Praise God, no more Lovenia.* I felt like a million. That is, until I entered the sanctuary. I looked out and there sat Lovenia; beside her was Maxine, who was also working her mouth as they looked at me. I thought, *O my Lord, this thing is spreading.* One time I had a dream that one Sunday I would look out there and the entire congregation would be whispering in tongues at me. A shiver really went through me when I looked at Dr. Reiff. I suddenly felt weak all over. He wasn't working his mouth at me, but he didn't look himself. He was leaning over, reading his Bible. He looked a little sick and with bloodshot eyes as if he'd been up all night. He sure had no resemblance to my champion, Dr. Col. William H. Reiff! No matter how hard I tried to ignore him, my eyes seemed glued to his face as I preached. I was all shook up.

"Has he got it...has he caved in yet? Does he or doesn't he?"

My dear friend, I just could not take the chance. I was overwhelmed with the urge to run! I cut the sermon in half, told the people that the choir would sing the benediction, pulled my robe up to my knees and made a rapid dash up the right aisle. I sped across the foyer, ran through the second floor of the education building, went out the exit, down the fire escape and entered the kitchen by the back door. I had the master key to all those doors. As I hid between two tall walk-in coolers, one of the cooks brought me a cup of hot tea with two bags; I was off coffee. I had drunk so much of it that I'd picked up heart *pre-matures.* Standing there, pressed back against the wall, I shook so hard I began to spill my tea. I thought, *She'll never find me here!*

Then I heard it. Lovenia—in the dining room, saying to the women who were waiting to pour, "Has the preacher been in here?" I stopped breathing.

"No, sorry, we haven't seen him."

Now, any sane person would have then said, "Well, we will see him later." But no, not Lovenia. I heard footsteps approaching—then she said in her deep manly voice, "Preacher, you in this kitchen?!!" I guess she had what she would call "a word of knowledge." How in heaven's name did she know I was in there??

The three of them then marched into the kitchen, Lovenia in front. Just as I pressed back to the wall as far as I could, she stopped between the coolers, turned toward me and said, "Boo!!"

I dropped my tea. She came closer.

"Preacher, I dare you to look behind me."

I leaned forward and squeaked, "Hi, Maxine."

Lovenia said loudly, "No, look behind Maxine!"

I wish I could fully describe what I beheld. There was Bill, the doctor, the colonel, with a shy grin on his pale face, standing there with this heavy Bible in his hand. As I stared at him, he stooped down a little and just from his ankles, began to spring up and down, over and over like a jack-in-the-box. He moved about two feet with each jump, going back and forth in front of me. All the while, these strange sounds were coming from his mouth, sorta like, "Abba, dabba doo, chu, chu, chu…laa-leek-alla-lu." Maxine was smiling broadly.

Lovenia was all reared back, chuckling, pointing at Bill with puffed up pride. She looked at me and said, "That's my boy, Bill!! Get a look at that! Look at him go—Go bill Go, 'Abba, Dabba, doobe, Shawndi, Sheloobbie.'"

She and Maxine were swaying, clapping and speaking in tongues.

I could not believe it, but, alas, I had now lost my champion. After a few minutes of this, Bill stopped and Lovenia said, "Well, Preacher, Bill got it. What do you say about that?!"

I put my hands out together toward Lovenia's face and said, "Lovenia, you win. Thy God shall be my God. Thy people, my people. Wherever thou goest, I will go. And where thou art buried, there will I be buried."

She turned to Bill and Maxine and said, "We got him. He's all ours."

Late the next Thursday afternoon, Allene and I were on our way to Tulsa with Lovenia, Bill and Maxine to keep an appointment with none other than the great Oral Roberts, an appointment that Lovenia had made three weeks earlier. She knew the very day I would come crashing down, ready to take the plunge. Lovenia drove the two-hour trip in her new yellow Cadillac. She had it loaded, including the six-way driver's seat which she had moved all the way up and all the way forward. The tilt steering wheel was all the way up. This is the only way that Cadillac could accommodate Lovenia; even then she could just barely see over the wheel to drive. Silence prevailed until we arrived at "Oral Land." The newly paved road wound past a large fountain accented by a row of lighted flags from every nation the ministry had reached. The prayer tower was ablaze with a golden glow, and everything was sparkling with lights. Farther into a wooded area was Oral and Evelyn's home. I turned to Allene and whispered, "See Allene, I told him these tongues would get him into trouble. Look at all this expensive property and these grand buildings. Imagine how much it took to build them and how much more it takes to run them. I'd hate to have to pay the light bill. Bet, poor soul, with all this heavy responsibility, he can't even sleep at night."

Allene cupped her hand over her mouth and whispered back so low I could hardly hear her, "Shut up, James. You're just having an attack of pea-green jealousy!"

As we arrived, Evelyn was at the door welcoming us all. Richard Roberts, then a high school student, was there with his guitar. Tommy Tyson was also there. As we were being seated, in came Oral, full of joy and laughter as he went around greeting everybody. He sat at the head, Allene on his left and I on his right. During the wonderful dinner, he mentioned our long friendship, beginning at Phillips, and how proud he was of our ministry in Oklahoma City. Afterward, we all gathered in the clubroom. Richard played his guitar and sang a couple of beautiful songs for us. Then Oral, who must have been briefed by Lovenia as to the agenda of the evening, got right to the point. He looked at me and said, "Well, well, Brother James, just why did you come up here?"

That was exactly the question he had asked me that day in Mrs. Hale's class twenty years earlier. I glanced at a smiling Lovenia, turned to Oral and said, "Brother Oral, I've come up here to receive the Holy Spirit."

"Well, praise the Lord! But James, do you want everything that the Holy Ghost's got for you?"

I knew that he was referring to the tongues. Again I looked over at Lovenia, who was smiling at me. This was the moment of truth. I either had to get all that Jesus had for me right then and there, or I was sure that Lovenia was going to kill me. There was no turning back now, for this was Oral Roberts who had asked the momentous question. So I said, "Yes, I do, Oral. I want everything the Holy Spirit has for me."

"Including your devotional language?" I had never heard tongues described that way.

I continued, "Yes, sir. Everything, including that."

Suddenly, I realized that I was right where I was supposed to be. The good Lord had chosen this man of God as the one person who was supposed to pray for me to get the baptism of the Holy Spirit. In a split second, these words raced through my mind: "I've got to have all of God; this is what I've really wanted long before those Nazarene days at Camp Grant. If I don't get this now, I'll probably die or quit the ministry, and my life will amount to nothing. I cannot go on a minute longer unless I seek and have all of God."

Oral broke in on these thoughts and said, "Come over here, Brother James, and let me pray for you."

So, I went over and knelt in front of him. He placed those miracle hands on both sides of my neck just under my ears, and looked down into my eyes—I felt into my very soul—and saw there the pain, the loneliness, the lostness, the grief; I was "weary totin' such a load" for so long. As he began to pray, tears came into his eyes. All of us in the room, including me, were fighting back the tears. His moving prayer went something like this: "Almighty God of love, this Your son, James, has taken a long and circuitous journey, over many miles and many years, seeking Your full will for his life." Then all those times as a child I longed for God, those hard years in the army, seeking the Spirit with prayer and fasting with the Nazarenes, the seven long years in college, the eleven years building a church in Virginia and almost two years of painful suffering at a great big church with so little happening flashed before me. He seemed to see all of this in the Spirit.

As I looked up into his eyes, now overflowing with tears, he continued, "Lord, my dear friend, Brother James, is sick and lonely and hungry for You. I beseech You, in the name of Jesus of Nazareth, to come right now and baptize him with Your mighty Holy Ghost. Give him his devotional language and all the gifts and the fruit of the Holy Spirit. And, Lord Jesus, we will be very careful to give you all the credit and the glory now and forever. Amen and Amen." (See Luke 11:11–13.) And everyone said amen.

In an instant, I felt the burden of those long years of seeking and searching fall away, and I was, for the first time in my life, really free of all care. Although I did not speak in tongues, and neither did anyone else, I felt light and full of peace and joy as I knelt there in front of him. Then everyone gathered around for hugs and blessings. There was a brief time of visiting during which I slipped out to the car and began to weep for joy but also for regret that I did not speak in my "devotional language."

Oral and Evelyn stood by the door, saying words of farewell and love to the Reiffs and to Lovenia. When Oral came to Allene, he held her hand and said, "Sister Pippin, you are the key to this whole situation. You will soon know what the Lord means by this."

Allene saw this as a word of prophecy given to Oral by the Holy Spirit.

We all piled in for the drive back to the City. We were rather quiet for most of the trip. Lovenia asked me if I would like to hear Maxine or Bill speak in tongues. I replied, "Not now." At the house, Allene expressed our deep thanks for the evening and the fine dinner. Then I said we would be in touch with them soon. We went quickly into the house. After consoling me that all things would work out in time and that I must remember Oral's words to her, Allene went on to bed.

I found a tape on "How to receive the Holy Spirit and speak in tongues by relaxation." So I lay down on the clubroom floor and put the tape on. The person on the tape assured me that if I would really relax and do as he said, I would be speaking in my devotional language at the end of the tape.

"So, get ready, here we go—relax toes, ankles, legs, arms, stomach. Now we come to the head, the most important part of the body—all five senses are here. First you must relax the jaw—so drop the jaw, shake it from side to side and go, Ah-aha-aha-aha. Now you must relax the tongue—so while the jaw is relaxed go, Blather-blather-blather. Now go, Ahh-aharr-aharr-aharr and bather-blather-blather-blather. Good. Now you are completely relaxed and fully ready to speak. I am going to count to three and snap my fingers; then I will start to speak and you are going to follow me."

He counted to three, snapped his fingers and started speaking some unintelligible sounds. I shook my head and continued saying "ahaaaa" and "blather, blather." After a few minutes of this, because I didn't speak, I cut off the tape, struggled up off the floor and staggered down the hall toward our bedroom, all the while going on with the ahrrr and blather noise. As I came to the bedroom, the light from the bathroom revealed a sight and sound I never thought I'd see or hear. There lay Allene, with her hands up in the air, her face wreathed in smiles, covered with tears, and—yes—she was speaking in a very strange language!

I tip-toed over to the bed, leaned over and with my jaw and tongue fully relaxed said, "Wha do ya thain ya ah doah? Wha is tha strane noi?"

"Well, honey, while you were listening to that tape, I've been back here—uh—praising the Lord and—uh—speaking in tongues!?"

I became un-relaxed, "O, please don't let me interrupt you. Go right ahead, and do it again, if you think you can."

She said, "Do it again? I am right now having great difficulty speaking in English." So, off she went again, speaking a beautiful new language that was impossible to describe.

Then I began mumbling to myself, "Well, well, well, what do you think about this? Wait a minute, *I* was the one who had gone these many years longing, pleading and praying for the Holy Spirit. Oral didn't even pray for her. And yet, here's this Presbyterian, the first lady of the manse, the wife of the Rev. James Clayton Pippin, lying there—speaking in tongues!"

But, you know what? I knew that if Allene was doing this, it had to be real. And if she could do it, I certainly thought I should be able to do it, too. Then it dawned on us just what Oral's prophecy meant when he said, "Sister Pippin, you are the key to this situation!"

But the good Lord overlooked my arrogance. While she continued to speak that night, I stood by the bed, and the more I listened, the more I felt something begin to happen within me. It was much like the experience I had when Oral prayed for me, only much more intense. I didn't speak, but I became light as a feather, feeling that I wanted to dance and run at the same time. The Holy Spirit really hit me, and I got what the Pentecostals call the "welling up." A sweet warm sensation began in my lower abdomen, and as it climbed slowly up through my chest, the hair stood up on the back of my neck. Then I began tingling all over; my arms were covered with goose bumps. I began to dance back and forth in the bedroom much as Bill Reiff had done in the church kitchen. Since it was late, and we were making quite a noise, I quickly danced over and closed the door. You see, the kids would tell on us, and if word of that scene got out, I was sure to be fired.

Once when Janet was asked in the youth meeting what her parents did at night for fun, she answered, "Well, after they put us to bed and think we're asleep, they go to the bedroom and have a few beers."

So I could just hear Janet say now in answer to that question, "Mom and Dad get back in their bedroom and go, 'bleetle, leettle, leettle, leetle' for about an hour."

Later, I complained to Lovenia that I did not get my devotional language. She said for me not to worry or doubt, for this would come in the Lord's good time. In just a few days, we understood why the Lord kept me from speaking in tongues. For one night, the church sent a delegation out to the house. The leader looked at me and said, "Brother Pippin, we have been told that Oral Roberts has been here to the church to visit you and that you have gone up to Tulsa and had dinner in his home. Is this true?"

"Yes, sir."

"Well, we have been sent to ask you if you speak in tongues, and are you thinking of going up there to work for Oral?"

"No, I do not and I am not. He was here to look at the architecture and interior of our church plant, since he is beginning to build his university."

My answer seemed to satisfy them. After they left, I trembled when I thought that Allene was sitting right beside me. If they had asked her, "Well, Mrs. Pippin, do you speak in tongues," she would probably have said, "Oh yes, and you all should try it sometime; it's really wonderful!"

Then it would have been all over. I would have been out of there fast, looking for a job. Thanks to the Lord and Allene, we were there six more years. But as the time passed, my desire to speak increased. During the few weeks after Allene spoke, I tried everything. My wife spoke every day and every night, yet not a squeak came from my lips. We went to numerous prayer meetings, and each time, they really "worked on me" to get me into the total Charismatic experience. But the gift of tongues still didn't come. Lovenia kept telling me, "Patience, patience, my young man; it will come."

Then one Saturday night about 1:30 A.M, I was kneeling by the piano bench in our living room, pleading with the Lord to show me exactly what I needed to believe, ask or do to receive a flowing devotional language. I knew that I could not get the gift by trying, for I had been trying very hard to speak every day and night for many weeks. I told the Lord that I was not going to fake it; it had to be real. While praying there, suddenly the exciting thought came to me that God was ready to help me. First, He reminded me that it must come from within and that He sends the Spirit through His Son Jesus Christ, who is the baptizer.

All at once, I saw a vision of the old staircase in our home on the hill in Round Oak. It had a wide solid oak banister on which Jack and I used to slide. At the bottom, there was a large oak ball. We always took this ball off, permitting us to slide all the way to the floor. A long steel screw came off with the ball. I wondered where in the world God was going with this rather strange vision.

Then God made it all clear as a bell. My head was like that solid oak ball—hard and full of too much intellectual nonsense. He understood that after seven years in college and seminary, plus many years "on the field," I, as an orthodox, mainline denominational minister, would have a lot of trouble accepting anything that smacks the least bit of the "Penney-costial," tongue-talking, holy-roller kind of religion. You will recall that I had resisted this "foolishness" years ago at Phillips when I first met Oral. There was a battle royal going on between my hard head, that is, my mind, and all that had happened in the spiritual realm at Oral's, including the miracle that had happened in our bedroom where my wife often chattered away in tongues like a magpie. You see, I was this educated person with my head full of Schleiermacher, Tillich, Hegel, Kant, Harnack and a little Nietzsche. All these doctrines filled my head full of rationalism, anti-supernaturalism and most all other bad "isms." We modern preachers wouldn't go near that touchy-feely emotional crowd that was "in love with Jesus." In fact, most of us didn't even know that the Holy Spirit was a Person—we called Him "it." On top of that, most of us preached only about God and rarely ever mentioned Jesus. If we did, He was called "the Lord Christ." To many of us of the cloth, speaking in tongues was unthinkable and went out of vogue ages ago with the apostles, leprosy and demons.

God knew all this teaching was blocking the Spirit, and He had been very patient with me as I kept seeking the gifts, including tongues. So, my loving Father had to work through this mental clutter in order to get me to stand still long enough to even ask for the gift of tongues. Now here I was, down on my knees like a child, trying to deal with the vision of a banister and a ball. I finally saw that I had to deal with all that modern doctrine of reason that was in my head so that my heart and soul could be filled with the Holy Spirit—that I was to remove that hard head just as we removed the solid oak ball from the banister. Then I seemed to hear Him say, "Do this, my son, and I will give you a joy a million times greater than the fun you and Jack had sliding down that banister."

So, though it felt like a very odd thing to do, in my imagination I reached up, cupped my right hand over my head and "unscrewed it." (The steel pin came with the ball.) Then I placed my "head" on the floor.

At that instant, I felt these funny sounds begin to bubble up in my inner self and come on up into my mouth. Then they began to freely flow out of my mouth as words that were strange and melodious. In my mind, I thought, *This is it! This is it! O Lord, I am speaking in tongues.*

As they continued, I pled with the Lord, to please, please, keep them coming…"O, don't let them stop, Father, keep them coming until I can get back and wake up Allene!"

The strange words continued to flood out of my mouth as I moved quickly to her bed. Although it was now about two in the morning, I leaned over and gently shook her. She slowly awakened and was so shocked to hear me speaking that she quickly sat up and joined me in tongues. For the next few minutes, we went back and forth. As I spoke a phrase to her, she would answer me back. And what was so amazing is that we seemed to know what we were saying to each other! Soon, we were both speaking together through a flood of laughter and tears. Then she slid off the bed, and we knelt there as we kept speaking for a few minutes after which, as if on cue, we both stopped simultaneously. Placing my arms around her, we had a very joyous "honeymoon hug."

The tears and laughter continued as she said over and over, "You got it! You got it! Praise the Lord, and hallelujah, James, you finally got your devotional language!"

So we went to bed that night and slept so sweetly; we were fresh and full of joy when we awakened Sunday morning.

As you can imagine, I just had to get to Lovenia as quickly as possible. So I showered, shaved, dressed and after a light breakfast, went on to the church alone. Well, as I walked into the foyer, there she was sitting by the bookrack. Our members checked out very few books on Sunday because when they picked a certain one and handed it to Lovenia, she would growl, "You don't want that book! It's no good. Here take this one; it'll bless ya."

Many would then say to let them think it over. Because of this, our books stayed new a long time since not much reading was going on. This morning I didn't care who read what. I was exploding to share with Lovenia what had happened the previous night.

I walked over to the stool where she sat with her face in the Bible. Well, she really sat *around* the stool, which was rather small and she was rather—ah, large. My plan was to stoop and reach around her, pull her up and give her a big hug and kiss. But it was a little difficult to hug Lovenia. Most folks bulge at the top and bottom and dip in the middle where the waist should be, but Lovenia was straight down all the way. So I reached around her and began to pull up on her. She didn't budge. We rocked back and forth, my lifting as much as I could each time, but no luck. She finally looked up, saw who it was, dropped the book, and with my help, stood up. Then I laughed and said to her, "Lovenia, I love you!"

As I hugged her tight and kissed her on her flabby cheek, she looked up, smiled and said, "You gotcha tongues, didn't cha?"

I said, "You are so right, sweetheart. I got it…the whole heart-bursting, life-lifting, joy-thrilling, saved, sanctified, *filled to overflowing THING*…with the music of the precious Holy Spirit bubbling up out of my mouth, my ears, eyes, nose and throat! O my dear Lord, Lovenia, why did I fight you and God so hard and so long?"

She and I both raised our heads back, laughed out loud and clinging together, began a little dance. Then she quickly calmed us down and said, "Let's go and find Maxine and Bill!"

"Oh no, Lovenia, we'll jump and giggle and make a scene. People will think we're drunk or that I've lost my mind. Just let me slip back into my study. But join me in prayer, for I want us to pray down an anointing so strong that the mighty Holy Spirit will preach this congregation a sermon like nothing this church has ever heard before."

After I prayed at my desk, I went into the sanctuary. As the service began, I looked up and saw the three of them together with their eyes glued on me and great big grins on their faces. Anyone who didn't know about all this and looked at us would have concluded that the four of us had just been notified that we had won the four-hundred-million-dollar lottery. As the opening hymn began, I smiled broadly, held my hymnal high, swayed back and forth and sang the opening hymn so loudly the congregation must have thought I had written it. The entire service was a total multicolored splash of glory. It flew by so fast I was shocked it was already time to preach. I had spent twenty to thirty hours of hard work on a sermon each week. Now, I spent much of that study time in prayer. Praise God, no more slaving away at sermon preparation! I was born a Georgia cracker; now I had become a Bible cracker. For the first few weeks, when I went to the pulpit to start the sermon, I held my Bible vertically in one hand and let it fall open. While looking at the congregation, I put my finger down on the page and proclaimed, "I'm gonna preach on that text—right there!"

I am certain that they looked at each other and whispered, "Oh, my, my, the minister is not prepared!"

Prepared? Praise God, I was never *more* prepared. I was full clear up to here with the Holy Spirit of the risen Lord. Just bubbling over! Most Christians never stop to think that the apostle Peter didn't study all night before he preached that sermon on Pentecost. He would have been afraid to have even shown his face the day before. But on Pentecost, every word came flowing up out of Peter's mouth in the power of the Spirit, and three thousand souls were added to the First Christian Church of Jerusalem that day! The day before, he was locked away with the other disciples, who were all pouting, shy and afraid for fear the Jews would kill them. But, O my Lord, on the Day of Pentecost, Peter became the great apostle, full of power, *preaching and speaking in every language of the thousands who were there!*

That first Sunday, and for the next few weeks, I preached the Word of God, both written and Living, the *rhema* and the *logos*. I got into parts of the gospel that I had never touched before, such as the blood of Jesus, sin, death, hell and heaven, the unspeakable riches of the Lord Jesus Christ, the joy of salvation and immortality, the powers of the world to come, and the eternal ecstasy we would enjoy in our glorified bodies for ages and ages and for eternity. Wow! Did the Holy Spirit bring His resurrection power that morning through me down into the hearts of those sweet people!? They knew something had happened to me, but they couldn't figure out what it was. Because I preached the Bible from cover to cover, I reminded myself of Mama's preacher, old Brother Williamson. I lifted up all nine of the fruit, and all *seven* of the gifts—yes *seven*, for I didn't dare get into tongues and interpretation.

When I shared the news with Oral he told me, "I am so very delighted that you and Allene have received your devotional language. Now you know why God told me that she was the key to all of this. But, Brother James, you should not mention the tongues part for a while. Your people will accept almost all of the full gospel but the speaking in tongues."

I was totally dumbfounded by the aversion and fear of the main-line denominations to this emotion of joy. Why this fear of the gifts of tongues and interpretation? It's biblical; the New Testament is crammed with new Christian faith and lifestyle. I longed to scream at them: "My dear glorified Lord, folks, *get over it! All the nine gifts are real; the New Testament is full of them. They are the Truth of God!*"

But, get this. When any of the "religious" got sick, they wanted me to pray for them to get well; if any member of their family was terminal, they asked me to call the prayer tower in Tulsa to see if I could get Brother Oral Roberts himself to pray for them to get a miracle healing.

Where and when did the New Testament Church lose its way? Was it the influence of the Jews who castigated Paul as he preached these truths all over the Mediterranean world? Was it the satanic influence in the first century that caused the enemies of the church to come against the ministries of the twelve apostles and have them put to death? Was it rationalism and anti-supernaturalism and deism in the early 1800s and 1900s? Prayer, faith, fasting and the belief that the Bible is the Word of God were thrown out the window with the baby and the bathwater, and Secular Humanism stuck up its ugly head and took center stage then and continues to do so today.

For the past several years, I have been teaching Church History at American Christian College and Seminary. I learned that much of the Christian Church in France accepted this rationalism from the religious elite of Germany. It became popular to deny or explain away the miracles of the Bible. Then greed and envy gave birth to class struggle, which caused France to suffer the revolt of the masses in the blood bath of the French Revolution. Everyone from corporal to king and queen lost their heads as the great, unwashed masses took control.

Yet, England avoided such a "revolution" later because of the rapid spread of Christianity under the great light of God that was John Wesley. The class struggle mind-set, which believes that one becomes a general by killing a general, that to become boss one kills the boss, never entered the mind of the British. They were taught the love of Christ. You go up the ladder by getting a good education, enjoying hard work, being honest and knowing that "the Golden

Rule is the only road to gold." Jealousy, greed and hatred for those who hired them were completely foreign to the mind of the Christians in Britain.

I wish the liberal modernists could catch a glimpse of what is happening through faith in Christ today in the U.S., in Europe and all around the world. If they would open their eyes and see, for instance, what is going on in Brooklyn, New York, at the Brooklyn Tabernacle, they would find a church of thousands, where hundreds are coming off the streets and off drugs and alcohol every month with no withdrawal pains whatsoever. If they could see these modern miracles, these enemies of Christ would exchange their Secular Humanism for a powerful relationship with the God and Father of our Lord Jesus Christ.

I wish I could relate all that happened in our personal lives and in the lives of many of the church members and visitors in the months and years that followed our trip to see Oral Roberts. All through the week and especially on Sundays, it was like Christmas Eve and Easter morning all wrapped into one. God's sweet love flowed down through all the nights and days of our new life in Christ. I will relate many of the happenings during those sparkling days. This part of the story could be the most exciting.

❋ 25 ❋

Primal Scream
at Mo Ranch

I felt that I was a new creature from the moment my feet hit the floor in the morning until nightfall, when Allene and I had our prayers and cut off the light. Those persons with whom I had the most conflict, including some of the staff, many of the church members and even those closest to me, now became my best friends. What used to be the daily grind, believe it or not, now became the daily grin; the days and nights were now filled with love, joy and delight. Because I became more sensitive to every person's need and pain and was willing to slow down long enough to really listen, my counseling appointments doubled. One of the greatest changes was the way I prayed for my members when they went into the hospital. Before, when I visited the sick, I would pray for God to give them a good appetite, to help them sleep well, to make their medicine work, to give them kind and loving doctors and nurses and to bring them home soon and back to church (so that they could pay up their church pledge). After the prayer, I would pat them on the hand and tell them to try not to worry. Then I was on my way.

Now, not only my prayers for the sick, but also all my prayers were filled with deep sympathy and love. Whenever I visited the sick, I asked what was the matter with them, laid my hand on them and asked for God, through His Son Jesus Christ and the mighty power of the Holy Spirit, to heal them instantly. Often they would have a miracle healing, and some were dismissed from the hospital a day or two later.

Although Mary Wells was the first miracle healing that happened in my new life in the Spirit, I did not know the amazing details of her great blessing until months later. So, what I called my first miracle happened just a few days after the prayer with Mary. One of our longtime members, Minona Cox, was in the hospital. Her son Everett, who was a deacon, phoned me and asked me to go see her. When I called on her and asked why she was there, she said to me in tears, "Brother James, I have developed a large blood clot in my right kidney. The doctors have tried for almost two weeks to dissolve it, with no results. They tell me that if they were to increase the strength of the medicine again, it would probably ruin both of my kidneys. I am so worried, and this pain is getting worse every day. I'm ready to call in another doctor."

At that point, I said, "Minona, I know of a physician who can take care of the problem in no time at all."

She sighed and said, "O thank God. Please tell me his name so that I can get him up here right away."

"My dear lady, He is already here. His name is Jesus Christ, the Great Physician."

She said through tears, "Oh, Him?"

"Yes, Him, but Minona, this is probably the first time you have ever done this kind of praying. I assure you that when you and I together in faith agree as touching this matter and then ask for your healing in Jesus' name, He has promised to make you completely well so that He might bring honor and glory to His Father. Will you believe and pray with me for that to happen right now?"

She was sobbing as she answered, "O yes, Brother James; I believe Jesus can and will heal me. I have no one else to turn to."

I stepped closer, placed my hand on her back, about where I thought the kidney was, and said this simple but specific prayer, "Almighty God, in the name of Your beloved Son, Jesus Christ, Minona and I believe that through the power of the Holy Spirit this clot will be dissolved, and beginning right now, she will have a perfect kidney."

Well, she passed the clot that night with no pain at all! The next morning she called me with the good news, and we praised God for His goodness and for His Son, the healing Christ. She and Everett both received the Holy Spirit, and their joy was full. For years I would often remind her that she was my very first miracle. Although Minona has recently gone to her eternal reward, Everett has witnessed many miracles in answer to his own prayers of faith. Also, God called him to an effective deliverance ministry.

The Spirit led me to do many of the things that Lovenia did. When people would ask me to pray for them about a certain need, rather than say as I did before, "I sure will pray for you," I'd say,

"Let's just pray right now." And no matter where we were, even if it was in line at a cash register in a store, I would step out of line with them, take their hand and in a low voice break into prayer. This was either an embarrassment or a shock to some, but they got used to this Spirit lifestyle right away. I became bold and was "not ashamed of the gospel," nor was I concerned about who thought what about this or that. Now, please don't think I was rude, arrogant, loud or a show-off. I just was not shy about loving Jesus Christ, and I wouldn't let custom, tradition or "they don't do it that way" prevent my ministering to a person in need. I believe that this testimony is also a bold witness to the "religious" who often say that they do not wear their faith on their sleeve. They do not think that we should talk about God in public. I have found that most of them don't talk about Him or to Him anywhere, anytime.

Once in a deep crisis, when they or a loved one is facing death, they will pray and ask everyone in town to join them. When our Lord, His disciples and the apostle Paul were out in public, they did not hold back or worry about their reputation. They did not have one. They and all of the martyrs are our examples that by the power of the Spirit, each of us can be used in a unique way to manifest Christ to the world. I lose my patience with those who think that they are great godly people, yet don't want anyone to know about it.

After our experience with the Holy Spirit, miracles and healings actually flooded our every day. Although I am relating the events of our life immediately after our baptism, for thirty-five years, Allene and I have enjoyed a life that has been led by the Spirit and filled with one miracle after another.

But at this time, an even more radical change came into my life and work. More than my bedside manner, my heightened awareness to a person's needs and my changed relationship to Jesus and God—my entire ministry was radically different. What was boring work before now became fun; that person who was hard to love melted when he or she sensed strong love coming from me. Before, I made at least an enemy a day. At the end of the year, I had three hundred sixty-five enemies. Now I experienced an ancient truth that had been there all the time: "A soft answer turns away wrath" (Prov. 15:1).

Then I found a way to put my lifestyle up against one of the greatest standards in the New Testament. The Spirit led me years ago to *put my own name* where the word *love* is in the thirteenth chapter of 1 Corinthians: "James is not puffed up, James does not seek his own way, James does not keep a record of wrongs…" Try it, and you will be blessed. This daily life of love may be a challenge to some, but this is the mark toward which we press.

I learned to pray in a new way, not only for the large needs, but also even for help with the little things, such as finding something that I'd misplaced. He still helps me do that today. In other words, I learned that I could appropriate into my own life the assurance of Paul's words, "I can do all things through Christ who strengthens me" (Phil. 4:13). Also, "In Christ, [you are] a new creation" (2 Cor. 5:17).

For sure, He did not completely change my type A personality, the fact that I've never met a stranger or my often uncontrollable urge to talk too much. But you can be sure that He took the rough edges off and toned me down quite a bit in order, to say with Paul, "In honor preferring one another." My thoughts, actions, desires and goals all became more and more God-centered and less and less me-centered. One of my guiding lights has been Charles M. Sheldon's book *In His Steps*, in which he asks, "What would Jesus do?" in every situation. But soon I began to add, "What would Jesus have *me* do?"

Even though my attitude had changed toward myself, my people and my work, little had changed as a result of my constant efforts to make a real church of this crowd, a ministry to which I thought I had been called. Before we were baptized in the Holy Spirit, Allene and I were not nearly spiritual enough, for we smoked, drank and went out dancing. Then we became filled with the Spirit and stopped all that—cold turkey. But as my story reveals, we will take a little wine under certain circumstances. But to our former "good-time crowd," we were too spiritual. It reminded me of what Jesus said to the Pharisees, "But to what shall I liken this generation? It is like children sitting in the marketplaces and calling to their companions, and saying, 'we played the pipe for you, and you did not dance; we mourned to you, and you did not lament'" (Matt. 11:16–17).

At first, we were popular with the liberal and social crowd, but severely criticized by the persons who were more committed to a walk with Christ. But I regret to say the social far outnumbered the serious in the church.

This change was the heart of what caused most of the trouble that lay dead ahead. My great desire was to lead them as individuals to become New Testament Christians and, by adding all of them together, bring into existence a modern day New Testament church. Although the miracles continued, the attendance increased and my sermons were more effective, I still saw very little spiritual growth toward the goal of changing the fragmented congregation into the unified body of Christ. I was confident that my main objective as minister was to lead them to see just what Christ placed His church in the world to be and to do.

So as the months drifted by swiftly, we continued to see many miracles daily. I was ever striving to bring this greatest miracle about: In addition to preaching sermons that called them to the devout and holy life, I constantly challenged them to a deeper walk with our Lord by stressing that they tithe, read their Bibles daily and experience the blessing of fasting that I had experienced with the Nazarenes.

I also encouraged them to be regular attenders at church school, worship services and the Wednesday night dinners and to dedicate themselves to be active in the departments and committees to which they had been assigned. As the new year dawned, I taught and preached what I felt would lead to the ideal Christian family: Prayer and Bible reading in the home, grace at the table and the effect of tucking the children into bed each night with a prayer by both parents. I called for parents and children to seek more time to pray together and to talk about Jesus and the Christian life. I also asked the couples to have their own private prayer time, being careful to never let the sun go down on their anger (Eph. 4:26).

I asked to be invited as a guest teacher to their classes in order to call them to Christian discipleship. Allene and I were already trying to do all of the above with our children and in our marriage. I used every opportunity to lift up the walk toward a life more dedicated to Christ. I stressed the value of study, worship, prayer, Holy Communion, serious giving of time, talent and treasure, service to the needy and the lost and the keeping of a spiritual journal. When all of this effort produced very little growth in the lives of the leaders and members of the church, I became more and more frustrated.

I welcomed the change in pace during the summer of 1966 when Allene and I flew to Washington, DC, to serve two weeks of chaplain training at the Pentagon. Because Bill and Roine Wilson had gotten to know Chaplain Brown earlier when he flew in for a party weekend at Lake Texhoma, they joined us in Washington for a visit with the chief and his wife, Ava Brown. We were delighted to see many of our chaplain friends, many of whom we had met at the Chaplain Retreat in Germany, and also Reserve Chaplain, Colonel James Roy Smith, minister of the Glebe Road Methodist Church in Arlington, for whom I preached on that previous Sunday. In all the eleven years that we were in Falls Church, James Roy was my closest minister friend. It was a delightful two weeks.

A MIRACLE A MINUTE

Because I had been invited by Brother Frank to go with him to Leach Lake to fish, Allene flew back with Bill and Roine while I flew to Kansas City Sunday night and spent the night with Frank. Before retiring from Community Church in July, he had spent a week in the hospital with a mild heart attack, but now was well and back at his apartment. He felt good and wanted to leave right away, so we left Monday in Frank's new Mercedes for our drive to Minnesota. We had a good first day, stopping about every three hours to get coffee, sandwiches and to stretch our legs. Half way there, just at sunset, we got a motel, had a delicious steak dinner and got some much needed sleep.

Tuesday morning, as we traveled north, we left the interstate because the many convoys on their way to summer camp were slowing us down. I went a mile east and picked up a good state road north. But then the air conditioning went out and it was getting very hot in the car. A few minutes later, I glanced at Frank. He had leaned back in his seat, was unconscious and turning blue. I knew what this meant. But, O my Lord, here we were out in the middle of nowhere! I continued to drive on in prayer and in tears, "Lord, he probably should never have come on this trip. But, Father, what shall I do? What he needs is oxygen and fast. Jesus, I must have oxygen to save his life. Please God, please help me, tell me what to do!!"

Just then, I glanced ahead, and over to the right off on a dirt road, I saw a truck with some men standing around it. I slowed, turned off on the road and sped over to the truck. I got out and ran, yelling to the men that I had a very sick brother in the car and I needed their help to get him onto the ground. As we were laying him down, one of the men, seeing his color, wheeled around and was back in a flash with a tank full of oxygen! These men were out there welding a pipeline that had burst. One of the men went to their radio and called 911. While another gave him CPR, I used a newspaper for a makeshift mask to give Frank the lifesaving oxygen he needed. In a few minutes, we brought him around! He started breathing on his own, and his color brightened just as the ambulance arrived. I sobbed as I thanked the men for saving his life. Then I jumped in the car and followed the ambulance to a hospital in Litchfield. The resident doctor quickly put him in a room and made him comfortable. He then turned to me, saying that Frank must not be moved for a week. Frank asked me to stay with him, so I checked into a motel; there we were in Litchfield, MN, for the duration of the vacation. No Leach Lake, no fishing, no kidding! But I really didn't mind; I just prayed constantly for Frank to get well.

Primal Scream at Mo Ranch

Wednesday morning, Charles "the Angel Foreman" who worked for the gas company and ran to get Frank the oxygen, came by to see him. Frank thanked him over and over for saving his life, and then they had a great time talking and laughing about World War II and fishing up on Leach Lake. His excellent doctor was also an old World War II heart specialist, so you can bet that he and Frank had many chats over decaffeinated coffee as they reminisced about the war and Gen. Patton. In a week, Frank was much better, so I drove him to the airport in Minneapolis, got a wheelchair and pushed him to the plane for Kansas City. Upon arrival, he was taken to St. Luke's hospital to finish recuperating.

I got the air conditioner fixed and drove his Mercedes the long, lonely journey back to Kansas City. Frank had called so often on his members who worked in the hospital at St. Luke's that he knew most of the nurses by name. I was not at all surprised that the pretty ones especially knew him and were always waiting on him. I found out later that some of the doctors were members at Community. I could see that he was getting better fast, so I said my farewells. The next morning I flew back to Oklahoma City. Although we never got to Leach Lake, we had a good time visiting in his private room in Litchfield, which was also brightened up by the nurses, the World War II Doctor and Charles the Angel Foreman.

Later in 1966, Brother Frank married Ann Hotchkiss, whom he met when he hired her to do some correspondence for him while he was staying at a hotel in Denver. She was beautiful, super intelligent, a Mensan and had been an outstanding administrative assistant to corporate executives. To Frank, she was a "beauty and a joy forever" because she challenged his mind and looked out for all his needs. They seemed to love each other and were very happy. He drove down to see us for a few days in March of 1967 and 1968. Sweet "Tops" always moved out of our master bedroom, so he could sleep back there with me in one of our twin beds. This made it easier for us to chat till the wee hours. The last time he came, he was on oxygen each night as he went to sleep. Because he was a retired lieutenant colonel not yet on Medicare, I drove him out to Tinker Air Force Base to get his tank refilled. He took Allene and me out to dinner twice at the Officers Club. He was still smoking moderately and had a "toddy" or two each night before dinner. Each afternoon, about five-thirty, as I walked in from the church, he would say, "Let's have a scotch and soda, Son."

He visited with "Tops" most of the afternoons, but would never go to the bar and help himself to a drink. After we sat down and began to chat awhile, he would hand me his empty glass and say, "Fix me another Son, and don't put so much water in it this time."

Allene and I always enjoyed being with Frank. I'm so glad that we were able to see him and Ozelle and later Ann every Thanksgiving. He loved to go walking in beautiful Swope Park, or the woods near "Ten Acres," where we would build a fire and sit there, talking for hours. During the last week in March, he came down for a few days and preached for me on Sunday. We had our dear friends Bill and Roine over the night before he left. After supper, he stood in the clubroom and recited poetry for almost an hour. I hated to see him go. I hugged him good-bye on March 28, 1968; it was the last time I saw him alive.

I was completely devastated when Ann called in late June with the sad news that Frank had had another heart attack. Although his doctor friends and the nurses tried desperately to save him, Frank passed away the afternoon of June 28, 1968, at the early age of sixty-two. He and Ann were together for the last twenty-two months of his life. On July 1, two years after his last sermon at Community and two years from the day that I arrived to go with him to Leach Lake, his body lay before the chancel at Community Christian. Allene, the girls and I drove up for the funeral. We had a good visit with Julia, who reminded us that her beloved daddy had suffered a total of seven heart attacks in seven years, and the seventh one took him from us. At the service, we saw many of the friends Allene and I made the two summers we served at Community Christian. I simply could not believe Frank had been taken from us so quickly and so early. I didn't realize how much I really loved him and how much I would sorely miss him until he was gone.

But how could any of us ever stop missing Brother Frank? I think of him almost every day, and I quote him often. So much of what I know and the person I have become, how I preach, how I write, how I talk and how I think I owe to my dearest friend and sweet Brother Frank. What I've said about General Patton, FDR, IKE, MacArthur, Bill Alexander and Reagan is also very true about Frank. No one anywhere or anytime will ever measure up to the likes of Frank Johnson Pippin. No one like him will ever pass this way again.

It was about this time that Allene and I sought to enlarge our lives and to bring a change to the daily routine. So starting in 1967, I began to lead tour groups to Europe and the Holy Land. By 1980, counting tours to the Passion Play in Germany, I escorted a total of about twelve groups. I also continued my active role as a reserve chaplain, being promoted from the rank of major, which I had when I came to the city, to the rank of lieutenant colonel in late 1968.

Less than two years after Frank's death, we lost Brother George, on February 4, 1970. Like Brother Frank, he had continued to smoke all of his adult life. He had an advanced case of emphysema, which took him from us also at the age of sixty-two. George and Vera had served churches in Eastman, Atlanta, Pittsburgh, Millcreek, MO, and Fayetteville, NC. A few months before he died, he and Vera came to Oklahoma and spent a few days with us. They were on a vacation but also looking for a church. From here, they went to interview for a church in Heavner, OK. The night before they left, he sat on the bed in his pajamas and called for me, loudly. Twice he called, "James! Brother James!!"

I answered from our bedroom. "Yes, Brother George, I'm coming."

As I walked into the room, he patted the bed next to where he sat and said, "Come on over here and sit down, Son, and let me tell you how much I love you."

That brought tears to my eyes then, and it does now. While I sat there, he put his arm over my shoulder and began to recall the past that meant so much to the both of us. He was so very proud of his little brother. He closed this special time by asking me, "Brother James, do you remember that time I came to the house in Round Oak, when you were about five years old, had you lie down on the running board of Papa's Model "T" Ford, closed and latched the luggage rack, and drove at top speed up and down that dirt road with you lying on the running board, holding on for dear life?"

"Yeah, and all the while, Mama was running up and down the road, chasing after the car and yelling at you, 'Stop, stop—you George, you stop right now, before you kill my baby!!'"

Allene, the girls, Vera and I had a good laugh about that. George just smiled, for if he laughed, he would lose his breath and start coughing. Out at the car, the next morning, we hugged and kissed them, and as they got in and drove away, it was the last time I'd see George alive.

What a senseless waste all my brothers' deaths were. They all died rather young except Ray, who lived to the ripe old age of eighty. I have often had deep, dark and lonely thoughts about them all, feeling that I was cheated out of the joy of sharing more of their lives. Each burned his candle at both ends. All of my dear brothers and precious sisters enriched my life much more that I can say. During the summer of 1971, when I was at Ft. Chaffee, AR, I longed so desperately to have them back to share those bygone years; I was so overcome with nostalgia that I walked down into the woods near my room. While standing under a giant pecan tree, I shouted each of their names up into that tall tree. What joy it would give me if they all could read this story. But because of my unshakable faith, I know that Mama, Papa and all of our family and close friends who have gone over are standing on yonder celestial shore waiting for our glad reunion.

> When we all get to heaven,
> What a day of rejoicing that will be!
> When we all see Jesus,
> We'll sing and shout the victory!
> —ELIZA E. HEWITT (1898, PUBLIC DOMAIN)

I think you will get much benefit out of what happened next. This experience put the finishing touch to my new life in the Spirit; it was "major surgery" big time! With the sad state of the church ever on my mind, I took one final step to turn it around. The second week of January 1970, I joined forty-three other ministers in a two-week retreat at Mo Ranch near Hunt, Texas. The National Council of Churches sponsored the seminar. We were all senior ministers who directed large staffs at large churches. The objective of the retreat was to increase our skills in serving the total needs of a large church. The retreat leaders were Christian men and women from the top executive levels of some of the nation's largest institutions and corporations, such as 3M, GE, AT and T, IBM and others. The seminar fee was $750 each.

But I was not at all ready for what the first three days would bring. We were divided into four groups of eleven for *sensitivity training.* Even though some of us were Spirit-filled, there were dark areas in most of our lives into which we were reluctant to let the light of the Holy Spirit shine. His pruning is "sharper than any two-edge sword…" We older pastors, especially, must not refuse to let that light in, or let that sword do its cathartic work. Those little fleshly secrets that only God knows must be laid bare before Him with Whom we have to do. (See Hebrews 4:12–13.)

Led by psychologists and psychiatrists, the sessions began at 8 A.M., and after a short break for lunch and dinner, went on until late at night. My group sat in a circle led by Herb—a short, bearded, wild-looking, Jewish psychologist. We used only our first names. He made it emphatically clear that he cared nothing for the size of our church, our many degrees or anything we had done in the past that caused us to feel that we were great. After taking our seats in the circle that first morning, he just sat there in silence waiting for some impatient nut to start off the session. Sometimes it would be several minutes. But always one of us just had to say something, which we often regretted by the time Herb got through with us.

Hour by hour, day by day, Herb drew each of us out, pulled the curtain on our fakery and made us come out of the dark dungeons and damp cellars in which we had been hiding. He left us standing there, feeling bare and naked with all our fat and our bellies showing, including our pomposity, prudishness, prejudices, hypocrisy and bad breath. In general, he uncovered for all to see our real selfish selves devoid of simple cleanliness, childlikeness, goodness and godliness. But, oh my Lord, did he brutally shut us up fast when he saw we were dodging his question or flat-out lying, bragging, crowing or claiming to be "this famous doctor of theology, Pastor So and So of the First Whatever Church, downtown on the corner by the filling station."

The moment one of us started whining or crying, he would come and stand over us and tell us, "Dry up! You are an adult now, so why don't you act like one?"

Whenever any of us began a sentence that started with "we," which was often, he would jump up and yell out, while stomping over to us, "We? We who? James, for God's sake, would you please for once in your miserable life cut the crap and just speak for yourself. Who made *you* the captain of the world? You surely cannot speak for these other persons here, and you sure as hell do not speak for me! And, by the way, in my entire career, I honestly do not believe I have ever known a person who talks as much as you do. You are the 'chief glibber,' the boldest type A personality I think I have ever seen in my entire life."

I dropped my head in total rejection. Near the end of these three days, I felt as if Herb had installed a large zipper that began at my bottom lip and went clear down to my pubic bone. He then proceeded to unzip me, and all of my guts fell out. He, and later the entire class, saw through me like a pane of glass. We were soon able to detect flaws in each other, and all of us were sorely embarrassed at the pompous jerks we really were.

What happened next caught us all off guard because by the third afternoon, the eleven of us became more than close friends. There developed among us an unexpected "David and Jonathan" type intimacy. We were "Oceans' Eleven" against the world, and they elected me team captain. We sat together at meals and had long sessions until the wee hours. We were completely open to each other and got deeply into each other's lives in ways we had never done with anyone before.

A MIRACLE A MINUTE

During class, we more and more sided with each other against Herb. Although he didn't show it, I felt that this was exactly what he had hoped would happen. But in a deeper sense, he wanted to open up the possibility that we would also develop just such relationships with our spouses, our family and, in time, with more and more of our church members. If this were to take place, it would drastically revolutionize our little world! Talk about becoming a new creature!

However, after that climax I just mentioned, the disaster of all the sessions came the last afternoon. It struck as a teeth-chattering, strong bolt of lightening, out of the blue. Ralph, a bald, short, sallow-faced Lutheran, had kept his mouth shut the entire time. He never said a word and never asked a question. We thought he had been overlooked by Herb. Nothing could be further from the truth. At about four P.M., Herb calmly walked over in front of Ralph and started in on him—quietly and mildly at first, but as he picked up steam, he began talking loudly and then often screaming at this poor man. As we all started looking around at each other, Herb hit the climax of his inexorable plan to entirely destroy the fantasy in this person, who had been for years a faker, this Rev. Dr. Ralph. None of us can ever forget what Herb said to Ralph that afternoon.

"First off, preacher, I want you to just sit there. Continue to keep that thin-lipped, corpse-like mouth of yours shut, and get the wax out of your ears so you can hear every word I have to say. Now—you think that you are one smart cookie, so nauseatingly dignified and so cock-sure and so boringly orthodox. But Ralph, you are actually this dumb animal, living in a little world that you have created for yourself, locked away in a world in which you have always thought you were safe and comfortable, a world in which you are king and a dismal world in which you have become absolutely sure that no one could ever penetrate. But it just so happens, little Mr. Ralphie, that I've got your number." Then when Herb continued, he shouted so loudly that we all jumped, "NEXT, SIR! You are a world-class THIEF! You have robbed us of your intelligence, your input and most supremely of all, your heart and your deep emotions. You are also a consummate and loveless liar! You have lied to us and yourself when you decided that you were way above all of this bunch of stupid non-Lutheran persons—sitting here listening to all this kindergarten crap from this Jew, this so-called 'psychologist.' Stuff that was to you, as cocky and cool as you are, a bunch of foolishness and not one bit of it could ever apply to that smug, totally self-involved, big ole ecclesiastical YOU. You have not been impressed in the slightest. You care nothing for me or any of these ten men. None of their life-gripping stories has touched your narcissistic existence even one little smidgen. You have given nothing, and consequently, you have received absolutely nothing. You have just been sitting there bored out of your mind, chafing at the bit to get the hell outta here!

"But hold on there for just a few seconds more, King Ralph. Are you aware that both your head and your heart are a solid ball of steel?! I am sure that you treat your little bitty wife, if you still have one, just like you have treated us. And what about those depraved children, if you were blessed with any, who have—never—ever—really had a father? I would wager that you have seldom, if ever, taken a single one of them, or your suffering, bored wife, up into your arms and hugged them tight and told them how very much you loved them."

Here, Ralph showed signs that he was about ready to crack. But long before Herb got this far, all of us had tears flowing down our faces, and my throat felt like it had a hot rock in it. I could not swallow. We all had to exercise great restraint to keep from putting into action our strong desire to come to Ralph's defense, to get up and try to put a stop to it all. Then it happened. Herb's last scorching statement did it. In a half whisper, as he put his face close up to Ralph's, he said, "Ralph, you know what? And I do not say this lightly, for I have never been more serious in my life. Sir, I think that you should drop outta here, go on back home tonight, resign your church immediately and let a real human being take your place as senior minister."

At that very instant, Ralph exploded. He hit the floor on his knees and looking up into Herb's face, filled the room with a loud scream. We were all deeply shocked and were trembling. Then amidst a flood of tears Ralph began to yell at the top of his voice, *"Stop it! Stop it, I tell you! Please, PLEASE,* have mercy and lay off me. Can't you see that I am falling apart? I am dying—I'm losing it—your sharp words of truth have forced me to see the awful, totally selfish, sick and depraved man that I actually am. Oh my dear God, I have had to live with this cesspool of a person all my adult life. Herb, oh Herb, is there any hope for me or my life—my soul? I must—I shall—change. Oh my Lord Jesus Christ, save me from a life that's worse than death."

As Ralph bent over and continued to weep, Herb reached down, took him by both hands, pulled him up, put his arms around him and held him close. Ralph continued to sob. We jumped to our feet as if by command and surrounded Herb and Ralph. We moved in as close as we could, and all of us put our hands on Ralph. We were all weeping. Now tears were even streaming down Herb's face. A few minutes later, each one of us slowly passed out of the room, leaving the two of them standing there alone.

As we sat at dinner, Herb came over and joined us for the first time. He was one of us now, so there was much talk and then a lot of laughter. That night after dinner, we had our final session. Herb was no longer "the enemy," and those two brief hours brought a shift, a sea change in each of our lives. After Herb dismissed the class, none of us seemed to want to leave. We embraced one another, and each of us gave Herb a great big bear hug. Before we went to bed that night, we learned what happened in the other groups. There was no doubt that we forty-four ministers went into the next seven days of the conference radically changed.

The leadership styles and skills that the corporate executives taught us during the remaining seven days gave us a solid superstructure built on the bedrock base gained in the sensitivity training. These layleaders stressed church growth that springs from the needs of all people who live in the area of the church, regardless of race, creed or color; pulling more persons into the decision-making process; and finding ways to make a church relationship more personal, satisfying and productive. The whole church-life spectrum was presented, including a meaningful worship service, briefer sermons that laypersons like to hear, a not-so-painful yet workable approach to stewardship, a forward-looking presentation of Christian education for all age levels, the importance of and the secret to effective evangelism, a more vital inner-city and world mission, sessions on property, budget, constitution and by-laws, and finally strong emphasis on goal-setting with short- and long-term planning.

Then, each of us was assigned to one of the leaders with whom we spent several hours being led through "The Haldane Exercise." We were asked to go back through our lives and cite our greatest successes, then list beside each the particular skill that caused that success. Next, we had to determine if there was a dominant skill that had been used in all of the successes. If so, our main goal then was to sharpen and further develop that skill because our next great success would most likely employ the same skill.

Dr. Alvin J. Lindgren, a Methodist theologian and author, was my faculty guide and became my good friend as he led me through the exercise. He also gave me much insight into solving the seemingly hopeless task I left back home—that of turning a group of scattered, preoccupied, mildly committed people into the body of Christ. He urged that I get all the leaders together to learn just what the church is and does, let the leaders voice the entire scope of their needs, and then build the church mission around the filling of those needs. If their stated needs left out a vital part of what the church should be doing, then we were advised to fill in the picture and add that need, according to the gospel of Jesus Christ and the teachings of the New Testament, even if the majority did not agree.

The two-week seminar quickly came to a close with a final dinner and a program where the faculty and some of the students led us in a summary. All forty-four of us seemed to feel that those ten days would provide lasting value to our total ministry and would impact our calling as servants of God for the rest of our lives. I deeply wished that the seminar could have continued for another week. If we had not come from all over the nation, I am certain we would have formed a permanent group, especially those who shared under Herb. I kept in contact with a few of them for many years.

✳ 26 ✳

A Trip Around the World

*B*ack in Oklahoma City, 17 January 1970, I felt more equipped to tackle the staggering task of putting more Christ into the First Christian Church. The attendance on Sunday mornings continued to increase. My sermons highlighted the need for all the members in the life and work of the church to feel the Holy Spirit's power. As I preached, people began receiving the Spirit while in their seats. One Sunday during the closing hymn, eighteen people came forward, all the way up onto the chancel, and several of them were speaking in tongues. I quickly moved among them, trying to calm them down and stop the speaking. Miracles were occurring all through the membership in the service, hospitals, homes and work places. I started attending a prayer meeting at the church that I had avoided before because it was made up of Spirit-filled women who called themselves "prayer warriors." Before I could come all the way out and reveal that I was one of those "Charismatics," I felt that I had to try with all my power to deepen the spiritual life of the members.

In late January 1970, we had an all-day core staff meeting during which I shared my experiences at Mo Ranch. They agreed that the people needed to grasp more firmly what the church was really all about. After much open discussion, we decided to conduct a seminar on the subject, "The Nature and Mission of the Church."

Over the next few days, the core staff got on the phones and enrolled seventy hand-picked church leaders who agreed to attend the seminar for thirteen Sunday nights. We were to meet in the dining room during March, April and May. At a pre-seminar meeting with the seventy, I explained the purpose, plans, dates and other details of the seminar. We passed out material for each to study in preparation for the sessions, which would begin the following

Sunday night. We agreed that broad support was needed for the seminar, so after we got the approval of the education departments, the elders and the official board, we announced it to the entire church and asked all of them to support the effort with prayer. A leading layperson was selected to chair the entire seminar. He would open and close with prayer and was asked to make a ten-minute weekly report and a final thirty-minute one on the closing night. All persons were asked to commit themselves to be on time and remain present for the entire session each night.

So for thirteen Sunday nights, we were off and running to study in-depth the NATURE and MISSION of the Church.

We met at six-thirty, and I or one of the staff conducted a fifty-minute lecture-discussion for the first six nights on the Nature of the Church. All were asked to take careful notes on each lecture. After a twenty-five-minute break for coffee, finger sandwiches and fellowship, we divided the seventy into seven groups of ten, which were then asked to go to their predesignated rooms, elect a chair and a secretary, and spend the next fifty minutes covering points of the lecture and that night's furnished material on the unique Nature of the Church. Then from 8:35 until 9:15, we gathered back in the dining room where each of the seven chairs of the groups was given five minutes to sum up their discussions. We collected the summary notes from each chair and printed them for reference the following Sunday night. All were asked to begin to firm up in their minds just what the nature of the church of our Lord was and what part each of us had to play to bring this nature into reality. Some key questions were the following: Should the Christian Church exclude anyone from the congregation? What people were welcome, and should we include those of the inner city and the poor? What does it mean to be the body of Christ? Who and what would Jesus ask us to be if He were our minister? Is He really the head of this body and the head of this church?

We then followed those six nights with the second set of six which studied in-depth the mission of the Church. We thought it was logical that the *mission* should evolve out of our newfound concept of the *nature*. The same time and program schedule were followed. During the second six Sunday nights, the smaller groups of ten began to take on some of the same closeness as the groups at Mo Ranch did. As we came to the final nights, however, I sensed a restlessness, even a growing division, in the thinking of some of the members of the groups. When the twelfth night was over, only few stayed back for fellowship. We all came face up with the bitter reality: Our church would have to change radically if it was to become the actual, living, functioning body of Christ. We got the message loud and clear what our mission should be:

> To make the church all inclusive; our doors should be wide open to all persons and no part of the nation or the world should be refused membership. Each member of this Body must have a "burden for lost souls," and each one should do his or her best to bring someone into fellowship each week.

Most of them were totally embarrassed when asked the following questions:

- "How long has it been since you have shared your faith with a non-Christian? Excluding your own family, has anyone here brought someone to Christ in the past month, six months, the past year?

- "What percent of your income do you or your family give to the work of the Church? Does this amount of giving show that you see it as the most important institution on earth? How many of you in this group will pledge to become tithers?

- "Is the daily reading of the Bible important? How many of you practice daily Bible reading in your homes? Do you have prayer together as a family every day or night, and does your family have grace at table?

- "Should regular attendance in church be the custom of a Christian?

- "Do we have a group that visits in prisons or calls on poor families with food and clothing?"

We covered most of the Christian graces that deepen the spiritual life. We discussed the Beatitudes, the fruit of the Spirit as described in Galatians 5:23 and 1 Corinthians 13 in-depth in the separate meetings. All of this gave them a lot to think and pray about for the next week. Before the twelfth night was over, some of us began to see more clearly the nature and mission of any group that called itself the church of Jesus Christ. Then in the light of all this, we saw the Christian lifestyle that we, as individuals, should seek to believe in and with the help of the Holy Spirit to put into practice everyday.

I felt shaky as they all left that night because these seventy were the most dedicated leaders of the church. I sensed a division in the group and that maybe many of them actually were not quite ready for all this. The staff felt that most of them had never been faced squarely as an individual and seriously challenged to accept the commitment it takes to become a full-fledged Christian. I became increasingly burdened. It helped when I went home and shared these feelings with Allene. She and I were in much prayer all that week.

That last Sunday in morning worship, I preached a sermon that stressed the seven steps each member should take to achieve a deeper walk with Christ as one of His disciples. These were studying, worshiping, praying, giving, serving, fasting and keeping a journal. Because I felt there was even some division in the core staff, I asked them to meet with me thirty minutes early Sunday night in my study for prayer.

Well, the last and fateful night was upon us, ready or not. As we walked into the dining room, the staff and I were restless and apprehensive at what the evening might bring. After one of the women led us in a brief devotional, the rest of the session was to be devoted entirely to the lay chair's thirty-minute summary of the findings of the seven groups. He had also been asked to give his recommendations and a summary of his own. After a time for comments and discussion, a message from me would end the seminar.

So, the chairperson went to the podium, gave a short talk and then said, "Pastor, members of the staff, all of the groups have seriously studied what the New Testament and other sources reveal the nature of the church should be. I think that all of us have also seen clearly what Christ said the mission of His church ought to be here and in the world. However, as we have come to understand the diverse make-up of that church, the deep commitment, disciplines, and works with all kinds of persons Christ expected of His followers, the majority of us have come to this conclusion: *We simply do not want to be that kind of church.*"

Without another word, the chairperson sat down. A deafening silence filled the room. As I glanced at the core staff, I saw that they were as pale as a sheet with looks on their faces that said, "What do we do now?" Everyone looked over at me. I whispered to myself, "James Clayton Pippin, this is it!!" My knees shook as I walked to the podium. *I knew that this was a moment of truth for this church and for me as the pastor.*

I paused, asked for the Lord's guidance and began, "Mr.

Chairman, sir, please let me get this straight. Am I to understand that in the past thirteen Sunday nights, all of you have seen clearly the true nature of our Lord's church, what He would have us be? And in the light of that nature, you also clearly see the mission of what Christ Jesus would have His church do. Am I hearing rightly that the majority of you don't want to be and do that?" The chairperson nodded.

I didn't know whether to laugh or to cry. My mind raced back through the history of this church and all our churches. How was this group of leaders able to come to this conclusion? I was baffled. The Lord's words came to my aid: Jesus said, "Many are called but few are chosen." I glanced at the staff and then looked into the eyes of those whom I knew were not on the side of the majority. Then I said, "My dear friends, the church is the Lord's idea. It is not our place if we are Christians to tell God and Christ what we will and will not do, who we will and will not be. The supreme guide for the nature and mission of the church is clearly spelled out in the New Testament. We must ever be moving up to His demands and clarion calls if we are to reap His blessings and inherit an eternal life that only He has to offer. If all of you have come to see that pattern and yet most of you do not want to follow it, then you are not a New Testament Christian.

"This is all very sad. Where do you think you will find the power to develop the gifts, or the fruit of the Spirit, or the miracle power to bring salvation to anyone? How does each of you plan to be able to cope day to day with what life brings? My friends, I say this with a broken heart: You'd better get over it, for there is no other kind of church possible. We must conclude, then, that this is not a saving and nurturing institution with Christ as the head and with the members as His body following His teachings and commands. I truly believe that most of you need to start all over again. Like the great prophet Jeremiah, you sorely need to have a fire ignited down in your bones, a white-hot heat to know and to do the will of God. You need the baptism of the Holy Spirit because only the Spirit can turn your eyes from the world to Jesus and cause you to begin to think of others instead of only yourselves."

My final words were mixed with tears. All the staff had their heads bowed. "All right then, you have spoken, and you are the elected leaders, but hear this well! You have spoken for only a part of this group present tonight and a very small part of this congregation. It may be hard for some of you to believe, but I know without a doubt that there are hundreds of persons out there in this congregation every Sunday morning who would strongly disagree with you! These are persons who want to be a vital part of a deeply thrilling, life-saving relationship that shares His resurrection power and a life forever in a glorified body like unto His own. Never forget that God is our forever Father, Christ is our forever Brother, and the church is our forever Family. Wherever you got such a watered-down and erroneous conception of what the church is, I have no idea. I can assure you all of this one thing—we shall not close the door on this serious matter tonight. You will be hearing much more about it later."

After a brief closing prayer, I dismissed the seminar. Allene and I did not get much sleep that night, and neither did any of the staff. We all did a whole lot of praying! The next morning, I called a staff meeting. None of us seemed to know what we should do now.

However, the next Sunday, the congregation heard more of this matter. My sermon was full of words on making Christ the real Lord of our hearts and on spotlighting "lukewarmness" and selfishness as the barriers that block our blessings and sap the joy from our life with Christ. I concluded that if this church was to survive, then all persons had to get much more of Jesus Christ into their thoughts and deeds through the Holy Spirit. It was a clear call to a more devout and holy life. In a word, my message shook the rafters. That Sunday, we sang all six stanzas of the invitation hymn, four between the bars and the two at the bottom of the page!

As I stepped to the center to say the benediction, I noticed that about thirty of the young people were gathered at the back of the church. They had just come back from a week at youth camp. Then, all of a sudden, I heard one of them shout, "GIVE ME A "J!!" The rest yelled, "J!!"

"GIVE ME AN "E!!" The rest of the youth yelled, "E!!"

And so on until they all ran down the aisle to the front of the church, turned and shouted, "J-E-S-U-S, J-E-S-U-S, J-E-S-U-S, JESUS, JESUS, JESUS—GLORY!"

Then as they all yelled haleluuuyaaaaahhhhhh!!!! to the top of their voices, they ran out of the sanctuary. The church sat stunned and silent.

I looked at my associate, Jim Sutherlin, and he put up his hands and shrugged. I looked back at him again—a look that shouted, "Jim, your brother is youth chairman!" He slowly shook his head. He wanted nothing to do with that insurrection.

A MIRACLE A MINUTE

The next night, there was a called meeting of the board of elders. The chairman shook his head hard as he faced me and said, "Dr. Pippin, did you or any of your staff have anything to do with that despicable scene that interrupted the worship service Sunday?"

"Mr. Chairman, no, we did not. I had no idea that was going to happen. However, it is entirely normal for young people to act in this way, especially if they have just come back from a week of no TV, no phone and a strong dose of Scripture and prayer. The youth retreat closed with many of them responding to the challenge to rededicate their lives to Jesus Christ. However, I am the senior minister, and I take full responsibility for it."

"Well, Preacher, can you assure us that this will never happen again?"

"I am sorry, sir, but I cannot. I saw this to be a move of the Holy Spirit, and I cannot and will not try to control or quench the Spirit. Many of those who worship here, and especially the youth, feel that this church needs more life in it. They are telling us to wake up! One cannot predict just what the Holy Spirit will do next around here."

"Well, we don't believe you can claim that all of the things that are going on around here are prompted by the Holy Spirit."

After I agreed that he had a point, he dismissed the meeting.

I thanked the Lord that Allene and I were going to be away from the church for the next month. For weeks before we left, I was involved as the regional director for the World Convention of Christian Churches, which was to be held in Adelaide, Australia, in August, 1970. I had always wanted to host a group on a tour around the world. Because we would be down under in Australia, halfway around, I felt this was the time to do it.

It was a welcomed change of pace and a needed diversion. I tried to get as many of our members in Oklahoma to go to the convention as I could. I got over fifty people to go, twenty-five of whom went with me on the trip around the world. I also planned a trip for Rev. Gene Whitley, then minister of the First Christian Church in Stillwater, to take a group for a shorter tour. Allene and I thought that both of us should not be gone for that long, so she left earlier with Gene's group to Adelaide where my group joined his at the convention.

Adelaide was an ideal place for the convention, a quiet but lovely city filled with wonderful people. We were blessed to get the rest we sorely needed. We were greatly challenged by the speakers at the programs, luncheons and dinners. Allene sang at a ladies' luncheon and at one of the evening services.

The convention was soon over, and Allene went one way and my twenty-five people and I the other, off like a flash on our trip around the world. From Adelaide, we toured Fiji, where I almost drowned, then Singapore, Bangkok, Hong Kong, Tokyo, New Delhi, Tehran, Athens, Rome, Paris, London, New York and home. Allene and Gene's group visited Honolulu, Hong Kong, Sydney, Adelaide, Fiji, Manila, LA and home. An entire chapter would not begin to relate all of the exciting things that Allene and I experienced on our tours.

But this I must share with you. Allene, and her roommate, Margaret, went first to Sydney, where in the hotel lounge, Allene met an Italian baritone named Alberto Rokie, who was the star of the evening. He came to their table, and learning that Allene was a soprano, asked her and Margaret to come with him to an open-air pavilion on the outskirts of Sydney, where he was to sing a concert. He wanted her to sing a few numbers with him. They went, and at the concert, Allene sang several duets with Alberto. The large crowd loved them both, so she and Margaret had a delightful evening.

Now for the rest of the story! Six years later, Allene and I joined Dr. Ralph Wilkerson and his wife, also named Allene, for a few days at Disney World. The four of us went to The Top of the World to have dinner. As the band came back from break and was playing, the featured singer walked out and greeted everyone. Yes, it was none other than Alberto Rokie in living color!! Allene almost fainted, and wow, it was hard for us to believe that this was really he, here halfway around the world on the very night we were there. At his first break, he came over to our table. He was as handsome as Allene had described him. But, alas, he said the club policy would not permit her to come up and join him. We all were very disappointed. Before his next break, he had Allene and all of us to stand, and he introduced us. Then he told the supper crowd the miracle story of how they had met and sang together in Australia six years earlier. Before we left, he visited with us again at our table, and we all had great fun. He was the life of the party. As we left, we joined hands with Alberto, and Ralph led us in prayer.

Most of those twenty-five persons had been with me on several tours earlier, so they were a delight to be with. I needed this seven-week break from the heavy schedule at the church and from the shock we got at the seminar. So, the trip was very thrilling and a refreshing rest indeed. As I said, it would take an entire book to relate the highlights of going around the world and visiting the world's fifteen largest cities. However, there was no way I could ever prepare for my final days at First Christian and for what was waiting for me in the next few weeks.

❀ 27 ❀

Sneaky Secret

Upon returning home, I settled back into the heavy routine. But I could not shake the memory of the results of that thirteen-week seminar. The staggering conclusion of the leaders bothered me so much that I often had trouble sleeping. A few weeks after the convention and the world tour, the Spirit seemed to move heavily upon me to take a very bold step. I mentioned in the weekly church paper, the worship bulletin and the pulpit that I would teach a class beginning the following Sunday night on "The Book of Acts: The Birth of the New Testament Church."

I followed up the announcement that Sunday with a sermon titled "The Kind of Church Christ Intended This Church to Be!"

Almost a hundred persons enrolled after the service to take the course. They were from across the entire spectrum of the church: youth, young adults, middle-aged couples and singles, and a good number of our senior couples and senior singles. The keen interest and the wide response resulted not only from the sermon, but also from rumors they had heard about what happened in the dining room during that fateful thirteenth night.

I intended for the class to meet only five Sunday nights. The entire core staff was invited to attend, but they were not to share in the teaching. The staff and the class members were asked to hold comments and questions until the last ten minutes, after the end of each fifty-minute lecture. This had been Dean Stephen England's policy for years.

The first and the second nights went super-great. On the third night, I described in detail what happened in the house of Cornelius where the Holy Spirit fell on the whole household and caused all those Gentiles to "speak in tongues" just as the Jews did on the Day of Pentecost (Acts 10:44ff). My purpose was to witness to the fact that the fruit and the gifts of the early Christians are available to us. To do this, I had to tell what happened to Allene and me. Since the majority of the leaders didn't want to be the true Body of Christ, the New Testament church, I knew that the only power that could change the church was the power of the Holy Spirit. So I was ready to go for broke. I felt that I could not hide our Spirit baptism and its results one day longer.

My next sentence sealed my doom as a minister of the First Christian Church (Disciples of Christ). It was a sentence that would slam the door in my face of almost every Christian Church (Disciples of Christ) in the nation.

After a deep breath, I clutched the sides of the podium and said, "What happened that day long ago in the house of Cornelius happened in the house of Pippin six years ago. So many of you have wondered these past few years just what set our hearts on fire for the Lord. It was in January 1966 that Allene and I both received the baptism in the Holy Spirit and have since then been blessed with our devotional language. Yes, we both have been blessed with the gift of speaking in tongues for the past six years."

Well, you would have thought that I was the president at a press conference, having just announced that we had made a pre-emptive nuclear strike against the Soviets! Upon hearing this startling statement, about one-third of the class (mainly the church leaders) sprang for the doors, ran down the hall and "phoned home." In the next instant, their spouses phoned their friends, who phoned theirs and so on. About one hour after my statement, probably the entire church knew that their minister and his wife were Charismatics, Holy Rollers, and Neo-Pentecostals who talked in those spooky tongues. I am sure that this comes as no surprise to you, but that night was the last meeting of that class!

I was fully prepared when I was called to a special elders' meeting at which I was told by the chairman, "Dr. Pippin, I am going to come straight to the point. We of the First Christian Church do not speak in tongues."

I answered, softly, "Mr. Chairman, in the very first First Christian Church of Jerusalem, they all spoke in tongues. On the Day of Pentecost, not only the one hundred twenty in the upper room, but also later that same day when the apostle Peter spoke, three thousand persons were added to the church, and they all spoke in tongues."

"Well, sir, that may well have been the case then, but we Disciples of Christ do not speak in those tongues."

I responded, "Sir, the disciples of Christ were the first ones to speak in those tongues."

"But, Pastor, we are not a Pentecostal church."

"Mister Chairman and Elders, I believe that all churches should be patterned after the New Testament and proud to call themselves Pentecostal."

"I don't think that we are getting anywhere. You don't seem to hear what I am saying. Let me put it bluntly and plainly: We all have voted and think that you need to find you a Pentecostal church where they speak in tongues."

I knew this was curtains for me. Even though I was sure that they could get the majority of the board to vote to dismiss me, I did not believe they could carry their will in a meeting of the congregation. But since I had no intention of splitting the church, I saw no further danger in getting a most important point across to these twenty dedicated elders. I was certain that this was my last opportunity. I looked around the table at each of them and said, "Mr. Chairman and members of the board, you know that I love all of you and this entire church dearly. We have been together for almost eight years. Since some of you were not in the class last Sunday night, I would like to tell you briefly about the miracle that happened to Allene and me. We both were baptized in the Holy Spirit, and she received the gift of speaking in tongues in January 1966. My gift of tongues came several weeks later. Both the speaking and singing in the Spirit have also occurred in the lives of many pastors and members of various churches all over the country.

"I am aware that our Brotherhood does not generally believe and practice this part of the gospel. However, I see the nub of our movement's problem in the fact that while Thomas and Alexander Campbell wanted to restore the New Testament church, they simply did not go far enough. But at the Cane Ridge camp meetings in western Kentucky beginning in 1801, there were several of our preachers standing on tree stumps scattered among a crowd of over twenty thousand. Every night for many weeks, thousands were saved, and the Holy Spirit fell at most of the meetings bringing unexpected manifestations called 'exercises.' These included laughing, falling, jerking, barking and running. But the singing exercise was the most rare of them all. Barton W. Stone, one of our earliest frontier leaders, describes this happening in his autobiography as the most amazing thing he ever saw. He recorded these events in the early 1800s.

A MIRACLE A MINUTE

"Stone and Dr. J. P. Campbell were 'attending' this lady as she began to make a most beautiful and melodious sound. The melody came not from her mouth or nose but entirely from her chest or bosom area. Such music brought silence to the entire crowd and attracted the full attention of all. The sound was most heavenly, and no one ever tried to stop her or ever tired of hearing it. Stone and Dr. Campbell said in all of their travels and meetings, this surpassed anything they had ever experienced. These kinds of camp meetings went on for years, and many of our pioneer Disciples of Christ members experienced a rare joy and many miracles and healings. However, the Christian Church was brought back to 'business as usual' by the leadership of the great intellectual father of our movement, Alexander Campbell.

"Although these kinds of experiences continued for awhile, they were not approved by some of our early leaders. Allene and I have learned that when the Holy Spirit falls on a house or church filled with worshipers, the people are overcome with laughter, singing, falling, speaking and singing in tongues. Miracles and healings break out, and many are filled with an ecstasy that is unspeakable, just like on the Day of Pentecost in the New Testament when Peter and the one hundred twenty who were in the upper room were accused by the Jews of 'being drunk on wine.' This helps to explain what occurred in the Cane Ridge camp meetings and also what is happening in most of such meetings in recent years in the mainline denominations. Please grant me just a few minutes longer.

"As I stated a moment ago, the church, which is patterned after the teachings of Christ and the apostle Paul, will neither resist nor forbid any of the nine fruit or nine gifts that are given by the sovereign will of God, through the Holy Spirit. Since these gifts are given by God it is very dangerous for you elders or anyone else to resist His will. The gifts are fully explained in 1 Corinthians, chapters twelve, thirteen and fourteen. You are going against the New Testament Scriptures when you tell me that I cannot be your pastor if I speak in tongues. In 1 Corinthians, chapter 14, verse 39, the apostle Paul says, *'Do not forbid speaking in tongues.'*

"Although Allene and I have been counted among the Charismatics for the past six years, I have not pushed tongues or any of the gifts on members of this church. Allene and I both are trying to become full-fledged New Testament Christians, part of an ever-increasing group which believes and teaches *all* of the gospel and that follows in faith and practice only that which is clearly taught in the New Testament. Although we fail or fall or sometimes backslide, as did Brother Lawrence, the seventeenth-century Carmelite friar who wrote the classic, *The Practice of the Presence of God*, we get right up and keep moving toward higher places in the Lord.

"In summary, I believe that all the gifts and the fruit are for today and are strongly supported by the Word of God. We who believe this are the norm, not the radical fringe, as we are so often characterized today. *Since the apostles did not give the gifts to the church, these gifts did not cease at their death.* I am absolutely certain that God and the gospel, the gifts, the fruit and Jesus Christ are all the 'same—yesterday, today and forever'" (Heb. 13:8).

After my statement, I observed that all of the elders took a deep sigh, but no one said a word. The chair then called them into "executive session," which meant I had to leave the room. A few nights later, I met with a committee of three who told me the elders had voted, and the official board of the church had ratified the vote that I should resign. The three had been sent to advise me that I should seek another church and that I would be given ninety days to find one.

In the weeks that followed, many of the visitors and some of the members began witnessing to others about their faith. We began having persons join whom the staff and the evangelism department had not officially visited. They came down without a membership card or a card for salvation! More and more non-members were coming to the front to accept Christ or to rededicate their lives. Some Sundays, the altar was almost filled with people who simply wanted prayer for their needs. Since such a response after the invitation hymn was not a general practice in the Christian Church, it widened the gap between where I was taking them and where the leadership wanted the church to go. My new leadership style, most of which I felt was led by the Spirit, caused much displeasure and serious criticism.

But I cannot and will not place *all* the blame on the Holy Spirit, the tongues or my new style of ministry for my being asked to leave. There were other reasons I was fired: the drastic changes I had made in the sanctuary and in the life and work of the church and my strong leadership style. I ran a tight ship where the staff was concerned, and some of the staff complained that I required too much of them. There was also my constant need for every member to share in the ministry; my call for staff and members to share the exciting vision I had of what a great impact that large church could have on the city, state and nation; my insistence that we lead the way in world missions; my belief that the church must be a place for all people. I also challenged our members to set the example for the smaller churches, and on balance, I continually endeavored to get all our members and all the churches and their ministers to grow and produce much fruit for the kingdom. As you can well imagine, this heavy agenda was a bit too much for some of the church members to swallow. I could hear the clamor loud and clear, "Just a little bit more of Jesus than I had bargained for, Preacher, Sir. After all, I'm just here two or three hours on Sunday. You're lucky I'm here. Don't ask me to do anything! Is the coffee ready yet? Let's have the benediction and go eat. Tithe! You just got to be kidding. Call? What do you think we hired you to do, Preacher? Besides, you got the evangelism department to do that; I'm on the finance department."

Because I perceived in most of our members' lives there was no real desire to commit themselves wholly to Christ, this time in my ministry was fraught with much frustration, deep stress and constant conflict. My days and nights were filled with the heavy load of a large congregation. I was spending a lot more time at the church during the day and in their homes and in meetings day and night than I was in my own home with Allene and the girls.

I was also sorely grieved those days at the recent loss of my two preacher brothers, Frank and George, who both died at sixty-two years of age and within months of each other. But added to all of this, when I came back from the two-week seminar in Texas, challenged and excited about taking the church to new heights in Christian discipleship, the response of most of my leaders was not only a crushing blow to me, but I also lost confidence in my ability to lead the church. I concluded sadly that I didn't really have a church and that I was not really their senior minister any longer, if I had ever been. I hit bottom and was at the lowest point of my entire life emotionally, physically, mentally and spiritually. I felt very angry at the church members and at life in general.

However, the final death to the hope that I could get them to follow my lead came when I learned that a few of the church leaders had a sneaky little secret. But it was no secret because I found out about it. Unknown to them, I was aware that for the past two years, this group wanted me to leave because they already had someone else waiting to replace me as senior minister. This situation made my continued effective leadership in my last two years an impossibility. It was their decision that I had served my time. They already had picked their new preacher. All of the above helped to open wide the door for the entry of "sin in the camp." So what happened next gave them the long-wanted grounds for dismissing me. What I did played right into their plans and into the plans of Satan.

I detest having to write this, and I am certain that you detest having to read it, but I am so sorry, I have to do it. It was just when I was passing through this my lowest valley that I permitted something to occur that I never thought could happen to *me*! Call it disenchantment, a sense of failure, an "I don't care attitude," a mid-life crisis, burnout, loneliness, grief or all of the above. Whatever the cause, I permitted an indiscretion to come into my life. Allene was aware of this, and in her forgiveness, she revealed just how much she loved me. News of this situation got out, I am sure, for I do not believe the leaders could have been as mean to me as they were those last few months had this not been known. All through that dark time, I asked God to forgive me and was hoping and praying that the majority of the congregation would try to understand and find it in *their* hearts to forgive me. I waited for the fruit of the Spirit: peace, love, joy and forgiveness, virtues I had continually preached and lived and qualities that should be a vital part in the life of every New Testament Christian and church. I waited and waited in vain for some of the dedicated leaders to come to me in the love of Christ and minister to me in my sin and brokenness and to restore the relationship I once had with them. How I needed their love for me to match my deep love for them during this period in my life! In tears and sleepless nights, I prayed and pled to God that they might find it in their hearts to forgive me. God, in Christ, forgave me; Allene and the girls forgave me, but some of the church leaders did not.

Brother Frank told me one time, "People demand virtues in others they do not have in themselves."

It was then I learned in a personal way that the church seeks often to punish and then to kill its wounded. But, as Scarlet wept and said in her last scene, "It's no use, it's too late." It was no use and far too late for me to hope for forgiveness because "somebody else is taking my place."

During that winter of my discontent, I found the truth in the old ballad, "They are writing songs of love, but not for me!"

So for many months, this old church had had no intention of keeping me as their minister, tongues or no tongues, and the infidelity came after they had selected my replacement. No matter what golden qualities I may have had, these had all turned to rust. They were restless and ready to move on with their stellar choice at the helm. That church and I had long ago come to a final parting of the ways. I came to the sad conclusion that I had been used, used as a fill-in, played second fiddle just long enough for them to be convinced that their real choice was fully ready to lead the church.

In the midst of the stygian night of thunderstorms that I caused by my sin, our God of love brought a bright sunrise that fully equipped me for the years ahead. Earlier in my need for more funds to maintain the lifestyle of the senior minister of the largest Christian Church in the state and the sixth largest in the nation and to provide for a wife and three growing girls, I began seeking ways to increase my income. I continued to be active as a reserve major; then in 1967, I began to conduct tours to Europe and the Holy Land. I also turned to the stock market, seeking to better our income by investing in solid quality stocks. Although I only had about ten thousand dollars, all the banks in town were more than glad to lend me money, a total of fifty thousand dollars, which I put into about five good stocks—*on margin!* Oh, I almost forgot. I also had one thousand shares at one dollar per share of a little unknown company called Toyota Motors!

However, beginning in 1968, the economy went into recession. My stocks went way down; the banks sold me out, and I lost about forty thousand dollars. I couldn't even pay the interest on the notes. Had I just used my own money and not borrowed from the banks or from the brokers, I would have been fine, for those were all great companies that are still there today. Things were black indeed. One morning, a bank president asked me over and told me that he was going to take our home and put us in the street. I staggered out, went back to the church and slowly walked out to the small prayer chapel we had recently placed at the bottom of the bell tower. I closed the door, fell on my knees and cried out to God to help me. I prayed with bitter tears: "Lord, I am tired to the bone and sick to death of all the pain I have suffered, not only in failing to move the church forward, but also in the pain, guilt and shame I have brought on my wife and girls and this church by my infidelity. I need the miracle of my life, Father. Please give me complete release from my great burden of sin, but also immediate help in the financial crisis that has now threatened to destroy me and take our home. I vow to You, Lord Jesus, that I am not going to leave this chapel until You take all my pain, weariness and guilt away and give me, instead, total peace and joy in my heart. Lord, I know You can do this, so in Your great mercy, please come to my rescue."

After two hours of praying and waiting, God stepped in and gave me one of His greatest miracles. I entered the chapel loaded, weary and ready to quit, but I walked out strong, confident and completely free from guilt, worry and stress. Then the Lord sent me back to the bank.

When I walked in, the president motioned for me to come into his office. He sat me down, poured us a cup of coffee and then gave me the news. In the past two hours, they had conducted a meeting, and the bank had decided to let me pay the interest only, in whatever amount I could, for the next six months. They would work with me, and I was to forget what he said about taking away our home! He walked me to the door, and I left on a cloud of peace, filled with joy unspeakable. I raced to share the miracle breakthrough with Allene.

So, praise God. With His complete forgiveness and His continued blessing with the added outside income, I finally paid back every dollar I owed those three banks, including the amount of the loans which their auditors had made them charge off. I was able to keep just one stock, The Southern Co., which in the twenty-five years I held it, increased over five-fold, paid a great dividend and made me back most of the forty thousand dollars I lost.

Now in the midst of all these revolting developments, I was not only asked to leave the church, but I was *persona non grata* in my denomination, immediately dropped from the board at Phillips University and removed from all other positions of state and national leadership. But strangely, all this mattered nothing at all to me. I still kept my peace and great joy.

One afternoon, during my last ninety days, Dr. Eulis Hill, our regional executive minister, came over to see me. After Vera brought us in some fresh coffee and we had a bit of pleasant chitchat, he warned me, saying, "James Clayton, I am going to come right to the point." When anyone ever says this to you, get ready; the point is on the end of the sharp knife that is about to be plunged to the hilt between your fourth and fifth rib! He said, "As long as you are involved in this 'glossalalia movement,' we cannot help you get another church." (*Glossalalia* is a highfalutin' Greek word for speaking in tongues.)

But I answered him, lightly chuckling, "Eulis, I don't think I want another church. After all I've been through with this church, I don't believe I have the strength left in me to stand another one." He smiled weakly, had a brief prayer and left.

A MIRACLE A MINUTE

My ninety days were about up, but the elders saw no signs of my leaving. So another committee of three was sent to me one Saturday afternoon to tell me that they wanted a firm terminal date. I told them that I would be out within the week. They were shocked. Their mouths dropped open as if I had pulled the pin on their jaws. They thought that I was going to be more difficult than that to get rid of or that I had another church already. They silently crept out, shaking their heads.

So I moved quickly; I wanted to get it all over with. At the close of our core staff meeting the next Tuesday morning, I asked Jim Sutherlin, my top associate, to stay back. After the staff left, I closed the door, pulled the drapes, lowered my voice and said, "Jim, I want you to promise me that you will keep this top secret. Don't tell anybody, not even your wife! I am going to resign at the elders' meeting tomorrow night."

He turned a bit pale. I continued, "I want you to sit right there and take down my letter of resignation. I do not want anyone to know but you that I am leaving until after I have resigned at the elders' meeting. Please go type this letter in your office now and bring it back to me. Do not make a copy. Turn in your penciled copy to me with the letter. Say, what do you think of my asking for ninety days' terminal pay?"

He responded, "Brother James, you have been here almost eight years. I urge you to ask for six months' full pay. You deserve it." So I took Jim's suggestion.

During the same time I was dictating the letter, Allene was on her way out to shop. All of a sudden, she pulled over and stopped. She started praying, weeping and speaking in her devotional language. Later, when I called to read her the letter that Jim had typed, I asked if she was sitting down because I had a very important letter to read to her. She asked me exactly the time that I dictated the letter. I told her; then she said, "That was the very same time that I was parked, praying, weeping and speaking in the Spirit!" The Spirit had given her a word of knowledge to pray for me.

I read her the letter, and she wept again. I didn't know if it was for sorrow or joy.

At the elders meeting Wednesday night, I read the letter, which stated how much I had been blessed by the years I had served with them, asked for the six months with full pay and told them that if they approved the letter, I would no longer be the senior minister as of that moment. They were stunned when I said that I would not go back into the pulpit for a farewell sermon and that I wanted no farewell reception. Since I was leaving Friday to go out of town to preach that weekend, I told them that I would clean out my study Monday and Tuesday of the next week. The instant I finished these words, a leading elder moved that the letter be accepted as written. It was seconded, and the vote unanimously carried. I pulled the large ring of church keys I had carried for almost eight years from my coat pocket and shoved them all the way across the thick, polished oak table into the hands the chairman. Then I got up and walked out without another word.

It was 8:30 P.M., Wednesday, January 5, 1972.

I stepped across the hall, entered my study for what was to be the last time, put on my overcoat, walked out, shut the door and stepped out onto the parking lot.

It was a cold, clear winter night, and the sky was full of stars. I raised my arms high over my head and let out a shout to an all-loving, all-forgiving and almighty God: "Praise God, Praise God, I'm free, I'm free! Praise God, I'm free at last."

I slowly drove off the lot and went home. There, in the den, were over fifty of our young people, including many of their friends, who started shouting and singing, "For He's the Jolly Good Fellow" over and over. I have wondered many times just how those young people knew how much I needed them to be there that night. Allene told me that the Lord sent them there. After I shared the news, we had a time of fellowship. Then each of them told us how much they loved us and were going to miss us. After some hot punch and cookies, many hugs and kisses and words of love, they all silently walked out.

My adjustment lasted about an hour. The church did not kick me *out*; they kicked me *up* into the kingdom. Pour the wine, start the music, turn on all the lights and flush all the toilets—for our Father God saw this sparrow fall!

Our new life then took off like a mighty eagle. A few weeks earlier, I had given my testimony at the Charismatic Tulsa Christian Fellowship where Bill Sanders and Chuck Farah were pastors. Without my knowing it, Bill sent the videotape to Dr. Ralph Wilkerson at Melodyland Christian Center in Anaheim, California. Ralph phoned me to come out immediately to spend the weekend and to preach for him Sunday. I left Thursday, the day after I "resigned." When I arrived, I was surprised to learn that there were two Sunday services. I preached at both of them to a total of more than five thousand persons! I tell you the truth, I sprained more than my orthodoxy that Sunday! After church, he and his wife Allene (same as my wife's name) took me and about twenty-five of his leaders and their spouses to a five-star hotel for a buffet like I'd never seen before.

Dr. Wilkerson received a "love offering" for me at each service, and Monday at the airport, he handed me a big fat check. Wow, this was a brand-new world, a world where the gifts and the fruit were in abundance, where everyone cared nothing for what you had done, but were only interested in who you were in Christ and where you were going! Talk about the extravagance of God! I never felt so loved in my entire life. Brother Ralph became, and still is, like a brother to me. I often slip and call him Brother Frank.

He and his lovely wife, Allene, sort of took us in, and his staff and deacons surrounded us with a lot of prayer and encouragement. I became one of Ralph's keynote speakers at the annual Charismatic clinics, and for years I was asked to come out there and speak about once a month. My Allene went with me most of the time and sang each Sunday. A few years later at Dr. Wilkerson's church, Melodyland Christian Center, I preached five services one Sunday to a total of fifteen thousand people! The church had a staff of two hundred fifty! In those days, I thought California and Melodyland were just a little lower than the kingdom of God.

Remember, I told the elders that I would pack up all of my books and my belongings and move out when I returned from California on Monday? Get this. When I got back to Oklahoma City Monday afternoon, I found that Vera had beat me to the draw and took it upon herself to personally move me out. The day after I resigned, she and one of the custodians threw all of my personal items, files, and books in boxes, then dumped two files of personal correspondence and four file drawers of my sermons into plastic bags, all of which the custodian put in a pile in the center of my garage on Saturday afternoon. I was sure that this mammoth task took her all of Thursday, Friday and half of Saturday. I have always felt that this decision of Vera to throw me out of my office while I was out of town meant that she was not only siding with the leaders of the church, but also that she was upset with me about many things, including the fact that I had not asked her to be in on the top-secret conference with Jim. More than this, she was very angry that she was not asked to type my letter of resignation. "Hell hath no fury…!"

The week I "resigned," *The Sunday Oklahoman* had a column on the front page, and the *Sunday Oklahoma Journal* had a long front-page story with a picture and the headline: *"PIPPIN SWITCH SETS CITY BUZZING!"*

Sneaky Secret

My new life was changed and so filled with love and joy that I soon forgot all of the hard work, heartbreak, rejection, and unhappy thoughts and things that occurred in those eight years at the big church. Because we tend to forget the bad and recall the good, all that I remember now are the incredible blessings, the happy times, exciting events, the love and joy that many of those precious folks extended to us, and the solid growth those years brought to Allene and me. And what about the indiscretion? The Lord really put wings to my spirit the day that He seemed to say to me, "I have forgiven you of that, so you forget it and go on with your life."

That summer, I was invited to three Charismatic clinics—in Anaheim, the Seattle-Tacoma area and Pittsburgh. There were about fifteen thousand persons enrolled for the week's event in each of them, including Charismatics who came from many of the leading denominations. I was on the program with pastors and layleaders, including many women, Catholic priests and sisters of all races, creeds and colors. In the Seattle-Tacoma area, we took a ferry over to Paulsbo (Little Norway) for one of our most exciting meetings. A few weeks later, I was in Pittsburgh, at Duquesne University, where I heard, for the first time, a group of nuns singing in tongues. It thrilled us all as if it were a canticle from heaven! After the meeting, I asked Father Bob Arrowsmith to take several of us to a room and have the nuns lead us into that angelic and lovely gift of singing in tongues. As Brother Kenneth Hagin says: "He did, they did and we did!!" But there are still many Spirit-filled churches where this precious blessing seldom or never occurs.

Almost immediately, I was on the road about three weeks out of the month, speaking coast to coast and border to border at small, medium and large churches, seminars and conventions. I was invited to speak at hundreds of meetings of the Full Gospel Businessmen's Fellowship, International (FGBMFI), including their regional seminars. I owe so very much to Demos Shakarian and to all those chapters and their leaders for their love and joy in the Lord during the thirty-five years that I have been speaking to them in almost every state in the U.S. Their monthly *Voice* magazine is a blessing to Allene and me. My testimony was printed in the January 1975 issue of *Voice*.

It was February 1972 when I again stepped out on faith. How would you like to go into the flower business? Big time?

Come on, let's do it! It's great fun! But I had to hog-tie and drag Allene all the way!

❋ 28 ❋

Miracles Galore!

*I*t didn't take me long to realize that "the road" full time was not good for the health or the family. I didn't want to have to be out there, trying to make enough income to support three growing girls and Allene. I wanted to go out when I felt like it and when it was in God's timing. So I asked my banker, George Grundy, to watch out for a business that would be somewhat compatible for a clergyman to get into. George called me about a week later, saying that there was someone in room 808 in the downtown Holiday Inn with a business proposition. Allene and I went down to see him and found that it was a franchise called "Flower Mini-mart," based in Minneapolis. They would come to your city, set you up in the new business and help in every way to get you started. The business was putting refrigerated flower cases in hospital gift shops. The gift shop would receive a percentage, and our shop would keep the case full of fresh, beautiful flower arrangements.

In February 1972, the company flew us up to frigid Minneapolis-Saint Paul, where they had twenty-two cases in the twin cities. We spent three days learning as much as we could about the operation. After we got back to the city, the company sent an executive and a designer who spent two weeks with us, helped us step by step to locate a place for the shop, went with me to sign up the two largest hospitals, helped me get a wholesaler to sell us the flowers and assisted me in leasing a large van. Our first day of business was March 15, 1972, with three cases placed.

Then we were on our own to serve the cases and to place more. In a few months, I had placed cases in seven of the hospitals in metropolitan Oklahoma City. We hired designers and a manager. I only missed speaking engagements for the few months it took us to develop a smooth operation. Allene was the owner-treasurer, and our middle daughter Anne, then a junior in high school, was soon head designer. Janet also became a top designer and helped us a lot when she was in town. Janet sold us on the idea of being open on Saturday. It was also her idea to put a person in a bunny rabbit outfit on the median out front with a sign: "Cash 'n Carry Roses—$12 per dozen." That bunny stayed on the street for the next twenty years. We were even given the nickname "The Bunny Roses Shop." The first Saturday we hired a bunny, Janet and Allene took in $236.50, money that we never had before. We stayed open on Saturday for the rest of the time we had the shop. Often when the bunny person did not show up, Janet got out there and cut such capers. On one Saturday, we took in over four hundred dollars! Janet and Anne were jewels, and they came up with many good ideas that brought customers in the door. Most of the years we had the shop, Beverly was always working somewhere. Since she was thirteen, she would go out and land a job on her own as a bus girl, food waiter, cocktail waiter, assistant at a local private airport, ticket agent for a small airline, then as a flight attendant for almost eleven years with American Airlines.

I promised First Christian that for one year I would not start a church that met on Sunday morning. So we rented space in the St. Francis de Sales Seminary out on the Northwest Expressway and started a fellowship that met at 5:30 P.M. on Sunday. We incorporated as a church and called it the "Charismatic Christian Fellowship." Our attendance ran from about one hundred to two hundred fifty on Sunday afternoons. I taught or preached for about fifty minutes, and then we went down to the dining room for a break and refreshments. I still remember those breaks for food and coffee, and all of those beautiful, young and older and new people who came out. Back upstairs, we'd go for another hour ministering to the needs of the group. For about two years, Sande and Billie Sanders sponsored a radio program that I broadcast from our home at eight A.M. Monday through Friday. Allene started the program with the song "I Believe" each day. Brother Kenneth Hagin came on before me, and Jimmy Swaggart followed me. I told my listeners that they were getting a "Pippin Sandwich" for breakfast.

In a few months, Allene felt led by the Lord to start a monthly luncheon on Saturday for Christian women. The Lord blessed it, and the attendance grew, often to over three hundred. She had many of the national leaders in to speak for the luncheon. After a year, we started Sunday morning services at the Tropicana Inn, at 39th and North May

Ave; then many of her speakers stayed over and spoke Sunday morning and night. The list of persons who spoke for the luncheon and/or the Fellowship included Patti Roberts, Bob Mumford, Derek Prince, Dick Mills, Vicki Jameson, John Osteen, Charles and Frances Hunter, Gene Neal, Lulu Roman, David du Plessis (Mr. Pentecost), Howard Conatser, F. E. Ward and Kenneth and Gloria Copeland.

One afternoon about six months after leaving the church, I was down on my knees at St. Anthony's hospital gift shop wiping out the bottom of the case that I had just filled with flower arrangements. I looked up and standing over me was Dr. Hill, the executive minister (bishop). He was not aware that I had started a business. He said with a smile, "Dr. Pippin, what on earth are you doing down there on your knees?"

"Eulis, I am down here praying. Naw, I'm really working to provide for my family."

I laughed, stood and shook his hand with my wet hand, then explained, "My wife and I have started a little business, kind of like Paul's tentmaking, but Allene and I are actually out of town most of the time preaching, singing and having the time of our lives. We have a good manager and designers, including two of our daughters, to help us run the flower business. Do you have a few minutes? I'd like to visit with you, briefly. Let's go over to the snack area and chat a while."

He agreed, and after I got us some coffee and we found a table over in the corner, I continued, "You know, Dr. Hill, I probably shouldn't say this, please don't tell anyone, but it is simply wonderful not to have twenty elders, one hundred fifty deacons and thirty deaconesses looking over my shoulder every day and night. I cannot believe that I used to have two hundred bosses! Let's make it two hundred one, counting you!"

We both laughed at this, but my laughter was a bit louder than his. I added, "Now I have only four bosses: God, Jesus, the Holy Spirit and Allene!

He replied, "I'm sure you are half-kidding, James Clayton, because I know you miss them all, and they miss you. You never really saw them as your bosses! You were one of our strongest and most effective leaders and always supported our regional and national programs. All of us over at the regional office and most of the ministers in the U.S. are going to miss you."

I said, "Eulis, I truly appreciate what you said. You and I were always close friends. But Dr. Hill, my leaders didn't think much of my idea of getting them to accept the gifts that come with the package of receiving the Holy Spirit. We Disciples are supposed to be a New Testament church, but even though Jesus said that all His followers 'will speak with new tongues' (Mark 16:17) and the apostle Paul told the early church, 'Do not forbid to speak with tongues,' (1 Cor. 14:39), I guess our brotherhood has chosen rather to follow the doctrine of the large mainline denominations rather than the New Testament."

"Well, James Clayton I guess it's all a matter of interpretation. Many believe that those gifts ceased with the death of the apostles."

"I am sure this is what most of our churches believe. But Eulis, my new life is not only filled with the Holy Spirit, but it is also now filled with speaking engagements, the Flower Mini-mart, Army Reserve activity, our little Charismatic Christian Fellowship and the tours I conduct to Europe and the Holy Land. And Dr. Hill, unlike some active ministers in the city and those who have retired in the region, I am keeping the ministerial code of ethics to the letter. I say no to every request I receive to marry, bury or visit the members of The First Christian Church at home or in the hospitals. I have not and will not try to get a single member of that church to join our Charismatic Christian Fellowship. So I give you my word. My remaining in the city will in no way affect Don Alexander's ministry there." He commended me for that and since it seemed he wanted to visit further, I continued, "Eulis, I know you realize that I will sorely miss many of the families of the church and also the fellowship I had with the ministers in the city, the state and nation. I also miss continuing the work I did for the region, serving on the board at Phillips University as honorary degree chairman and the national program. But I'm sure that is the price one pays when he becomes a 'glossalalia Pentecostal,' and years later, for a moment, slips and falls."

He followed all that chatter with a warm response saying, "Brother James Clayton, please remember that the Christian Church here in Oklahoma and at large is going to sorely miss your leadership and your wife, Allene, and her lovely voice. I have truly enjoyed our visit. Let's keep in touch now and have lunch sometime soon."

Dr. Hill was very sincere, and I am sure he and his entire staff loved Allene and me dearly.

In the business world we often hear the phrase "follow the money." Brother Frank used to say, "Brother James, don't ever forget that everything comes to market by price."

A MIRACLE A MINUTE

I seriously answered, "Why, Brother Frank, surely this is not true among Christians?!"

He laughed. Although in high social circles money is seldom mentioned, it seems to run strongly just beneath the surface in the lives of the rich, the near or new rich. Family members who have always been close will find out who each other really is, when, at the death of the parents, they gather for the reading of the will. When not treated as they thought they should have been, many members have walked away from such meetings and have never again spoken to each other. I mention this because of what Jesus teaches in the Gospels: a few hundred or even a few thousand dollars are not worth breaking off a family relationship. But greed, hate, anger or selfishness often rule the hour and also the hearts of some members of a family and sometimes in the hearts of some "members" of the church. The bountiful hand of God returns gifts to those who give. Jesus says that we will receive "good measure, pressed down, shaken together and running over" from a loving Father above "who gives thee the power to get wealth!" (See Luke 6:38; Deuteronomy 8:18.) So, I really believe that this attitude that came from some of the leaders was partly caused by the miracle of an abundance of finances that the Lord sent into our lives beginning the very week we were fired from the church.

The honoraria from the love offerings wherever I preached or taught were more than liberal; those loving people of that small Charismatic Christian Fellowship paid me over five hundred dollars per week, which was more than the big church paid me. Add to this the Reserve Army pay, income from tours and profits from the Flower Mini-mart, and the result is a total that is over three times what I received from the church although I had been there eight years and worked often seventy to eighty hours per week. We also served the Charismatic Fellowship for eight years and were in the wholesale and retail flower business for twenty years. In 1980, I retired from the U.S. Army Reserve after thirty-six years.

Even after all that labor, the constant agony of trying to get the church to be the church, and my heartache in being fired, I never held a grudge, was not bitter (for long), and I believe, before God, that I completely forgave them, collectively and individually, for everything that was ever said about me or done to hurt me.

In the summer of 1973, the Lord sent us an angel who brought a new and exciting dimension into our lives. One afternoon I was teaching at a Charismatic Clinic at The Calvary Community Church in San Jose, California, when a lovely Chinese lady came up to me after class. She was holding in her small hands her new book, *For Those Tears.* As she bowed, she said, "I would be greatly honored if you would please read my book."

The pretty lady was Nora Lam, a Chinese missionary who made her home in San Jose. After Allene and I read the book, Allene asked her and her husband, S.K., to be guests in our home and to speak at her luncheon in the fall of 1973. She stayed over Sunday to preach at the Fellowship. We became very fond of Nora and S. K. and were delighted when she asked Allene to go and to sing in her Summer Crusade to Taiwan, Korea and Hong Kong in 1974. Then in August of 1975, Nora took Allene and Beverly, our thirteen-year-old daughter to China. Beverly's pretty green eyes were filled with excitement at the sounds and sights and the people she met on that wonderful trip. Those people Bev met included Ming Rhen Hsu, a handsome Chinese boy who worked with his dad at a jewelry shop on the sidewalk across the street from her hotel. They became close friends, and before she left, he presented her with several beautiful pieces of costume jewelry. He and Bev continued their friendship for months and exchanged many letters.

Then in September of 1975, I went with Nora, her mother and S.K. to Taiwan and other cities where her crusades were to be held that next summer. It was a great spiritual experience as I got to meet the president of Taiwan and the president of China-TV, who sold Nora weekly TV time. She was the first Chinese-American missionary to be honored in this way. Because the President and founder of Taiwan, Chiang Kai-shek, had recently passed away, we four made a visit to his gravesite in the mountains south of Taipei. Nora was a very close friend of Madam Chiang, who graduated from the same school as Allene did, Wesleyan Conservatory of Music, Macon, Georgia. She and her husband, President Chiang Kai-shek, were devout Christians. She had Nora to tea every time they came to Taiwan. The Chinese people were so warm and friendly to me, especially after Nora taught me to use chopsticks. The hotels were grand, and the food was delicious. The food in Taiwan and Hong Kong was different from U.S. Chinese food; it was much better.

Upon returning to San Jose, Nora added me to her official board, and I have been on it for the past twenty-five years. From 1974 until 1991, Allene and I went many times to Southeast Asia with Nora and her sons Paul and Joe and her daughter Ruth. Allene sang and I helped in the crusades in several ways, including the communion and ordination services. Crusades were conducted in Taipei, Seoul, Tokyo, Hong Kong, Bangkok, Manila and Singapore.

We did not go with Nora for three years because we were sponsored into Amway. Though we just used the products until 1979, we began having meetings in our home and in the homes of active persons we signed up. We broke Direct in 1980, then became profit-sharing Directs for the next three years. We had loads of fun, held meetings in several cities and met lots of great people. Our Amway family reached a total of thirty-six hundred by 1982. I was ready to help three couples break Direct under us, when in January 1982, I began having acute angina pains and had to call a halt to most of my activities. It was so bad that I could not get through shaving without having an attack. Of course, my doctor did the usual tests. He wanted to check me into the hospital to do an angiogram and bypass surgery. I refused, and he fumed.

My reason was that a few months before this, my sister Mary had this same problem, underwent bypass surgery and never regained consciousness. She died of cerebral hemorrhage at sixty-seven years of age. At the time of my angina, I was still in grief at her passing and was in no mood to take a chance on the same thing happening to me. My doctor asked me what in the world I planned to do. If I refused the operation, I might drop dead any day. When I told him that I had heard of an alternative, he said that was quackery and not legit. After much prayer, I went to a nutritional food store and learned that there were several good books on an alternative to bypass surgery. After reading a couple of them, I felt a great load lift from my life. My new doctor was listed in one of the books as one of the best holistic physicians. His offices were in south Oklahoma City; his name, Charles H. Farr, an M.D. with a Ph.D. in nutrition.

After extensive tests, he prescribed a drastically modified lifestyle, which included better nutrition, vitamins, exercise on a rebounder, increased intake of distilled water, decrease of stress and twenty chelation treatments given by IV once a week for twenty weeks. It took about three hours at his clinic. After all of his direction and the reading of the books, I developed a plan for myself and my friends that I designated as the VWWWW program: steps to prevent heart surgery. This protocol began giving me relief from the angina attacks in three weeks; in about six weeks, the attacks ended. That was in 1982, and I have had no angina since.

After I finished the chelation, I began to share this information with friends and groups as only a suggested lifestyle, not a prescription and not a guaranteed cure since I am not a medical doctor. A few years ago, Dean Ornish, M.D., Ph.D., wrote a fabulous book that scientifically sums up all one needs to know about the alternative to bypass surgery. He operates a clinic in California in which he has led many persons suffering from heart trouble to a life free from pain and free from the need for surgery. His book, which contains many recipes, is now in paperback at most bookstores. I will briefly share my VWWWW formula, which I have adopted from all my research and from Dr. Farr's treatments.

Before following any of these suggestions, consult a holistic M.D. or a certified nutritionist to determine the doses that are right for you. VWWWW stands for:

V: Vitamins—A-C-E-S. The S stands for selenium, which is vital. I also take garlic, pantothenic acid, potassium, zinc, Barley Green, and a multiple B vitamin. I have taken 1,000 milligrams of E and 10,000 of C (calcium ascorbate), a day for twenty-five years, but you should begin by taking E in much lower doses to begin with.

W: Distilled water. Drink at least 3 quarts a day, even better, a gallon. Better not to drink water 30 minutes before a meal or 30 minutes after.

W: Walking. Walk at least five days a week. Start gradually: 5 minutes warm-up, 5 cool-down; get your time up to 30–40 minutes of fast walking. Always slow down if you sense the slightest discomfort.

W: Watch what you eat. Cut down on your intake of fat, salt and raw sugar. Limit or eliminate pizza, sausage, pickles, rich desserts, doughnuts, and most fast foods.

W: Work daily, hourly on your *worry*. This is our great enemy. You must resist becoming an adrenaline junkie. Take a short break, flat on your back, alone, twice a day; take deep breaths to help clear your mind of all stress, anxiety, worry, fear and hate. Be still, relax, get that adrenaline DOWN. Work smarter, not harder. Pray with, love and hug your spouse and children a lot. Buy a Jack Russell terrier, feed him and love him till he becomes your dog! Try not to discuss stressful things at meals or near bedtime, certainly not around the children.

All of the above have greatly enhanced Allene's and my life. I'll be eighty my next birthday, but I look, feel and act like I am under sixty…in every room of the house. I told our prayer meeting friends that Allene and I were going to take a second honeymoon. When they asked where we were going, I said, "VIAGRA Falls!"

Beginning again in 1983, Allene and I went with Nora and her group into mainland China to Kwangchow (Canton), Shanghai, Beijing and other large cities. Our first trip into mainland China was by train from Hong Kong to Kwangchow. The first time we arrived, there were no taxicabs; we went by bus straight to the only fine hotel, the White Swan. On the way there, I saw that many of the buildings were crumbling, and single light bulbs hung from high ceilings. People on bicycles or on foot filled the streets with a solid river of shiny black hair. There were only a few motor scooters and few, if any, personal autos. At the hotel, we were not allowed outside unless we were on the bus. No phone calls could be made to anyone in the city; only room-to-room calls in the hotel were allowed. Prices for everything we purchased were very low. A full breakfast was one dollar, including juice and coffee!

In 1984, however, everything began to change dramatically. Each year, there were more motor scooters, personal autos, taxicabs and five-star hotels. We were given the freedom to go where we pleased, see the cities and use the phone to call anywhere locally or globally. And, of course, the prices went up a little each year. The old buildings began to be kept in better repair. The electric systems were more modern, and construction was nonstop on new buildings and large hotels. Their great five-star hotels had spacious rooms, grand lobbies with waterfalls and several restaurants that served delicious cuisine from every country.

Each year, the size of Nora's groups and the attendance at the crusades increased. Many times we had over three hundred on the trip. At the meetings conducted in the cities, there were large numbers of persons who confessed Jesus Christ as Savior, were healed by the power of the Holy Spirit and were ministered to in whatever ways that were needed. We worshiped with the underground churches, visited the jails and brought gifts and offerings to the orphanages. We ministers and some laypersons in the group preached or taught in the local churches on Sunday.

In our largest crusade, there were over two hundred fifty thousand people present, and one night, over one hundred thousand came forward for salvation and ministry. A full-length movie of Nora's second book, *China Cry*, was shown in theaters nationwide and is still frequently repeated on Trinity Broadcasting Network by Paul and Jan Crouch, both of whom went with Nora to China many times. Nora, S. K. and their family have brought many rich blessings to untold numbers of persons all over the world, and also to Allene and me since the afternoon she gave me that copy of her first book over twenty-five years ago.

The 60s through the 90s were filled with God's blessings and many miracles as Allene and I hosted tour groups to cities all over Europe and Israel and went with Nora to Southeast Asia, Taiwan and mainland China. During all of these trips, we were constantly in the midst of miracles that occurred on the planes, in the cities, on the buses, in the hotels and even on the streets. Israel was one of the most frequent places for the supernatural. Almost every trip we took, persons were healed in both the upper room and at the Garden Tomb where Jesus was temporarily placed after His death. Often when we were in prayer in the Garden Tomb, members of the tour with various illnesses began to be healed instantly. I remember a man whose arms were swollen almost as large as his legs. As he walked out of the tomb, he noticed that both of his arms were completely normal! He ran around to all of us, crying and laughing as he hugged every person in the group. But thank the good Lord we never took any of the healings or miracles for granted. There was always a chorus of praise to God, Christ and the Holy Spirit for the big and the small miracles.

I have to share with you one amazing story about the way God often provided funds for people to go on the tours with Nora. When people would tell me that there was no way they could go because they had no money, I challenged them to decide to go regardless of their financial condition, to go ahead and send in the deposit and then stand on tip-toe, looking and praying in faith for the rest of their funds to come in. Many told us of how enough funds came in from unexpected sources so they could go.

One lady who had garnered only half of the funds needed held out till the very last. She flew from her home to San Francisco anyway. On the shuttle bus to our overseas airline, she was ready to give up because she saw no shred of hope that she would be on Nora's plane to China. She sat there and prayed, struggling to hold the tears back. Suddenly, a man came up to her as he was getting off the bus and said, "My dear lady, I have never done anything like this in my life. But, suddenly, I have this strong feeling that I have to do what I am doing. I have never seen you before, but take this envelope. In it you will find the rest of the money you need to take your trip."

The man got off before she could thank him. When this dear woman opened the envelope and counted the money, it was more than she needed! She then hastened to give Nora the money and ran to our gate to tell us her amazing story. Well, we all began shouting and laughing, and some of us began to jump up and down. We raised our hands over our heads and lifted up vocal praise in word and song in the Spirit to the *El Shaddai*, the God of more than enough! You can imagine that for her and all of us, it took awhile for this wonderful miracle to sink in. Events such as this one and all the other "signs and wonders" do not happen without faith and the direct hand of God. These kinds of "happenings" gave most of us a quantum leap in the level of our personal faith. Whenever our faith increased, all kinds of God-things began to fall around and in the group, and also in our personal lives during and after the trips.

With all of the activities Allene and I were involved in and all the travel we did in Europe, Israel and Southeast Asia, this last decade has flown by so quickly that it passed before we realized it. Although I do not now serve a church and I have reduced my times of going out to speak, Allene and I are still involved in ministry and see miracles almost every day. For the eight years we had the Fellowship, I had Bible study every Tuesday night at the motel and prayer meeting every Thursday night in Fred and Helen Singleton's home. In both meetings, there were many persons saved, healed and filled with the Holy Spirit, and most received their devotional language. It took me five years to lead about seventy members of the Fellowship through the entire New Testament.

Seven years ago, we began a prayer group in our home that meets every Thursday night. We have five couples who make up the core, plus a few individuals who visit, seeking answers to prayer. Almost everyone in the group has received a major healing, and we have praise reports of miracles almost weekly! As I finished each chapter of this book, I read it to the group. They have patiently listened, made good suggestions and given me much encouragement. Also for the past five years, I have been teaching at The American Christian College and Seminary, located here Oklahoma City. It is fully accredited, offering bachelor's, master's, master of divinity and doctor of ministry degrees.

You will recall that I received the honorary doctor of divinity degree in 1966 from Phillips University. But in an accredited institution, all professors must have an *earned* doctor's degree to be able to teach graduate students. So, after over three years of writing, teaching and studying, I received the doctor of ministry degree in January 1999. The D. Min. degree required a major writing project and a total of thirty three additional hours beyond the master of divinity degree. Now, with my D. Min. degree, I am able to teach both graduates and undergraduates.

As we near the end of our long journey together, I must relate a precious little miracle that happened only a few months ago. At about five P.M. on a Saturday afternoon, I felt badly as if I had a cold. I was in my pajamas in bed. A strong wind a few days before had ripped off about three feet of the ridge-row on our roof. A severe storm was predicted to hit us in about an hour; it could be seen out in the southwest, roaring this way. I could not get up there and fix it myself. Besides it was late Saturday, and I figured no one was available. So I lay there and started asking Jesus what in the world I could do to get the roof fixed to prevent the leaking and possible serious damage to our home. All I could do was pray: "Lord, You tell me exactly what to do. I promise I will do it. It seems impossible to me, but this is so easy for You."

Suddenly, Jesus seemed to speak to me in my spirit. He clearly told me to get up, put on my overcoat and go get in the car. As I was backing out, I asked Him which way. He said for me to just go. I turned west on our street, Chapel Hill Road, and then south on Lakehurst Drive. I was looking for a person with a truck and a ladder on it to help me. As I drove along, I could hear the thunder in the distance and knew the rain was not far away. I was looking left as I passed each long street, and there was not a truck anywhere in sight. Then, as I got to the fifth street, I looked left. Down at the end of the long block was a truck with a ladder on it! I wheeled left and raced to reach the truck. Just as I arrived, the truck started to drive away. I daringly went around and pulled in front of him, as if I were a cop. As I got out, I was sure he could see my pajamas sticking out around the top of my overcoat. But I walked up and told this good-looking young man my plight, pleading that he was the only one who could help me. He asked me where I lived. I told him, and he said, "Let's go!" In the minute after we pulled up in front of our house, he was up on the roof, wearing a roofer's large leather belt that contained nails and a hammer. He was not even working on a roof that day; he just "happened" to have his belt on the front seat of his truck. He called down, "Sir, where is the ridge-row?"

A MIRACLE A MINUTE

Before I could answer him, he yelled, "Oh, here it is over on the other side of the roof."

In less than five minutes, he had the piece of ridge-row nailed down solid. He then hopped down off the roof, grabbed his ladder, threw it up on the rack, jumped in his truck and was ready to drive off.

I ran over and tried to pay him.

He said nothing doing!

I asked if he was a Christian.

Yes, he was a deacon in his Assembly of God church.

I ran in and brought him a tape of my testimony and one of Allene's cassettes. After getting his name and phone number, I trotted across the yard and thanked him over and over as he slowly drove away.

Fifteen minutes after I prayed that little prayer and had the simple faith to foolishly go get in the car and follow the Lord's leading, I was back in my bed and the roof was all fixed. Within a few minutes, the storm hit with hard rain and hail, but I rested back on my pillow with a broad smile. I knew that Jesus had fixed our roof and all was well. But most important of all, I had made a roofer friend for life. While the rain was pouring, Allene came back to our room with a big smile on her face. She said, "You are something else, James Pippin! That took a lot of faith!"

"No," I smiled and said, pulling up the covers under my chin, "a little faith and a great big God!" By the way, I was cured of my cold that day.

I know that you now believe me when I say that I could sit here the rest of my life and share with you the small and the great miracles that have sprung out of the fruit and the gifts of the Holy Spirit since 1966. Allene and I will never lose our faith for miracles. Janet, Anne, Beverly and Alecia, our granddaughter, and most of our close friends also have had miracles in their lives and in the lives of their friends. I might even make my second book, *A Book of Miracles*, somewhat like a daily devotional. Do you believe that I could relate three hundred sixty-five miracles? You know that I can. Though time may not be on my side, God is! So watch the bookstores, for

> It is no secret what God can do,
> What He's done for others
> He will do for you.
> With eyes wide open,
> He'll pardon you.
> It is no secret what God can do!

Miracles Galore!

I am going to adapt a verse of the Gospel of John to fit my feelings as I come to the end of our journey together:

> James and Allene and the girls have witnessed many other things that are not written in this book, "but these are written that you may believe that Jesus is the Christ, the Son of the Living God, and believing, you may have LIFE; [Life abundant and eternal,] in His name."
>
> —JOHN 20:31

I also thank God daily for what the apostle Paul said in Hebrews 13:8: "Jesus Christ the same, yesterday, today and forever!" I cannot say "farewell" to you, but maybe this will do: "So long until we meet again."

✵ *Epilogue* ✵

Our Journey Ends

I wrote the first draft of the first four chapters of this book in 1972. I have written many parts of it in my mind, and threads of it have been with me all these years, especially in the night hours.

I have always loved the night. Mark Twain said, "None of us is quite sane in the night."

I agree. The night hours are so very different from the day ones.

The ancient Visigoths used to plan their battle strategies in the day to be sure they were correct. Then they would go back over them at night when they were half drunk to make sure that they were daring.

So, this partially explains some of it; I have written most of this late at night. Though I was not physically drunk, I was often drunk in the Spirit.

During many of the nights, I doubt that I was fully sane.

I have had serious attacks of nostalgia as I have remembered most of the best parts of this story. My heart would actually ache to go back there to those long ago years.

I would never have believed this, but writing this book has caused the nostalgia to almost completely disappear.

In Beryl Markham's splendid book, *West with the Night*, she wrote, "There is no opiate for nostalgia." I feel sure that after she finished her book, much of her nostalgia had also disappeared.

For the past five years, I have fought for small bits and pieces of time to write the best of my life. But often, the living of the rest of my life got in the way.

My past has become my close companion for so many years.

Now that I have gotten round to finishing it so late in life, a sad realization has moved in over me like a cloud. So many of those who were close to me and with whom I would love to have shared my book have passed away.

When I think of those who were with me in school, in the Army, in college, those sweet children and the great men and women in the churches we have served, the dedicated and loving teachers I have sat under, the many students that have sat in my classes, and last but not least, my entire Pippin family, all these I so much would have wanted to read this, but so many of them are no longer with us. I often feel that I have been cheated because so few of them stuck around to share these glorious times with me.

This fact has also brought me a little of the feeling that Dr. Samuel Johnson had when he finished his mammoth dictionary in 1796. When that great work was finally ended, he mentioned to James Boswell, his biographer, that much of the joy had now faded because so many of his dearest friends with whom he could have shared his great feat were no longer living.

Well, any sadness I may have is fleeting. Indeed, my faithful and patient reader, I pray that you and those who join you will far out-number the friends and family who have passed. What little sadness is left is quickly swept away by the large number of new friends like you I am making in the publication of this book. Actually, my greatest joy and honor is to have been given the privilege to share my life with you.

You and I have traveled a long, long journey together since we started this story of a poor, little Georgia boy born in Round Oak. Again I say to you, thank you very much for giving me the good pleasure of writing the major events of my life for you.

I feel that even while you have been reading this story, our Father has already begun to work miracles in *your* life. I have faith that since you have now seen all these grand works of the hands of Jesus Christ, you can say that you also are now *"Living a miracle-a-minute life."*

I think you might be interested in my sharing with you some of the important lessons I have learned along the way.

I began early to stoop down when I spoke to children and say to them in words they could understand that they are loved and that I was expecting great things from them. One is never so tall as when one stoops to love and encourage a child.

My early life was impacted by times of illness and pain. I learned patience, received love and was ever being drawn closer to God.

Every person I have met or have come to know is a unique cre-ation of God. Each person knows something that I do not. I have tried to learn that from each of them. (Just a little touch of Emerson there.)

> Since I have lived so long, this may be my greatest asset to you:
> I know so many ways that will not work.
> From this I have learned a few of the things that will.
> We are young only once, but we can remain immature all of our lives.
> Life is a journey of joy toward maturity.
> We are forever becoming; we can never count ourselves to have arrived.
> But we must press on.

My travels to Israel, the Mediterranean and all over Europe have helped prepare me to understand life and people better. They also have assisted me to teach subjects in Bible history and religion with firsthand knowledge gained from visiting those countries.

Travel in Southeast Asia and China have shown me what free enterprise and competition can do to improve lifestyle. In China and East Germany, I saw firsthand what Socialism and Communism can do to utterly destroy a country by stealing away the freedom of its people.

These forms of government have never worked, but the liberal elite keep trying. If we remain silent, do nothing and refuse to vote, the Socialists' tireless efforts will succeed in taking over our nation and destroying our freedom.

I asked a popular minister friend, who could sway thousands, if he and his wife voted in the last presidential election. He said, "Nah, we didn't bother. They're all alike!"

Hey feller, I am sorry, angry and very sad, *but they're not all alike!* The person who seeks to keep you from voting steals your vote. That person is the enemy of the people! I recently heard one of our major newscasters who is, of course, a flaming liberal tell an audience of millions, "You know, the two major parties are so much alike that it really doesn't pay the American people to go to the polls and vote."

Oh!! Wouldn't she like you and me to believe that!

Well, the majority of Christians must have been brainwashed into believing this, for they stayed away in droves. Only 50 percent of registered Christians voted in the 2000 presidential election! As we look back years from now, wouldn't it be devastating to know that the "Christians" caused us to lose our country? God forbid. The vote is about all we have left.

Epilogue—Our Journey Ends

As I traveled to those parts of the world in which people are not free, my desire to keep America ever alert has greatly increased. Now I watch out for all those who would steal our birthright of freedom; despots and dictators, Socialists, atheists and secular humanists who would put us in chains and with the help of their followers, overthrow our government and then move to put all free nations into slavery. They are ever stalking the streets of our cities, the classrooms of our schools and colleges, our halls of Congress and the pages of history, seeking whom they may devour.

There are so many things we as a people can do better for ourselves so much cheaper than an intrusive government can.

I repeat here for emphasis what I recently heard Milton Friedman say, "Socialism is the most inefficient system of government on earth."

Of each dollar that the government spends on welfare, only about twenty-three cents gets to the "poor."

However, the main lesson that my years, studies and travels have taught me is this: The Light of Truth will never fail to shine in this world or in the kingdom of God. I have stood with sadness as I looked over the ruins of the great empires of the past, including the decline and fall of Egypt, Persia, Greece and Rome. More recently, we have seen the decline of the Soviet Union and certain parts of Eastern Europe.

Now we see that this slow moral rot is beginning its stench most drastically in the heart of our large cities, where in both North and South America, the inner cities are awash with drugs. I believe that all this decay has occurred because the majority of the people of each of these nations have turned their backs on the God who created the world and on Jesus Christ, the Prince of Peace, who came to save it from itself. He is a Savior who empowers Christians to stand in the path of those bent on destroying the church and the nation.

The lack of morals and values in some of the leaders of the branches of government, of some of the military and even of some of America's large denominations, will bring any nation that will tolerate this slow rot inexorably closer and closer to the gates of death and destruction.

In these dark days of deceit, each of us must learn to hang on to the truth that "God is still on the throne"; someday, if the freedom-loving refuse to give up, "all will be right with the world."

In the midst of and in spite of all of this evil, a person must maintain a hopeful and positive outlook.

A MIRACLE A MINUTE

Never ignore the vital importance of a keen sense of humor.

Brother George used to say, "James, don't glum up on me!"

President Lincoln was criticized for his laughing at jokes while many of our men were being killed in battle. He said in response to these attacks that if he didn't pause and laugh once in awhile, he would go absolutely mad. He said that every day he attempted to experience the wisdom of the Good Book that "laughter works on the heart like a medicine." (See Proverbs 17:22.)

I try to remember that the very best joke is the one I tell on myself. I have been given the gift of always recognizing the ridiculous in life. But I stand still and silent during those precious moments when I know that I am in the presence of Almighty God.

Share the blessings that Allene and I have had as we read and re-read such books as Brother Lawrence's *Practicing the Presence of God*, Catherine Marshall's *To Live Again*, Charles Sheldon's *In His Steps* and Francis Shaeffer's *How Should We Then Live*, sub-titled "The Rise and Decline of Western Thought and Culture."

The recent death of our oldest daughter, Janet, has forced Allene and me, Anne, Beverly, and our only granddaughter, Alecia, to lean day and night on the bosom of our Good Shepherd, the Lord Jesus. Each of us has learned that we can do all things through Christ and the Holy Spirit, who strengthens us and whom the glorified Christ sent back to all who believe and ask. (See Luke 11:11ff.) That mighty yet very tender Spirit is our Comforter, and He is the Treasure in our earthen vessels.

He has often lifted us from the stygian dungeon of night, from depression and grief, out into the joy of Christ's marvelous light. The Spirit also brought sanity to us during those early days of almost uncontrollable sorrow when life seemed unfair and made no sense.

Janet Diane was struck by a car in Arlington, Texas, April 18, 1998, and killed instantly at the early age of forty-three. Janet was a lover of animals, especially horses and Arthur, her dog of twelve years. She was a computer genius, a master hair designer, an expert in hair coloring, a guitarist, a writer of songs, a member of a band, a super flower designer, poet and gourmet cook. She was a ray of sunshine to all who knew her. Her death has been hard, but we have been greatly comforted by our Christian friends, our prayer group and also a group we meet with monthly, "The Compassionate Friends," an organization that meets once a month to help persons work through the grief one has in the loss of a child.

The experience of the death of a child whom we have loved and lost teaches us that "this too shall pass." Get and stay ready for the death of your loved ones, but get ready for your own death first. That word from the apostle Paul comes to mind and helped us by faith not only to know where Janet is, but also to be ready to join her ourselves: "To be absent from the body is to be present with the Lord" (2 Cor. 5:8).

Many of us have heard William H. (Bill) Alexander say, "While you are teaching people how to die, do not forget to teach them to live."

Frank Johnson Pippin encouraged us when he said in words that sound like the apostle Paul, *"Faith makes all things possible. Love makes all things easy."*

I read in the spurious Gospel of Thomas a possible lost saying of Jesus: *"Life is a bridge from this world to the next. Just don't stop to build a house on the bridge."*

An anonymous poet has said:

> Just one short life, 'twill soon be past,
> Only what's done for Christ will last.

I believe that the following is the greatest of all of the sayings of Jesus:

> This is My commandment, that you love one another as I have loved you. Greater love has no one than this, than to lay down one's life for his friends. You are my friends if you do whatever I command you.
>
> —JOHN 15:12–14

God is our Forever Father, Jesus Christ is our Forever Friend, the Holy Spirit is our Forever Comforter and the church is our Forever Family.

I now leave you in the presence of this, our Great Eternal Friend, our Divine Elder Brother, Jesus Christ, the Lamb of God, the Ancient of Days, who is able to be right there with you and here with me all at the same time. He is truly the "same yesterday, today and forever" (Heb. 13:8).

"Holding forth the Word of Life"

Near Hitler's "Eagle's N
—1965

Lecture in
Germany — 1965

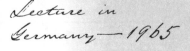

Welcome
Protestant Chaplains
Retreat

Germany, Arlene's
opening sermon & song
—1965

Germany, Chaplain
Conference — 1965

My retur
from Germa
—1965

From left: Me,
Allene, Raine &
Bill Wilson,
Major General
Charlie Brown &
Eva his wife at
a reception in
NY — 1965

Carna Kaiser, Bill
& Raine — 1966

Oral and Evelyn Roberts — 1966

Ray Pippin &
his brother
Dr. Frank
Johnson
Pippin — 1965

The famous "Bridge of Sighs," in Venice with Oma — 1967

Overlooking Haifa, Israel — Nov, 1968

Me floating in the Dead Sea (the water is dense with minerals) — 1968

Spain, Dottie Armbrust, Allene & her mother — 1968

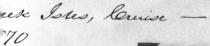
reek Isles, Allene's
first ride — 1969

Donkey ride on
the Greek Island
of Santarini —
1969

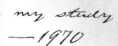
reek Isles, Cruise —
70

my study
— 1970

Flowers from the Holy Land

Pressed Flowers
of Jerusalem — 1971

Ray, Mae &
at Taj Maha
Agra, India
— 1970

Christmas in
Jerusalem
at the Garden
Tomb — 1971

HEADQUARTERS
353ᵈ ENGR GP (C)

Headquarters
— 1974

At home with the 4
Pippin Dogs — 1974

Mary Pippin Marr
(Age 65) — 1977

Mary, James, Myrtle,
Mae, Ray & Arlene
— 1980

Vera & Allene
(Vera was the
one who told me,
"Go see that girl
who sings on the
radio!") —1981

Pippin Reunion
Daniel Jack[...]
(back row, [...]
and Billy
(back row, [...]
—1981

Pippin Reunion, August, 1982
(Note "Pippin Road" named in our honor!)

Allene, Anne,
Alecia, Beverly
me—1982

Lovenia James (on the
right) Phyllis Baker
(on the left) at
Beverly's Wedding
—1984

Me, Allene,
Oretha, Bro.
Kenneth Hagin
and "Doc" &
Jerry Horton
—1984

First Trip to
Mainland
China with
Nora Lam
—1984

Premier of
"China Cr—
—with Nora
Lam, Julie
Nickson
(who play—
Nora in th—
movie) and
me—1985

Eight
orphans
I brought
from
China for
Nora Lam
—1988

This is the
whole family!
Bev, Janet & Ann
in the back row,
Allene, me & Alec
front row — 1988

Allene & me — 2001

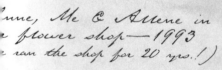

...nne, Me & Allene in
...e flower shop — 1993
...e ran the shop for 20 yrs.!)

"Here's
looking at
you, kid!"
Our 50th
Wedding
Anniversary
May 6, 2001

Thanksgiving: Back Row: Martha Ann (Jack's daughter) Alecia, Anne, Front Row: Don, Beverly, Allene & me—200

Our prayer group (to whom I read most of the chapters of this book—2001

Anne Pippin
& daughter
Alecia
—2001

...mes Clayton
Pippin
—2001

❦ *Postscript* ❦

Just a few words to you, my faithful reader, about the tragedy that occurred Tuesday, September 11, 2001. It is my firm belief that the only Power that can carry us safely through these sad and critical days is our close and personal relationship with Jesus Christ. I have lived through the Great Depression, several wars and the assassination of John F. Kennedy and other great leaders. Yet those tragedies pale in contrast to the terror and destruction our nation suffered on the 11th of September—a dark day that changed the world; a day that will be remembered for the rest of our lives; the day when we were brought face to face with Satan himself, who always comes to kill, steal and destroy. The former wars were "over there"; this war brought senseless murder and destruction "over here."

We must be on high alert to prevent other strikes that could tragically cripple us in many ways, including our electric and water supplies. Some of our past leaders have allowed our nation to become so vulnerable, our borders so open, that our enemies have infiltrated us for years with little resistance. So we must be prepared to be in this for the long pull. As mentioned in this book, forty years of mistakes in so many areas of our national life cannot be corrected in forty days. We must act with great speed and yet with great caution. We must not precipitate a third world war.

I earnestly beseech you to join me in daily prayers that the Lord will guide the president and the members of his cabinet, Congress, our governors and mayors, and all of our churches, synagogues and mosques during these critical days, that together we all may do His will and usher in a new era of peace without terror.

Sincerely,
Your friend in Christ,
James Clayton Pippin

To contact the author, please write:

Dr. James Pippin
3017 Chapel Hill Road
Oklahoma City, OK 73120-4431
E-mail: drjcpippin@aol.com
Fax: (405) 842-2549